The Collected Works of J. Krishnamurti

Volume VII

1952–1953

Tradition and Creativity

COLLECTED WORKS VOLUME 7

Photo: J. Krishnamurti, ca 1950 by D.R.D Wadia

P.O Box 1560, Ojai, CA 93024

Website: www.kfa.org

Printed in the United States of America

ISBN 13: 9781934989401
ISBN: 1934989401

Contents

Preface

Jiddu Krishnamurti was born in 1895 of Brahmin parents in south India. At the age of fourteen he was proclaimed the coming World Teacher by Annie Besant, then president of the Theosophical Society, an international organization that emphasized the unity of world religions. Mrs. Besant adopted the boy and took him to England, where he was educated and prepared for his coming role. In 1911 a new worldwide organization was formed with Krishnamurti as its head, solely to prepare its members for his advent as World Teacher. In 1929, after many years of questioning himself and the destiny imposed upon him, Krishnamurti disbanded this organization, saying:

Truth is a pathless land, and you cannot approach it by any path whatsoever, by any religion, by any sect. Truth, being limitless, unconditioned, unapproachable by any path whatsoever, cannot be organized; nor should any organization be formed to lead or to coerce people along any particular path. My only concern is to set men absolutely, unconditionally free.

Until the end of his life at the age of ninety, Krishnamurti traveled the world speaking as a private person. The rejection of all spiritual and psychological authority, including his own, is a fundamental theme. A major concern is the social structure and how it conditions the individual. The emphasis in his talks and writings is on the psychological barriers that prevent clarity of perception. In the mirror of relationship, each of us can come to understand the content of his own consciousness, which is common to all humanity. We can do this, not analytically, but directly in a manner, Krishnamurti describes at length. In observing this content we discover within ourselves the division of the observer and what is observed. He points out that this division, which prevents direct perception, is the root of human conflict.

His central vision did not waver after 1929, but Krishnamurti strove for the rest of his life to make his language even more simple and clear. There is a development in his exposition. From year to year he used new terms and new approaches to his subject, with different nuances.

Because his subject is all-embracing, the *Collected Works* are of compelling interest. Within his talks in any one year Krishnamurti was not able to cover the whole range of his vision, but broad amplifications of particular themes are found throughout these volumes. In them he lays the foundations of many of the concepts he used in later years.

The *Collected Works* contain Krishnamurti's previously published talks, discussions, answers to specific questions, and writings for the years 1933 through 1967. They are an authentic record of his teachings, taken from transcripts of verbatim shorthand reports and tape recordings.

The Krishnamurti Foundation of America, a California charitable trust, has among its purposes the publication and distribution of Krishnamurti books, videocassettes, films, and tape recordings. The production of the *Collected Works* is one of these activities.

Ojai, California, 1952

First Talk in The Oak Grove

I think most of us are aware that some kind of change is necessary not only in our individual lives but as a group, as a race, as a nation. We see the importance of a radical change, a change that will bring lasting hope, that will give an assurance, a certainty not of the mind but of something which is above and beyond the mind. Surely, most of us feel—those of us, at least, who are serious—that within ourselves there must be this vital transformation, but transformation is not of the mind because the mind can never solve any human problem. The more we investigate the process of thought and seek to resolve our problems by the sanctions of the mind, the greater are the complications. There is more and more degradation and suffering, and less of creative existence. Yet it is obvious that a vital change is necessary, and that is what I would like to discuss during the course of these talks—how to bring about not a superficial reformation or a casual adjustment to some immediate challenge but a change, a revolution, a radical transformation that will give us direct experience of something which is fundamental, eternal, not of time, and which may be called truth, God, or what you will. I feel this is the only essential study, the only fundamental inquiry, especially now that we are in a state of crisis, both individual and historic. To look for transformation to some philosophy, to some teacher, to some ideal or example, or to analyze our own complexities and try to do something about them within the field of the mind, within the field of time, is so utterly futile.

Let us see, then, if we cannot, during this and the subsequent talks, peacefully, tentatively, and deeply go into the matter of how to change, how to bring about a real transformation within ourselves. One can see the importance, the necessity, the urgency of such a change because mere reformation, superficial adjustment to an idea, to a particular end in view, is not a change at all. Most of us are concerned only with the immediate changes; we do not want to go more deeply, more fundamentally into the problem. Our desire for change is brought about through superficial thought, and in the process of our changing, there is constant mischief in action. I am sure most of us are aware of this, and yet we do not know how to go beyond it; and, if I may suggest, I would like these talks to result in the discovery for each one of us, including myself, of how to touch that source which is not of the mind, which is not of time, which has nothing to do with any particular philosophy or political system, with any organized religion, code of ethics, or social reform. Religion is the discovery of that which is unnameable, and if we can directly experience it and let that operate, let that be the impetus, the drive, then that will bring about this transformation which is so essential.

May I add here that there is a right way of listening. Not that you must accept or reject what I am saying, but you want to find out, do you not? Surely, that is why you are here—not to spend a pleasant afternoon amongst friends whom you have probably met after many years. You can do all that afterwards. You have taken the trouble to come, and you must be somewhat serious. The art of listening is not to be merely vague and receptive but to find out what it is I want to convey. Together—and I mean this—together we can discover it, discover something which is not merely at the verbal level; something which is not an idea to be opposed by another idea; something which is not mere knowledge, which you cannot acquire, but which you and I together can experience directly; something which is the only transcendental value, which gives you extraordinary confidence, a confidence that no theory, no political or religious argument can evoke.

So, these talks are not mere lectures for you to listen to and for me to expound, but let us undertake a journey together to find out for ourselves that which is not made up by the mind. I can invent, speculate, and so can you. I can put out some idea, and you can oppose it by another idea, a different argument; but surely, if I want to find something which is not of time, which is not of the mind, which is not merely the response to a particular challenge—if I really want to find out, I must go beyond the responses, the casual, superficial reactions.

To listen properly, then, is very important. We are discussing, talking over together problems which are very difficult and which face all humanity, every individual; and that requires a very subtle, hesitant, inquiring mind, a mind that is capable of going deeper and deeper, and not merely coming to a conclusion and adhering to it. So, if I may suggest, after each of these talks go away by yourself, think about it; do not immediately get agitated and begin to talk about when and where you last met—you know the kind of superficial conversation that goes on.

What is important is to find out how to bring about a radical change in ourselves. I do not know if this is a problem to you. Probably it is not because most of us are caught in inertia, in habit, in tradition. We have given ourselves over to a particular political or religious conviction, and we pursue that, hoping it will bring a lasting, fundamental change, a transformation, a revolution within us. Having committed ourselves to a certain pattern of thought, we pursue it for years, and we think we are changing. Surely, fundamental change is not to be found in the pursuit of a pattern of thought, however noble, nor in compliance with tradition, nor in the acceptance of any idea, belief, or example; but what is required is a change that is not of the mind. So, please listen carefully and do not immediately translate what I am suggesting into the pattern with which you are familiar, whether it is of some book which you have read or of a particular society or religious group to which you belong. Let us put aside all those things and think of the problem anew.

Now, I see the immense importance of a fundamental change in myself. I may be ambitious, I may be greedy, I may tell lies. How are these things to be changed completely? I see that ambition is a very destructive process, both individually and collectively; though one must have sufficient, the whole spirit of acquisitiveness—the craving for more, more, more, the self-defenses which ultimately end up in lying, deception, illusion—all this is creating havoc in the world. Seeing all these patterns—the reactions, the stupidity, the vanity, the prejudices in which we are caught—how is one to transform them not just verbally but actually? Those of us who have experimented with these things have already tried several ways, have we not? We have disciplined ourselves through action of the will, we have followed teachers, leaders, worshipped authority; and yet, in spite of various kinds of effort to be free from these things, we remain shallow, empty. Our problems are still there in a different form. I may cease to be a liar or give up being ambitious—but what? I may be very kind, affectionate, considerate, but that spark, that flame, has still never been touched, that thing which gives a quality of life I have never known. So until I touch that, until there is the experiencing of that, all superficial reformation, the outward capacity to adjust, has very little meaning because mere adjustment on the outside does not give that faith, that hope, that conviction, that certainty, that tremendous feeling of something eternally new. And I feel if we can touch that, then the change will have an extraordinary meaning. Surely, that is the search for reality, for God, or what you will. Without having touched that, we are doing everything in our endeavor to shape, to alter, to mold the mind. That is why when so-called religions have failed, as they inevitably do, political parties become all-important; they offer a vision, a conviction, a hope, and we jump at these things because in ourselves we have lost the source, the spring of that which is unnameable.

So, it is not a question of mere social reformation, superficial change, but of how to bring about an experience which gives lasting faith—if I can use that word *faith* without introducing all the superstitious sentimentality that goes with it—an experience which brings confidence stripped of all our stupidities and selfish arrogances, a confidence born of clarity, of that thing which cannot be destroyed and for which we live and die. There is a certainty, a peculiar quality which gives, not the superficial hope in something, but a feeling which is in itself the flowering of something beyond the functioning of the mind. It is that that we have to touch, and if we are really in earnest, it is our problem, yours and mine, to find it. Without touching that, we shall be everlastingly in misery, in confusion; there will be endless wars, perpetual conflicts between nations, races, groups, individuals; without that, there is no compassion, no love.

Now, you and I are not brilliant, we are not cursed with immense knowledge, we are ordinary people; perhaps there are some on the outskirts who are unbalanced, but that doesn't matter. Is it possible for ordinary people, for you and me, to go into this and to experience not something which the mind invents and then experiences but something which is not of the mind at all? That is what we are going to find out—which may entail a great many denials, sacrifices, the putting aside of various personal ambitions, the desire to become great, for a mind that is caught in its own patterns of thought can never experience the eternal. If we are to inquire earnestly into this, we must study the mind—not the universal mind or the mind of another, however great, but the mind that you and I have, with which we think, with which we operate, and in the reactions of which we are caught. The mind is the only instrument we have, and without knowing how it works, merely to find out what is beyond the mind only leads to illusion; and most of us are caught in that illusion, especially the so-called religious people, the people who are seeking God.

So, if I want to understand, to experience directly something which is not of the mind, the first step is to understand the process of the mind, which is thinking. Only by penetrating, by going deeply into the process of thought, can thought come to an end.

After all, our thinking has not led us very far; our ideas have not brought peace to the world or happiness to ourselves. Thought is a process of reaction, a conditioning of the past, and it is ever creating patterns which we instinctively follow. All that has to be understood, which means going into and dissipating the traditions, the prejudices, the particular patterns and peculiarities of the 'me', stripping the mind, laying it bare, so that it becomes really still. Such stillness is not induced, it is not cultivated, it cannot be brought about through discipline because all those processes are still part of the mind. It is only a quiet mind, a still mind, that can experience that which is not of the mind, and it is one of the most difficult things for the mind to be quiet. When the mind is as nothing, only then is there God. But we have cultivated the mind for centuries, it is the one thing that we worship, and therefore we have to understand the process of the mind. We will go into this at every talk. As we begin to discover, as we become aware of the process of our own thinking, through that understanding, through that awareness, there comes a tranquillity of the mind itself in which there is no longer any effort towards a particular end; and only then is the mind capable of receiving or experiencing something which is not a projection of itself. When there is the experiencing of that, however little it may be, then from that there is a transformation, from that there is a change—not the change of a shallow mind which ends in mischievous action.

Question: Unity seems essential for the well-being of man. How is one to achieve this unity in a group or in a nation?

KRISHNAMURTI: How do we generally achieve unity as it is practiced in the various nations? Superficial unity is brought about through propaganda, through education, through various forms of compulsion; you are ceaselessly reminded that you are an American, a Hindu, a Russian, a German, and so on. Through various forms of conditioning—religious, social, economic, climatic—we are forced to unite; and that, we feel, is essential. We think that if we are identified with a particular group and give our life to it, we shall establish unity.

Now, is unity of the mind? Is unity limited to a particular group or nation? When, out of economic necessity or for any other self-protective reason, we identify ourselves with any group or nation, is that unity? Or does all self-protective action bring about conflict within ourselves and therefore outwardly? When do we feel the sense of unity? When do you feel united with another? Surely, only when the self is absent. When the 'me' and the 'mine'—my hurts, my prejudices, my tendencies—when all that is absent, then there is a possibility of unity with another. As long as the 'me' is present, there is disunity, there is separation, is there not? Our education, our social distinctions, our economic, national, and racial barriers all indicate the separativeness of the 'me'; the "me first" runs through it all, and over that we try to find unity. That is our problem, is it not? We try to establish superficial unity without love, and love is something which cannot be when the self is. With one hand we strengthen the self, and we try to find unity at the same time. There is a conflict between the 'me' and the ideal, and therefore society, like the individual, is everlastingly in conflict.

So, unity cannot be brought about by any superficial means. No psychological training, no inculcation of ideas, no special form of education, however carefully worked out, can bring about unity until we really dissolve the separating element, that process in which the 'me' is predominant. Surely, that is what we are going to find out—how to eliminate completely, if we can, the 'me'. Do not say it is impossible, that it cannot be done. Let us find out, let us inquire.

Question: Ever since I began reading you a number of years ago, I have been attempting to be complete, but I find that it eludes me. In what wrong process of thinking am I caught?

KRISHNAMURTI: Let us go into this matter as fully as we can and find out for ourselves whether completeness is possible, even for a fleeting second, and what the experiencing of it implies.

Why do we want to be complete in ourselves? Because we are incomplete, we are insufficient, we are inwardly poor, miserable, we have innumerable conflicts; we want love, we want praise, we want peace, we want to be patted on the back, we want to be told what wonderful beings we are, we want to worship, we want somebody to help us. Being incomplete, we strive after completeness; we want to be self-sufficient, not dependent, inwardly rich, unfettered, without a shadow of sorrow, and so on and so on. But we are fettered; we are in sorrow, and without understanding what we are, we try to pursue something which we are not. The thing we are pursuing, which we call completeness, becomes an illusion because without understanding what we are, which is the fact, we pursue something which is not a fact. We think it is much easier to pursue that which is not a fact and imitate it than to tackle and dissolve what we are. Surely, if I knew how to face this incompleteness, how to understand it, if I saw what are its colorations, its implications, those things which are not merely of the word—if I understood all that and knew how to deal with it, then I would not pursue completeness. So when, knowing that I am incomplete, I pursue completeness, there is a wrong process set going because that pursuit is an escape into an idea, into a fancy, into an unreality. The fact is, I am inwardly poor, I am lonely, I am in conflict, in sorrow; my mind is petty, shallow; I indulge in mischief. That is what I am. Though occasionally I may have a glimmer of something which is not all this, the actual fact is, I am these things—it may be ugly, but it is so. Why can't I deal with it? How am I to understand it and go beyond it? That is the problem, not how to be complete. If you say, "Well, I once caught a glimpse of something which is more than this; therefore, I am going to pursue it," then you are living on the dead. As a boy I may have had an experience of something beautiful, but if I live in that, I am incapable of understanding the fact of what I am.

So, to go beyond what I am, I have to understand it; I have to break it down, and not try to become complete because when that which I am is not, there is completeness; I don't have to look for it. I don't have to look for light when I can see; it is only when I am caught in darkness, in misery, in travail, that I think of something beyond it. What is important, then, is to find out if I can understand the thing which I am. Now, how do I set about it? I hope I am making this very clear because the pursuit of completeness is a wrong process altogether. If I pursue completeness, it will always elude me, for then it is an illusion, an invention of the mind. The fact is what I am, however ugly or beautiful. I can deal with the fact, but not with the illusion. So, how can I look at the fact in order to understand it and go beyond it? That is my problem. Have I the capacity to look at it? Can I actually see that I am poor, insufficient, and not invent ideas about the fact? The fact is one thing, and the idea about the fact is another. When I look at the fact, I am full of ideas about it, and the ideas frighten me, they prejudice me, they help me to run away from incompleteness through worship, drink, amusement, and other forms of escape. So, we have to understand the idea about the fact.

Let us say I am dishonest, ambitious, a liar, what you will. I am that. Now, can that be transformed without the idea? Please follow this because the moment I introduce the idea of what I should or should not be, I am not bringing about a fundamental transformation; I am only dealing with it superficially. But I want to deal with the fact fundamentally, to transform it with a different force altogether. If I deal with it superficially, I may cease to be ambitious or jealous or envious—but then what? I am still empty, I am still striving, I am still incomplete. I see, then, that when the mind acts upon the fact, it cannot fundamentally alter it; it can modify it, it can cover it up, it can move it to another place, but it cannot transform the fact and go beyond it.

So, is it possible to experience a fundamental change which is not a result of the mind? And how am I to bring about such a transformation in the thing which I have called ugly, or whatever it is, so that there is a different action altogether upon it which is not a calculated, self-assertive, self-deceptive action of will? I hope I am making myself clear. It is rather difficult to explain this.

Let us suppose I am ambitious, and I see all the implications of ambition as well as its obvious manifestations in society, in relationship, everywhere. I see that an ambitious person, like an ambitious nation, is destructive, shallow, bringing misery and conflict to others and to himself. Now, how am I to be free of ambition without controlling, subjugating, without trying not to be ambitious? That is the problem, is it not? If I struggle against ambition, I am still ambitious in a different direction; I am ambitious not to be ambitious because I think that by being free of ambition, I shall achieve some other thing: peace, tranquillity, God, or what you will. So, how am I to be free from ambition without the exertion of will? For, the moment I apply will, it is a motive, it has a tail attached to it, an acquisitive tentacle, and yet I see the immense necessity, the urgency of really changing that thing which I have called ambition. So, I have to inquire into the problem of change, what change implies. Change brought about by the mind is still very shallow; therefore, there is always conflict in it. Then what am I to do? As it is a problem to me because I really want to go into this and be free of ambition, I have to study not ambition but the question of change—whether change is in time or from a point which has nothing to do with time. So, I have to discover or experience a state which is not of time. And can I experience that—a state which is not of memory, which is not of accumulated knowledge? Can I experience something eternal, which is beyond time? And if I can experience it, then the problem of change, of trying to resolve ambition, has completely gone.

So, what is important is not how to be complete but how to bring about a transformation which is not of time, and that, as I said, we will talk over in all these meetings.

August 2, 1952

Second Talk in The Oak Grove

Perhaps we can continue with what we were considering yesterday afternoon—the problem of change, of fundamental or radical transformation, and how it is to be brought about. I think it is very important to go into this question fully, not only this morning, but in the subsequent talks that are going to take place. I do not know if you have further considered the matter, but the more one regards the problem, the more one takes it into consideration, the vaster and more complicated one discovers it to be. We see the importance and the absolute necessity of changing—changing ourselves in our relationships, in our activities, in the process of our thinking, which includes the mere accumulation of knowledge. Yet when one considers the implications of change, one sees how, though we attempt to change ourselves, there is no radical transformation. I am using the word *transformation* in its simple meaning, not in any grandiose sense, the superphysical, and all the rest of it.

We see the necessity of change not only in world politics but in our own religious attitude, in our social relationships, in our individual, everyday contacts with the familiar, with each other; but the more we attempt to change on the small scale, the more superficial our thinking becomes, and the greater the mischief in action. The closer we look at the problem, the more we are aware of this. Seeing the necessity of change, we project ideals, and according to that pattern, we hope to transform ourselves. I am narrow, petty, superstitious, shallow, and I project the ideal of something vast, significant, deep; and I am continually struggling, adjusting, molding myself according to that pattern. Now, is that change? Let us look at it a little closely. When I project an ideal and try to live up to that ideal, constantly adapting myself to a particular pattern of thought, does that process bring about the fundamental change which you and I recognize as essential? But first of all, do we in fact recognize that it is essential to bring about a fundamental change in our orientation, in our outlook, in our values, in our contacts, in the manner of our behavior, in the way of our thinking? Do we see the importance of that? Or do we merely accept it as an ideal and try to do something about it?

Surely, it is obvious to any person who is at all thoughtful that there must be a revolution in our thinking and in our action because everywhere there is chaos, misery. In ourselves and outwardly there is confusion, there is an incessant striving without any release, any hope; and perhaps, being aware of it, we think that by creating an ideal, a projection outside of us of something which we are not, or by following an example, a leader, a savior, or a particular religious teaching, we can bring about a fundamental change. Of course, in following a pattern certain superficial modifications take place, but obviously that does not bring about a radical transformation. And yet most of our existence is spent in that way—trying to live up to something, trying to bring about a change in our attitude, to change according to the pattern which we have projected as an ideal, as a belief.

Now, let us find out if the pursuit of an ideal really does bring about a change in us or only a modified continuity of what has been. I do not know if this is a problem to you. If you are satisfied with merely trying to live up to an ideal, then there is no problem—though that has its own problem of constant conflict between what you are and what you should be. This struggle, this ceaseless effort to adjust to a pattern, is still within the field of the mind, is it not? Surely, there is a radical transformation only when we can jump, as it were, from the process of time into something which is not of time. We will go into that as we discuss.

For most of us, change implies the continuation of ourselves in a modified form. If we are dissatisfied with a particular pattern of ideas, of rituals, of conditioning, we throw it aside and pick up the same pattern in a different milieu, a different color, with different rituals, different words. Instead of Latin, it is Sanskrit or some other language, but it is still the old pattern repeated over and over and over again; and within this pattern we think we are moving, changing. Because we are dissatisfied with what we are, we go from one teacher to another. Seeing confusion about us and in ourselves, seeing perpetual wars, ever-increasing destruction, devastation, and misery, we want some haven, some peace; and if we can find a refuge that gives us a sense of security, a sense of permanency, with that we are satisfied.

So, when the mind projects an idea and clings to it, struggles towards it, surely that is not change, that is not transformation, that is not revolution because it is still within the field of mind, the field of time. To clear away all that, we must be conscious of what we are doing, we must be aware of it. And it must be cleared away, must it not? Because, with all that burden, with all that impetus of the mind, obviously we cannot find the other; and without experiencing the other, do what we will, there will be no change. But what generally happens? We say that individually we can do nothing, we are helpless; therefore, let us do something politically to bring about peace in the world; let us have faith in the vision of one world, of a classless society, and so on and so on. The intellect worships that vision, and to carry out that vision, we sacrifice ourselves and others. Politically, that is what is happening. We say that in order to end wars we must have one society, and to create that society, we are willing to destroy everything—which is using wrong means to a right end. All this is still within the field of the mind.

Also, are not all our religions man-made, that is, mind-made? Our rituals, our symbols, our disciplines, though they may temporarily alleviate, bring about an uplift, a feeling of well-being, are they not all within the field of time? When we regard the political and religious ideals by means of which we hope to bring about a change—to educate and discipline ourselves to be less selfish, to be less ambitious, to be more considerate, more virtuous, to renounce, not to acquire so much, and so on—when we look at this whole pattern, do we not see that it is a process of the mind? The mind, which is also the will, is the source of effort, of intentions, of conscious and unconscious motives; it is the center of the 'me' and the 'mine', and whatever it may do, however far it may endeavor to go, can that center ever bring about a fundamental change within itself?

I want to change, but not superficially, because I see that in the process of superficial change, there is mischievous action taking place. So, what am I to do? Isn't that your problem also, if you are really serious about all this? One may be a communist, one may be a socialist, one may be a reformer, or a religious person, but that is the core of our problem, is it not? Though we may have a hundred explanations of man, of his responses and activities, or of the universe, until we change fundamentally, no explanation has any value. I see that, not just casually, I see the importance of a radical change in myself. And how is that to be brought about? There is revolution only when the mind has ceased to function within the field of time, for only then is there a new element which is not of time. It is that new element which brings about a deep, lasting revolution. You can call that element God, truth, or what you will—the name you give to it is of no importance. But until I touch it, until I have a sense of that which will cleanse me completely, until I have faith in that which is not self-induced, not of the mind, obviously every change is a mere modification, every reformation has to be further reformed, and so on—infinite mischief.

So, what is one to do? Have you ever asked yourself this question? Not that I am asking you or you are asking me, but if we are at all intelligent, if we are at all aware of our own problems and those of the world, isn't this the first question to put to ourselves? Not what kind of beliefs, religions, sects, new teachers we should have—they are all so utterly empty and futile. But surely, this is the fundamental question that one ought to put to oneself—how to bring about a change which is not of time, which is not a matter of evolution, which is not a matter of slow growth. I can see that if I exercise will, control, if I discipline myself, there are certain modifications; I am better or worse, I am changed a little bit. Instead of being bad-tempered or angry or vicious or jealous, I am quiet; I have repressed all that, I have held it down. Every day I practice a certain virtue, repeat certain words, go to a shrine and repeat certain chants, and so on and so on. They all have a pacifying effect; they produce certain changes, but these changes are still of the mind, they are still within the field of time, are they not? My memory says, "I am this, and I must become that." Surely, such activity is still self-centered; though I deny greed, in seeking nongreed I am still within the self-enclosing process of the 'me'. And I can see that it leads nowhere, do what I will; though there may be change, as long as my thinking is held within the process of the 'me', there is no freedom from struggle, pain.

I do not know if you have inquired into this. The problem of change is very important, is it not? And can this change be brought about through a process of thinking, through disciplines, through rituals, through various forms of sacrifice, immolation, denial, suppression?—which, if you observe, are all tactics, designs of the mind. However much the self, the 'me', struggles to be free, can it ever be free? Whatever effort it makes, can it ever absolve itself from its own activities? If it cannot, then what is it to do? I hope you see the problem as I see it. You may translate it differently in words, but that is the core of our problem.

Now, since we do not see any outlet, any way of release from the process of the 'me', we begin to worship reason, the intellect. We reject everything else and say that the mind is the only important thing, the more intellectual, the more cunning, the more erudite, the better. That is why knowledge has become so important to us. Even though we may be worshippers of God, essentially we have denied God because our gods are the images of our own minds; our rituals, our churches—the whole business is still within the field of the mind. We say, "Since there is only the mind, let us make man according to the mind, according to reason." Our society, our relationships, everything we do conforms to the pattern of the mind, and whoever does not conform is either liquidated or otherwise denied.

Seeing all this, are we not concerned to find out how we can jump over that intangible barrier between the process of time and the timeless, between the projections of the mind and that which is not of the mind? If that is really an earnest question which we have put to ourselves, if it has become an urgent problem, then surely we will lay aside the obvious activities of the mind—the ideals, the rituals, the churches, the accumulation of knowledge—we will completely wash them out of our system. It is through negation that we will find the other thing, not through direct approach, and I can negate only when I begin to understand the ways of my own mind and see that I seek refuge, that I am acquisitive, that there is not a single moment when the mind is really quiet. The incessant chattering, the images, the things that I have acquired and hold on to, the words, the names, the memories, the escapes—of all that I have to be aware, have I not? Because, with that burden, which is of time, how can I experience something which is timeless? So, I must purge myself completely of all that, which means I must be alone—not alone in an ivory tower, but there must be that aloneness in which I see all the processes, the eddies of the mind. Then, as I observe, as I become more and more aware and begin to put aside without effort the things of the mind, I find that the mind becomes quiet; it is no longer curious, searching, groping, struggling, creating, and pursuing images. All those things have dropped away, and the mind becomes very quiet, it is as nothing. This is the thing that cannot be taught. By listening a hundred times to this statement, you are not going to get it; if you do, then you are mesmerized by words. It is a thing that must be experienced, that must be directly tasted, but it's no good hovering at the edge of it.

So, when the mind is still, not made still by self-discipline, control, by greed to experience something which is not of the mind, when the mind is really still, then you will find that there comes a state which brings a revolution in our outlook, in our attitude. This revolution is not brought about by the mind, but by something else. For this revolution to take place, the mind must be quiet; it must be literally as nothing, stripped, empty; and I assure you, it is not an easy job. That emptiness is not a state of daydreaming; you cannot get it by merely sitting still for ten hours or twenty-four hours of the day and trying to hold on to something. It can come only when the mind has understood its own processes, the conscious as well as the unconscious—which means one must be everlastingly aware. And the difficulty for most of us is inertia. That is another problem which we will not go into now. But the moment we begin to inquire and see the importance of change, we must go into all this. That means we must be willing to strip ourselves of everything to find the other, and when once we have even a slight glimmering of the other, which is not of the mind, then that will operate. That is the only revolution, that is the only thing that can give us hope, that can put an end to wars, to this destructive relationship.

Question: How is one who is superficial to become serious?

KRISHNAMURTI: Let us find out together. First of all, we must be aware that we are superficial, must we not? And are we? What does it mean to be superficial? Essentially, to be dependent, does it not? To depend on stimulation, to depend on challenge, to depend on another, to depend psychologically on certain values, certain experiences, certain memories—does not all that make for superficiality? When I depend on going to church every morning, or every week, in order to be uplifted, in order to be helped, does that not make me superficial? If I have to perform certain rituals to maintain my sense of integrity or to regain a feeling which I may once have had, does that not make me superficial? And does it not make me superficial when I give myself over to a country, to a plan, or to a particular political group? Surely, this whole process of dependence is an evasion of myself; this identification with the greater is the denial of what I am. But I cannot deny what I am; I must understand what I am, and not try to identify myself with the universe, with God, with a particular political party, or what you will. All this leads to shallow thinking, and from shallow thinking there is activity which is everlastingly mischievous, whether on a worldwide scale or on the individual scale.

So, first of all, do we recognize that we are doing these things? We don't; we justify them. We say, "What shall I do if I don't do these things? I'll be worse off; my mind will go to pieces. Now, at least, I am struggling towards something better." And the more we struggle, the more superficial we are. So, I have to see that first, have I not? And that is one of the most difficult things—to see what I am, to acknowledge that I am stupid, that I am shallow, that I am narrow, that I am jealous. If I see what I am, if I recognize it, then with that I can start. Surely, a shallow mind is a mind that escapes from what it is, and not to escape requires arduous investigation, the denial of inertia. The moment I know I am shallow, there is already a process of deepening—if I don't do anything about the shallowness. If the mind says, "I am petty, and I am going to go into it, I am going to understand the whole of this pettiness, this narrowing influence," then there is a possibility of transformation; but a petty mind, acknowledging that it is petty and trying to be nonpetty by reading, by meeting people, by traveling, by being incessantly active like a monkey, is still a petty mind.

Again, you see, there is a real revolution only if we approach this problem rightly. The right approach to the problem gives an extraordinary confidence which I assure you moves mountains—the mountains of one's own prejudices, conditionings. So, being aware of a shallow mind, do not try to become deep. A shallow mind can never know great depths. It can have plenty of knowledge, information, it can repeat words—you know, the whole paraphernalia of a superficial mind that is active. But if you know that you are superficial, shallow, if you are aware of the shallowness and observe all its activities without judging, without condemning, then you will soon see that the shallow thing has disappeared entirely without your action upon it. But that requires patience, watchfulness, not an eager desire for a result, for a reward, for achievement. It is only a shallow mind that wants an achievement, a result. The more you are aware of this whole process, the more you will discover the activities of the mind, but you must observe them without trying to put an end to them because the moment you seek an end, you are again caught in the duality of the 'me' and the 'not-me'—which is another problem.

Question: I read the Buddha because it helps me to think clearly about my own problems, and I read you and some others in the same way. You seem to suggest that such help is superficial and does not bring about a radical transformation. Is this a casual suggestion on your part, or do you mean to indicate that there is something very much deeper which cannot be discovered through reading?

KRISHNAMURTI: Do you read in order to be helped? Do you read in order to confirm your own experiences? Do you read in order to amuse yourself, to relax, to give your mind, this constantly active mind, a rest? The questioner says he reads because it helps him to solve his problems. Are you really helped by reading?—it does not matter who it is. When I go out seeking help, am I helped? I may find temporary relief, a momentary crack through which I can see the way, but surely, to find help, I must go within myself, must I not? Books can give you information about how to move towards the door which will solve your problems, but you must walk, must you not? You see, that is one of our difficulties—we want to be helped. We have innumerable problems, devastating, destructive problems in which we are caught, and we want help from somebody: the psychologist, the doctor, the Buddha, whoever it is. The very desire to be helped creates the image to which we become a slave, so the Buddha, or Krishnamurti, or X becomes the authority. We say, "He helped me once, and my goodness, I am going back to him again"—which indicates the shallow mind, the mind that is seeking help. Such a mind creates its own problems and then wants somebody else to solve them, or it goes to somebody to help it to uncover the process of its own thinking. So, unconsciously, the one who seeks help creates the authority: the authority of the book, the authority of the state, the authority of the dictator, the authority of the teacher, of the priest, you know, the whole business of it. And can I be helped, can you be helped? I know we would like to be. Fundamentally, can you and I be helped? Surely, it is only by understanding ourselves patiently, quietly, unobtrusively that we begin to discover, experience something which is not of our own creation, and it is that which brings about help, which begins to clear the field of our vision. But you cannot ask for that help; it must come to you darkly, uninvited. But when we are suffering, when we are in real psychological pain, we want somebody to give us a hand, and so the church, the particular friend, the teacher, or the state, becomes all-important. For that help, we are willing to become slaves.

So, we have to go into this problem of how we are caught in our own sorrows, we have to understand and clear it up for ourselves; for reality, God, or what you will, is not to be experienced through another. It must be experienced directly, it must come to you without any intermediary; but a mind that is seeking help, that is petitioning, that is asking, begging—such a mind can never find the other because it has not understood its own problems, it has not studied the process of its own activities. It is only when the mind is quiet that there is light. That light is not to be worshipped by the mind; the mind must be utterly silent, not asking, not hoping for experience. It must be completely still. Only then is there a possibility of that light which will dispel our darkness.

August 3, 1952

Third Talk in The Oak Grove

The last two times we met, we were considering the problem of change, and I would like, this afternoon, to go into the question of power, and whether power, as we know it, can bring about a fundamental, psychological transformation within oneself. The difficulty in going into this problem lies, I think, in understanding the usage of words. That is one of our major difficulties, is it not? Words like God, love, discipline, power, communist, American, Russian, have a very specific psychological significance in our lives, and when they are touched upon, we react nervously, emotionally; there is a psychological response. So, if we are to go further into this problem of change, I think we also have to consider the fact that certain words have a psychological influence on each one of us. We have built about ourselves so many verbal barriers, and it is very difficult to transcend those barriers and see the significance that lies beyond the word. After all, words are a means of communication, but if particular words cause a neurological or psychological reaction in us, then it becomes very difficult to communicate. And surely, this is another of our difficulties—that in trying to understand the problem of change, we have to strip ourselves of all ideals because conformity to a particular pattern, however reasonable, however logical and well thought out, is not a change at all, is it? Change implies a complete transformation, not the continuity of a modified thought. So, there are many factors to be considered in this whole problem of how to bring about a fundamental change, not only psychologically within ourselves but also outwardly.

I see the necessity of certain changes in myself, and I can either deal with the problem superficially or go into it very profoundly and find out what are its implications. When I see that I have to change, that it is a necessity, I generally exercise the will, do I not? Any process of change implies resistance, the application of effort, which is will. With that we are familiar. That is, I perceive in myself a state which is socially not good, or a state which brings conflict within me, and I want to go beyond it; I want to break down that particular quality or condition, so I suppress it, or I discipline myself to resist it, which necessitates a certain power of the will. We are accustomed to that process, are we not? So we think power in different forms—social, political, economic, inward, spiritual, and so on—is a necessity.

Now, is not this whole process of will a self-centered activity in which there is no release from the condition in which I am caught, in which the mind is held, but only a covering up and a continuity of the same thing in a modified form? And our education, our reforms, our religious thinking, our psychological struggles are all based on this process, are they not? I am this, and I want to become that, and in becoming that, I must employ a certain force of will; there must be resistance, control. And is not this process of control, of discipline, a self-centered activity which engenders a sense of power? The more you discipline, control yourself, the more there is of a certain concentrated activity, but is not that activity still within the field of the self, of the 'me' and the 'mine'? And is reality, God, or what you will, the outcome of self-centered activity? Yet do not all your religious books, your teachers, the various sects or societies to which you belong—do they not all imply, fundamentally, that change can be brought about through compulsion, through conformity, through the desire for success, that is, to achieve a certain result? But is not that whole process an activity of the 'me' in its desire to be something more? And can we, realizing it, bring that process to an end?

I do not know if you see the problem as I see it. All this activity, however reasonable, however noble or well calculated, is still within the field of the mind; it is the activity of the self, the result of desire, of the 'me' and the 'mine', is it not? And can the self, that consciousness which is always within the limits of the mind and therefore always in conflict—can that self ever go beyond itself? Will that self not always create conflict between individuals and therefore between groups, between nations?

Now, it seems to me very important to understand this, but is it a problem to each one of us? We see that a radical change is necessary in society, in ourselves, in our individual and group relationships, and how is it to be brought about? If change is through conformity to a pattern projected by the mind, through a reasonable, well-studied-out plan, then it is still within the field of the mind; therefore, whatever the mind calculates becomes the end, the vision, for which we are willing to sacrifice ourselves and others. If you maintain that, then it follows that we as human beings are merely the creation of the mind, which implies conformity, compulsion, brutality, dictatorships, concentration camps—the whole business. When we worship the mind, all that is implied, is it not? If I realize this, if I see the futility of discipline, of control, if I see that the various forms of suppression only strengthen the 'me' and the 'mine', then what am I to do? Have you ever put yourself that question? I see that to exercise any power over myself is evil; it is merely a continuation of the 'me' in a different form, and I also see that the 'me' must entirely cease if there is to be peace in the world and in myself. The 'me' as a person, as an entity, as a psychological process of accumulation, the 'me' that is always struggling to become something, the 'me' that is assertive, dogmatic, aggressive, the 'me' that is kind, loving—that is the center from which arise all conflicts, all compulsion, all conformity, all desire for success, and it is only in bringing it to an end that there is a possibility of peace within myself and outwardly. When I realize this, what am I to do? How am I to put an end to the 'me'?

Now, if this is a serious problem to each one of us, what is our response to it? Naturally, we cannot all give our replies, but we can see that any movement of the self in order to become better, nobler, any movement of suppression, any desire for success must come to an end. That is, the mind, which is the center of the 'me', has to become very quiet, has it not? The mind is the center of sensation; it is the result of memory, the accumulation of time, and any movement on the part of the mind to become something is still within the limits of the 'me', of sensation. And can the mind, which is sensation, which is memory, which is tradition, which is the calculating machine of the 'me', which is everlastingly seeking security, hiding behind words—can that mind, out of its own desire, by any exercise of its own will, come to an end? Can it cease by its own volition?

So, I must study my own mind, I must be aware of all its reactions—just be aware of my mind without any desire to transform it. Is that not the first necessary step?—if I can use that word step without introducing the idea of time. To be aware of the process of my mind without condemnation, to observe the fact without judgment, to be merely aware of *what is*—is it possible to do that? Some may say yes, some may say no—but what others say about this matter is of very little importance, is it not? You have to experiment with this, experience it, and is it possible to experience without building up images, symbols? That is, we generally experience only the things that we recognize, do we not? We are conscious of experiencing only when we recognize the experience, and if we are not capable of recognizing it, there is no experience. So, the factor of recognition is essential to what we call experience. Now, is God, truth, or what you will, a matter of recognition? If I can recognize something, it implies that I have already experienced it before, does it not? That which I have experienced before becomes a memory, and when there is a desire for the continuation of that experience, I project that memory and recognize it, experience it. That is, through memory, through recognition, through experience, I build the center of the 'me'.

So, for most of us, it is extremely arduous to go into this problem of change and really bring about a transformation within ourselves. Can I change if I am constantly experiencing through the process of recognition, whether on the verbal level or the psychological level? That is, when I meet you for the first time, I do not know you, but the second time I meet you, I have certain memories of you; there is like or dislike, pain or pleasure. So, through the dictates of pain and pleasure, I say I have met you; there is a process of recognition. That recognition is established verbally or psychologically, and if I am to go beyond and discover a state which is not mere recognition, recollection, memory, must not the center of the 'me', which is the process of recognition, come to an end? There is this entity as the 'me' which is everlastingly craving experience, seeking more of what it has known, whether outwardly or psychologically, and as long as the 'me' continues to exist, whatever I experience only strengthens the 'me', does it not? Therefore I create more and more problems, endless conflict. And is it possible for the mind to be so still that the process of recognition ceases? After all, that is creation, is it not?

Please, in listening to these talks it seems to me that what is important is not to accept all this but to let the significance of the words penetrate and see whether they have any validity, any truth. It is that quality of truth which liberates, not the verbal denial or assertion, and so it is very important to listen rightly, that is, not to be caught in words, in the logic of certain statements, or in your own experiences. You are here to find out what another says, and to find out you must listen, and to listen rightly is one of the most difficult things to do, is it not? Because when I use words like *experience, truth,* and so on, you immediately have certain responses— certain images, symbols come up, and if the mind gets caught in those symbols, you cannot go beyond.

So, our problem is how to free the mind of this self-centered activity not only at the level of social relationships but also at the psychological level. It is this activity of the self that is causing the mischief, the misery, both in our individual lives and in our life as a group, as a nation, and we can put an end to it only if we understand the whole process of our own thinking. Can thought bring about a vital change? Up to now we have relied on thought, have we not? The political revolution, whether of the right or the extreme left, is the result of thought. And can thought fundamentally change man, change you and me? If you say it can, then you must see all the implications—that man is the product of time, that there is nothing beyond time, and so on and on. So, if I am to create a fundamental change in myself, can I rely on thought as an instrument to bring about that transformation? Or, can there be a fundamental change only when there is the ending of thought? My problem, then, is to experiment, to find out, and I can find out only through self-knowledge, through knowing myself, watching, being aware in moments when I'm off guard. It is only when I begin to understand the process of my own thinking that I can find out whether or not there is a possibility of a fundamental change; until then, mere assertion that I can or cannot change is of little significance. Though we see the importance of a radical change in the world and in ourselves, there is very little chance of such a change as long as we do not understand the thinker and his thought. The economist and the politician are never revolutionary. It is only the truly religious person that is revolutionary, the man who is seeking reality, God, or what you will. Those who merely believe, who follow a pattern, who belong to a particular society, sect, or group—they are not seekers; therefore, they are not real revolutionaries. We can bring about a transformation within ourselves only when we understand the process of our own thinking.

Question: What do you mean by ambition? Would you consider any improvement of oneself ambitious? At what point does ambition begin?

KRISHNAMURTI: Do we not know when we are ambitious? When I want something more, when I want to assert myself, when I want to become something, is that not ambition? Can we say where it begins and where it ends? Is not all self-improvement a form of ambition? I may not be ambitious in this world; I may not want to be a leader with great political power or a big businessman with a lot of property, position, but I may be very ambitious spiritually. That is, I want to become a saint, I want to be free from all pride. Is not the very assertion of wanting to be something the beginning of ambition? The desire not to be ambitious—is that not self-improvement, and therefore self-centered activity? If I am proud and, seeing the implications of pride, I cultivate humility, is not that cultivated humility a self-centered activity? And is that not ambition? And if you are not to cultivate humility, then what are you going to do with pride? How is one to deal with it? The very desire to get rid of one thing in order to be something else—is that not a self-centered activity, which is ambition? Please see how extremely difficult it is, when you know what you are, not to struggle to be something else. This process of struggle, this trying to become great or humble or generous is called evolution, is it not? I am this, and I am going through a struggle to become that. From thesis I proceed to antithesis, and out of that create synthesis. This process is called growth, evolution, is it not? Now, in that is implied self-centered activity, the improving of the self, the 'me'. But can the 'me' ever be improved? It may be improved within its own field, but if I want to go beyond and find out if there is something which is not of the 'me', will self-improvement help to bring about that discovery? So, being ambitious, what am I to do? Should I suppress ambition? And is not the very suppression of ambition a form of ambition which negatively strengthens the 'me', and in which there is a certain sense of power, dominance?

I see that I am ambitious, and what am I to do? Is it possible to be free from it?—which does not mean that I must become nonambitious. Is it possible to be free from ambition? I can think it out logically, see the conflicts, the ruthlessness, the brutality of ambition in my relationships, and so on. And will that help me? Will explanations of the perniciousness of ambition help me to be free from ambition? Or, is there only one way, which is to see all the implications of ambition without condemnation, just to be aware of the fact that I am ambitious not only at the conscious level but at the deeper levels of my own thinking? Surely, I must be completely aware of it, without any resistance, because the more I struggle against it, the more vitality I give it. Ambition has become a habit with me, and the more I resist a habit, the stronger it becomes. Whereas, if I am aware of it, merely see the fact of it, does that not bring about a radical change? I am no longer concerned with suppressing ambition or with putting it aside, nor am I satisfied with any explanation—I am directly concerned with the fact of ambition. So, when I look at it, what do I see? Is ambition mere habit? Am I caught in the habit of a society which is based on ambition, on success, on being somebody? Am I stimulated by challenge, by the sense of achievement, and without that stimulation do I feel lost, and so I depend on stimulation? Is it not possible to be aware of all this, to see the implications of it and not react—just see the fact? And will that perception not bring about a radical change? If I acknowledge that I am ambitious and see the implications of it not only at the verbal level but also inwardly, which means that I am aware of the influence of habit, sensation, tradition, and so on, then what has happened? My mind is quiet with regard to that fact, is it not? My mind does not react to it any more—it is a fact. And the quiet acceptance of *what is* is a release from that fact, is it not?

Please do not accept this. Experiment with it and you will see. First be aware that you are ambitious, or whatever it is, and then see all your reactions to it, whether those reactions are habitual, traditional, verbal. Merely to oppose the verbal responses by another series of words will not free you, or if it is tradition, in the mere cultivation of a new tradition or habit you will not find release. The very desire to suppress ambition is a trick of the mind to be something else—which is part of ambition. So, when the mind sees that any movement it makes with regard to a particular quality is part of the process of its own sustenance and security, what can it do? It cannot do anything; therefore, it is immediately quiet with regard to that quality. It is no longer related to it. But this is an arduous task, is it not?

A revolutionary inward change is essential, and if we are to understand the problem of change, we must go into all this and study the problem of the 'me' from different angles.

August 9, 1952

Fourth Talk in The Oak Grove

In talking about the necessity of fundamental and radical change, should we not consider the problem of method, of the "how"? For most of us, the means, the method, the system, becomes very important. We see that a change is essential, and so our minds immediately turn to the problem of how to change, how to bring about the radical transformation which is so obviously necessary. Let us for a moment consider whether the "how," the technique, is important. What happens when we are concerned with the technique, the "how"? The cultivation of the "how," the practice of a particular method with the intention of success, does that not induce inertia? Is that not one of the primary causes of inertia in ourselves? The moment I have found the "how," the system, I begin to practice it, which implies a conformity brought about by the desire to succeed, to achieve a certain result. So, for most of us, the "how" becomes very important—how am I to change, what system am I to follow, how am I to meditate, what discipline should I practice? Don't we ask this question all the time? Are we not constantly seeking the "how"?

Now, is that important—the "how," the method? And is it not far more important to be aware that the mind is demanding the "how" and to see why it is seeking a method? If you want a method, a technique, you will find it, for every religious teacher offers a certain form of discipline, control, or a system of meditation. What happens in this process of self-control, in the process of trying to follow a particular discipline? I do not know if you have practiced any disciplines. If you have, are you not aware that the mind is conforming to a pattern of thought? And in doing so, does not the mind produce its own limitations? Surely, though it is able to live and function within a certain field of thought and action, such a mind is bound by conformity, in which there is no freedom to experience anything anew. So, by practicing a discipline with an end in view, by gradually conforming in the hope of success, the mind induces inertia, does it not? Obviously, that is one of our greatest problems—the laziness, the extraordinary inertia of the mind, and the more we want to break down this inertia, the more the mind inquires "how." That is why the "how" becomes so extraordinarily important for most of us.

If we do not seek the "how," the method, the technique, what are we to do? Suppose I see the falseness of this pursuit of the "how"; I see that to find and practice a method is mere repetition, which essentially dulls the mind. If I see that, see the falseness of it, then what happens? Then the mind is really watchful, is it not? To see the implications of practicing any particular method, to be aware of the significance of it, not only at the superficial level, but fundamentally, deeply—does that not quicken the mind, is there not greater alertness? And is that not one of our problems when we are considering the question of fundamental change? Because, it seems to me that the desire for a method, the search for a technique which will bring about a radical change in ourselves, induces a slowing down, a deadening of the mind. A method, a technique may produce certain experiences, but are not those experiences merely the result of a very careful training, are they not the projections of a mind which has constantly followed a particular pattern of thought and action? And is reality, God, or what you will, to be experienced through any pattern? Surely, it can come only when the mind is free of desire, the invitation to further experience.

So, when we are discussing the question of change, should we not inquire into this complex problem of technique, effort? If you watch your mind, you will see how quickly it falls into a particular habit of thought; because it has once experienced a pleasant sensation, a feeling of joy, there is a desire for its repetition, and so the mind cultivates it, practices a discipline, hoping to recapture that pleasure. And is not this repetition, with its desire, one of the primary causes of inertia? Through technique, through discipline, through a method, can there be a fundamental change? Is not this fundamental change brought about not through any manipulation of thought but only when the mind understands its own activities, its self-centered movements, and so comes to an end? For that, one needs constant watchfulness, not a discipline, a technique.

Perhaps some of you practice various forms of discipline, and so you may be listening rather guardedly, you may be resisting. You will say, "What shall I do without a discipline? My mind will be all over the place." But if you want to understand something which I am trying to convey, will you resist what I am saying? Or, will you try to find out the truth of the matter for yourself? Not that you should accept what I am saying, but do you not want to find out what is true in this affair? And to find out, your mind must not be in a state of resistance, in a state of fear. Because you have practiced a discipline for a number of years doesn't mean that it's right; there may be the fear that if you remove the fence which you have so carefully built around yourself, the mind will overflow and get lost. And to find out what is true, one must obviously listen not according to one's desires, promptings, and wishes but with an inquiring mind, a mind that is in a state of discovery. I think that brings about its own discipline, which is not the discipline imposed by the mind in order to achieve a certain result.

Take, for example, the problem of integration. We are in a state of contradiction at different levels. Each level is in conflict within itself and with the other levels of our being; there is conflict at both the conscious and the unconscious levels. Please follow this; do not try to feel integrated or inquire how you are to arrive at the state of integration. If you will listen and not try to achieve a result, then perhaps the thing will come without your asking.

We are aware of contradiction at different levels within ourselves, and there are various methods of bringing about the so-called unification of these contradictions—analysis, hypnosis, constant introspection, and so on—all of which entail a struggle to establish the integration of our whole being. I recognize that a sense of unity, a sense of inner completeness is necessary, and I also see that this integration cannot be brought about by avoiding contradiction, by enclosing the mind in a particular pattern of thought and action. A state of integration is obviously necessary because only in that state is there freedom from conflict, which enables the mind to discover, to experience, to feel things out anew. If, seeing the importance of integration, of that state of inner unification, that state of completeness, I do not inquire how I am to get at it, am I not then aware of all the contradictions? And does not that awareness allow the unconscious, the deep layers of myself in which there are contradictions, to come out? There is no resistance. I simply want to find out, and so I watch my dreams, my waking consciousness, every hint of conflict, every incident that awakens a contradiction. My concern is not integration, but to be aware of these contradictions in different layers, at different levels. So, what happens? Since I am not seeking a particular state but am just being aware of the different contradictions in myself, observing them from moment to moment, does not this watchfulness bring about an integration which is not that of desire, not that of a mind which has sought integration? What have I done? I have understood conflict, not run away from it; I have let it come out from the very bottom of my being, and then, perhaps, one has a flash of this integration which is not induced but which comes of itself. When there is a flash of integration, the mind proceeds to live in the memory of that experience and thereby sets going the machinery of imitation, conformity. That memory is not integration; it is merely a memory. So, one has again to be aware of how the mind, having experienced a sense of integration, instead of being integrated, now lives in memory. And so the question arises how to maintain, through memory, a living quality, which then becomes our problem.

So, when we consider the problem of change, we have to go into this question of memory, the cultivation of a particular habit or pattern of action. The mind can never be free when it is seeking or cultivating the "how." To listen to my own contradictions, to see that my mind is pursuing memories, cultivating habits in order to be secure, and is thereby held in the self-centered activity of the 'me'—to be really aware of all that without going with it or battling against it is much more important, requires far greater energy, greater alertness than to cultivate a particular pattern of discipline. Conformity obviously leads to inertia, and as most of us worship success in others and in ourselves, we naturally want to conform. Is it not one of our traditions to live in a state of conformity, in a state of discipline? Please do not think I am against discipline; that is not the problem. We are considering the question of change, revolution within ourselves, and can that revolution, that fundamental transformation be brought about through discipline? Obviously it cannot—at least for me, it cannot. Discipline can only make me more conforming, and conformity does not bring about a change. I have to understand why the mind seeks conformity, and can the mind ever be free from this pressure of tradition, not only the external, but the constant, self-created tradition which is memory? As we have seen, whatever the mind does, however erudite, however extensive, however cunning, however speculative it may be, it cannot produce a fundamental change; and a fundamental change is necessary, is it not? No reason, no logic, no discipline can bring about this lasting, radical transformation. It is only when the mind is quiet that there is a possibility of something else coming and transforming us. But we cannot seek it—it must come, and it can come only when the mind is capable of receiving it, which is when the mind is no longer thinking in terms of time. For all thinking is a process of time, is it not? We cannot put an end to thinking, but we can understand the movement of thought, and as long as there is a 'me', a thinker apart from the thought, obviously we are thinking in terms of time. When the mind seeks to go beyond time through discipline, it only creates barriers, strengthens time.

So, when you listen to all this, is it not important to find out how you are listening? Is it not important to see your own reactions, to study your own mind and begin to know yourself? After all, what I am saying is what each one of us is thinking, more or less, but we cannot go beyond the verbal level if we do not see the truth of this, and with patience and watchfulness, become aware of the movement of our own thought. If we do that, then, perhaps, some other element, some other quality which is not of the mind will come in, but it can come in only when there is no desire for it, when the mind is not caught in the process of recognition.

Question: Of all the spiritual teachers, you are the only one I know of who does not offer a system of meditation for the attainment of inner peace. We all agree that inner peace is necessary, but how can we attain it without practicing a technique, whether of Eastern yoga or Western psychology?

KRISHNAMURTI: Isn't it too bad that there are teachers, spiritual teachers and followers? The moment you have a teacher and you become the follower, have you not destroyed that flame which must constantly be kept alive if you are to find out, to discover? When you look to a teacher to help you, does not the teacher become more important than the truth you are seeking? So, let us put aside the teacher-and-follower attitude; let us get it out of our systems completely and regard the problem itself as it is affecting each one of us. No teacher can help you to find truth, obviously; one has to find it within oneself; one has to go through the pain, the suffering, the inquiry; one has to discover and understand things for oneself. But in becoming the follower of a particular teacher, have you not cultivated inertia, laziness, is there not a darkening of the mind? And, of course, the various teachers with their various groups are in contradiction, competing with each other, doing propaganda—you know all the nonsense round it.

So, the whole question of followers and teachers is ridiculous and childish. What is important in the question is this: Is there a method, whether Eastern or Western, to attain peace? If peace is attained through practicing a certain method, that which you have attained and which you call peace is no longer a living quality; it is a dead thing. You know by formulation what peace should be, and you have laid down a path which you follow towards it. Surely, that peace is a projection of your own desire, is it not? Therefore, it is no longer peace. It is what you want, a thing opposite to that which you are. I am in a state of conflict, of misery, of contradiction; I am unhappy, violent, and I want a refuge, a state in which I shall not be disturbed. So I go to various teachers, guides; I read books, practice disciplines which promise what I want; I suppress, control, conform in order to gain peace. And is that peace? Surely, peace is not a thing to be sought after—it comes. It is a byproduct, not an end in itself. It comes when I am beginning to understand the whole process of myself, my contradictions, desires, ambitions, pride. But if I make of peace an end in itself, then I live in a state of stagnation. And is that peace?

So, as long as I am seeking peace through a system, a method, a technique, I shall have peace, but it will be the peace of conformity, the peace of death. And that is what most of us want. I have had a glimmer of something, an experience which cannot be put into words, and I want to live in that state; I want it to continue; I want an absolute reality. There may be an absolute reality, or there may be experiences of greater and greater significance, but if I cling to one or the other, am I not cultivating slow death? And death is not peace. So, I cannot possibly imagine what peace is in this state of confusion, in this state of conflict. What I can imagine is the opposite, and that which is opposite to what I am is not peace. So, a technique merely helps me to obtain something which is the opposite of what I am, and without understanding what I am—going into it completely, not only at the conscious, but also at the unconscious levels—without understanding the whole process of myself, merely to seek peace has very little significance.

You see, most of us are lazy; we are so inert; we want teachers, monasteries to help us; we do not want to find out for ourselves through our own constant awareness, through our own inquiry, through our own experience, however vague, however subtle, elusive. So we join churches, groups, we become followers of this or that—which means there is a struggle on one side, and the cultivation of inertia on the other. But if one really wishes to find out, experience directly—and we can discuss what that experiencing is at another time—then surely it is imperative that one put aside all these things and understand oneself. Self-knowledge is the beginning of wisdom, and that alone can bring peace.

Question: Can the mind ever be still, and should it be still?

KRISHNAMURTI: Let us find out. Why should the mind be still? And can I make the mind still? Is the 'me' who is trying to still the mind an entity apart from the mind? Who is the 'me' that is trying to control the mind? And who is the 'me' that asks if the mind should be still? Is not the thinker, the questioner, part of the mind? Why is there this division in the mind as the thinker and the thought, the 'me' and the not 'me'? Why is there this division? Please, that is the problem, is it not? I do not know whether the mind can be still or whether it should be still, but I want to find out, and I shall find out only when I have inquired into who the entity is that is asking this question. Is he different from the mind? For most of us, he is, is he not? There is the discipliner, the thinker, the controller, the experiencer, the observer apart from the observed, apart from the experience, apart from the thought. Having brought about this division, we then ask how the thinker is to control his thoughts, and from that arises the question of technique.

Now, is the questioner, the thinker, an entity apart from thought? Please let us go into this, not for the sake of argument, not so that you can oppose my ideas by your ideas, but let us find out together what is the truth of this matter. First of all, we do not know whether the mind should be still or even whether it is capable of being still, but before it can experience stillness or find out if it is possible to be still, must not the mind bridge this gulf between the thinker and the thought? Who is this entity that is always trying to control—the censor, the judge, that says this is right, that is wrong? Is he different from the thing which he is observing in himself? For most of us he is different, he is an entity quite apart who is watching, guiding, shaping, controlling, suppressing thought. Now, why is this entity different, apart? But first of all, are you not aware that there is a different entity, the higher self controlling the lower?—you know, the whole business of it. There is in each one of us a thing apart which is guiding, shaping, watching every thought. We know that, do we not? Now, how has that separate entity come into being? Is it not the result of the mind, the result of thought? Obviously it is; it is not different from thought. If I had not thought about it, it could not exist, so it is a product of thought, is it not? And can that which is a product of thought be a spiritual entity, apart from thought? Can it be a timeless entity, something eternal, beyond the thought process? If it is a timeless entity, I cannot think about it because I can only think in terms of time. But I do think about it, for it is I who have set it apart; I am related to it; therefore, it is a projection of my own memory, a product of thought. It is not something apart from me, yet I have set it apart. Why? I see that my thoughts are transient, that everything around me is impermanent, that there is death, decay; everything is in movement, in a state of flux. So I say there must be something in me which is permanent, and I want that permanency; therefore, I create the entity, the thinker, the judge, who is apart from me. That is, thought separates and establishes part of itself as a permanent entity who is watching, guiding, shaping; and then the problem arises of how this entity, the thinker, is to bridge the gap and integrate himself with his thoughts. Until I really understand and solve this problem, it is not possible to have a still mind or to find out if the mind can ever be still.

So, please just listen to what I am saying, and try to find out if it is possible for the observer and the observed to be one, for the thinker and his thought to be integrated. As long as they are separate, the mind cannot be still. As long as I am apart from my thought, as long as I am away from the experience and observing it, as long as I am conscious that I am still, there cannot be peace, there cannot be stillness. Until I understand and resolve this fundamental problem, to search for peace or to ask whether the mind should or should not be still has very little meaning.

So, I am broken up into various fragmentary states, and how is all that to become one? Can I do anything about it? That is, the thinker, the actor, the maker of patterns of action—can he do anything about it? And if he does, is there not then another fragment to be brought into focus and absorbed? As long as there is the maker of patterns, the thinker, can he bring about integration? Surely, it is impossible, is it not? So, I have to find out how this separate entity as the thinker comes into being; I have to see how it accumulates memory, wealth, knowledge, property, flattery, insult—I have to be aware of the whole thing. It is when I am more and more aware of its reactions, its implications, that I begin to find out whether it is possible for this extraordinary integration to take place, this stillness which is not of the mind, which is not the product of discipline, of control, of conformity to a particular pattern of thought or action. What is that state? When the mind is no longer separating itself as the thinker and the thought, can it be called "still"? Is there not then a different kind of movement which is not of time, a different kind of becoming which is not of the 'me' and the 'mine'? We know stillness only as a reaction within the activity of the 'me', but is there not a stillness which is not of the 'me'? But that state cannot possibly be conceived as long as there is a division between the thinker and the thought, as long as the thinker is trying to experience stillness. It comes only when the thinker is the thought.

August 10, 1952

Fifth Talk in The Oak Grove

May I request those who are so anxious to take photographs of me to refrain from doing so. I do not give autographs, nor do I want to pose for photographs, and please don't embarrass yourself by asking me about it.

If we can this evening talk over together this problem of fundamental change, I think it will be very profitable. As there are so many of us and we cannot discuss it individually, perhaps you will kindly listen to me and try to find out what I mean. I feel that this radical change demands a certain attitude of mind, a certain state of consciousness, and I want to talk it over so that you and I together understand both the problem and its resolution. I feel we have so far dealt with the problem of change merely on the level of active consciousness. We see that a change, a psychological change, is necessary, and we set about to find ways and means to achieve that change. Such a pursuit is still on the level of active consciousness, on the superficial level of the mind, is it not? And sometimes we feel that if we could only get at the unconscious, resolve or bring to the surface all its hidden motives, pursuits, and urges, then perhaps, a vital change would be brought about. I feel there is quite a different way of approach to this problem, and I would like to talk it over hesitantly and rather tentatively with you.

To consider this problem fully we must go into the question of what is consciousness. I wonder if you have thought about it for yourself, or have merely quoted what authorities have said about consciousness? I do not know how you have understood from your own experience, from your own study of yourself, what this consciousness implies—not only the consciousness of everyday activity and pursuits, but the consciousness that is hidden, deeper, richer, and much more difficult to get at. If we are to discuss this question of a fundamental change in ourselves and therefore in the world, and in this change to awaken a certain vision, an enthusiasm, a zeal, a faith, a hope, a certainty which will give us the necessary impetus for action—if we are to understand that, isn't it necessary to go into this question of consciousness?

We can see what we mean by consciousness at the superficial level of the mind. Obviously, it is the thinking process, thought. Thought is the result of memory, verbalization; it is the naming, recording, and storing up of certain experiences so as to be able to communicate, and at this level there are also various inhibitions, controls, sanctions, disciplines. With all this we are quite familiar. And when we go a little deeper, there are all the accumulations of the race—the hidden motives, the collective and personal ambitions, prejudices—which are the result of perception, contact, and desire. This total consciousness, the hidden as well as the open, is centered round the idea of the 'me', the self.

When we discuss how to bring about a change, we generally mean a change at the superficial level, do we not? Through determinations, conclusions, beliefs, controls, inhibitions, we struggle to reach a superficial end which we want, which we crave for, and we hope to arrive at that with the help of the unconscious, of the deeper layers of the mind; therefore, we think it is necessary to uncover the depths of oneself. But there is everlasting conflict between the superficial levels and the so-called deeper levels—all psychologists, all those who have pursued self-knowledge are fully aware of that.

Now, will this inner conflict bring about a change? And is that not the most fundamental and important question in our daily life: How to bring about a radical change in ourselves? Will mere alteration at the superficial level bring it about? Will understanding the different layers of consciousness, of the 'me'—uncovering the past, the various personal experiences from childhood up to now, examining in myself the collective experiences of my father, my mother, my ancestors, my race, the conditioning of the particular society in which I live—will the analysis of all that bring about a change which is not merely an adjustment?

I feel, and surely you also must feel, that a fundamental change in one's life is essential—a change which is not a mere reaction, which is not the outcome of the stress and strain of environmental demands. And how is one to bring about such a change? My consciousness is the sum total of human experience, plus my particular contact with the present, and can that bring about a change? Will the study of my own consciousness, of my activities, will the awareness of my thoughts and feelings and stilling the mind in order to observe without condemnation—will that process bring about a change? Can there be change through belief, through identification with a projected image called the ideal? Does not all this imply a certain conflict between what I am and what I should be? And will conflict bring about fundamental change? I am in constant battle within myself and with society, am I not? There is a ceaseless conflict going on between what I am and what I want to be, and will this conflict, this struggle, bring about a change? I see a change is essential, and can I bring it about by examining the whole process of my consciousness, by struggling, by disciplining, by practicing various forms of repression? I feel such a process cannot bring about a radical change. Of that one must be completely sure. And if that process cannot bring about a fundamental transformation, a deep inward revolution, then what will? I hope I have made myself clear so far.

Do we see that the struggle to change what one is will not bring about a revolution, an inward transformation? If I see that, then what is the next step, what am I to do? Before I can find out the truth of this matter, must I not be very clear that such a process—the restrictions, moralities, compulsions, and thoughts which are continually imprinted upon me by the society in which I have been brought up and conditioned—can never bring about a fundamental change? I must be very clear about that, must I not? And I doubt if we are.

So, I think it is important to see very clearly for oneself that the way we have been attempting to change ourselves is utterly false, for if that process is seen to be false, then we shall be in a state of mind to discover what is the true way of changing. But if we do not see the content of the false in our minds, in our habits of thought, and so on, then how can we ever find the other? So, should we not find out for ourselves, first of all, whether the pursuits with which we are familiar can ever bring about a radical change? Discipline, suppression, control, analysis, going through various forms of hypnosis to release the unconscious, adherence to a belief, conformity, the constant developing of a particular quality, the struggle to follow an ideal—is not this whole process utterly false? And if it is false, then should we not look at it, understand it, go into it and be completely free of it? Surely, it must be completely put away from us, and only then is there a possibility of discovering the new, which will bring about a transformation.

To convey verbally how to bring about a radical change is comparatively simple, but to actually experience that new element, that transforming quality, is entirely different. That is why I feel you should listen not merely to hear what I am saying but to find out for yourself whether the disciplines you have practiced, the ambitions, the jealousies, the envies you have felt, the various ideals and beliefs you have followed, the analysis you have gone through, the introspection and struggle in which you have been caught—whether these things have any validity. And if they have not, then what is the state of the mind that has seen through and finished with them all?

Let us put the problem differently. However much I struggle to be different, to change, is not that struggle still part of the 'me' that is desirous of a result, that is seeking a continuity of happiness, the perpetuation of a particular state? I am greedy or envious or acquisitive, and I see the implications of it, so I discipline myself against it, I suppress it, try to inhibit certain reactions. This desire, this struggle to change greed into something else, is it not still an activity of the 'me' that is attempting to become a better 'me'? And the 'me', the 'I', this center of the accumulating process, can it ever be "better"? And we know those moments, those rare occasions when the 'me' is absent, completely absent, in which there is a timeless state, a sense of happiness that is not measured by this mind.

So, our problem is, how to bring about a change without effort? We are used to effort, are we not? We have been brought up in the habit of effort. Not liking this, we make effort to change it into that. Seeing myself to be ugly, selfish, or what you will, I make tremendous effort to change it. That is all we know. Now, realizing all this, being aware of the workings of the mind, is it possible not to make effort—and see what happens? Our effort is always towards success and conformity, is it not? We work towards a desired end, and to achieve it, we must conform. That is all we know in various degrees, negatively or positively. And is it possible to free the mind from this habit, that is, to make no effort, but merely be in a state in which the mind sees the fact and does not act upon the fact in order to transform it?

If we can look at ourselves without any desire to change, then there is a possibility of a radical change. But that is extremely difficult, is it not? It is not easy to observe oneself without the desire to do something about it. When we have a pleasant experience, we want to continue in that experience. If I had a pleasant experience yesterday, I want to continue it today; my mind lives on that experience of yesterday, and so it is everlastingly making an effort to recapture the past or to create the future from the memory of yesterday. Is it not possible for the mind to be aware of all this? And if you are not aware, you cannot be quiet, you cannot but make effort. You have to know the various activities of the mind, you have to be conscious of them, aware of what the mind is doing, and being aware, seeing how every kind of effort is still within the field of struggle, of trying to become something, and therefore of conformity—being aware of all that, is it not possible to observe without effort, to look without any desire to change what you are into something else?

It is extremely difficult to talk about this, to convey in words the thing that actually happens when you do not desire any particular change. After all, that is what we mean by integration, is it not? When you see the whole process of the mind, when you are aware of the various struggles, divisions, cleavages, and in the center there is no movement to transform or to bring these cleavages together, then the observer is essentially quiet. He does not wish to transform anything, he is merely aware that these things are happening—which requires enormous patience, does it not? But most of us are so eager to change, to do something about ourselves; we are impatient for an end, for a result. When the mind is aware of its own activities, not only the conscious, but also the unconscious, then you do not have to examine the unconscious to bring the hidden things to the surface—they are there. But we do not know how to observe. And don't ask, "How am I to observe, what is the technique?" The moment you have a technique, it is finished, you do not observe. The quietness of the center comes only when you are aware of all this, and you see that you cannot do anything about it; it is so. As long as the mind is active in its desire to transform itself, it can only be a model of its own projection; therefore, there is no transformation. If you really see the truth of this, then there comes a state of mind which is not concerned with change at all—and therefore a change does take place.

As I said, this is a very difficult subject to talk about. It is more a question not of verbal or so-called intellectual comprehension but of feeling out for oneself how the activities of the mind do impede the radical change. I will try to answer some of these questions.

Question: I think all mysticism is foolish, and your talks seem to have a mystical undertone. Is this your intention, or is my reaction to your talks a peculiar one based on my own prejudices exclusively?

KRISHNAMURTI: What do we mean by "mysticism"? Something hidden, mysterious? Something that comes out of India? Something you feel when your mind is irrational? Something vague, unclear, of which the prophets and teachers have spoken? Or, is it the experiencing of something real, something which is the summation of reason and yet is beyond reason, which is not verbal, an experience which is not a mere projection of the mind? Is it not important to find out the truth of the matter, without condemnation or acceptance?

We live in experience, do we not? We know life only as experience. And what do we mean by that word *experience?* Something which we can recognize, do we not? Something which we can name, which we can communicate to others. I have an experience only when I am capable of recognizing it. Otherwise, I have no experience. Once having had a certain experience, I store it in memory, name it, give it a particular term, and when a similar experience comes, I recognize it, I give it the same term which I have used before. So, is not all experience that we are aware of based on recognition? And is truth, God, that something which is unnameable, a matter of recognition? That is, can reality be recognized? To recognize it, I must have had an experience of it before. Having had a previous experience of it, I say, "There it is again"; therefore, what I experience is never new.

Is it not important to inquire into this question of recognition and experience? If I am capable of recognizing an experience, does it not indicate that I have already experienced it? Therefore the experience which I now have is not new, it is already the old. As that which is reexperienced, recognized, is never new but always the old, can it be reality, God? Must not this process of recognition come to an end before the new can be? And can that which is the new be verbalized, put into words? If it cannot, then is mysticism the experiencing of that which is beyond the verbal level, beyond the recognition of the mind? Surely, to be aware of that state, whatever it is, must we not go beyond all images, all knowledge? To find reality, God, or what you will, must we not go beyond the symbols of Christianity, of Hinduism, of Buddhism? Must we not free the mind from all habits, traditions, from all personal and collective ambitions? You may call this "mysticism" and say that it sounds foolish, but it is only when the mind is as nothing that it is capable of receiving the new. If we rely entirely on the mind for our guidance, if our action is based exclusively on reason, on logic, on conclusions, on materialistic reactions, then we will obviously create a brutal, ruthless world. Seeing all this, is it not possible for the mind to go beyond and discover that which is new, the timeless?

Question: I find it extremely difficult to concentrate. Would you please go into this matter.

KRISHNAMURTI: Let us go into this matter together and see if we cannot understand what it is to concentrate without making an effort to be concentrated. Actually, what happens when you are attempting to concentrate? There is a conflict, is there not? You are trying to fix your mind on a particular thought, and your mind goes off, so there is a division, a cleavage in the mind between what it wants to concentrate upon and what it is interested in. There is this constant battle going on. We try to discipline the mind; we practice focusing our thought on a particular idea, phrase, image, or symbol, and the mind is always wandering off. With that we are familiar, are we not?

Now, how is the mind to be concentrated? If it is interested, is there an effort to concentrate? And why is there this division between various thoughts, pursuits, desires? If that can be understood, then there will be natural concentration, will there not? Why is there this division of attention between the thing in which I am trying to be interested and a thought which is apart from that? And what happens when we are aware of this division? We try to bridge the gap so that the mind can be concentrated on only one thing.

So, is not our problem that of the thinker and the thought? I want to think about one particular thought, and I put my mind on it, but another part of me wanders off. I pull it back and try to concentrate, and again it wanders off, so I keep this conflict going. I never try to find out why there is a thinker apart from the thought, why the thinker is always trying to control the thought, bring it back. Why is there this division? That is the problem, is it not? If there is no thinker apart from the thought, then every thought is concentration, is it not? Please observe your own thinking and you will see. There is the thinker trying to control his thought, trying to do something about his thought, trying to change it, dominate it. Now, why is there this division? And can the thinker ever dominate all his thoughts? He can do it only when he is completely absorbed in one particular thought, wholly identified with one belief, one symbol. Such a state obviously leads to insanity, does it not?

Now, can we understand why the thinker chooses between various thoughts and tries to dwell upon one particular thought? If we can understand that, which is to understand the process of choice, then we shall come naturally to a concentration in which there is no conflict. So, we have to understand the problem of choice, why the thinker chooses one thought and rejects another. When the thinker chooses a particular thought, various other thoughts are always impinging, and he is always pushing them aside. So, does choice lead to concentration? Is the mind concentrated when it is constantly choosing, excluding, rejecting? Is concentration a process of narrowing down the mind so that it can be completely identified with a particular thought? Yet that is what we generally mean by concentration, is it not? We mean a state in which the mind is so completely absorbed in a particular idea, a chosen thought, that no other thoughts disturb it, no other reactions come in, and yet there is a conflict of choice going on all the time.

So, in order to understand concentration, must we not first understand the problem of choice? As long as we choose one particular thought and try to dwell on it, is not conflict with other thoughts inevitable? Must we not examine, be aware of every thought, rather than choose one and reject others? You will say, "I have no time to do that." But have you time to struggle against the army of impinging thoughts? And is that not a waste of time?

As every thought arises, look at it; do not choose, do not say, "This is good, that is bad; I am going to hold to the good and reject the bad." Without condemnation, be aware of each thought as it arises, and then you will see there comes a concentration which is not exclusive, which is not the result of choice, which is not the narrowing down of the mind. Such concentration is extensive, and only then is it possible for the mind to be quiet, for the mind to be still. Stillness is not the outcome of concentration, it is not the result of choice. Stillness comes about spontaneously when we understand the whole process of choice with its various activities, struggles; and in that stillness there is the unrecognizable, an experience which is not of the past.

August 16, 1952

Sixth Talk in The Oak Grove

We have become accustomed, I think, to the idea that struggle is inevitable, and that through struggle we shall come to understanding, we shall have peace, we shall realize something beyond the problems which evoke conflict. It seems to me important to understand this question of struggle, the conflict within and about us, and to find out whether it is necessary to creative understanding and to the release of human happiness. We accept struggle as an integral part of our daily existence, of our social contacts, of our inward, psychological being, and we think that without struggle, conflict, we shall stagnate. There is the fear of stagnation, of being nothing, of destroying ourselves if we do not make an effort, if we do not struggle towards an object, a goal, an end. We think that without struggle, without inward stress and strain, the ultimate happiness is not attainable. So we accept struggle as part of life, and through struggle we think we can bring about a radical change in ourselves. This morning let us find out, if we can, whether struggle is necessary, whether conflict contributes to understanding, enlightenment, and human happiness.

We see that struggle is necessary in certain directions, at certain levels: struggle with the earth, struggle in resolving objective problems. At certain levels of existence, struggle seems to be necessary, but we carry on that struggle into the psychological realm, where it becomes the acquisitive survival of the 'me', and it is there that we have to find out whether struggle contributes to one's own happiness, to human welfare, and to the creation of a peaceful society. This conflict in relationship is a complex problem, is it not? For centuries we have accepted it as inevitable, and it is therefore very difficult to examine the whole question anew, to go into it deeply and discover its full significance. If we can, let us try this morning to see how far it is valid, and whether struggle must end if we are to understand the further reaches of the human heart.

Why do we struggle psychologically, inwardly? We struggle in order to conform to a pattern of action; we struggle to express certain feelings or because we have a problem which through struggle we hope to resolve; we struggle in order to achieve a continuity, a survival of the 'me' as an entity. Now, this struggle to conform, to survive, expresses itself in belief, in the ideal, does it not? We project the ideal and strive to conform, to adjust ourselves to it, hoping through that struggle, through that adjustment to improve, to be happier, kinder, and so on. That is, we create a pattern of action through the desire to achieve a certain result, and thereby we establish the habit of constant inward or psychological struggle between the various layers of our consciousness. We struggle with problems, both personal and collective; having problems, we examine them, analyze, go into them as fully as possible, hoping in this way to resolve them. We struggle with the trivialities of our mind in order to banish them, to put them aside and go beyond. Our life is a series of never-ending struggles; we are always inquiring, always struggling to find out. We start to find out, but gradually establish the habit of a particular pattern of action, or if we are more deeply concerned, we think that through struggle we shall be creative, that we must go through this process of conflict in order to achieve a certain peace of mind. All this is our life, the familiar pattern of our daily existence, and we need not go into it in more detail.

Now, I want to find out if struggle is necessary, if struggle can produce the radical inward change which is so essential. When we have a psychological problem, a problem of relationship, why do we struggle to solve it? Can such a problem be solved through struggle, through conflict? We struggle with a problem only when we want a particular result, a particular answer to that problem, but if our intention is to understand and go beyond the problem, surely this conflict with the problem will not help us, will it? We can understand the problem only when we are capable of looking at it without condemnation, justification, or any desire to find an answer outside of it. The moment we try to conform to a particular pattern which the mind has projected in the hope of solving the problem, there is a state of struggle, and the more we struggle, the more complex the problem becomes. So we see that to understand a problem profoundly, there must, first of all, be no effort to find a particular answer to it.

When I have a problem, am I not always seeking a particular answer to that problem? I am not concerned with understanding the problem, I want an answer to it, so a conflict is established. Whereas, if I would really understand the problem, I must be aware of the whole content of it, which is possible only when I am not identifying myself with a particular answer, when I am not judging, when I am not condemning. Being fully aware, the mind is quiet, and only then is the problem resolved, not when there is a struggle to find an answer. At one level we want an answer, and at another level we do not. We seek a particular solution to a problem, and yet we know, deeply, that the search for a particular solution involves conflict within oneself, and therefore only increases the problem in another direction. So, what is required is insight into the problem, which means understanding the whole of one's consciousness, the total process of oneself.

We see, then, that struggle to resolve a problem does not bring about freedom from that problem. On the contrary, it only makes the problem more complex. You can observe this for yourself.

Now, we think that survival is possible only through struggle, through contention, through conflict; and yet we see that where there is conflict between individuals, between groups, between nations, there is no possibility of survival at all; war and mass destruction are inevitable. As long as we are struggling for psychological security, there must be outward conflict, which results in war. We struggle to be psychologically secure, to survive acquisitively, to be the more; and as long as we are acquisitively struggling to be the 'more', either in this world or in the psychological realm, there must be conflict, there must be incessant battle within and about us.

We struggle to be secure, to be certain, because the mind is afraid to be uncertain, to be in a state of constant inquiry, constant understanding, constant discovery. There can be discovery, understanding, only when there is a state of deep uncertainty. But the mind dislikes to be uncertain, so it proceeds from memory to memory in order to be secure; it builds for itself various virtues, qualities, attributes, habits, patterns of action in which it can function. Unconsciously as well as consciously, most of us are seeking this psychological survival, which denies survival in the physical world. As long as the 'me', the self, the 'I', is cultivated, given nourishment, strength, there must be everlasting conflict.

So, that is our state, is it not? And if we want to change radically, then the walls which the mind has built around itself—the walls of virtue, belief, ideas, the desire for immortality, and so on—must all be broken down so that the mind is completely free to discover what is real.

What is necessary, first of all, is to perceive for ourselves without persuasion or argumentation how we move from memory to memory, from knowledge to more knowledge, and this movement we consider a revolution.

Tradition, environment, education, conditioning can all be modified—and that is what every outward revolution tries to do, whether it be capitalist, communist, or fascist. They all try to change the environment, the conditioning, the tradition. It can be done, of course, but it does not release man from suffering, does it? And it is that we are considering—how to free the mind from sorrow, and whether sorrow can ever be solved through struggle. Does not the struggle itself strengthen the cause of sorrow, which is the 'me' with its self-centered activities? When I struggle to be virtuous, is that virtue? Though we have been brought up to believe that a virtuous state can be achieved through struggle, through conflict, through discipline, through influence, through education, does not that whole process strengthen the 'me', which is the very cause of misery? When I try to discipline myself to be more generous, am I not strengthening the 'me', which is the cause of greed? When I struggle to be humble, without pride, is that not a self-centered activity?

This is a very complex problem, and it cannot be dealt with casually, at only one level. Seeing this complex problem and being aware that the root of suffering is the 'me', the 'I', the self, and ego—what name you give it is of no importance—how can that foundation, how can that basis be broken, destroyed? How can this self, the 'me', be put aside without struggle? That is the real problem, and it is there that the revolution, the change, the transformation must take place. Is this transformation brought about through conflict? Do I resolve the 'me' by trying to impose upon it various regulations, compulsions? Or, does its resolution come about when the mind is aware of this whole complex problem and becomes nonactive with regard to it? After all, it is the mind that is the center of the 'me', is it not? Perhaps most of us have not thought about this problem. As long as the self exists, there must be conflict, misery; as long as the self exists, there can be no creative being. But most of us accept the self and cultivate it in various ways. Now, if we realize the nature of the self, if we are extensively aware of its complex problems, is it not possible for the mind to be nonactive with regard to them so that it does not contribute to the 'me', give it nourishment?

I am concerned with the dissolution of the 'me', of the 'I', the negation of the self. How is it to be achieved without becoming an end? I see that suffering, frustration, conflict are inevitable as long as my mind is consciously or unconsciously occupied with the 'me' and its activities. Now, how is all that to be resolved? Will the identification of myself with a nation, with an idea, with a belief, with what we call God resolve it? Such identification is an activity of the 'me', is it not? It is only an extension of the 'me', an escape from the 'me' of trivialities to what I call the immense, the universal—which is still part of my petty mind. So, identification does not resolve the 'me', does not break down the walls of the 'me', nor does discipline, the practice of a particular pattern of action, nor does prayer, supplication, nor the constant demand to resolve it. All this only strengthens the 'me', gives it continuity—the 'me' being a bundle of memories, experiences, pleasures, struggles, pains, suffering. Nothing will resolve the 'me' as long as the mind is active in its resolution, for the mind is incapable of breaking down the barriers, the walls that it has created. But when I am aware of this whole complex structure of the 'me', which is the past moving through the present to the future, when I am aware of the inward as well as the outward, the hidden as well as the open—when I am fully aware of all that, then the mind, which has created the barriers in its desire to be secure, to be permanent, to have continuity, becomes extraordinarily quiet; it is no longer active, and only then is there a possibility of the dissolution of the 'me'.

Now, in listening to a statement of that kind, how you listen matters, does it not? Because, after all, what are we trying to do in these talks? We are not trying to superimpose one set of ideas on another or substitute one belief for another or follow one teacher, renouncing another. What we are trying to do is to understand the problem, talk it over, and in talking it over, you are open to suggestions, you see the implications, and thereby you discover directly for yourself the falseness of this struggle. You do not make a conscious effort to change. The transformation comes when there is direct understanding, and therefore there is a certain spontaneity without any sense of compulsion. But that is possible only when you are capable of listening very quietly, inwardly, without any barriers. If you change because of argumentation, because logically it is so, because you are influenced, then you are only conditioned in a different direction, which brings again its sorrow. Whereas, if you understand this problem of sorrow as a whole, as a totality, and not as something to be escaped from superficially, then the mind becomes very quiet, and in that quietness there takes place a transformation which is not induced, which is not the result of any form of compulsion, of desire. It is that transformation which is essential, and that transformation is not possible through influence, through knowledge. Knowledge does not resolve our suffering—knowledge being explanations. Only when knowledge is suppressed completely, when we are no longer looking to knowledge as a means of guidance, only then is there a possibility for the mind to experience the unnameable, which is the only factor that brings about a radical transformation, a revolution.

Question: Great minds have never been able to agree on what is the ultimate reality. What do you say? Does it exist at all?

KRISHNAMURTI: What do you say? Is that not much more important—what you think? You want to know if there is an ultimate reality, and you say that great minds have said there is or there is not. Of what value is that? You want to find out, don't you? You want to know if there is an absolute reality, something which is not changeable, which is permanent, which is beyond time. Now, how are you to find out? With what instrument are you going to find out? You have only the mind, have you not?—the mind being the result of time, the residue of memory, of experience. With that mind, you are going to find out if there is an ultimate reality. You have read about these matters, and what you have read has strengthened your own prejudices, opinions, or objections, and with that mind you are going to find out. Can you? And is this not really a foolish question to ask? If I said there is or there is not an ultimate reality, what significance would it have? Actually, what significance would it have in your life? It would merely strengthen your particular conception, your particular experience, your particular knowledge. But the strengthening of your idea, the corroboration of your belief, is not the ultimate reality, is it? So, what is important, surely, is for you to find out, and to find out, your mind must be in a state of creative experience, must it not? Your mind must be capable of discovering—which means it must be completely free from all knowledge as to whether there is an ultimate reality or only a series of ever more extensive and significant experiences. But your mind is crammed with knowledge and information, with experience, with memories, and with that mind you try to find out. Surely, it is only when the mind is creatively empty that it is capable of finding out whether there is an ultimate reality or not. But the mind is never creatively empty. It is always acquiring, always gathering, living on the past or in the future or trying to be focused in the immediate present; it is never in that state of creativeness in which a new thing can take place. As the mind is a result of time, it cannot possibly understand that which is timeless, eternal. So, our job is to inquire not if there is an ultimate reality but whether the mind can ever be free from time—which is memory—from this process of accumulation, the gathering of experiences, living on the past or in the future. That is, can the mind be still? Stillness is not the outcome of discipline, of control. There is stillness only when the mind is silently aware of this whole complex problem, and it is such a mind that can understand if there is an ultimate reality or not.

Question: With what should the mind be occupied?

KRISHNAMURTI: Here is a very good example of how conflict is brought into being: the conflict between 'what should be' and *what is*. First we establish 'what should be', the ideal, and then try to live according to that pattern. We say the mind should be occupied with noble things, with unselfishness, with generosity, with kindliness, with love; that is the pattern, the belief, the 'should be', the 'must', and we try to live accordingly. So there is a conflict set going between the projection of 'what should be', and the actuality, the *what is*, and through that conflict we hope to be transformed. As long as we are struggling with the 'should be', we feel virtuous, we feel good. But which is important: the 'should be', or *what is?* With what are our minds occupied—actually, not ideologically? With trivialities, are they not? With how one looks, with ambition, with greed, with envy, with gossip, with cruelty. The mind lives in a world of trivialities, and a trivial mind creating a noble pattern is still trivial, is it not? So, the question is not with what should the mind be occupied but can the mind free itself from trivialities? If we are at all aware, if we are at all inquiring, we know our own particular trivialities—incessant talk, the everlasting chattering of the mind, worry over this and that, curiosity as to what people are doing or not doing, trying to achieve a result, groping after one's own aggrandizement, and so on. With that we are occupied, and we know it very well. And can that be transformed? That is the problem, is it not? To ask with what the mind should be occupied is mere immaturity.

Now, being aware that my mind is trivial and occupied with trivialities, can it free itself from this condition? Is not the mind, by its very nature, trivial? What is the mind but the result of memory? Memory of what? Of how to survive, not only physically, but also psychologically through the development of certain qualities, virtues, the storing up of experiences, the establishing of itself in its own activities. Is that not trivial? The mind, being the result of memory, of time, is trivial in itself, and what can it do to free itself from its own triviality? Can it do anything? Please see the importance of this. Can the mind, which is self-centered activity, free itself from that activity? Obviously, it cannot; whatever it does, it is still trivial. It can speculate about God, it can devise political systems, it can invent beliefs, but it is still within the field of time, its change is still from memory to memory, it is still bound by its own limitations. And can the mind break down that limitation? Or, does that limitation break down when the mind is quiet, when it is not active, when it recognizes its own trivialities, however great it may have imagined them to be? When the mind, having seen its trivialities, is fully aware of them and so becomes really quiet—only then is there a possibility of these trivialities dropping away. But as long as you are inquiring with what the mind should be occupied, it will be occupied with trivialities, whether it build a church, whether it go to prayer or to a shrine. The mind itself is petty, small, and by merely saying it is petty, you haven't dissolved its pettiness. You have to understand it; the mind has to recognize its own activities, and in the process of that recognition, in the awareness of the trivialities which it has consciously and unconsciously built, the mind becomes quiet. In that quietness there is a creative state, and this is the factor which brings about a transformation.

Question: I find I am a snob. I like the sensation, but I feel it is a wrong attitude. How am I to be free from this snobbishness?

KRISHNAMURTI: We all like to be superior or to feel that we are superior, do we not? We want to have friends who are prominent, who are in the center of things, we want to know the great. We all want to be identified with the great or be seen with the great or be ourselves the great, either through heredity or through our own particular endeavor. From the clerk to the highest of the land, we all want to be somebodies, so the snobbishness, the sense of importance, begins. And though the questioner says the feeling of being somebody is pleasurable, he wants to know how to be free from that snobbishness. Surely, it is very simple to be free from that snobbishness, is it not? Be nobody. No, sirs, don't laugh and pass it off. It is very difficult to be nobody because our education or social environment, our religious instruction all encourage us to be somebody. Inwardly, don't you want to be somebody? Don't you want to be a good writer or to know somebody who writes extraordinarily well and is popular, famous? Don't you want to be the first painter, the greatest musician, the most beautiful person, or the most virtuous saint? To know, to acquire, to possess—isn't that what we are all striving after? If we are honest with ourselves, it is. All our struggle, our everlasting conflict, is to achieve that—to be somebody. It gives great impetus, great energy, does it not? Ambition is a great spur, and we are caught in that habit of thought. Can you easily deny all that and be as nothing? And yet we must be as nothing—but not through discipline, not through compulsion. We are as nothing when we know what it is to love, but how can a man love when he is concerned with his own importance?

So, it is easy to say, "I must be as nothing," but to bring it about requires enormous vitality, energy. To break down the habits, the customs, the traditions, the educational influences, the sense of competition—to break down all those encrustations requires a great deal of watchfulness, alertness, not only at the superficial level, but profoundly, deeply. But to be conscious that you are as nothing is to be something. To be as nothing is a state which comes without invitation, and one knows that state only when there is love. But love is not a thing to be sought after; it comes when there is inward revolution, when the self is not important, when the self is not the center of one's existence.

August 17, 1952

Seventh Talk in The Oak Grove

I think it is possible, in talking, to expose oneself and one's own inward thoughts, and if we can do that this evening, perhaps it will be worthwhile; for then this will not be a lecture, a talk to which you are listening, but an exposing of the problems and difficulties that one confronts in going into the question of transformation, this inward revolution which is so essential. We see around us the disintegration of the world, and we are aware of our own extraordinary processes of deterioration as we grow older—lack of energy, the settling into grooves of well-established habit, the pursuit of various illusions, and so on—all of which create a barrier to the understanding of our own fundamental and radical change.

In considering this problem of change, which we have been doing for the last three weeks, it seems to me that the question of incentive is very important. For most of us, change implies an incentive. I need an incentive to change. Most of us require an incentive, an urge, a motive, a purpose, a vision, or identification with a particular belief, utopia, or ideology, do we not? And does incentive bring about a radical change? Is not incentive merely a projection of one's own desires, idealized or personified or put away in the future in the hope that by pursuing that self-projection, we can somehow bring about a change? Is not this problem of change very profound, and can it be solved by the superficial incentives which societies offer, which religious organizations dangle before us? Can a fundamental transformation be brought about by the revolutionary ideologies which give logical reasons for change and offer the incentive of a better world, a heaven on earth, a society in which there are no class distinctions? We identify ourselves with these incentives and give our lives for the things which they promise, and does that bring about a radical change? That is the problem, is it not?

I do not know how much you have thought about all this or how deeply you have gone into the question of changing oneself, but unless we understand from what point of view, from what center the transformation must take place, it seems to me that mere superficial changes, however beneficial socially and economically, will not resolve our extraordinarily complex problems. The incentives, the beliefs, the promises, the utopias—to me, all these are very superficial. There can be a radical change only at the center, only when there is complete self-abnegation, complete self-forgetfulness, the complete putting aside of the 'me', the self. Until that is done, I do not see how a fundamental transformation can take place. And is this radical change at the center brought about through an incentive of any kind? Obviously not. And yet all our thinking is based on incentive, is it not? We are continually struggling to gain a reward, to do good, to live a noble life, to advance, to achieve. So, is it not important to find out what this self is that wants to grow, to improve?

What is the self, the 'me'? If you were asked, what would be your response to that question? Some would say, perhaps, that is the expression of God, the higher self enclosed in material form, the immense manifested in the particular. And probably others would maintain that there is no spiritual entity, that man is nothing but a series of responses to environmental influences, the result of racial, climatic, and social conditioning. Whatever the self may be, should we not go into it, understand it, and find out how it can be transformed at the center?

What is the self? Is it not desire? Please, I would like to suggest these things for you to observe, not to contradict or accept, because I feel the more one is capable of listening, not so much with the conscious mind, but unconsciously, effortlessly, the more there is a possibility of our meeting and proceeding together further and more deeply into the problem. If the conscious mind merely examines an idea, a teaching, a problem, then it does not go beyond its own level, which is very superficial, but if one can listen not with the conscious mind, as it were, but with a mind that is relaxed, observing and is therefore able to see what is beyond the words, the symbols, the images, then there is a possibility, I think, of a quickening of direct experience and understanding, which is not a process of conscious analysis. I think we can do that at these talks if we do not meet idea by idea. What I am saying is not a set of ideas to be learned, to be repeated, to be read over, or communicated to others, but if we can meet each other not at the conscious, reasoning level, which we can do later, but at that level where the conscious mind is neither opposing nor struggling to understand, then there is a possibility, I think, of seeing something which is not merely verbal, not merely intellectual.

So, what is the self that needs fundamental transformation? Surely, it is there that a change must take place, not on the superficial level, and in order to bring about a radical change there, must we not find out what this self is, the 'me'? And can we ever find out what the 'me' is? Is there a permanent 'me'? Or, is there a permanent desire for something which identifies itself as the 'me'?

Please don't take notes; do please listen. When you take notes you are not really listening; you are more concerned with putting down what you hear so that you can read it over tomorrow or convey it to your friends or print it somewhere. What we are trying to do is something quite different, is it not? We are trying to find out what this thing is which we call the self, the center of the 'me', from which all activity seems to spring, for if there is no transformation there, mere change on the periphery, on the outside, on the surface, has very little meaning.

So, I want to find out what this center is, and whether it is possible to really break it up, transform it, tear it away. What is the self with most of us? It is a center of desire manifesting itself through various forms of continuity, is it not? It is the desire to have more, to perpetuate experience, to be enriched through acquisition, through memories, through sensations, through symbols, through names, through words. If you look very closely, there is no such thing as a permanent 'me' except as memory, the memory of what I have been, of what I am and what I should be; it is the desire for more—the desire for greater knowledge, greater experience, the desire for a continued identity, identity with the body, with the house, with the land, with ideas, with persons. This process goes on not only at the conscious level but also in the deeper, unconscious layers of the mind, and so the self, the center of the 'me' is sustained and nourished through time. But none of that is permanent in the sense of a continuity, except through memory. In itself it is not a permanent state, but we try to make it permanent by clinging to a particular experience, a particular relationship, or belief—not consciously, perhaps, but unconsciously we are driven to it through various desires, urges, compulsions, experiences.

So, all this is the 'me', is it not? It is the self, the 'I', which is ever wanting the 'more', which is never satisfied, everlastingly groping for further experience, further sensation, cultivating virtue in order to strengthen itself at the center; therefore, it is never virtue, but only the expansion of itself in the guise of virtue. So, that is the 'me', the 'I'; it is the name, the form, and the feeling behind the symbol, beyond the word, which in its struggle to acquire, to hold, to expand, or to be less, creates an acquisitive society in which there is contention, competition, ruthlessness, war, and all the rest of it.

Unless there is a transformation at the center, not substitution, but a radical uprooting of the 'me', no fundamental change is possible. Realizing this, how is one to bring about a deep inner change? That is the problem, is it not?—for a serious person, not for the superficial who are seeking some comforting illusion, gurus, teachers, and all the rest of the nonsense. So, how can that center transform itself? Sirs, people who see that a change must take place and do not know how it should come about are easily caught by incentives, are they not? They are distracted by ideological utopias, by the Masters, by worship, by churches, by organizations, by saviors, and so on and on and on; but when I put aside all distractions because they will not transform the center, and I am concerned only with the transformation of the center—when I really see the urgency, the necessity of that, then all these superficial reformations have very little significance.

Now, when all incentives, pursuits, and desires have been put aside, is one then capable of transforming the center? You and I are considering this problem as two individuals, I am not addressing a group. You see the problem, do you not? There must obviously be a change not at the superficial or abstract level but at the very center; there must be a new flow, a new state of being which is not of time, of memory; there must be a change which is not the result of any theory or belief, whether of the left or of the right, a change which is not the conditioning of a believer or a nonbeliever. I see this complex problem, and how is it possible for a spontaneous change to take place at the center—a change which is not the result of compulsion, of discipline, which are mere substitutions? I do not know if you have put the question to yourself in this manner, and if you have, what do you find, how are you to bring about that change, that transformation? Is the understanding of these distractions, incentives, pursuits, desires merely verbal, intellectual, superficial, or is it real—real in the sense that incentives no longer have any value, and therefore they have dropped away? Or, knowing their immature promptings, are you still playing with them?

So, I have first to find out what is the state of my mind that sees the problem and tries to seek an answer, have I not? Am I making myself clear? There is the problem which we all know and of which we are fully aware at different moments of our existence; there are occasions when we see the significance, the depth of it. And as we discuss it together, what is the state of one's mind that is looking at the problem? Isn't that important? The state of the mind as it approaches the problem is very important because that state of mind is going to find the answer. So, I first see the problem, and then I have to see what the state of my mind is that looks at the problem. Please, these are not first and second steps—the problem is a whole, a total process. It is only in putting it verbally that it has to be broken up in this way. If we approach the problem in stages, first seeing the problem, then inquiring what the state of the mind is, and so on and on, we shall get lost, we shall wander further and further away from the central issue. So, it is very important for me to be fully aware of the whole state of my mind as I approach the problem.

First of all, I do not know if I want to have a fundamental change, if I want to break all the traditions, values, hopes, beliefs that I have built up. Most of us do not, obviously. Very few want to go so deeply and fundamentally into the problem. They are quite satisfied with substitutes, with a change of belief, with better incentives. But, going beyond that, what is the state of my mind? And is the state of the mind different from the problem? Is not the problem the state of the mind? The problem is not apart from the mind. It is my mind that creates the problem, my mind being the result of time, of memory, the seat of the 'me', which is everlastingly craving for the 'more', for immortality, for continuity, for permanency here and in the hereafter. So, can the mind detach itself from the problem and look at the problem? It can abstractly, logically, with reason—but actually, can it separate itself from the thing it has created and of which it is a part? This is not a conundrum, this is not a trick. It is a fact, is it not? My mind, seeing its own insufficiency, its own poverty, proceeds to acquire properties, degrees, titles, the everlasting God, so it strengthens itself in the 'me'. The mind, being the center of the 'me', says, "I must change," and it proceeds to create incentives for itself, pursuing the good and rejecting the bad.

Now, can such a mind see the problem and act upon the problem? And when it does act, is it not still within the field of incentives, of desires, of time, of memory? So, is it not important for me to find out how my mind looks at the problem? Is the mind separate from the problem as the observer apart from the observed, or is the mind itself the totality of the problem? With most of us, that is the point, is it not? I am observing the problem of how to dissolve radically and deeply that center which is the 'me', so the mind says, "I am going to dissolve it." That is, the mind, the 'I', separates itself as the observer and the observed, and then the observer acts upon the observed, the problem. But the observer is the creator of the problem; the observer is not separate from the problem. He himself is the problem. So, what is he to do? If we can really feel this out, just stay with the problem and not try to find an answer, a quick solution, or reach for a quotation from some teacher or book, or rely on our past experience; if we can simply be aware of this total problem without judgment, then I think we will find the answer—not an answer at the verbal level, but a solution which is not invented by the mind.

So, my problem is this, and I hope it is yours also—I see that a fundamental revolution must take place at the center, not on the surface. Change on the surface has no meaning. Becoming better, nobler, acquiring more virtue, having much or little property—these are all superficial activities of a very superficial mind. I am not talking about those changes; I am concerned only with a change at the center. I see that the 'me' must be completely dissolved. So I inquire what the 'me' is, I become aware of the 'me' not as a philosophical abstraction but from day to day. From moment to moment I see what the 'me' is—the 'me' that is always watching, observing, gathering, acquiring, rejecting, judging, hating, breaking up, or coming together in order to be more secure. The change has to take place there; that center has to be rooted out completely. And how is that to happen? Can the mind, which is the creator of the problem, abstract itself from the problem and then act upon it in the name of God, in the name of the higher self, for a utopia, or for any other reason? And when it does that, has it dissolved the center? Obviously it has not. Therefore, my problem is: Can the mind bring about a fundamental revolution through dialectics or through knowledge of historical processes? This is an important question, is it not? Because, if a radical change can take place at the center, then my whole life has a different significance; then there is beauty, then there is happiness, then there is creation, then there is quite a different state of being; there is love, which is everlasting forgiveness.

So, can that state be brought about by the mind? If you say, "No," you are not aware of the problem. That is a very quick, a very superficial answer. And if you say, "I must look to God, to some high spiritual state which will transform all this," again you are relying on words, on symbols, on a projection of the mind. So, what is one to do? Is this not a problem to you? Looking at this complex problem of the 'me' with all its darkness, its shadows and lights, its tensions and stresses, can I, the observer, affect this thing that is observed? Please listen to the problem; don't look for an answer or try to solve it; just listen to it; let it soak into you as the soft rains that enrich the earth. If you are really with the problem, if it is your daily concern from moment to moment to see how that change can be brought about, and if you are negatively putting aside those things which you have thought to be positive, then I think you will find the element that comes into being so darkly, without your knowing. This is not a promise. Don't smile as though you had understood.

So, what we have to do, surely, is to be aware of the totality of this problem not merely consciously but especially unconsciously; we have to be aware of it inwardly, deeply. The superficial mind can give reasons, explanations; it can logically work out certain problems, but when we are concerned with a profound problem, the superficial approach has little value. And we are concerned with a very profound problem, which is how to bring about a change, a revolution at the center. Without that fundamental transformation, mere changes on the surface have no meaning and reforms need constant reform. If we can look at this problem as a whole, taste it, smell it, unconsciously absorb it, then we shall be familiar with all the activities and tricks of the 'me'; we shall see how the observer is separating himself from the observed, rejecting this and accepting that. The more we know of this total process, the less the superficial mind will act. Thought is not the dissolver of the problem. On the contrary, thought must come to an end. It is the observer who judges, justifies, accepts and rejects, all of which is the process of thinking. Thought has created our problem—the thought that seeks the more in property, in things, in relationship, in ideas, in knowledge; and with that thought we are trying to solve the problem. Thought is memory, and the calming of memory is the stilling of the mind, and the more the mind is still, the deeper it will understand this problem and resolve the center.

Question: Does not this process of constant self-awareness lead to self-centeredness?

KRISHNAMURTI: It does, does it not? The more you are concerned about yourself, watching, improving, thinking about yourself, the more self-centered you are, are you not? That is an obvious fact. If I am concerned with changing myself, then I must observe; I must build a technique which will help me to break up that center. There is self-centeredness as long as I am consciously or unconsciously concerned with a result, with success, as long as I am gaining and putting aside—which is what most of us are doing. The incentive is the goal I am pursuing; because I want to gain that end, I watch myself. I am unhappy, I am miserable, frustrated, and I feel there is a state in which I can be happy, fulfilled, complete, so I become aware in order to gain that state. I use awareness to get what I want, so I am self-centered. Through awareness, through self-analysis, through reading, studying, I hope to dissolve the 'me', and then I shall be happy, enlightened, liberated, I shall be one of the elite—and that is what I want. So, the more I am concerned with gaining an end, the greater is the self-centeredness of thought. But thought is ever self-enclosing anyhow, is it not?

So—what? To break down the self-centeredness, I must understand why the mind seeks an end, a goal, a particular result. Why does my mind go after a reward? Why? Can it function in any other way? Is not the movement of the mind from memory to memory, from result to result? I have acquired this, I don't like it, and I am going to get something else. I don't like this thought, but that thought will be better, nobler, more comforting, more satisfying. As long as I am thinking, I can think in no other terms, for the mind moves from knowledge to knowledge, from memory to memory. Is not thinking self-centered in its very nature? I know there are exceptions, but we are not discussing the exceptions. In our everyday life, are we not consciously or unconsciously pursuing an end, gaining and avoiding, seeking to continue, putting aside anything that is disturbing, that is insecure, uncertain? In seeking its own certainty, the mind creates self-centeredness, and is not that self-centeredness the 'me', which then watches over and analyzes itself? So, as long as we seek a result, self-centeredness must exist, whether in an individual, in a group, in a nation, or a race. But if we can understand why the mind seeks a result, a satisfying end, why it wants to be certain—if we understand that, then there is a possibility of breaking down the walls that enclose thought as the 'me'. But that requires an astonishing awareness of the total process not only of the conscious but also of the unconscious levels, an awareness from moment to moment in which there is no gathering, no accumulation, no saying, "Yes, I have understood this, and I am going to use it for tomorrow," a spontaneity which is not of the mind. Only then is there a possibility of going beyond the self-enclosing activities of thought.

August 23, 1952

Eighth Talk in The Oak Grove

I would like to continue this morning with what we were discussing yesterday afternoon—the necessity of change and the problem involved in changing. I think most of us see at least superficially, and sometimes perhaps deeply, the importance of change in the outward world where there is so much misery—war, starvation, class distinctions, snobbishness, the appalling difference between the rich and the poor, eighty or ninety percent of Asia going to bed without proper food, while here you are well fed. There must obviously be a complete transformation, a vital change, and many people have tried to bring it about in different ways—through bloody revolution, through economic adjustments, through various superficial reforms, and so on. But it seems to me that the fundamental revolution cannot take place unless there is complete self-abnegation, a total dissolution of the 'me', of the self; and yesterday I somewhat went into the problem and the processes involved in the dissolution of this 'me' that is everlastingly struggling to assert itself, positively or negatively.

This morning I would like to discuss desire and whether desire can ever be changed, for I think that desire is one of the major problems that confront each one of us in considering the question of fundamental transformation. Surely, until we understand the whole process of desire—the longing, the striving, the conscious or unconscious pursuit of a particular object, however noble—until we go into and understand that process, mere superficial reform or violent revolution will have very little significance. And again, as I said yesterday, please do not regard this as a talk to which you are listening; do not argue with me in your own mind, opposing one idea by another idea. What we are trying to do is to see the complex problem involved in this process of desire. I am talking to you as an individual, not to a large and heterogeneous group of people who are not particularly interested in all this. We are discussing the problem as one individual to another, without opposition, to see how far we can go into it, how deeply we can bring about a radical transformation in ourselves. In talking it over with you, I am merely exposing the problem and how I feel it may be approached, and I think it is much more important to listen, as it were, unconsciously, rather than with a conscious effort to understand.

For most of us, desire is quite a problem—the desire for property, for position, for power, for comfort, for immortality, for continuity, the desire to be loved, to have something permanent, satisfying, lasting, something which is beyond time. Now, what is desire? What is this thing that is urging, compelling us?—which doesn't mean that we should be satisfied with what we have or with what we are, which is merely the opposite of what we want. We are trying to see what desire is, and if we can go into it tentatively, hesitantly, I think we will bring about a transformation which is not a mere substitution of one object of desire for another object of desire. But this is generally what we mean by "change," is it not? Being dissatisfied with one particular object of desire, we find a substitute for it. We are everlastingly moving from one object of desire to another which we consider to be higher, nobler, more refined, but however refined, desire is still desire, and in this movement of desire there is endless struggle, the conflict of the opposites.

So, is it not important to find out what is desire and whether it can be transformed? What is desire? Is it not the symbol and its sensation? Desire is sensation with the object of its attainment. Is there desire without a symbol and its sensation? Obviously not. The symbol may be a picture, a person, a word, a name, an image, an idea which gives me a sensation, which makes me feel that I like or dislike it; if the sensation is pleasurable, I want to attain, to possess, to hold on to its symbol and continue in that pleasure. From time to time, according to my inclinations and intensities, I change the picture, the image, the object. With one form of pleasure I am fed up, tired, bored, so I seek a new sensation, a new idea, a new symbol. I reject the old sensation and take on a new one with new words, new significances, new experiences. I resist the old and yield to the new which I consider to be higher, nobler, more satisfying. So, in desire there is a resistance and a yielding, which involves temptation, and of course, in yielding to a particular symbol of desire, there is always the fear of frustration.

If I observe the whole process of desire in myself, I see there is always an object towards which my mind is directed for further sensation, and that in this process there is involved resistance, temptation, and discipline. There is perception, sensation, contact, and desire, and the mind becomes the mechanical instrument of this process in which symbols, words, objects are the center round which all desire, all pursuits, all ambitions are built; and that center is the 'me'. And can I dissolve that center of desire—not one particular desire, one particular appetite or craving, but the whole structure of desire, of longing, hoping, in which there is always the fear of frustration? The more I am frustrated, the more strength I give to the 'me'. As long as there is hoping, longing, there is always the background of fear, which again strengthens that center. And revolution is possible only at that center, not on the surface, which is merely a process of distraction, a superficial change leading to mischievous action.

So, when I am aware of this whole structure of desire, I see how my mind has become a dead center, a mechanical process of memory. Having tired of one desire, I automatically want to fulfill myself in another. My mind is always experiencing in terms of sensation, it is the instrument of sensation. Being bored with a particular sensation, I seek a new sensation, which may be what I call the realization of God, but it is still sensation. I have had enough of this world and its travail, and I want peace, the peace that is everlasting; so I meditate, control, I shape my mind in order to experience that peace. The experiencing of that peace is still sensation. So, my mind is the mechanical instrument of sensation, of memory, a dead center from which I act, think. The objects I pursue are the projections of the mind as symbols from which it derives sensations. The word *God*, the word *love*, the word *communism*, the word *democracy*, the word *nationalism*—these are all symbols which give sensations to the mind, and therefore the mind clings to them. As you and I know, every sensation comes to an end, and so we proceed from one sensation to another, and every sensation strengthens the habit of seeking further sensation. So, the mind becomes merely an instrument of sensation and memory, and in that process we are caught. As long as the mind is seeking further experience, it can only think in terms of sensation, and any experience that may be spontaneous, creative, vital, strikingly new, it immediately reduces to sensation and pursues that sensation, which then becomes a memory. Therefore, the experience is dead, and the mind becomes merely a stagnant pool of the past.

If we have gone into it at all deeply, we are familiar with this process, and we seem to be incapable of going beyond. And we want to go beyond because we are tired of this endless routine, this mechanical pursuit of sensation, so the mind projects the idea of truth, of God; it dreams of a vital change and of playing a principal part in that change, and so on and on and on. Hence there is never a creative state. In myself I see this process of desire going on which is mechanical, repetitive, which holds the mind in a process of routine and makes of it a dead center of the past in which there is no creative spontaneity. And also there are sudden moments of creation, of that which is not of the mind, which is not of memory, which is not of sensation, of desire. So, what am I to do?

As I said yesterday, I think it is important to listen to what I am saying and merely be aware of what I am trying to imply. I am not trying to convince you or to impress upon you a particular pattern of thought, which only leads to superficial thinking and so to mischievous action. To see how far what I am saying is true, as you listen be aware of the process of your own thinking without judgment, and the moment you are aware of something that is true, it will act if you give it a chance. But if you listen to something that is true without letting it act upon you, it becomes a poison, it brings about a state of deterioration. Consciously or unconsciously, most of us avoid finding out what is true; we do not want to listen to something which is not habitual, which is not the traditional pursuit of thought. So, if I may suggest, please listen not with a view to being convinced but listen to find out how your own mind operates. The moment I see how I am thinking, how I am acting, I do not want another to convince me of what I am. Self-knowledge brings wisdom, and wisdom is not conviction, opinion, information, knowledge. It is something which is not measurable by the mind. All that I am trying to convey is the process of our own thinking and how to be aware of it, and in the process of being aware of itself, the mind captures the significance that lies beyond the words, beyond the symbols, and their sensations.

So, our problem is to understand desire—not how far it should go or where it should come to an end but to understand the whole process of desire, the cravings, the longings, the burning appetites. Most of us think that possessing very little indicates freedom from desire—and how we worship those who have but few things! A loincloth, a robe, symbolizes our desire to be free from desire, but that again is a very superficial reaction. Why begin at the superficial level of giving up outward possessions when your mind is crippled with innumerable wants, innumerable desires, beliefs, struggles? Surely, it is there that the revolution must take place, not in how much you possess, or what clothes you wear, or how many meals you eat. But we are impressed by these things because our minds are very superficial.

So, your problem and my problem is to see whether the mind can ever be free from desire, from sensation. Surely, creation has nothing to do with sensation; reality, God, or what you will, is not a state which can be experienced as sensation. When you have an experience, what happens? It has given you a certain sensation, a feeling of elation or depression. Naturally, you try to avoid, put aside the state of depression, but if it is a joy, a feeling of elation, you pursue it. Your experience has produced a pleasurable sensation, and you want more of it; and the 'more' strengthens the dead center of the mind, which is ever craving further experience. Hence the mind cannot experience anything new; it is incapable of experiencing anything new because its approach is always through memory, through recognition; and that which is recognized through memory is not truth, creation, reality. Such a mind cannot experience reality, it can only experience sensation; and creation is not sensation, it is something that is everlastingly new from moment to moment.

Now, I realize the state of my own mind; I see that it is the instrument of sensation and desire, or rather, that it is sensation and desire, and that it is mechanically caught up in routine. Such a mind is incapable of ever receiving or feeling out the new, for the new must obviously be something beyond sensation, which is always the old. So, this mechanical process with its sensations has to come to an end, has it not? The wanting more, the pursuit of symbols, words, images with their sensations—all that has to come to an end. Only then is it possible for the mind to be in that state of creativeness in which the new can always come into being. If you will listen without being mesmerized by words, by habits, by ideas and see how important it is to have the new constantly impinging on the mind, then perhaps, you will understand the process of desire, the routine, the boredom, the constant craving for experience. Then I think you will begin to see that desire has very little significance in life for a man who is really seeking. Obviously, there are certain physical needs: food, clothing, shelter, and all the rest of it. But they never become psychological appetites, things on which the mind builds itself as a center of desire. Beyond the physical needs, any form of desire—for greatness, for truth, for virtue—becomes a psychological process by which the mind builds the idea of the 'me' and strengthens itself at the center.

So, when you see this process, when you are really aware of it without opposition, without a sense of temptation, without resistance, without justifying or judging it, then you will discover that the mind is capable of receiving the new, and that the new is never a sensation; therefore, it can never be recognized, reexperienced. It is a state of being in which creativeness comes without invitation, without memory—and that is reality.

Question: I happen to be a successful businessman of considerable means. I dropped by casually last Sunday to hear your talk, and I saw at once that what you are saying is perfectly true. It has created in me a serious conflict, for my whole background and occupation are diametrically opposed to the kind of life which I now realize is essential. I don't see how I can return to my business. What am I to do?

KRISHNAMURTI: I wonder why some of you laughed? Was it a nervous reaction to cover up your own conflict of a similar kind? This man has asked a serious question, and you brush it off with a laugh. He is concerned, he wants to know what to do. What should he do? If he is serious and not carried away by words, by the mere sensation of a pleasant morning, obviously he has to act drastically, has he not? He may have to give up his business because what he has realized is much more important than the business, than making money, than position, prestige, family, property. Can he go back to an occupation which is not what he wants, which he realizes is not his life? But we generally cover up this struggle, this discontent, by words, by explanations, justifications, and slip back to the former state. We realize that the life we have been leading as a businessman, or what you will, is unworthy, corrupting, destructive—we realize that, we feel it in our bones and blood. But instead of acting, thinking it out, pursuing what we think, we are afraid of the consequences, and so there is an everlasting conflict going on between what we have realized and what we should do according to the dictates of society. So we invite psychosomatic diseases, we invite the deterioration of the mind, the conflict underground. You have felt the stirring of something real, of something which you know to be true, but you are caught in a machine of making money or ritualism or what you will. If you fully realize that and not just verbally accept it, then there will be drastic action, a breaking away from the old habits. But you see, very few ever come to that realization. We are getting old, our habits are settled, we want comfort, we want people to appreciate us, to love us, to be kind in the pattern of action to which we are accustomed. So, instead of taking the drastic action, we cover up our conflict and get lost in words, in explanations. The more you are attached to possessions, to responsibilities, the vaster are the implications and the more difficult it is to act. But if you realize that it has to be done, there is the end of the matter, you will do it. When you perceive what is true, that very perception is action.

Question: After stripping away all the stimulations, sensations, hopes, and beliefs, one is left with a sense of utter dullness. Since you say that the thinker can do nothing about this dullness, one feels frustrated. How is one to go beyond the dullness without doing something about it?

KRISHNAMURTI: I think most of us feel this way, do we not? We consciously strip ourselves of beliefs, of hopes, of sensations because we want greater hopes, more stimulating sensations, more satisfying beliefs. We do not see the significance of hope, of belief, of sensation as a total process; we merely see that certain beliefs, sensations, hopes are futile, empty, without meaning, so we push them aside, we strip ourselves of them or resign from certain societies. In stripping itself in order to gain more, naturally the mind becomes dull. It is still acting within the pattern of hope, of belief and sensation, so it feels frustrated, and then the problem arises: "How am I to be free of frustration?" Without understanding the total process of belief—which is the desire to be secure, to be certain, to take shelter in an idea, in a sensation—without understanding all that, going into it, being aware of all its implications, its nuances, we strip away one belief and pursue another. Whereas, if one is aware of how the mind creates a belief and clings to it, how it is everlastingly seeking sensation through experience—if one sees the full significance of that, then there is no problem of frustration. Then the mind is not dull—it is alert, it is constantly watching to find out, to discover where it lurks in its own security. It is fully aware of itself, ceaselessly observing its own processes; and how can such a mind be dull? How can such a mind ever feel frustrated? You feel frustrated because you want to fulfill yourself in certain sensations, in certain beliefs, certain hopes. Where there is the desire to fulfill, there is fear, which is frustration.

In its desire for sensation, happiness, security, certainty, the mind is creating at the same time the fear that they will not be. In pursuing its own projections, it gets caught in the fear of not fulfilling, of not being secure. It is this whole process that we have to understand, and understanding comes when we are aware of this process, when we observe it without judgment. The mind observes itself in action; there is no such entity as you observing the mind. The mind is aware of itself, of all its thoughts, of its hidden and open pursuits. Such a mind can never be dull because there is never a moment of achievement, of success, of conformity. It is only when the mind conforms in its desire to succeed that it becomes dull, weary. A mind that is not seeking to extend itself through sensation, through further experience, has no blockage, no hindrance in which it feels frustrated. If you and I can understand this process, if the mind can see itself in operation from moment to moment in our daily life, then I think the problem of dullness, of frustration, will disappear completely.

Question: I have had an experience of God, and I know for myself that God exists. Though it is a belief, it is not a mere escape but is based on an actual experience. I listened to you for the first time last week, and I feel you are wrong when you say that all belief is a hindrance. Is not belief based on direct experience a help to the realization of reality or God?

KRISHNAMURTI: What do we mean by a belief? A conviction? Please, I am not trying to define it according to the dictionary. You have beliefs. What are they based on? On experience, are they not? And your experience is the result of your tradition, of your background, of your education, and the influence of your society. The influence of your environment conditions your belief. You have been brought up as a Christian, and you believe according to that tradition, according to that background. Another is brought up in a society where God is taboo, is regarded as absurd, illogical, unreal; and he also believes according to his background. So, you experience according to your background as he will experience according to his. You experience that which you have unconsciously and deeply cultivated. You have been educated according to a certain pattern of thought which has been inculcated, built into you from childhood, and naturally you experience God according to that pattern, and your experience then becomes a reality to you, and you say it is no longer a matter of mere belief but is based on knowledge, on conviction, on truth. Will such a belief help you to experience further what you call God? Of course it will. But that which you experience according to your conditioning—is it God, is it truth? And will not that experience strengthen your belief, which is your conditioning? You may say that this is not an escape, but are you not reacting according to your conditioning as another will react according to his conditioning?

So, what is important is not whether you believe or disbelieve in God but to free the mind from its conditioning, and then discover. If, without freeing itself from its own conditioning, the mind asserts that there is or that there is not God, what significance has it? So, the mind must free itself from its conditioning, that is, from its self-projections, its desires, its longing for certainty, for security, for its own continuity, whether in the state or in God. Only then is it possible to say whether there is an absolute reality or a series of ever-expanding and more significant experiences. Surely, that is the important point, not whether your belief strengthens your conditioning or whether your experience is of God. The moment the mind recognizes God, it is not God; the word is not the thing. Memory is not reality. That which is unnameable cannot be recognized; it is not a sensation; it is something completely different which comes into being from moment to moment; therefore, there is no continuity. As long as my mind seeks continuity, it is conditioned by its own desires; therefore, it experiences that which gives it continuity, which it may call God, but which is not God. So, what is vital in this question is how the mind can free itself from its own background, conditioning; and is it ever possible to be free? That is the problem, not continued belief or disbelief or whether belief will help you. We want God to help us in our pettiness, in our ambitions, in our pursuits. Such a God is not a help but a hindrance.

So, our problem is—can the mind free itself from its conditioning, the background in which it has been brought up, educated, controlled, shaped? To be free, one has first to be aware that one is bound. The mind has to be aware of its own conditioning, of the conscious as well as of the hidden, underground conditioning, which is not a process of analysis. That is, if one part of the mind analyzes itself, goes deeply into the problem through analysis, it is not possible to free the mind from its conditioning. The mind can free itself only when it is aware of the total process of its conditioning and of why it accepts this conditioning, and you can be aware of it; it is not very difficult. If the mind is constantly aware of its conditioning in its relationship with nature, with people, with ideas, with things, then the whole of existence is a mirror in which you can discover without analyzing. Analysis may temporarily open the door to a few difficulties, but to free the mind from its background, from conditioning, from tradition, so that it is made new—that is possible only when we are aware from moment to moment without struggle, when we see without effort what is happening within the corridors, the recesses of the mind. Only when the mind is new, free, is it capable of receiving that which is unnameable, the timeless.

August 24, 1952

Ninth Talk in The Oak Grove

Those who have attended these talks fairly regularly will know that we have been considering the very complex problem of change. This evening I would like to discuss, if possible, the power that brings about change, and what it is, and whether there can be a direct experiencing of that power, the energy, or what you will. I think we realize that some kind of energy, force, or power is necessary for change. Politically we see it very clearly. There are the extreme forms of tyranny, and also the more persuasive methods of bringing about a reform through the power of organization. Most of us rely on some form of compulsion, on political, religious, or social coercion, because we are caught in inertia, we are lazy, slothful. For most of us, change implies danger, and so we are unwilling to go through this psychological revolution which is so essential if we are to create a world in which human beings can act cleanly, decently.

We have been considering the various approaches to this problem of change, and it seems to me that we inevitably come to the central question as to what it is that brings about this change. What is that power, that energy, that force? Compulsion, self-discipline, any kind of coercion, creates resistance; and resistance does produce energy, power, which brings about a certain form of change. You must have noticed in your own life that the more you resist something, the more energy you have; the more you discipline, the more concentrated, focused you are, the greater the power. But does that bring about a fundamental change? Is that the power that is necessary for this inward, psychological revolution? Does the cultivation of the opposite bring about this essential transformation? If I hate, will the cultivation of love bring about a radical change? Is not the opposite of hate still within the field of hate? Is goodness the opposite of evil? Must I go through evil to find goodness? Is goodness the outcome of any form of compulsion, any form of discipline, coercion, suppression? Does not the cultivation of goodness, of compassion, of kindliness, merely emphasize the 'me', the self? That is, suppose I hate, and realizing its implications, I sedulously cultivate goodness, kindliness; does not that process strengthen the 'me', the self? The cultivation of goodness obviously brings about a certain change; there is power, there is energy. But surely, that change is still within the field of the 'me', of the self, of the mind, is it not? And as I have pointed out, the more you cultivate goodness and become conscious that you are good, the more evil there is, for evil is the outcome of the self.

Let us say you realize all this, and you also see the necessity of a fundamental transformation. How are you to bring about that revolution? What is the power, the creative energy that brings about that revolution, and how is it to be released? You have tried disciplines, you have tried the pursuit of ideals and various speculative theories—that you are God, and that if you can realize that godhood or experience the atma, the highest, or what you will, then that very realization will bring about a fundamental change. Will it? First you postulate that there is a reality of which you are a part and build up round it various theories, speculations, beliefs, doctrines, assumptions, according to which you live; and by thinking and acting according to that pattern, you hope to bring about a fundamental change. Will you?

Suppose you assume, as most so-called religious people do, that there is in you, fundamentally, deeply, the essence of reality; and that if, through cultivating virtue, through various forms of discipline, control, suppression, denial, sacrifice, you can get into touch with that reality, then the required transformation will be brought about. Is not this assumption still part of thought? Is it not the outcome of a conditioned mind, a mind that has been brought up to think in a particular way, according to certain patterns? Having created the image, the idea, the theory, the belief, the hope, you then look to your creation to bring about this radical change.

So, one must first see the extraordinarily subtle activities of the 'me', of the mind, one must become aware of the ideas, beliefs, speculations and put them all aside, for they are really deceptions, are they not? Others may have experienced reality, but if you have not experienced it, what is the good of speculating about it or imagining that you are in essence something real, immortal, godly? That is still within the field of thought, and anything that springs from thought is conditioned, is of time, of memory; therefore, it is not real. If one actually realizes that—not speculatively, not imaginatively or foolishly, but actually sees the truth that any activity of the mind in its speculative search, in its philosophical groping, any assumption, any imagination or hope is only self-deception—then what is the power, the creative energy that brings about this fundamental transformation? I do not know if you have come so far in your meditations, in your thoughts, in your daily awareness as to have rejected completely all assumptions, all imaginations, all speculative hopes, fears, and demands. Surely, any person who is really seeking must come to that, must he not? And if you have come so far, what happens? What then is the force, the energy, the creative something that brings about a radical change?

You see, as long as I pursue an idea, however noble, however imaginatively godly, theoretically supreme, there is always the duality of the seeker and the thing which he seeks, is there not? There is the entity who hates, and the entity who is pursuing peace, love; the one who is good, and the other who is evil. That is our struggle, our conflict, and I think that is the central problem—how to bridge the duality, how to go beyond. That is, suppose I hate, I have no affection in my heart. My heart is full of the things of the mind; it is cunning, devious, calculating, and I realize it. Also I feel that there can be a transformation in the world only when there is more love, a state of compassion, and therefore I pursue love. So there is in me the duality of love and hate with its struggle—the private thought and the public life, that which I am, and that which I am trying to be. There is a constant inward battle, conflict—and if we can understand that, then perhaps we shall find out how to awaken the energy, that creative something which will bring about a transformation. To understand that the thinker and the thought are one—to experience it, not repeat it verbally, which has no meaning—that, it seems to me, is the central problem. The self, the 'me', is made up of this struggle of duality, is it not? There is the 'me' and the 'not me', the bundle of memories, of conditionings, of hopes, and what it wants to be. The struggle between *what is* and 'what should be', the everlasting conflict between what I am and what I want to be, not only consciously, but deep down, unconsciously, in the obscure recesses of my mind and heart—is not that very struggle the process of the 'me'? But if I can really experience that the thinker is the thought, the observer is the observed, then there is a release of that creative energy which brings about a fundamental transformation.

So, if you are at all aware of yourself, you will know that there is this constant struggle going on which only emphasizes, gives nourishment, strength to the 'me', to the 'I-ness', to the ego, to the self—whether it be the higher or the lower self, it is all the same because it is all within the field of thought. And is not the thinker created by thought? Is the thinker separate from thought? As long as the thinker is trying to control thought, shape it, give it a certain direction, which is the process of discipline, that very struggle gives strength to the thinker and so gives vitality to the 'me'; and it is on this center of the 'me' that the revolution, the change must take place. And how is that to come about? I see clearly that no form of compulsion, no discipline, no incentive, no hope, no vision can bring it about because in all these there is a duality—the *what is* and 'what should be', the observer and the observed—and as long as the observer exists, there must always be the struggle to achieve the thing which he has observed, which he has thought out. This struggle gives strength to the thinker, which is the 'me', the self. I see that very clearly, so what am I to do?

Perhaps, in coming to this point, we have used the conscious mind; we have followed the argument, we have opposed or accepted it, we have seen it clearly or dimly. That is, the conscious mind is active in pursuit of what the speaker is saying. But to go further and experience more deeply requires a mind that is quiet and alert to find out, does it not? It is no longer pursuing ideas because if you pursue an idea, there is the thinker following what is being said, and so you immediately create duality. If you want to go further into this matter of fundamental change, is it not necessary for the active mind to be quiet? Surely, it is only when the mind is quiet that it can understand the enormous difficulty, the complex implications of the thinker and the thought as two separate processes—the experiencer and the experienced, the observer and the observed. Revolution, this psychological, creative revolution in which the 'me' is not, comes only when the thinker and the thought are one, when there is no duality as the thinker controlling thought, and I suggest it is this experience alone that releases the creative energy which in turn brings about a fundamental revolution, the breaking up of the psychological 'me'. But this is an extremely difficult thing to realize because the mind is so conditioned to struggle, to be separate, to be secure, to be permanent, that it is afraid to think of the problem anew. We have probably never experienced this state in which the thinker is absent, in which the observer is not, because we are so conditioned by the idea, so accustomed to the feeling that the thinker is always separate from his thought, and you are not going to experience it by merely listening to me. But if you have earnestly followed these talks and have really experimented with yourself during the past weeks, you are bound to come to the point when you are fully aware that there is this extraordinary division between the thinker and the thought. Most of us are still unaware of this division. We are caught up in the conflict between the thinker and the thought, in the everlasting battle of the 'me', the self, to acquire, to reject, to suppress, to become something. With that we are very familiar, but we are not aware of the division. If, becoming aware of the division, the thinker seeks to destroy it, to bridge it over, he increases the division because then the thinker is again seeking to be something which he is not, thereby giving himself greater strength, greater security.

So, how is it possible for you and me, as individuals, to come to this experience, to this realization? We know the way of power—power through domination, power through discipline, power through compulsion. Through political power we hope to change fundamentally, but such power only breeds further darkness, disintegration, evil, the strengthening of the 'me'. We are familiar with the various forms of acquisition, both individually and as groups, but we have never tried the way of love, and we don't even know what it means. Love is not possible as long as there is the thinker, the center of the 'me'. Realizing all this, what is one to do? Surely, the only thing which can bring about a fundamental change, a creative, psychological release, is everyday watchfulness, being aware from moment to moment of our motives, the conscious as well as the unconscious. When we realize that disciplines, beliefs, ideals only strengthen the 'me' and are therefore utterly futile—when we are aware of that from day to day, see the truth of it, do we not come to the central point when the thinker is constantly separating himself from his thought, from his observations, from his experiences? As long as the thinker exists apart from his thought, which he is trying to dominate, there can be no fundamental transformation. As long as the 'me' is the observer, the one who gathers experience, strengthens himself through experience, there can be no radical change, no creative release. That creative release comes only when the thinker is the thought—but the gap cannot be bridged by any effort. When the mind realizes that any speculation, any verbalization, any form of thought only gives strength to the 'me', when it sees that as long as the thinker exists apart from thought there must be limitation, the conflict of duality—when the mind realizes that, then it is watchful, everlastingly aware of how it is separating itself from experience, asserting itself, seeking power. In that awareness, if the mind pursues it ever more deeply and extensively without seeking an end, a goal, there comes a state in which the thinker and the thought are one. In that state there is no effort, there is no becoming, there is no desire to change; in that state the 'me' is not, for there is a transformation which is not of the mind.

Question: One must obviously know the bad in order to know the good. Does this not imply the process of evolution?

KRISHNAMURTI: Must we know drunkenness to know sobriety? Must you go through hate in order to know what it is to be compassionate? Must you go through wars, destroying yourself and others, to know what peace is? Surely, this is an utterly false way of thinking, is it not? First you assume that there is evolution, growth, a moving from bad to good, and then you fit your thinking into that pattern. Obviously, there is physical growth, the little plant becoming the big tree; there is technological progress, the wheel evolving through centuries into the jet plane. But is there psychological progress, evolution? That is what we are discussing—whether there is a growth, an evolution of the 'me', beginning with evil and ending up in good. Through a process of evolution, through time, can the 'me', which is the center of evil, ever become noble, good? Obviously not. That which is evil, the psychological 'me', will always remain evil. But we do not want to face that. We think that through the process of time, through growth and change, the 'I' will ultimately become reality. This is our hope, that is our longing—that the 'I' will be made perfect through time. What is this 'I', this 'me'? It is a name, a form, a bundle of memories, hopes, frustrations, longings, pains, sorrows, passing joys. We want this 'me' to continue and become perfect, and so we say that beyond the 'me' there is a 'super-me', a higher self, a spiritual entity which is timeless, but since we have thought of it, that "spiritual" entity is still within the field of time, is it not? If we can think about it, it is obviously within the field of time, is it not? If we can think about it, it is obviously within the field of our reasoning.

Please, if I can think about the spiritual state, if I know what it looks like, what it tastes like, what its sensations are, it is already within the field of my knowledge, and my knowledge is based on memory, on conditioning. Surely, that which I can think about is not spiritual, timeless. Thought is the result of the past, of memory, of time, and thought has created this so-called spiritual entity because I am conditioned to accept that theory, I have been brought up from childhood to think in that way. Perhaps others are conditioned not to believe in a spiritual entity—which is actually happening in the world. They will deny that there is a spiritual entity because they have been conditioned to think in those terms.

The mind, seeing its own impermanency, its own transiency, craves a permanent state, and the very craving creates the symbol, the sensation, the idea, the belief to which we cling. So, there is the 'me' who is transient, and the 'super-me', the higher self, which we consider to be permanent; and the mind is pursuing the permanent, thereby creating duality, the conflict of the opposites. In dividing thought into the superficial 'me' which is impermanent, and the 'me' which is concealed, far away, timeless, spiritual, with all the various degrees between the two, I have given birth to the conflict of duality; and to achieve the timeless, I say I must have time, there must be a psychological growth, a becoming. In this process there is always the 'me', the observer, and the thing which he observes and is going to gain; and in giving himself to this struggle, he strengthens his longings, his desires. And to achieve what he is after, he must have time, the future; therefore, he has reincarnation—if not now, tomorrow. But if we can cut across all that, then we will see that as long as there is the thinker apart from the thought, the observer separate from the observed, there must be conflict; and through conflict there can be no understanding, no peace.

Now, is it possible for the thinker and the thought, for the observer and the observed, to be one? You will never find out if you merely glance at this problem and superficially ask me to explain what I mean by this or that. Surely, this is your problem; it is not my problem only; you are not here to find out how I look at this problem or the problems of the world. This constant battle within, which is so destructive, so deteriorating—it is your problem, is it not? And it is also your problem how to bring about a radical change in yourself and not be satisfied with superficial revolutions in politics, in economics, in different bureaucracies. You are not trying to understand me or the way I look at life. You are trying to understand yourself, and these are your problems which you have to face; and by considering them together, which is what we are doing in these talks, we can perhaps help each other to look at them more clearly, see them more distinctly. But to see clearly merely at the verbal level is not enough. That does not bring about a creative psychological change. We must go beyond the words, beyond all symbols and their sensations—the symbol of love, the symbol of God, the Hindu and the Christian symbols—for though they create certain responses, they are all at the verbal level, at the level of images. We must put aside all these things and come to the central issue—how to dissolve the 'me' which is time-binding, in which there is no love, no compassion. It is possible to go beyond only when the mind does not separate itself as the thinker and the thought. When the thinker and the thought are one, only then is there silence, the silence in which there is no image-making or waiting for further experience. In that silence there is no experiencer who is experiencing, and only then is there a psychological revolution which is creative.

Question: What are the essentials of right education?

KRISHNAMURTI: Surely, this is a very complex problem, is it not? And do you think it can be answered in a few minutes? But perhaps we can see what is important in this question.

For what are we educating ourselves and our children? For war? For greater knowledge so that we can destroy each other? For techniques so that we can earn a livelihood? For information, culture, prestige? Actually, why are we educating our children? We really don't know, do we? How can we know when we ourselves are so utterly confused? Practically everything we do leads to war, to the destruction of our neighbors and ourselves. We are educating the child to compete, strengthening the 'me', conditioning him so that he can survive in this battle, and we throw in various forms of information, knowledge. That is what we call education. Or, we condition the child to think along certain lines and act according to established patterns; we want him to be a Catholic, a Christian Scientist, a Communist, a Hindu, and so on and on. So, first of all, is it not important that the educator himself be educated? Surely, education is not the mere teaching of facts—anyone can pick those up in an encyclopedia if he knows how to read. What is essential is to awaken intelligence so that the mind is able to question, to find out, and to meet life without getting caught in any form of conditioning—religious, social, or political—and for that, both the teacher and the parent have to be intelligent, have they not?

As this is a very complex problem which must be approached from different angles; we cannot merely lay down what are the essentials of right education, but we can see that what we are now doing throughout the world is false, destructive, uncreative. Creativeness is not the mere production of pictures, of inventions, it is not the writing of poems, of essays, books. That may or may not be creative. But what is important is this inward creativeness in which there is no fear, no desire for self-extension, no aggressiveness, no psychological dependence, a state in which there is a freedom, a sense of aloneness which is not loneliness. This is the truly creative state, and it is only when we have awakened it in ourselves that we can help the student in his gifts, in his studies, in his relationships, without emphasizing the 'me'. But to break down the self-enclosing activities of the mind and come to that creativeness requires an enormous watchfulness, a constant alertness within oneself.

So, our problem is not easy, but we must begin with ourselves, must we not? Self-knowledge is the beginning of wisdom, and wisdom is not the mere repetition of someone else's experience or phrases. Wisdom has no authority; it comes into being as the mind begins to understand the depths and extensions of its own nature, which cannot be speculated upon. To discover that which is creative, we must come to it anew; the mind must be empty, free from all knowledge, from all memory. Only then is there a possibility of a new relationship and a new world

August 30, 1952

Tenth Talk in The Oak Grove

As this is the last talk of the present series, perhaps it might be as well if I briefly went over what we have been discussing for the past several weeks; but in doing so, I am not making a résumé, which would imply recollection of what has been said and repeating it, and that is not my intention.

What we have been discussing is the problem of change. I think most of us realize the necessity of change, not only outwardly in the economic and social world, but primarily at the psychological level of our existence. When we consider change, we generally think in terms of the superficial level. We mean the change that must take place in the relationship of nations, of groups, of communities, of races. We talk of economic and social revolution, and how to bring it about—and there the majority of us stop. We are satisfied with intellectual concepts, verbal formulations, or with the vision of a new world to which we can give our faith and for which we can sacrifice ourselves. So, we see the necessity of change, but I feel a radical change can take place not at the periphery, on the outside, the circumference, but only at the center, that is, at the psychological level. In discussing this problem, we have considered it from different points of view, and perhaps this morning we can approach it from the point of view of authority, and how authority prevents a fundamental change. There is the authority of knowledge, the authority of one's own experience, the authority of memory, the authority of what others say, the authority of the interpreter; and wherever the mind clings to authority, is hedged about by it, obviously there can be no radical change.

I think authority is one of the greatest hindrances that prevent this inward transformation which is so essential if there is to be an outward change in which the problem of war and starvation can be resolved. Until there is a psychological revolution, a fundamental transformation in each of us, mere outward reformation will not bring about the desired end, and this inward change is prevented when you and I as individuals cling to authority. Most of us are afraid of change. We want things to remain as they are, particularly at the physical level if we are well off. We have a house, a little bit of property, and we are afraid of change there. We are also afraid of change in belief because we are uncertain of the future. However intelligent, clever, so-called intellectual the mind may be, it clings to some form of belief. Belief becomes the authority, the ideal, the vision. In our relationships, in experience, there is the desire to be secure, to continue in a particular psychological state, and we are afraid to have a fundamental change along these lines. Being afraid, the mind creates authority—political authority, the authority of religion, of belief, of dogma, the authority of one's own experience, and so on.

Is it not important to find out how the mind is constantly creating its own barriers of authority, which prevent a radical transformation? Has not each one of us a subtle form of authority? There is the authority of the book, which is knowledge, and must not knowledge be completely set aside if the mind is to be free to see the new? And can the mind ever be free from this acquisition of knowledge? By knowledge we mean information concerning what has been said by the clever, the intellectual, the people who are capable of expressing ideas very clearly, subtly, and does not the mind, in its fear, make of this an authority to which it clings? And do we not make our own experience into authority, a pattern of action according to which we function? Do we not make belief into an authority? Because we ourselves are uncertain, fearful of change, of what might happen, there is always the belief, the ideal, the ultimate reality, the authority of a book, of another's experience, and of our own hope. Most of us are seeking something to which the mind can cling, round which the mind can build its own security, its own continuity, are we not? And can the mind ever be free from this pursuit, from the erection of these walls which hold it? Can the mind, being smothered by authority, ever change? Is this not one of our problems, yours and mine? Can the mind ever be free from authority, even at the superficial level?

You may not make an authority of me because, after all, I am not saying anything which you cannot find out for yourself if you are eager, if you are alert, inquiring, but the desire for authority is always there. Being confused, you depend on interpreters to tell you what I am trying to say or not to say; you find interpreters of the truth. In yourself you are so uncertain, lost, confused, and you want someone to lead, to help you. The moment you rely on another, however great or absurd he may be, there is no freedom; hence there is no possibility of a radical change. In its own uncertainty, in its own confusion and desire to find security, the mind gradually sets up the authority of the church, of the political party, of the leader, the teacher, the book; and realizing this, the church, the state, the politicians, the cunning people seize the authority and tell us what to think. Most of us are satisfied with authority because it gives us a continuity, a certainty, a sense of being protected. But a man who would understand the implications of this deep psychological revolution must be free of authority, must he not? He cannot look to any authority, whether of his own creation or imposed upon him by another. And is this possible? Is it possible for me not to rely on the authority of my own experience? Even when I have rejected all the outward expressions of authority—books, teachers, priests, churches, beliefs—I still have the feeling that at least I can rely on my own judgment, on my own experiences, on my own analysis. But can I rely on my experience, on my judgment, on my analysis? My experience is the result of my conditioning, just as yours is the result of your conditioning, is it not? I may have been brought up as a Mohammedan or a Buddhist or a Hindu, and my experience will depend on my cultural, economic, social, and religious background, just as yours will. And can I rely on that? Can I rely for guidance, for hope, for the vision which will give me faith on my own judgment, which again is the result of accumulated memories, experiences, the conditioning of the past meeting the present? Can I analyze my own problems? And if I do, is the analyzer different from the thing that he has analyzed?

Now, when I have put all these questions to myself and I am aware of this problem, I see there can be only one state in which reality, newness, can come into being, which brings about a revolution. That state is when the mind is completely empty of the past, when there is no analyzer, no experiencer, no judgement, no authority of any kind. After all, is this not one of our deep problems? As long as the mind is crippled by the past, burdened with knowledge, with memories, with judgments, the new cannot be; as long as the mind is the center of the self, the 'me', which is the result of time, there is no possibility of the timeless. I do not know what the timeless, that ultimate reality is, but I see that I cannot possibly be aware of anything other than my own creations as long as the mind is merely in a state of experiencing, analyzing, judging, following.

So, if I am really anxious to find out whether there is anything new, the mind must see the nature of its own creations, its own illusions. And I think this is one of our greatest difficulties because our whole education is to worship the intellect, the mind. So many books have been written about the mind, and everything that we have read is guiding, shaping, conditioning us. This is not a matter of agreement or disagreement with me, but are you not aware of these things in your own life? And a mind which is crippled by the past, by one's own experiences, by one's own motives, urges, demands, ambitions, beliefs, by the everlasting striving to be something—how can such a mind ever be capable of seeing the new? If you are at all aware of your own inner problems and see that the political, religious, and economic crises of the whole world are inter-related with the psychological conflicts, you are bound to put these questions to yourself. Any change that takes place without freeing the mind of the past is still within the field of time, therefore within the field of corruption, and surely, such a change is no change at all, it is merely a continuation of the old in a different form.

Being aware of all this, I ask myself, as you must also, whether the mind can possibly be free, completely empty of the past, and so, capable of seeing something which is not of its own projection, of its own manufacture. To find out if it is possible, you have to experiment—which means that you must distrust completely any form of authority, self-imposed or imposed by outward circumstances. And authority works very subtly. You are being influenced by me, you are bound to be. But if you are only being influenced, then there will be no radical change—it's merely a sensation which will react and throw off this influence, taking on another. Whereas, if you are deeply concerned with the problem of fundamental change, then you will see directly for yourself that this change must come about if there is to be peace in the world, if there is to be no starvation when many are well fed. If there is to be the universal well-being of man, there must be a change not at the superficial level but at the center. The center is the 'me', the 'I', which is everlastingly accumulating, positively or negatively, and one of its ways of acquisition is through authority. Through authority it has continuance. So, if you and I realize this, then the problem arises: Can the mind empty itself of its whole content, can it be free of all the things that have been put upon it, imposed and self-imposed? It is only when the mind is empty that there is a possibility of creation, but I do not mean this superficial emptiness which most of us have. Most of us are superficially empty, and it shows itself through the desire for distraction. We want to be amused, so we turn to books, to the radio, we run to lectures, to authorities; the mind is everlastingly filling itself. I am not talking of that emptiness, which is thoughtlessness. On the contrary, I am talking of the emptiness which comes through extraordinary thoughtfulness, when the mind sees its own power of creating illusion and goes beyond.

Creative emptiness is not possible as long as there is the thinker who is waiting, watching, observing in order to gather experience, in order to strengthen himself. And can the mind ever be empty of all symbols, of all words with their sensations so that there is no experiencer who is accumulating? Is it possible for the mind to put aside completely all the reasonings, the experiences, the impositions, authorities so that it is in a state of emptiness? You will not be able to answer this question, naturally; it is an impossible question for you to answer because you do not know, you have never tried. But, if I may suggest, listen to it, let the question be put to you, let the seed be sown, and it will bear fruit if you really listen to it, if you do not resist it, if you do not say, "How can the mind be empty? If it is empty, it cannot function, it cannot do its daily job." And what is its daily job? Routine, boredom, tiresome continuity. We all know that. So, it seems to me important to find out for yourself, and to find out, you must listen, inquire. When I am talking, I am helping you to inquire; I am not putting something across or over to you. I also am inquiring. That is the purpose of these talks.

After all these weeks of talking, of going into this problem of change, we must ultimately come to this question, whether the mind can ever be empty so that it can receive the new. It is only the new that can transform, not the old. If you pursue the pattern of the old, any change is modified continuity of the old; there is nothing new in that, there is nothing creative. The creative can come into being only when the mind itself is new, and the mind can renew itself only when it is capable of seeing all its own activities not only at the superficial level but deep down. When the mind sees its own activities, is aware of its own desires, demands, urges, pursuits, the creation of its own authorities, fears; when it sees in itself the resistance created by discipline, by control, and the hope which projects beliefs, ideals—when the mind sees through, is aware of this whole process, can it put aside all these things and be new, creatively empty? You will find out whether it can or cannot only if you experiment without having an opinion about it, without wanting to experience that creative state. If you want to experience it, you will, but what you experience is not creative emptiness; it is only a projection of desire. If you desire to experience the new, you are merely indulging in illusion. But if you begin to observe, to be aware of your own activities from day to day, from moment to moment, watching the whole process of yourself as in a mirror, then, as you go deeper and deeper, you will come to the ultimate question of this emptiness in which alone there can be the new. Truth, God, or what you will is not something to be experienced, for the experiencer is the result of time, the result of memory, of the past, and as long as there is the experiencer, there cannot be reality. There is reality only when the mind is completely free from the analyzer, from the experiencer, and the experienced.

Now can you not just listen to this as the soil receives the seed and see if the mind is capable of being free, empty? It can be empty only by understanding all its own projections, its own activities, not off and on, but from day to day, from moment to moment. Then you will find the answer, then you will see that the change comes without your asking, that the state of creative emptiness is not a thing to be cultivated—it is there, it comes darkly, without any invitation, and only in that state is there a possibility of renewal, newness, revolution.

Question: I read recently of a Hindu girl who could easily solve problems in higher mathematics which were difficult for even the greatest mathematicians. How can you explain this except by reincarnation?

KRISHNAMURTI: Isn't it very odd how we are satisfied by explanations? You have a particular theory of continuity, which is reincarnation. You have that belief, that conviction. I don't know why, but you have it—or rather, we do know why—because you want to continue. Having that belief, that explanation, you want to fit everything round it, and the authority of your belief cripples your discovery of the new. This girl's extraordinary faculty may or may not be the result of reincarnation, but surely what is important is to find out your own state, not that of the girl, why your mind is caught and crippled by words, explanations. Good gracious me, there can be a dozen explanations for this, but why do you as an individual choose the particular explanation that satisfies you? That is important to find out, is it not? Because, if you go into it, you will discover how your mind is crippled by belief, by sensation, by the desire for your own continuity. Surely, that which continues cannot be the new. Only in dying is there the new. But we don't want to die, we want to continue. Our whole social structure, all our religious beliefs are based on this continuity of the 'me', of the 'I', which means we are afraid of death, of coming to an end. Being afraid, we have innumerable explanations to cover up that fear, and the more we cover it, the more it festers. And what is this fear? Please follow this: What is this fear of not being, of not continuing? What is the 'you' that wants to continue? Is it not your property, the things that you have gathered in your house, the furniture, the radio, the washing machine, the qualities, the virtues you have struggled to gain, the name, the reputation, the memories, and experiences? And if you really go into it, look at it earnestly, what are all these things? What are they but empty words, symbols that give you sensations, and these sensations we cling to. It is that we want to continue, and so there is never the new; there is never a death, but a postponement. It is only in dying that you see the new; it is only in putting an end to the old that there is a possibility of something creative. And is it possible to die from day to day? Is it possible not to hoard resentments, ideas, goals, to put an end to this process of achievement which gives birth to everlasting strife? Fear is a thing which we have never really looked at; death we have never faced. We watch other people die, but we don't know what death means because we are afraid of it, so we run away through explanations, through words, through ideas, beliefs. And can the mind face fear? Can the mind look at it? What is this fear? Is it a word or an actuality? Please listen, find out. The thing which we are afraid of, is it the word *fear* or something which is actual? There is the fact of death, but we have ideas, opinions about death. The ideas about the fact create the fear. It is the word about the fact that creates the fear—not the fact itself. And can the mind be free of the word and look at the fact? Which means, really, looking at the fact without the activity of the mind. The mind is active only in words, in symbols, in opinions, so the mind creates the barrier and looks through the barrier at the fact, and therefore there is fear. Can the mind look at the fact without having an idea about it, without an opinion, a judgment? If it can, then there is a complete revolution, is there not? Then there is a possibility of going beyond death.

Question: What is suffering?

KRISHNAMURTI: Let us inquire and find out. There is the physical pain which gradually becomes a mental suffering, and which the mind uses to create situations, problems, either to strengthen or to diminish itself. Then there is the suffering caused by not being loved sufficiently, by wanting love; there is suffering through death, when you love somebody and that somebody is gone; there is suffering through frustration, the suffering which comes when you are ambitious and cannot achieve your ambition; there is suffering through the loss of your property, through ill health. What does all this indicate? What is this thing that we call suffering? Is it not that through these activities of the mind the self-enclosing process of the 'me' becomes more and more accentuated, strengthened? When you become aware that you are enclosed, held, is that not suffering? Does not suffering exist when you are conscious of yourself, of your battles, of your strivings, of your frustrated ambitions? The more you are caught in the conflicts of the self, the more there is of suffering. So, suffering is a reaction of the self, and to understand the implications of suffering is to go into the whole process of the 'me', of the 'I'—which is what we have been doing in these talks.

Suffering is an indication of the activities of the mind. Suffering is not to be denied, but most of us try to cover it up; we run away from it through explanations, through satisfying words. We do not go into the problem of suffering, which is to expose the 'me' in its nakedness, and when it is suddenly exposed, we do not dwell with it, we do not watch it, we try to escape. In escape there is resistance, and that very resistance creates further conflict, further struggle, so we are caught in this everlasting process of suffering. Whereas, if, when suffering comes, we are capable of looking at that nakedness, that loneliness, that emptiness which is the self, only then is there a possibility of going beyond it.

Question: What is meditation?

KRISHNAMURTI: Perhaps you and I can find out together what meditation is, so let us go into it. You are not waiting for an answer from me so that you can be satisfied by words, by explanations. You and I are going to find out what meditation actually is.

What is meditation? Sitting quietly, cross-legged, or lying down, relaxed? Obviously, there must be relaxation of the body, but though your body is relaxed, your mind is very active, chattering away endlessly. Being aware of this, you say, "I must control it, I must stop it, there must be a certain sense of quietness." So, you begin to control, to discipline your mind. Please follow all this, and you will see. You spend years in controlling, disciplining your chattering mind; your energy is spent in making the mind conform to a desired pattern, but you never succeed, and if you do succeed, your mind becomes so weary, lethargic, empty, dull. Obviously, that is not meditation. On the contrary, the mind must be supremely alert, not caught in a routine of habit, discipline.

So, I see that my mind, though it is chattering endlessly, cannot be disciplined, made to fit into a particular pattern of thought. Then how is it to be calmed? How is the chattering mind to be quiet? Just see the implications of the problem. If the observer, the analyzer, imposes a discipline on the chattering mind, then there is a conflict between the observer, the analyzer, and the thing he has observed, analyzed. The thinker is struggling to make his thought conform to the pattern which he desires, which is to calm the mind, so he disciplines it, he controls, dominates, suppresses it, in which is involved the conflict of duality. There is a division between the observer and the observed, and in that division there is conflict, and meditation is obviously not an endless process of conflict.

So, how is the mind, which is ceaselessly chattering, to be quiet? When I ask that question, what is the state of your mind? Please watch yourself. What is the state of your mind when I put that question? You are accustomed to discipline, control, but now you see its absurdity, its illusory nature; therefore, the state of your mind is that you do not know how to quiet the mind. You are finished with explanations, with knowledge, which is conditioning; the actual fact is that your mind is chattering, and you do not know how to quiet it. So, what is the state of your mind? You are really inquiring, are you not? You are watching, you have no answer. All that you know is that your mind is chattering, and you want to find out how the mind can be quiet—but not according to a method. Surely, the moment you put to yourself the question, "How is the mind to be quiet, cease from chattering?" you have already entered the realm in which the mind is quiet, have you not? You know that your mind is active, ceaselessly battling, one layer against another layer, the observer fighting the observed, the experiencer wanting more; you are aware of the incessant vagaries of thought, and you actually do not know how to reduce it, how it is to be quiet. You reject all methods because they have no meaning. To follow a method, to copy a pattern only cripples the mind through habit. Habit is not meditation. The routine of a discipline does not free the mind so that it can discover the new. So, you reject all that completely, but you still have the question, How is the mind to be quiet? The moment you put that question to yourself really, vitally, actually, what then is the state of your mind? Is it not quiet? It is no longer chattering, analyzing, judging; it is watching, observing, because you don't know. The very state of not knowing is the beginning of quietness. You discover that as long as there is the struggle between the desired pattern and that which you are, there must be a battle, and this battle is a waste of energy, which creates inertia. So, the mind sees the falseness of all that and rejects it. As it observes, the mind becomes quiet, yet there is still the problem of the thinker apart from thought, so there is again a battle.

Meditation is all this process, not just a limited process with a particular end. It is this vast searching, groping, not being caught in any particular idea, belief, or experience, being aware that any projection of the mind is illusion, hypnosis. And if you go into it more and more deeply, not with a motive, not with any desire for a particular result, but simply watching the whole process of yourself, then you will see that without any form of compulsion, suppression, or discipline, the mind becomes creatively empty, still. That stillness will not give you any riches in this world—do not translate it so quickly into dollars. If you approach it with a begging bowl, it will offer you nothing. That stillness is free from all sense of continuity; in it there is no experiencer who is experiencing.

When the experiencer is there, it is no longer stillness, it is merely a continuation of sensation. Meditation is all this process which brings about a state in which the mind is still, no longer projecting, desiring, defending, judging, experiencing. In that state the new can be. The new is not to be verbalized; it has no words to explain it; therefore, it is not communicable. It is something that comes into being when the mind itself is new, and this whole complex process of self-knowledge is meditation.

August 31, 1952

Rajghat School, Banaras, India, 1952

The Foundation for New Education (formerly known as The Rishi Valley Trust) has schools and colleges at Rajghat-Banaras, and at Rishi Valley in South India.

J. Krishnamurti delivered these Talks at Rajghat-Banaras, on the banks of the river Ganga during the month of December 1952 to boys and girls of the ages of 9 to 20.

First Talk at Rajghat

I suppose most of you understand English because I am going to talk, as you know, every morning at 8:30, and we are going to talk over the many difficulties that are involved in education.

Have you ever thought why you are educated, why you are learning history, mathematics, geography? Have you ever thought why you go to schools and colleges? Is it not very important to find out why you are crammed with information, with so-called knowledge? What is all this so-called education? Your parents send you here because they have taken certain degrees and have passed certain examinations. Have you ever asked yourselves why you are here, have the teachers themselves asked you why you are here? Do the teachers themselves know why they are here? So, should you not try to find out what all this struggle is to pass examinations, to study, to live in a certain place, to be frightened, to play games, and so on? Should your teachers not help you to inquire into all this and not merely teach you to pass certain examinations?

Boys pass examinations because they think they will have to get a job, they will have to earn a livelihood. Why do you girls pass examinations? To be educated in order to get better husbands? Do not laugh; just think about this. Or, are you a nuisance at home, and therefore your parents send you away to a school? By passing examinations, have you understood the whole significance of life? Take, for instance, a boy who passes a certain examination, some stupid examination—because you people are very clever in passing examinations—this does not mean he is a very intelligent person. Some people who do not know how to pass examinations may be very intelligent, may be capable with their hands and with their minds; they may think out more than the person who merely crams and learns some subject very well in order to pass examinations.

Some boys pass examinations to get jobs, and their whole outlook on life is the getting of a job. What happens afterwards? They get married, they have children, and they are caught in a machine, are they not? They become clerks or lawyers or policemen. They are caught in that machine for the rest of their lives. They keep on being clerks, lawyers; they have an everlasting struggle with the women they marry, with their children, a constant battle; and that is their life until they die.

As regards you girls, what happens to you? You get married, don't you? That is your aim or concern; your parents get you married and you have children. You marry a clerk or a lawyer, and for the rest of your life, if you have a little money, you are concerned about your saris and how you look and what people will say and about the quarrels between you and your husband.

Do you see all this? Are you not aware of this in your family, in your neighborhood? Have you noticed how it goes on all the time? Must you not find out what is the meaning of education, why you want to be educated, why your parents want you to be educated, why they make speeches about education—as you heard the other day—elaborate speeches about what education is doing in the world? You may be able to read Bernard Shaw's plays, you may be able to quote Shakespeare or Voltaire or some new philosopher, but if you yourself are not intelligent, if you are not creative, what is the point of education?

So, is it not important for the teachers as well as for you students to find out, to inquire, how to be intelligent? Education does not consist in being able to read; any fool can read, any fool can pass examinations. If you know how to read, are you educated? Surely, education consists, does it not, in cultivating intelligence. Must you not find out what it is to be intelligent? I do not mean cunning, I do not mean trying to be clever to outdo somebody. Intelligence is something quite different, is it not? Intelligence obviously comes when you are not afraid, when there is no fear. You know what fear is? Fear comes when you think about what people may say about you or what your parents may say, when you are criticized, when you are punished, when you fail to pass an examination, when your teacher scolds you, when you are not popular in your class, in your school, in your surroundings. Fear gradually creeps in, does it not?

So, fear obviously is one of the barriers to intelligence, is it not? Is not the essence of education to free the student—that is, you and me—from fear and to make him aware of the causes of fear so that he can live free from it? Is it not one of the essential aims of education, from the very beginning of your life, from childhood until you go into the world, to help you to be free so that you are able to understand fear and the causes of fear?

Do you know that you are afraid? You have fear, have you not? Or, are you free from fear? Do you know what fear is? You do not know? Are you not afraid of your parents, of your teachers, of what people might think? Suppose you do something of which your parents do not approve, of which the society around you does not approve. Would you not be afraid? Suppose you did not marry a person of your caste or class; you would be afraid, would you not, of what people might say? Would you not be afraid if your future husband did not get the right amount of money or position or prestige? Would you not be ashamed? Would you not be afraid if your friends did not think well of you? Are you not afraid of death, of disease? So, most of us are afraid. Do not say no so quickly. We may not have thought about it, but if we do think about it, we will notice that almost everybody in the world, grown-ups as well as children, has some kind of fear gnawing at his heart. And, is it not the aim, the purpose, the intention of education to help each one, each individual, to be free from that fear so that he can be intelligent? I do not know if this school is going to do that or is doing it. That is what we want to do here, which means really that the teachers must be free from fear. It is no good teachers talking of fearlessness, and themselves being afraid of what the neighbors may say, afraid of their wives or women teachers being afraid of their husbands.

If one has fear, there is no initiative. You know what initiative is? Is it so difficult to find out? To have initiative is to do something original, spontaneously, naturally, without being guided, forced, controlled, to do something which you love. You often walk in the streets and you see a stone in the middle of the road and a car goes bumping over it. Have you ever removed that stone? Or, have you, as you walked, seen the poor people, the peasants, the villagers, and have you done something spontaneously, naturally, kindly, out of your own heart, instead of being told what you have to do? You see that if you have fear, then all that is shut out; all that goes out of your life; you are unconscious of and do not observe what is going on around you. If you have fear, you are bound to follow tradition, some person, some guru. When you follow tradition, when you follow a husband or wife, you—as an individual, as a human being—lose your dignity.

Is it not the purpose of education to free you from fear, and not merely make you pass some examinations which may be necessary? Essentially, deeply, is it not the vital aim of education to help you from childhood until you go into the world? Should not such education help you to be completely free inwardly from fear so that you are an intelligent human being, full of initiative? Initiative is destroyed when you are copying, when you are merely following a tradition, following a political leader, or a religious swami. To follow anybody is surely detrimental to intelligence. The very following creates a sense of fear, shuts out the understanding of the extraordinary complications of life with all its struggles, with its sorrows, with its poverty and riches and its beauty, the birds and the sunset on the water. When you are frightened, all this is shut out.

It is the function, obviously, of every teacher to help each one of his students to be completely free from fear so that he is awakened to do things of his own accord without being told, without being guided.

I have talked for twenty minutes and I think it is enough. If I may suggest, you should ask your teachers to tell you what we have been talking about, to explain it. Will you do it? Find out for yourself if the teachers have understood what I am talking about; it will help them to help you to be more intelligent, not to be frightened. Because, in subjects of this kind, we want teachers who are very intelligent—intelligent in the right sense, not in the sense of passing the M. A. or B. A. examinations. If you are interested in it as students, discuss this with your teacher, have a period during the day in which to talk about this. Because, you will have to grow up; you will have to have husbands, wives, and children; you will have to know what life is, the struggle to earn, starvation, death, and the beauty of life—all this you will have to know. And this is the place to find out all these things. If the teachers merely teach you mathematics and geography and history and science, that is not enough.

So, if I may suggest, during the time I am here for the next three or four weeks, set aside a period to talk over what I have said so that tomorrow when you come, you may ask questions and find out more about it, so that you are awake, so that you want to question, you want to find out, so that your own initiative may be awakened.

December 10, 1952

Second Talk at Rajghat

I wonder if you thought any more about what we were talking about yesterday morning. Did you have an opportunity to discuss with your teachers the problem of fear, or did you forget about it with your day's activities?

May I continue with what we were talking about yesterday morning? This is not just a polite question. I want to know if you are interested in what we have been talking about, or do you want me to talk about something else?

I will go on with what I was saying; then as we go along for several days, perhaps we can talk more easily.

Yesterday, we were talking about fear. It is fear that prevents initiative because most of us, when we are afraid, cling to things like a creeper that clings to a tree. We cling to our parents, to our husbands, to our sons, to our daughters, to our wives. That is the outward form of fear. Because inwardly we are afraid, we dread to stand alone. We may have a great many saris or clothes or property, but inwardly, psychologically—do you know what "psychologically" means?—we are very poor. The more poor we are inwardly, the more we intrigue outwardly, the more we cling to parents, to things, to property, to clothes. When we are afraid, we cling to outward things as well as to inward things such as tradition. Have you noticed old people and the people who are inwardly insufficient, inwardly empty? To them tradition matters a great deal. Have you noticed that amongst your friends, parents, and teachers? Have you noticed it in yourself? The moment there is fear, inward fear, you try to cover it up by respectability, by following a tradition; and so you lose initiative. Because you are just following, tradition becomes very important—tradition of what people say, tradition that has been handed down from the past, tradition that has no vitality, no zest in life, tradition which is only a mere repetition without any meaning.

When one is afraid, there is always an inclination, a tendency, to imitate. Have you noticed that? You know what "imitation" is? Being afraid, you cling to tradition; you cling to your parents, to your wives, to your brothers, to your husbands. There is always the desire to imitate. Imitation destroys initiative. You know, when you paint a tree, you do not merely imitate the tree, you do not copy it exactly as it is; otherwise, it is merely photography. But to be free to paint it, you have to feel what the tree or flower or sunset conveys to you; you have not merely to copy it in black and white but to feel the significance, the meaning of the sunset. It is very important to convey the significance, and not merely to copy it; then you begin to awaken the creative process. And for that, there must be a free mind, a mind that is not burdened with tradition, with imitation. Look at your own lives and the lives about you, how empty everything is!

At certain levels of life you must imitate, must you not? Unfortunately, you have to be imitative in the clothes you put on, in the books that you read. They are all forms of imitation, but it is necessary to go beyond this—that is, to feel free so that you can think out things for yourselves, so that you do not merely accept what somebody says—it does not matter who it is, your teachers, your parents, great teachers. To really think out things for yourselves, not to follow, is very important because the moment you follow somebody, the very following indicates fear, does it not? Somebody offers you something you want—paradise, heaven, or a better job. So long as you are wanting something, there is bound to be fear, and fear cripples the free mind. Do you know what a free mind is? Have you ever watched your own mind? Is it free? No, it is not, because you are always watching to see what your friends say. Your mind is like a house enclosed by a gate or by a barbed wire. In that state no new thing can take place. A new thing can only come about when there is no fear. And it is extremely difficult for the mind to be free from fear—which means really free from imitation, from the desire to imitate, from the desire to follow, from the desire to amass wealth or to follow a tradition—which does not mean that you do something outrageous.

Freedom of mind comes into being when there is no fear, when the mind is not intriguing for position, for prestige, to show off. Therefore, in it there is no sense of imitation. It is important to have a mind which is really free, free from tradition, which is the habit-forming mechanism of the mind. Is this all too much, is it all too difficult? This is certainly not as difficult as your geography or mathematics. It is much easier, only you have never thought about it. You spend most of your lives in school acquiring information. You are in school for about ten to fifteen years, yet you never have time to think about any of these things—not a week, not a day to think fully, completely, of all these things—and that is why these things seem difficult. It is not at all difficult. On the contrary, if you give time to it, then you can see how your mind works, operates, functions. So you see, while you are very young—as most of you are here—it is very important to understand all this because if you do not, you will grow up following some tradition without much meaning; you will imitate and so keep on cultivating fear, and so you will never be free.

Have you noticed in India how tradition-bound you are? You must marry in a certain way, your parents choose the husband or the wife. You must perform certain rituals; they may have no meaning, but you must perform them. You have leaders whom you must follow. Everything about you, if you have observed it, is a way of life in which authority is very well-established. There is the authority of the guru, the authority of the political group, the authority of parents, the authority of public opinion. The older the civilization, as in India, the greater the weight of tradition, the weight of a series of imitations. So, your mind is never free. You may talk about freedom, political freedom or any other kind of freedom; but you as an individual are never free to really find out for yourself; you are always following somebody, following an ideal or some guru or some teacher or some tradition.

So, your whole life is hedged in, limited, confined to ideas, and deep down within yourself there is fear. How can you think freely if there is fear? So, what is important is to be conscious of all these things. If you see a snake, you know that it is poisonous and you run away, you put it aside. But you do not know the series of imitations which prevent initiative; you are caught in them unconsciously. But if you are aware, if you are conscious of them, if you have thought out how they hold you, if you are aware of the way you yourself want to imitate because you are afraid of what people may say, because you are afraid of your parents or of your teachers; if you are aware of the series of imitations, you will push them aside. Once you become conscious of these series of imitations, then you can look at them, you can examine them, you can study them as you study mathematics or any other subject. Are you conscious of why you put on *kumkum?* Why do you do it? Not that you should or should not. Why do you treat women differently from men? Why do you treat women contemptuously? At least men do it. Why?

Why do you go to a temple, why do you do rituals, why do you follow a guru?

So, when you are aware of all these things, then you can go into them, then you can question, then you can study them, but if you blindly accept everything because for the last thirty centuries it has been so, it has no meaning, has it? So, what we need in the world is not mere imitators, not mere leaders and more and more followers. What we need now are individuals like you and me who will keep on thinking of all these problems, not superficially, not casually, but more deeply so that the mind is free to be creative, free to think, free to love.

Education is a way of discovering our relationship to all these things, our relationship to human beings, to nature. But the mind creates ideas, and these ideas become so strong, so vital, that they prevent us from looking beyond. So, as long as there is fear, there is tradition. As long as there is fear, there is imitation. A mind that merely imitates is mechanical, is it not? It is like a machine that is functioning, it is not creative, it does not think out problems. It may produce certain actions, certain results, but it is not creative. So, here in this school, what we want to do—you and I as well as the teachers and the trust members and the managers—what we all should do is to go into all these problems so that when you leave school, you may be a mature human being, capable of thinking problems out for yourself and not dependent on some traditional stupidity, so that you may be a human being with dignity, a human being really free. That is the whole intention of education, not merely to pass some examinations and then be shunted off for the rest of your life to do something, to live to become clerks or housewives or breeding machines. You should demand from your teachers, you should insist that education should help you to be free, to think freely without fear, to understand, to inquire. Otherwise, life is a waste, is it not? You are educated, you pass the B.A. or the M.A. examination, you get a job which you dislike and which you do not want to do, you are married, you have to earn money, you have children, and so you are stuck for the rest of your life. You are miserable, unhappy, quarrelsome; you have nothing to look forward to except babies and more starvation, more misery. That is not education. True education should help you to be so intelligent that with that intelligence you can choose a job which you love, or starve, but not do something stupid which would make you miserable for the rest of your life.

While you are young, you should create the flame of discontent. While you are young, you should be in a state of revolution. This is the time to inquire, to grow, to shape. So, insist that your teachers and your parents educate you properly. Do not be satisfied merely to sit in a classroom and learn some information about some king or about some war. Be discontented, go and find out, inquire from your teachers—if they are stupid, you will make them clever, you will make them intelligent by inquiring—so that when you leave this school, this atmosphere, you will be growing to maturity, to intelligence; you will be learning right through life until you die so that you are a happy, intelligent human being.

Question: How are we to gain the habit of fearlessness?

KRISHNAMURTI: Look at the words he uses. "Habit" implies a movement which is repeated over and over again. If you do something over and over again, does that insure anything except monotony? Is fearlessness a habit? You understand? He asks, "How am I to gain the habit of fearlessness?" He wants to be fearless, and so he asks whether it will come through doing something habitually, constantly, repeatedly, imitatively. Fearlessness comes only when you can meet the incidents of life not as a habit but when you can thrash them out, when you can see them and examine them, but not with a jaded mind that is caught in habit.

If you have habits, then you are merely an imitative machine. Mere habit creates imitation, doing the same thing over and over again, building a wall round yourself. If you have built a wall round yourself through some habit, you are not free from fear; you live within the wall which makes you afraid. So, you can only be free from fear when you have the intelligence to look at every problem, every incident, everything that happens in life, every emotion, every thought, every reaction; if you are capable of looking at it, examining it, then there is freedom from fear.

December 11, 1952

Third Talk at Rajghat

The last two times, we have been talking about fear and how to be free from it, how fear perverts the free mind which is creative and which has the enormous quality of initiative. I think we should also consider the question of authority. You know what authority is, but do you know how authority comes into being? The government has authority, has it not?—the state, the police, the law, the soldier. Your teachers have authority over you, have they not? Your parents have authority over you, making you do what they think you ought to do—to go to bed at certain times, to eat certain right kinds of food, to meet the right kind of people. They discipline you, don't they? Why? They say it is for your good. Is it for your good? We will go into that. But before we go into it, we must understand how authority—the power over another, the coercion, the compulsion of a few over the many or of the many over the few—comes into being.

We have to go into it, but before we can understand the process of authority, we have to find out how authority comes into being. Because you are the father or the mother, the parent, what right have you over me? What right has somebody over me, to treat me like dirt, as if they were superior? What makes for authority? What do you think makes for authority? First, obviously, the desire on the part of each one of us to find a way of conduct, the desire to find what to do. I do not know what to do, I am confused, I am worried, so I go to you, to the priest, to the teacher, to the parent, to somebody. I am seeking a way of conduct, so I go to you, and you tell me what to do. Because I think you know better than I do, I go to you. I go to the guru, to the teacher, to some priest, to some so-called learned man, and I ask him to tell me what to do. So, the desire in me, the desire to find a way of life, a way of conduct, a way of behavior, the very desire in me creates the authority. Does it not? Say, for instance, I go to a guru; I think he is a great man, he gives me peace, he knows the truth, he knows God. I do not know anything about all this, but I go to him, I prostrate myself, I put flowers before him, I pour milk into his throat, I give him devotion. I have the desire to seek comfort, to seek knowledge, so I create an authority. Authority does not exist outside of me.

While you are young, the teacher says that you do not know. But if the teacher is at all intelligent, he will help you to grow to be intelligent, to be without authority. He will help you to understand your confusion and, therefore, not to seek an authority outside.

Then there is the authority of the state, the police, the law. I create this authority outwardly because I have a piece of property which I want to protect. The property is mine, and I do not want you to have it. So I create the government, a government which protects what is mine! So, the government becomes my authority; it is my invention to protect me, to protect my idea, my system of thought. So, I establish gradually through centuries a system of law, of authority—the police, the state, the government, the army—to protect me and mine!

Then, there is the authority of the ideal which is not outward but which is inward. In my mind, I create the authority of an ideal. I say, "I must be good," "I must not be envious," "I must feel brotherly to everybody." So, I create the authority of an ideal, don't I? I am intriguing, I am stupid, I am cruel, I want everything for myself, I want power. That is what I am, and because religious people have said so, because it is convenient to say so, because it is profitable to say so, I think I must be brotherly. I create that as an ideal. I am not that; I want to be the ideal, and so the ideal becomes the authority.

So, there is the authority which is compulsion outside. There is also the authority which is compulsion, coercion, inside—which we call an ideal. Now, in order to live according to that ideal, I discipline myself. I say, "I must be good." I feel very envious of your having a better coat or a better sari or more titles, so I say, "I must not have envious feelings, I must be brotherly." The ideal becomes my authority, and according to that ideal, I live. So, what is happening in my life? I am greedy, I am envious; I have an ideal according to which I am living; I discipline myself according to that ideal, and my life becomes a constant battle between what I am and what I should be. So, I invent discipline, don't I, the discipline to live according to the ideal. So I discipline myself, and the state disciplines me. The state, whether it is a communist state or a capitalist state or a socialist state, has ideas as to how I should behave. They say the state is all-important. I am simplifying it to make you understand. If I, living in that state, do anything contrary to the state, I am coerced by the state—the state being the few controlling the state.

There are two parts of us, the conscious part and the unconscious part. You understand what that means? You are walking along the road and you are talking to a friend; your conscious mind, the mind that is talking, continues when you are talking. But there is another part of you which is absorbing unconsciously the trees, the leaves, the sunlight on the water, the birds. There is the impact going on from the outside on the unconscious all the time, though your conscious mind is occupied; and what the unconscious absorbs is much more important than what the conscious absorbs. The conscious mind can absorb very little. You can only absorb what has been taught in the school; that is not very much. But the unconscious is also being treated in the school, the interactions between you and the teacher, between you and your friends; all that is going on underground. That matters much more than the mere absorption of facts on the surface.

Similarly, this talk every morning is important in that the unconscious is absorbing. Later on during the day or week, you will constantly remember what has been spoken about. That will have a greater effect on you than merely listening, actually or consciously.

You see we create authority—the state, the police. Similarly, we create the authority of the ideal, the authority of tradition. My father says, "Do not do this." I have to obey him because he gets angry, because I am dependent on him for my food. He controls me through my emotions. Doesn't he? So, he becomes my authority. Similarly, there are traditions—you must do this or that, you must wear your sari this way, you must look that way, you must not look at boys, or at girls. There is the tradition which tells you what to do. And tradition is, after all, knowledge, is it not? There are books which tell you what to do, the state tells you what to do, parents tell you what to do, tradition tells you what to do; society, the church, the temple, religions, all these tell you what to do. So, what happens to you? You are just crushed, you are just broken. You are never thinking, acting, living vitally, for you are afraid of all these things. You have traditions, authority, parents, and you say that you must obey; otherwise, you will be helpless.

So you create the authority because you are seeking a way of conduct, a way of living. The very desire, the very pursuit of a way of conduct creates authority, and so you become merely a slave, a cog in a machine, living without any capacity to think, without any capacity to create. I do not know if you paint. If you paint, generally the art teacher tells you what to paint. You see a tree and you copy it. But to paint is to see the tree and to express what you feel about the tree and what the tree signifies—the movement of the leaf, the whisper of the wind in the trees—and to do that, you must be very sensitive to catch the movements of light and shade. How can you catch anything of the swift wind if you are all the time afraid saying, "I must do this," "I must do that," "What will people say?" So gradually, any feeling of sensitiveness, of seeing something beautiful, is destroyed by authority.

So, the problem arises whether a school of this kind should discipline you. See the difficulties which the teachers, if they are true teachers, have to face. You are a naughty child, girl or boy; should I discipline you? If I discipline you, what happens? Because I am bigger, have more authority, and all the rest of it, because I am paid to do certain things, I force you to do them. Then, you obey. Have I not crippled your mind? Am I not beginning to destroy your mind, to destroy your intelligence? If I force you to do a thing because I think it is right, am I not making you stupid? You like to be disciplined, to be forced. I know you do because if you are not forced, you think you would be naughty, you would be bad, you would do things which are not right. Therefore, you say, "Please help me to behave rightly." First, should I force you, or should I help you to understand why you are naughty, why you are this or that? This means what? It means that I must have no sense of authority as a teacher or as a parent. I want you to understand; I want to help you to understand your difficulties, why you are this, why you are bad, why you want to run away; I want you to understand yourself. If I force you, I do not help you. So, if I am a teacher, I must help you to understand yourself—which means, I can only look after a few boys and girls. I cannot have fifty boys or fifty girls; I must have only a few so that I can pay individual attention to every child, so that as a teacher I do not create authority which coerces you to do something which you will probably do yourself if you understand.

So, I see, and I hope you see, that authority destroys intelligence. After all, intelligence can only come when there is freedom, freedom to think, to feel, to observe, to question. But if I compel you, I make you as stupid as I am; generally, this is what happens in a school; the teacher thinks he knows everything, and you do not know. What does the teacher know? Nothing more than mathematics or geography. He has not solved any problems, he has not questioned the enormously important things of life, he thunders like Jupiter or like a sergeant major.

So, what is important in a school of this kind is that, instead of merely being disciplined to do what you are told, you are helped to understand, to be intelligent and free so that you can meet all the difficulties of life. That requires a competent teacher, a teacher who is really interested in you, who is not worried about money, about his wife and children; and it is the responsibility of the students as well as of the teachers to create such a state of affairs. Do not obey; just find out for yourself how to think about a problem. Do not say you are doing a thing because your father says so, but find out what he is trying to say, why he thinks it is bad or good. Question him so that you not only become intelligent but you help him to be intelligent. Generally what happens is, if you begin to question him, he will discipline you; he has not the patience; he is occupied with his own work; he has not the love of sitting with you and talking over with you the enormous difficulties of existence, of earning a livelihood, of having a wife, a husband. He has not the time to go into all this, so he pushes you away or sends you to a school. And the teachers are like everybody else. It is the responsibility of the teachers, of the parents, and of you all to help to bring about this intelligence.

Question: How to be intelligent?

KRISHNAMURTI: You ask, "How to be intelligent?" Look at what is implied in that question. You want a method, which means that you know what intelligence is. That is, when you want to go to Banaras and you ask the way to Banaras, you know already the destination, and you only want to know the way. Similarly, when you say, "How can one be intelligent?" you know what intelligence is; at least, you think you know what intelligence is, and you want a system by which you can be intelligent. Intelligence is the very questioning of the method. Fear destroys intelligence, does it not? Fear prevents you from examining, from questioning, from inquiring, from finding out what is true. If there is no fear, probably you will be intelligent. So, you have to inquire into the whole question of fear and be free from fear, and then there is the possibility of your being intelligent. But, if you say, "How am I to be intelligent?" you are merely cultivating a method, and so you become stupid.

Question: Everybody knows we die. Why are we afraid of death?

KRISHNAMURTI: You are saying you are afraid of death. Why are you afraid of death? Because you do not know how to live? If you knew how to live fully, you wouldn't be afraid of death. If you love the trees, the sunset, the birds, the leaf, if you see women and men in tears, poor people, and really feel love, would you be afraid of death? Would you? Do not be persuaded by me. Let us think about it together. Because you do not live, you do not enjoy life, you are not happy, you are not seeing things vitally, you ask what is going to happen when you die. Life is sorrow, and you are much more interested in death. You feel that perhaps there will be happiness after death. But that is a tremendous problem. I do not know if you want to go into that. After all, fear is at the bottom of it. Fear of dying, fear of living, fear of suffering, fear is at the root of it. So, if you cannot understand what it is that creates fear, and you are not free from that, then it does not matter whether you are living or dying.

Question: How can we live happily?

KRISHNAMURTI: Are you not living happily? You say you do not know if you are living happily. Don't you know when you are suffering, when you have pain, when you have physical pain, when somebody hits you? You know when somebody is angry with you. You know suffering. Do you know when you are happy? Do you know when you are healthy? Happiness is the state of which you are unconscious, of which you are not aware. The moment you are aware that you are happy, you are not happy, are you? But most of you suffer, and being conscious of that, you want to escape from that suffering into what you call happiness. Therefore you want to be happy consciously, and the moment you are consciously happy, it is gone. Can you ever say that you are joyous? It is only a moment afterwards that you say, "How happy I am, how joyous I have been." It becomes a memory. In the moment of actual happiness, you are unconscious of it, and that is the beauty of it.

December 12, 1952

Fourth Talk at Rajghat

You remember we were talking the day before yesterday about the problem of discipline. It is really quite a complex problem because most of us think that through some kind of discipline, we shall have freedom. You know what discipline is, don't you? It is the cultivation of resistance, is it not? Is this too difficult a word? You see, by resisting, building something against something else, we feel we shall be more capable of understanding, of being free, of being able to live fully, but that is not a fact, is it? The more you resist—that is, push away—the more you struggle against something, the less the comprehension. I do not know if you have talked about all this, but if you have, you will see that only when there is freedom, real freedom in which you can think, in which you can be, it is only in that state that you can find out anything, that you can know love. But freedom does not exist and cannot exist in a frame. Most of us live in a world enclosed by ideas, don't we? Is this too difficult? For instance, you say your parents or your teachers know what is right or wrong; at least you think they know what is right, what is wrong, what is bad, what is beneficial. You know what people say, what people do not say, what religion has said, what the priest has said, what your parents have said, what you have learned from the school, what tradition says; in that, you live; in the enclosure you live, and living in that enclosure, you say you are free. Are you? Can a man who lives in a prison be ever free?

So, one has to break down walls and find out for oneself what is real, what is true, what is really beneficial. One has to experiment, one has to find out, not merely follow somebody; however good, however noble, however exciting, however happy one might feel in that person's presence, it has no meaning. But what has meaning, what has significance, is to be able to examine all values, all the things that people have said are good, are beneficial, are worthwhile, and not to accept. Because the moment you accept, you begin to conform; then you begin to imitate, and a person who imitates, who copies, who merely follows, can never be happy.

Older people say that you must discipline yourself. Discipline is imposed upon you either by yourself or by somebody from outside. In school, you are told to do this or that. But it is important to find out how to be free so that you begin to find out for yourself. Unfortunately most people do not want to find out, most people do not want to think; they have a closed mind. To have a mind which is thinking, discovering, finding out, going into things, is very difficult; it requires a lot of energy and perception and inquiry. Most people have not the energy nor the inclination to find out; they say, "It is right; you know better than I do; you are my guru, my teacher." It is very important that in a school of this kind, right from the very beginning, right from the most tender age to the time when you leave school, you should be free to find out, and not be enclosed by a wall of do's and don't's because if you are told what to do and what not to do, where is your intelligence? You just walk into a career; you are a thoughtless entity, and your parents tell you to marry or not to marry, to become a clerk or to become a judge. That is not intelligence. You may pass examinations, you may have very good saris, you may have plenty of jewels, friends, and position, but that is not intelligence.

Surely intelligence comes when you are free to discover, when you are free to think out, when you are free to question every tradition so that your mind becomes very active, your mind becomes clear, so that you are an individual, integrated, functioning fully—not a frightened entity not knowing what to do and therefore obeying, inwardly feeling one thing and outwardly conforming to another. Inwardly, you have to break away from every tradition and live on your own, but you are enclosed by the parents' ideas of what you should do and should not do, by the traditions of society. So, inwardly, there is a conflict going on. You know this, don't you? You are all young, but I do not think you are too young to be aware of this. You want to do something and your parents and teachers say, "Don't." Your aunt or your grandfather says, "Don't," and yet you want to do it, and so there is struggle going on, is there not? As long as you do not solve that struggle, you are in conflict, pain, sorrow, wanting to do something and prevented from doing it.

So, if you go into it very carefully, discipline and freedom are contradictory. If you are seeking freedom, then there is quite a different process of understanding which brings its own clarification so that you do not do certain things. So, what is important, while you are young, is to be free to find out and to be helped to find out what to do in life. If you do not find out while you are young, you will never find out, you will never be free. The seed must be sown now so that you have initiative, so that you are free to find out. How often you have passed the villagers carrying heavy things! What is your feeling about them? Do you have any feeling about them, those poor women with torn clothes, smelling, dirty, without enough food, day after day working without any security, earning a pittance? You have seen them, haven't you? What do you feel about them? Are you so frightened, so concerned about yourself, about your examinations, about your looks, about your saris, that you never pay any attention to them? You feel you are much better, you are of a different class; therefore, you have no regard for them, and when you look, when you see them go by, what do you feel? Don't you want to help them? No? Do you help them? That indicates how you are thinking. Are you so dead or dull because of tradition, of fathers, of mothers, of centuries of crushing down, because you happen to be a boy or a woman of a certain class, and therefore you feel you must not look at them? Are you actually so suffocated that you do not know what is happening around you?

So, gradually, fear—fear of what the parents say, what the teachers say, fear of tradition, fear of life—destroys sensitivity, does it not? You know what sensitivity is? To be sensitive, to feel, to receive impressions, to know, to have a feeling for those who are suffering, to have sympathy, to have affection, to be aware of the things that are happening around you. You hear the temple bell ringing; are you aware of it? Do you listen to the sound? Do you see the sunlight on the water? Are you aware of the poor people, the villagers who have been controlled, trodden down for centuries by exploiters? Are you sensitive to all the things around you? When you see a servant carrying a heavy carpet, do you give him a hand? All that implies sensitivity. You see that sensitivity is destroyed when anyone is disciplined, is fearful or is concerned with himself. You know what it is to be concerned with oneself? To be concerned with oneself implies to be concerned about one's own looks, one's own saris, to think about oneself all the time—which most of us do in some form or another—so that one's mind, one's heart becomes enclosed, and one loses all appreciation of beauty.

To be really free implies great sensitivity. There is no freedom if you enclose yourself by various disciplines. As most of your life is an imitation, you lose that feeling of sensitivity, that freedom. Is it not very important, while you are here, to sow the seed of freedom so that all through life there may be intelligence which is freedom? With that intelligence you can examine all the problems of life.

Question: Is it practicable for a man to keep himself apart from the sense of fear and at the same time to keep himself with society?

KRISHNAMURTI: What is society? What would you say is society? A set of values, a set of rules and regulations and traditions? You see the conditions outside and you say, "Can I be here and have a practical relationship with that?" Why not? After all, if you merely fit into that condition, into that framework of values, are you free? What do you mean by "practicable"? Do you mean earning a livelihood? Then, what does it mean to be able to live with it, to be able to do something about it? Take this for example—I do not want to take up a complex problem—you have to earn a livelihood, and there are many things that you can do to earn a livelihood; if you are free, can you not choose what you want to do? Is that practicable? Or, would you consider it practicable to forget your freedom and just fit into anything, become a lawyer, a banker, a merchant, or a road sweeper? Or, would you say, "I am free, and I have cultivated my intelligence. I am going to see what is the best thing for me to do. I shall set aside all traditions and do something which I like; it does not matter whether my parents or society approve or disapprove. Because I am free and because there is intelligence, I shall do something which is completely my own, as an integrated man." Does that answer your question?

Question: What is God?

KRISHNAMURTI: Do you really want to have an answer to this question? How are you going to find out? Are you going to accept somebody else's information? Or are you going to try to see what God is? It is easy to ask questions, but to find out requires a great deal of intelligence, a great deal of inquiry and search.

Now the first thing is, are you going to accept what anybody says about it, either Krishna or Buddha, it does not matter who? I might be mistaken, and so might your own pet guru. So, the first thing you must have, in order to find out any real deep truth, is that your mind must be free to inquire, not to accept, but to directly find out. I can give you a description of the truth, but it will not be the same thing as your seeing the truth. Most books give a description; all sacred books describe in words what God is, but that may not be God. The word *God* is not God. Is it? So, to find out, you must never accept, must you? You must never be influenced by what the books, teachers, or others say. Because if you are influenced by them, you will find what they want you to find. So, outwardly, you must not be influenced by any book, by any teacher, by any guru; and inwardly, you must know that your mind can create what it wants; it can imagine God with a beard, with one eye; it can imagine him blue or purple. So, you have to guard against your own desires because your desires, your wants, your longings can project and create in your own mind the things which you want. If you long for God, it will be according to your wishes, won't it? That will not be God, will it? If you are in sorrow, if you want comfort, if you feel that you have been crushed in life, if you feel destroyed, if you feel sentimental and romantic, eventually you will create a God who will supply you all that. But it will not be God. So, your mind must be completely free; then only can it find out—not by the acceptance of some superstition or the reading of some sacred book or the following of some guru. It is only when you have that freedom—that real freedom from external influences, from your own desires, and from your own longings—and when your mind is very clear, is it possible to find out what God is. But when you sit down and speculate, your guess is as good as your guru's guess, and your speculation is useless, is absurd.

What is important is to be conscious, to be aware of the influences outside which force you in a certain direction, and also to be aware of your conscious as well as unconscious desires and to be free from all those so that the mind is clear, uninfluenced.

Question: Can we be aware of our unconscious desires?

KRISHNAMURTI: First of all, are you aware of your conscious desires? Do you know what desire is? Do you know that you do not listen to somebody who says something contrary to what you believe? Your desire prevents you from listening. You desire God. Somebody says to you that God is not the outcome of your frustrations and fears; it is something quite different. Will you listen to him? Of course not. You want one thing, and the truth is something else. You shut yourself within your own desires; gradually, you are half conscious of your own desires, you are closed in. You are not conscious of your waking desires, conscious desires, are you? To be conscious of the desires that are deeply hidden is much more difficult. You know, it is like wanting to find out what is hidden. You cannot find out what is hidden unless the mind which is looking is fairly clear, fairly free; otherwise, you cannot discover what your own motive is. So, the first thing is to be consciously aware of your desires on the surface; then, as you become conscious of them, go deeper and deeper.

Question: Why are some people born in poor circumstances and some rich and well-to-do?

KRISHNAMURTI: What do you think? Karma? Instead of asking me and waiting for my reply, why do you not find out what you feel? Do you think it is some mysterious process? In a former life, I have lived nobly and therefore I am rewarded, and therefore I have plenty of wealth, saris, and position! Or, I have acted very badly in a former life, I am paying for it in this life!

You see, this is really a very complex problem. It is the fault of society, the society in which the greedy and the cunning exploit and rise to the top. We also want the same thing, we also want to climb the ladder and get to the top. So long as everybody wants to get to the top, what happens? We tread on somebody, and the man who is trodden on, who is destroyed, asks "Why is life so unfair? You have everything and I have no capacity, I have nothing." As long as we climb the ladder of success, there will always be the ill and the unfed. The desire for success has to be understood, and not why there are the poor, why there are the rich, why some have talents and others have no talents. What has to be changed is the desire to climb, the desire to be a big man, to be a success. We all aspire for success, don't we? There lies the fault, and not in karma or any other nonsense. The actual fact is that we all want to be on the top, perhaps not quite on the top but halfway to the top. So, as long as there is that drive to be great, to be somebody in the world, we are going to have the rich and the poor, the talented and those without talent.

Question: Is God a Mr., a Miss, or a mystery?

KRISHNAMURTI: Is God a man or a woman or something completely mysterious? I have just answered that question. I am afraid you did not listen to the answer. This country is full of men and the dominance of men. Suppose I said God is a lady, what would you do? You would reject it because you are full of the idea that God is a man. So I say that really you have to find out, but to find out, you must be free of all prejudice.

December 14, 1952

Fifth Talk at Rajghat

We have been talking the last three or four times about fear, and as it is one of the fundamental causes of our deterioration, I think we ought to look at it from a different angle, from a different point of view.

Are you interested in all this? I wonder if you think over these talks afterwards. Or, do you think it is a morning outing and forget about it?

You know we are always told what to think and what not to think. Books, teachers, parents, the society around us all tell us what to think, but that never helps us to find out how to think. There is a difference, is there not, between what to think and how to think. Now what to think is comparatively easy because from early childhood and as we grow into maturity and depth, our minds are conditioned in words, in phrases, in attitudes, in prejudices, in the way to think, in what to think. I do not know if you have noticed how the minds of older people are already set, like clay in a mold. Their minds are set already, and it is very difficult to break through that mold. So the molding of the mind is the conditioning of the mind.

Here in India, you are conditioned to think by centuries of tradition, by economic reasons, by religious reasons. So the mind here is set in a certain pattern, in a certain mold; it is conditioned according to all these causes. In Europe, it is conditioned in one way, and in Russia, after the revolution, the political leaders have set their minds in a certain other way. So, the mind is conditioned. Do you understand what I mean by conditioned?—conditioned not only superficially in the conscious mind but also in the hidden mind, conditioned by the race, by the climate, by unverbalized and unuttered imitations.

The mind can never be free if it is molded. Most people say that you can never free the mind from its conditioning, and that it must always be conditioned. That is, you must always have certain limitations, certain ways of thinking, certain prejudices, so that there can be no release, no freedom for the mind to be other than conditioned. The older the civilization, the more weighed down it is by tradition, by authority, by discipline. An old race like in India is more conditioned than in America where there is more freedom because of economic and social reasons and also because they have been pioneers. Here, we are enclosed.

A conditioned mind can never be free. Such a mind can never go beyond its border, its barrier; that is obvious. It is difficult for a mind which is conditioned, built round, to free itself from the conditioning and go beyond. And this conditioning is not only imposed by society, but it is also liked by you because you dare not go beyond. You are frightened at what the mother will say or what the father will say, with what the teacher will say or what the society will say, what the priest will say. You are frightened; therefore, you create barriers that hold you. So you are always telling your children, and your children will, in their turn, tell their children not to do this or that.

The mind is always held in, especially in a school where you like a teacher. Because, if you like the teacher, you want to follow him. You want to do what he does. So, conditioning becomes much more settled, much more permanent. Say, for instance, there is a teacher who does puja, and you are in a hostel under him. You may like the show of it or the beauty of it, so you begin to do it. So, you are being conditioned. That conditioning is very effective because when one is young, one is eager, creative, alive. I do not know if you are creative because your parents will not allow you to go beyond the wall to look. You are married off and are fitted into a mold, and there you are for the rest of your life.

While you are young, you are easily conditioned, shaped, forced into a pattern. If you give a child—a good, intelligent, alert child—to a priest, then within seven years the child will be so conditioned by him that for the rest of his life, he will be the same, with certain modifications. And so in a school of this kind where the teachers are not unconditioned, they are just like everybody else. They have their puja, their fears, their desires for gurus, their rituals; they do all these things, and unconsciously you, being under them and because you like the teacher and because you see something beautiful, want to do it, and within a couple of months, you are caught, your imitation begins.

Why do older people do puja? I do not know, you do not know, and they do not know. They do it because their fathers have done it and also because they think it gives them a certain feeling, certain sensations, because it makes them quiet. They chant some *slokas.* They feel that if they do not do it, they are lost. Therefore, they do it. And you young people copy them and your imitation begins. If the teacher goes into it, thinks about it, which very few people do, if he really uses his intelligence—which is to investigate, to question and not to be prejudiced—then he will find there is no meaning in it. But to find out what the truth of the matter is requires a great deal of freedom; then only can you investigate and find out the truth. If you say you like it and then try to investigate, it means you are only going to strengthen your likes, and that is not investigation. If you are already prejudiced in favor of it and then you proceed to investigate it, you only strengthen your bias, your prejudice.

So, surely it is very important in a school of this kind that the teachers not only must be unconditioning themselves but must also help the children never to condition themselves, and when they know the conditioning influence of society, of parents, of the world, they must help the child not to accept but to investigate, to find out the truth of the matter. As you grow, you will begin to see how various influences are beginning to mold you, not helping you how to think, but telling you what you should think. Ultimately, you become an automatic machine, functioning without much vitality, without much original thought, like a cog in a vast social machine. All of you are afraid that if you do not fit into society, you will not be able to earn a livelihood. Your father is a lawyer and you must be a lawyer. If you are a girl, you must be married off. So, what actually happens? You start out as a boy or girl with a lot of vitality, with a lot of vigor which is cruelly destroyed by the teacher who is conditioned by his prejudices, by his fears, by his superstitions, by his pujas, by his guru. You go out of the school filled with information which you can pick up at any time, but you have lost the vitality to inquire, the vitality to revolt against your parents or society.

You listen to all this and what is going to happen? You know very well what is going to happen when you pass your B.A. or M.A. examination. You will be like the rest of the world because you dare not be otherwise. You will be so conditioned, so molded, that you dare not strike out. Your husbands will control you, your wives will control you, or society will control you, and so generation after generation of imitation goes on. There is no initiative, there is no freedom, there is no happiness; there is nothing but slow death. What is the point of being educated? Why not just learn to read and write, get married and carry on like machines? That is what parents want, that is what the world wants. The world does not want you to think, to be free to find out, because then you will be a dangerous citizen, because then you will not fit into a pattern. No real thinker can ever belong to any particular country or class or type of thinking. Freedom means not only freedom here but everywhere, right through. To think along a particular line is not freedom.

So while you are young, it is very important to be free not only consciously but also deep inside, to be watchful of yourself when you see the influences controlling or dominating you, to investigate, never to accept but always to question and to be in revolt.

Question: How can we make our minds free when we live in a society full of tradition?

KRISHNAMURTI: First, you have to have the urge to be free, the demand to be free. It is the demand of the bird to fly, of the waters of the river to flow. Have you such a feeling to be free? If you have it, then what happens? Your parents, your society are going to force you to a certain mold. Can you resist them? You find it difficult because you are afraid. You are afraid you will not find the right husband, you will not have the right wife, you will not have a job, you will starve, people will talk about you. As you are afraid, you are not going to resist, though you want to be free. Your fears of what people may say, what your parents may say, block you, and you do what they want you to do. Can you say, "I want to know. I do not mind starving. I do not mind battling against this rotten set of barriers. I want to be free to find out"? This does not mean to be free to do whatever you want. That is not freedom. You may want to be free, but when you yourself are frightened, can you withstand all these barriers, all these impositions? Is it not very important even from childhood not to encourage fear but, on the contrary, to help the child to see the implications of fear and to help him to be free? If you are frightened, there is an end to freedom.

Question: We have been brought up in society. How is it possible to be free?

KRISHNAMURTI: Are you conscious of the fear? Are you aware that you are frightened? If you are, what are you going to do? How are you going to be free from fear? You and I have to find out. How are you to find out? First you must be conscious that you are afraid. Are you? Then what are you going to do? Do think it out with me. What are you going to do when you are conscious that you are frightened? What do you do, actually? You run away from it, don't you? You pick up a book or go out for a walk; you run away from it. You are afraid of your parents, of society; you are conscious of that fear, and you do not know how to solve it. You are really frightened even to look at it, so you want to run away from it. That is why you all want to be educated, to keep on passing examinations until the last moment when you have to face the inevitable and act. So, you continually escape from your problem. That will not help you to dissolve your difficulty. You have to look at it. Can you look at it?

If you want to look at a bird, you must go very close to it, observe it, see the shape of the wings, the legs, the beak; you must examine it. Similarly, if you are afraid, you must look at your fear. You are so frightened that you increase fear. Say, for instance, you want to do something which you feel is good for you. But there are your parents, and they tell you not to do it, or they will do something terrible to you. They will not give you money. So you are frightened of what they are going to do to you. You are so frightened that you dare not look at the results of it. So you give way and your fear continues.

Question: What is real freedom? How to acquire real freedom?

KRISHNAMURTI: Real freedom must be the product of intelligence. Freedom is not to be acquired. You cannot go out and buy it in the market. You cannot get it by reading a book or by listening to some talk. It is a thing that comes with intelligence. But what is intelligence? Can there be intelligence when there is fear, when the mind is conditioned? You understand what I mean by conditioned? When the mind is prejudiced, when you think you are a marvelous human being, or when you are very ambitious and want to go on succeeding, can there be intelligence? When you are concerned about yourself—which expresses itself through ambition in different forms, not only worldly ambition, but ambition to be spiritually great—when you follow somebody, when you worship somebody, can there be intelligence? When your mind is crippled with authority, can there be intelligence? So, intelligence comes when there is freedom from all this. Then only can there be freedom. So, you have to set about it; the mind has to set about to free itself from all this, and then there is intelligence which brings freedom. You have to find the answer. What is the use of someone else being free, someone else having food when you are hungry? You want freedom really to be creative.

To have initiative there must be freedom, and for freedom there must be intelligence, and you have to ask and find out how to create that intelligence and what prevents that intelligence. You have to investigate life, social values, everything—not accept anything because you are frightened.

December 15, 1952

Sixth Talk at Rajghat

Perhaps, this morning, we can approach the problem of fear from another angle. Fear does extraordinary things to most of us. It creates all kinds of illusions, problems, and until we really understand it, go into it very, very deeply, fear always distorts our actions throughout life; it twists our ideas, the way of our life; it creates barriers between people; it certainly destroys love. So, I think the more we understand it, the more we go into it, the more we really are free of it, the greater is our contact with what is around us. Our contacts, what we can touch in life, are at a very few points, are they not? But if we can have contacts, wide contacts, deep understanding, deep sympathies, love, and consideration, great will be the extension of our horizon. So perhaps we can talk about fear from a different point of view.

I do not know if you have noticed that most of us want some kind of safety. We want some kind of security, somebody on whom to lean. As a small child holds on to the mother's hand, so we want something to lean on, somebody to love us. Without a feeling of security, without a feeling of safety, without a mental safeguard, we lean, do we not? Because we have leaned on others, looked to others to guide us, to help us, we feel confused, we are afraid, we do not know what to do, what to think, how to act. So, when we are left to ourselves, we are completely lost, we feel insecure, uncertain. From that arises fear, does it not? Now, there are different kinds of safeguards, different kinds of feelings of certainty, the feeling that one is being protected as when the parent protects the child. We want something to give us certainty. So we have outward protections and inward protections, outward securities and inward safeguards. Have we not? When you close the windows and the doors of the house and live inside, you feel very secure, you feel safe, unmolested. But life is not like that. Life is constantly knocking on the door, trying to push the windows open all the time so that you may see more, but if there is fear and you close all the windows, the knocking grows louder. So, the more outward securities you cling to, the more life comes and pushes you. The more you are afraid, the more you are enclosed, the greater the suffering, which is knocking, which is dominating, which is the questioning of life. Life won't leave you alone. You like to be left alone, you like to close all the windows, the lattices, everything completely, to be safe inside. But the more you enclose yourself, the more life comes and breaks your windows, and so the struggle begins. You want to be secure and life says, "You cannot." So outwardly, you want security, and society, tradition, fathers, mothers, wives, husbands, push and break through. And inwardly you seek security, comfort, in an idea. You know what ideas are, how ideas come into being? You have an idea to go out for a walk, to see something. You read a book and you get an idea. You must find out what an idea is, and then see how the idea becomes a means of security, of seeking safety, something to which you cling. Have you ever thought about an idea? If you have an idea and I have an idea, I think my idea is better than your idea, and we struggle, don't we? I try to convince you and you try to convince me. The whole world is built on ideas, and if you go into it, you will find that merely clinging to an idea has no value. Have you noticed how your fathers, your mothers, your teachers, your aunts cling to what they think?

Now, how does idea come into being? How do you have an idea? When you want to go out for a walk, how does it come? That is an idea, is it not, a very simple idea. The idea that you should go out for a walk, how does that come? It is very interesting to find out how that comes. If I watch it, I see that an idea arises, and I cling to it and push everything else aside. So, you must find out, must you not, how that comes, the thought of your going out on a walk. That is a response to a sensation, is it not? Is this too difficult? There is the feeling which is a sensation, and that sensation comes because I have seen something which I want to do. Then, thought is created and then put into action. I see a car. There is a sensation, is there not? It is a beautiful car, it is a Buick, a Ford; there is sensation which comes from the very look of it. The perception creates the sensation. From the sensation there is the idea, and then the idea becomes very prominent. I want the car. It is my car.

There are outward securities of ideas and inward securities of ideas. I believe in something, I believe in God, I believe in rituals, I believe that I should be married, I believe that there is reincarnation, life after death; these beliefs are all created by my desires, by my prejudices; and to these beliefs I cling. So, I have outside of me, outside the skin as it were, ideas of security and also inward securities; remove them or question those ideas outside and inside of me, and I am afraid. So, I will battle with you, I will push you away so that you do not touch my ideas.

Now, can there ever be any security? You understand? We have ideas about security—the feeling of being safe with my father, with my mother, in a job, the way I think, the way of my life, the way I look—with these I feel very satisfied; I feel very content in being enclosed in safe ideas. Can I ever be safe, can I ever be secure, however many the safeguards are which I may have outwardly or inwardly? How can there be security if my bank fails tomorrow, if my father or mother dies tomorrow, if there is a revolution? Inwardly is there any safety within my ideas? I like to think that I am safe in my ideas, in my beliefs, in my prejudices, but is there safety? They are walls which are not real; they are just my ideas, my sensations. I see for myself when I look into both the outward and the inward securities, that there is no safety at all. I like to believe that there is God who is looking after me. I like to think that I am going to be born more rich, more noble. But it may be or it may not be.

Inwardly there is no certainty, and outwardly there is no certainty. If you ask the refugees that have left Pakistan or any of the refugees from Eastern Europe, they will tell you that there is no security. But inwardly they feel that there is security, and so they cling to it. You may remove the outward security, but still inwardly you are very eager and build your security because you do not want to let that go. That implies greater fear. Supposing tomorrow, or in a few years' time, your parents tell you to do what they want, to marry or not to marry. Would you be frightened? Of course you would not be frightened because up to now you have been brought up to do exactly what you were told to do, to think along certain lines, to act in a certain manner, to follow certain ideas. If you are asked to do what you like, would you not be completely at a loss? If your parents told you to marry whom you liked, you would shiver, would you not? Because you have been conditioned—as I explained yesterday, by tradition, by fears—you will soon find that, if you are left to yourself, to be left alone is the greatest danger. You never want to be alone. You never want to think out anything for yourself. You never want to go out for a walk by yourself. You all want to be like active ants, talking, talking, doing something. When you are left alone to think out any problem, to face any of the things that life demands, you who have been brought up sheltered in ideas, sheltered by parents, by priests, by gurus, you are totally at a loss and are frightened; being frightened, you do most chaotic things, most absurd things; you accept like a man with a begging bowl, who will accept anything thoughtlessly.

So, seeing all this, really thoughtful persons begin to be free from any kind of security, inward or outward. This is extremely difficult because it means that you are alone, that you are not dependent. The moment you depend, there is fear, and where there is fear, there is no love. Where there is love, you are not alone. The sense of loneliness is only when you are frightened, when you do not know what to do. When you are controlled by ideas, isolated by beliefs, then there is fear, and when there is fear, you are completely blind. So, in a school of this kind, the teachers and the parents have to solve this problem of fear, but unfortunately, parents are afraid for you and what you are going to do if you do not get married, if you do not get a job. They have fear of what people might say, the fear of your going wrong or right; because of this fear, they make you do something. Their fear is couched, is clothed, in what they call love. They want to look after you; therefore, you must do this. But if you go behind that wall, behind the so-called affection and consideration, there is their fear for your safety, and you are also equally afraid because you have depended on people so long. So, you are frightened.

Is it not very important, in a school of this kind, that you should, from the very tender age right through life, break down these feelings of fear and question them so that you are not isolated, so that you are not in fear, so that you are not enclosed in ideas, in traditions, in habits, but you are free human beings with creative vitality?

Question: Why are we afraid, though we know that God protects us?

KRISHNAMURTI: You have been told that God protects you. Look what is happening. Your father, your brother, your mother have told you that God protects you, which is an idea, and that idea you cling to, and yet, there is fear. So, you have an idea that God protects you—an idea, a thought, a feeling. But the actual fact is you are afraid. The actual fact is the real thing, not your idea that you are going to be protected because your father, your mother, your tradition, hope that God will protect you. But what is actually happening? Are you being protected? Look at the millions of people who are not protected, who are starving. Look at the villagers who carry weights, who are dirty, smelling, with torn clothes. Are they protected by God? Because you have more money than the rest, because you have got a position, because your father is a *tahsildar* or collector or a merchant who has cheated somebody, should you be protected while there are millions in the world going without food, without proper clothes? Really, there is no protection even though you like to feel that God will protect you. It is just a nice idea, which is to pacify the fear, so you do not question, but just believe in God. If you really go into the question of fear, then you will find out whether God will protect you or not. To start with, the idea that you are going to be protected by God has no meaning. You start with the hope that the suffering, poor, starving human being is going to be protected by the state, by his employer, by society, by God, by tradition, but they are not going to protect him. When there is the feeling of affection, there is no fear; then there is no problem.

Question: What is shyness?

KRISHNAMURTI: Do you not know what it is? Do you not know when you feel shy? If you feel shy, I ask you what is shyness? Here is a large group of people, and you are not used to getting up and talking, and you feel a little bit sensitive to expose yourself to criticism. You are shy of your bad speech, your incapacity to pronounce English properly, and so on. In other words, you are afraid to expose yourself to all of us; we might laugh at you, we might criticize you. It is your shyness, it is your feeling of inadequacy, a feeling that you cannot speak properly, that we will all laugh at you. Therefore, you either say you would like to speak in Hindi, or keep quiet. But if you felt very sure, you would express yourself. To be able to express yourself gives you a feeling of a certain assurance, does it not?

Question: What is society?

KRISHNAMURTI: What is society? What is the family?

Let us find out step by step how society is created, how it comes into being. What is the family? When you say, "It is my family," what do you mean? My father, my mother, my brother, my sister, the feeling of closeness, the feeling that we are living in the same house, the feeling that my father and my mother are going to protect me, the ownership of certain property, of jewels, saris, clothes. That is the beginning of the family. There is another family like that living in another house, feeling the same things I feel—the sense of my house, my clothes, my car, my wife, my husband, my children—and there is another family over there feeling exactly the same thing so that ten such families living on the same piece of earth, feeling the same thing, have a feeling that they must not be invaded by other families. So, they begin to make laws. The powerful families build themselves into positions, they have big properties, more money, more clothes, more cars. So the ten families get together and frame laws; they tell us what to do. So, gradually, a social entity comes into being with laws, regulations, policemen, the soldier, the navy, the army. Ultimately, the whole of the earth becomes peopled by various kinds of social entities. Then, people get ideas and want to overthrow those who are established, who have all the means of power. They break down that society and then form another society.

Society is the relationship with people, the relationship between one family and another family, between one group of people and another group, between individuals and society. So, relationship is society; the relationship between individuals, between you and me, is society. If I am very greedy, very cunning, if I have great power, authority, I am going to push you out, and you are going to do the same to me. Then, laws are made by you and me, and others come and break our laws and establish another series of laws, and that goes on all the time. In society and in relationship, there is constant conflict. This is the simple basis of society; it becomes more and more complex as human beings become more and more complex in their ideas, in their wants, in their mechanical institutions, in their industry.

Question: Can you become free, living in this society?

KRISHNAMURTI: While living in society, can you be free? If you depend on society for your security, for your comfort, can you ever be free? If I depend on my father for affection, for money, for initiative to do things, if I depend on him or on my guru, am I free? I am not. If I depend similarly on society—society being the instruments that give me a job, that give me protection, that give me various sets of comforts—am I free? So, is it possible to be free when I am dependent? It is only possible when I have capacity, when I have initiative, when I can think freely, when I am not afraid of what anybody says, when I want to find out something which is true, when I am not greedy, envious, jealous. As long as I am envious, greedy, I am depending; as long as I am depending on society, I am not free; but if I am free from greed, I am free. I do not mind what I do, what kind of job I get, but if I insist that because I have been educated, because I am this or that, I must become only a certain type of worker, a clerk, a glorified clerk under the government, if I demand that I should work only in certain directions, then of course, I depend on society. Then, I am not free.

Question: Why do people want to live in society? They can live alone.

KRISHNAMURTI: Can you live alone?

Question: I live in society because my father and mother live in society.

KRISHNAMURTI: To have a job, to live, to earn a livelihood, to do anything, have you not to live in society? Can you live alone? For your food you depend on somebody; for your clothes you depend on somebody; even if you are a sannyasi, you depend for your food, for your clothes, for your shelter, on someone. You cannot live alone. There is no entity which is completely alone. You are always related; it is only in death that you are alone. In living, you are always related—to your father, to your brother, to the beggar, to the roadmender, to the *tahsildar,* to the collector. You are always related, and because you do not understand that relationship, there is conflict. But if you understood that relationship between one man and another, there is no conflict, and there is no problem of living alone.

Question: When we are related to one another, that means we cannot be free. Is it not absolutely true?

KRISHNAMURTI: We do not understand what relationship is, right relationship. Suppose I have to depend on you; suppose I depend on you for my life, for my comfort, for my security; how can I ever be free? But if I do not depend, I am still related, am I not? I depend on you because I want some kind of emotional or physical or intellectual comfort. I depend on my parents because I want some kind of safety. So, my relationship to my parents is that of dependence, and if I depend, there is fear, and my relationship to my parents is based on fear. So, how can I have any relationship which is free? I can only have relationship which is free when there is no fear. So, I have to set about freeing myself from that dependency so as to have right relationship, for in that right relationship, I am free.

Question: How can we be free when our parents depend on us?

KRISHNAMURTI: Why do your parents depend on you? Because they are old, they depend upon you to support them. Then what happens? They depend on you—for you to earn a livelihood, for you to clothe them—and if you say, "I want to become a carpenter although I may not earn any money at all," they say that you must not do so because you have to support them. Just think about it. I am not saying it is good or bad. If I say it is good or bad, then we put an end to thinking. So, the father's demand that you should provide for him prevents you from living your life, and the living of your life is considered bad, selfish; you thus become the slave of your parents.

The state should look after old people through old age pensions, through various means of security. But when there is a country where there is overpopulation, insufficiency, lack of productivity, and so on, the state cannot look after old people. So, parents depend on the young, and the young always fit into the groove of tradition and are destroyed. So, it is not a problem to be discussed by me; you have to work it out and you have to think about it. Look, I want to support my parents within reasonable limits. Suppose, I also want to do something which may not pay, which may not bring me money. Suppose I want to become a religious person, to find out what God is, what life is; that way, I may not have much money, and if I pursue it, I may have to give up my family, and they will probably starve like other millions of people. But as long as I am frightened of what people say—that I am not a dutiful son, that I am not a worthy son—I never will be a creative being. To be a happy, creative human being, I must have a great deal of initiative.

Question: Will it be good on our part to see our parents starving?

KRISHNAMURTI: You are not putting it in the right way. I want to become an artist, a painter, and I know painting will bring me very little money. What am I to do? Sacrifice my urge to paint and become a clerk? That is what happens. I become a clerk and I am in great conflict, I am in misery; and because I suffer and am frustrated, I will make miserable my wife and children. So, what am I to do? I say to my parents, "I want to paint, I will give you what little I can from the little I have, that is all I can do."

You have asked questions like, "What is society?" "What am I to do if my parents are dependent on me?" "What is freedom?" "Can I be free in society?" and I have answered them. But if you really do not think about them, if you do not go into them for yourself more and more deeply and approach them from different angles, if you do not look at them in different ways, then you will only say, "This is good. This is bad. This is duty. That is not duty. This is right. That is wrong."—and that will not lead you any further. But if you and I sit down, think about these problems, if you and the teacher discuss them, go into them, then your intelligence is awakened; then when these questions arise in daily life, you will be able to meet them. You will not meet them if you only accept what I am saying. My answers to your questions are only to awaken your intelligence so that you will think these questions out, so that you will be able to meet life rightly.

December 16, 1952

Seventh Talk at Rajghat

You know I have been talking about fear; it is very important that we should be conscious and be aware of it. Do you know how fear comes into being? We notice throughout the world that people are perverted and twisted in their ideas, in their beliefs, in their activities. So, we ought to go into it from every point of view, not only from the moral and economic point of view of society, but also from the point of view of the inward psychological struggles.

We have been talking of how fear twists the mind and, as I said yesterday, how fear for outward security and inward security distorts our thinking. I hope you have thought a little more about it today because you see that the more you consider, the more you will be free from all dependence. The older people in the world have not created a marvelous society; the parents, the ministers, the teachers, the rulers, the fathers, the priests, they have not created a beautiful world. They have created an ugly, frightful, brutal world in which everybody is fighting somebody else—one group fighting another group, one class against another class, one nation against another nation, one idea fighting another idea, one belief against another belief. The world in which you are growing up is an ugly world, it is a sorrowful world; and the older people try to smother you with their ideas, beliefs, with their ugliness; and, if you are merely going to follow the ugly pattern of the old people that have made this world, what is the point of being educated, what is the point of living at all?

If you look throughout the world, you see appalling destruction and human misery. You do not know anything about wars in this country except what happened when partition took place. You may read about wars in history, but you do not know the actuality of it, how houses are completely destroyed, how there are the latest bombs, hydrogen bombs, which when thrown on an island cause the whole island to disappear; you know what that means, the whole island vaporizes into steam. Ships are bombed and they go up into thin air. There is appalling destruction due to this so-called improvement, and into this world you are growing. You may have a good time when you are young, a happy time, but when you grow older, unless you are watchful and very alert, you will always create another world of battles, of ambitions, a world where each one is competing with the other, where there is misery, starvation, overpopulation, and disease. Unless you are very watchful of your thoughts, of your feelings, you will perpetuate this world, you will continue the ugly pattern of life.

So, is it not very important for you, while you are young, to think about all these matters, and not be taught by some stupid teacher to pass some stupid examinations but be helped by the right teacher to think about all these things? Life is sorrow, death, love, hate, cruelty, disease, starvation. You have to think about all these things. That is why I feel that it is good to think out these morning talks together so that you and I can explore, can think out, can go into these problems, so that you can intelligently have some ideas, some feeling about all these things, so that you need not just grow up to be married, to become a clerk, and then lose yourself like a river in the sand.

One of the causes of fear is ambition, is it not? You are all ambitious, are you not? What is your ambition? To pass some examination? To become a clerk? To become a governor? Or if you are very young, to become an engineer or to drive engines across the bridge? You are all ambitious. Why are you ambitious? What does it mean? Have you ever thought about it? Have you noticed older people, how ambitious they are? In your own family, have you not heard your father, your mother, your uncle talk about getting more salary or occupying some prominent position? Everybody is doing that. In our society—I explained what our society is—in our society, everybody is trying to be on the top of the others. Are they not? They all want to become somebody—a governor, a minister, a manager. If they are clerks, they want to become managers; if they are managers, they want to become bigger, and so on and on and on—the continual struggle to be something. If I am a teacher, I want to become the principal; if I am the principal, I want to become the manager, and so on. If you are ugly, you want to be beautiful, you want to have more money, more saris, more clothes, more dresses, more and more and more. Not only outwardly—furniture, houses, clothes, property—but also inwardly you want to be somebody, though you clothe or cover that ambition by a lot of words. Have you not noticed this? You have, and you think it is perfectly right, don't you? You think it is perfectly normal, justifiable, right.

What has ambition done in the world? So few have ever thought about it. When somebody is struggling to be on the top of somebody else, when everybody is trying to achieve, to gain, have you ever found out what is in their hearts? If you will look at your own heart and see when you are ambitious, when you are struggling to be somebody, spiritually or in the world, you will find that there is the worm of fear inside it. The ambitious man is the most frightened man because he is afraid to be what he is, because he says, "If I am what I am, I shall be nobody. Therefore, I must be somebody, I must become the engineer, the engine driver, the magistrate, the judge, the minister." If you examine this very closely, if you go beyond the wall of words, behind the wall of ideas, positions, and ambitions, you will find there is fear because he is afraid to be what he is. Because he thinks that what he is, is so insignificant, so poor, so ugly, so lonely, so empty, he says, "I must go and do something outside." Either he goes after what he calls God—which is just another form of ambition—because he is afraid, or he wants to be somebody in the world. So, what happens is that this fear is covered up, this loneliness—this sense of inward emptiness of which he is really frightened—is covered up. He runs away from it, and the ambition becomes the emotions through which he can escape.

So, what happens in the world is that everybody is fighting somebody. One man is lesser than another man. There is no love, there is no consideration, there is no thought. Each man wants to become somebody. A member of parliament wants to become the leader of the parliament, to become the prime minister, and so on and on and on. There is perpetual fighting, and our society is one constant struggle of one man against another, and this struggle is called the ambition to be something. Old people encourage you to do that. You must be ambitious, you must be something, you must marry a rich man or a rich woman, you must have the right kind of friends. So, the older generation, those who are frightened, those who are ugly in their hearts, try to make you like them, and you also want to be like them because you see the glamour of it all. When the governor comes, everybody bows down to the earth to receive him, gives him garlands, makes speeches; he loves it, and you love it because you feel you are honored, you know his uncle or you know his clerk, so you want to bask in the sunshine of his ambitions, of his achievements. So you are easily caught in it, in the web of the older generation, in a world which is most ugly, most monstrous. Only if you are very careful, if you are watchful and if you question all the time, if you do not accept and are not afraid, then you will not be caught in it, then you will create a different world.

That is why it is very important that you should find the right vocation. You know what "vocation" means? Something which you will love to do, which is natural. After all, that is the function of education, of a school of this kind, to help you to grow independently so that you are not ambitious but can find your true vocation. The ambitious man has never found his true vocation. If he had found it, he would never be ambitious. Is it not the function of the teacher, of the principal, of the manager, of the trustees of this place to help you to be intelligent?—which means, not to be afraid—so that you can choose, you can find out your own vocation, your own way of life, the way you want to live, the way you want to earn your own livelihood. This means, really, a revolution in thinking because, in the world, the man who can talk, the man who can write, the man who can preach, the man who can rule, the man who has a car, is thought to be in a marvelous position; and the man who digs in the garden, who cooks, who builds a house, is despised. Have you noticed your own feelings, how you look at the mason, the man who builds, who mends the road, the driver of a taxi or a rickshaw, how you regard him with absolute contempt? To you he does not even exist, but when you look at a man with a title, an M.A., or a B.A., a little clerk, a banker, a merchant, a pundit, a minister, immediately you respect him and disregard the *tongawala*. But if you really found your true vocation, then you would break down this system completely because then you might be a gardener, a painter, because then you would be doing something which you really love with your being. That is not ambition, to do something marvelously, completely, truly according to what you think; that is not ambition; in that there is no fear. But it is very difficult because that means that the teacher has to pay a great deal of attention to teach each one of his boys to find out what he is capable of, to help him to find out, to help him not to be afraid but to question, to investigate. You may be a writer, you may be a poet, you may be a painter, and if you love that, you have no ambition because, in that, you want to be, to create; it is a thing which you love. In love, there is no ambition.

So, is it not very important when you are young, when you are in a place like this, to help you to awaken your own intelligence so that you naturally find your vocation? Then, if you find it and if it is a true thing, then you will love it right through life. In that, there will be no ambition, no competition, no struggle, no fighting each other for position, for prestige; and perhaps then you will be able to create a new world. Then, in that world, all the ugly things of the old generation will not exist—their wars, their mischief, their separative gods, their rituals which mean absolutely nothing, their government, their violence. In a place of this kind, the responsibility of the teacher and of you is very great because you can create a new world, a new culture, a new way of life.

Question: What is calamity?

KRISHNAMURTI: Why are you asking that? Do you want the dictionary meaning? May I suggest then that you look it up in a dictionary. What is behind the question? Don't be nervous. What do you mean? Is it not a calamity to see the villager carrying a tremendous weight on her head? To be a villager with dirty clothes, starving—is it not a calamity? It is a calamity to the villager, and if you are at all sensitive, it is a calamity also to you. I do not see what the problem is which makes you ask this question.

Question: If somebody has an ambition to be an engineer, does it not mean that he is interested in it?

KRISHNAMURTI: Would you say being interested in something is ambition? We can give to that word *ambition* any meaning. Ambition, as we generally know it, is the outcome of fear. Now, if I am interested as a boy in being an engineer because I love it, because I want to build beautiful houses, because I want to have the best irrigation in the world, because I want to build the best roads, it means I love the thing; therefore, that is not ambition. In that, there is no fear.

So, ambition and interest are two different things, are they not? I am interested in painting, I love it, I do not want to compete with the best painter or the most famous painter, I just love painting. You may be better at painting, but I do not compare myself with you. I love what I am doing when I paint; that in itself is sufficient for me.

Question: What is the easiest way of finding God?

KRISHNAMURTI: I am afraid there is no easy way because to find God is one of the most difficult things, one of the most arduous things. Is not God something which the mind creates? You know what the mind is. The mind is the result of time. The mind can create anything, any illusion; it has the power of creating ideas, of projecting itself in fancies, in imagination, in accumulating, discarding, choosing; being prejudiced, narrow, limited, the mind can create God, can picture a God, can imagine what God is. Because some teachers, some priests, some so-called saviors have said there is God and they have described him, the mind can imagine God. But that is not God. God is something that cannot be found by the mind.

So, to understand God, you must understand your own mind first—which is very difficult. It is a very complex business, it is not easy. But it is very easy to sit down and go into some kind of dream and have various visions, illusions, and think that you are very near God. The mind can deceive itself enormously. So, to really find that which you call God, you must be completely quiet, and that is not easy. Have you not found how difficult it is? Have you seen older people, how they shake, how they jiggle with their toes and with their hands, how they never sit quiet? How difficult it is physically to sit still, and how much more difficult it is for the mind to be still! You see, if you force the mind to be still, if you follow gurus, the mind is not still. It is like a child that is made still. It is a great art, one of the most difficult things, for the mind to be completely still without coercion. Then only is there a possibility of that which you call God, to be.

Question: Is God everywhere?

KRISHNAMURTI: Are you really interested in this, or have you been put up to ask this question? You ask questions, and I notice you then subside; you do not listen. Have you noticed how the older people never listen to you? They are so enclosed in their own thoughts, in their own emotions, in their own achievements, in their own sorrows, that they never listen to you. I am glad you notice a lot of things. Now, if you know how to listen, really listen, you find out a lot of things not only about people but about the world.

Here is a boy who asks if God is everywhere. He is too small to ask that question. He does not know what it really means. Probably, he has a vague inkling about it—the feeling of beauty, the feeling of the birds in the sky, of waters running, a nice smiling face, the dance of the leaf in the wind, a woman carrying a burden, anger, noise, sorrow, all that is in the air—and he is interested and anxious to try to find out what life is; probably, the little boy feels it vaguely; he discusses it with older people; he hears them talking about God, and he is puzzled. It is very important, is it not, for him to ask that question and for you to seek an answer because, as I was telling you the other day, you may unconsciously, deep down, be able to catch the meaning of all this inwardly and, as you grow, you will have hints of other things besides this ugly world of struggle. The world is beautiful, the earth is beautiful, rich, but we are the spoilers of it.

Question: What is the real goal of life?

KRISHNAMURTI: It is, first of all, what you make of it. It is what you make of life.

Question: As far as reality is concerned, it must be something else.

KRISHNAMURTI: What is the goal of life? Find out the truth of it, and until you find the truth of it, do not stop, because apparently, "What is the goal of life?" interests you.

Question: I am not particularly interested in my goal, but I want the goal of life for everybody.

KRISHNAMURTI: How will you find it out, who will show you? Can you find it out by reading? If you read, one author may give you a method, another author may give you a different method. If you go to a man who is suffering, he will say the goal of life is to be happy because he is himself suffering; for him, the goal of life is to be happy. If you go to a man, to a person, who is starving, who has not had a full meal for years, his goal of life is to have his tummy full. If you go to one of the politicians, his goal is to become one of the directors, one of the rulers of the world. If you ask a woman, she will say, "My goal is to have a baby." If you go to a sannyasi, his goal is to find God. The general desire, the goal of people is to find something that is very comfortable, to find some security, to find safety in something so that they have no fear, so that they have no anxiety, no doubt, no questions. They want something permanent to which they can cling. Is it not so?

So, the general goal of life for a man is some kind of hope, some kind of safety, some kind of permanency. You cannot say, "Is that all?" That is what is happening. You must be fully acquainted with that first. You must question all that, which means, you must question yourself. The general goal of life is embedded in you because you are part of the whole of life—you want safety, you want permanency, you want happiness, you want something in which to cling. Now, to find out something beyond that, some truth which is not of the mind nor of the illusions of the mind, all this must be finished; that is, you must understand all this and put it aside; then only, you will find out the real thing, whether there is a goal. But to stipulate that there must be a goal, to believe that there is a goal, is merely another illusion. But if you can question all the conflicts, the struggles, the pains, the vanities, the ambitions, the fears, the hopes and go through them, go beyond and above them, then you will find out.

Question: Then I must develop higher influences and ultimately find out the real goal of life.

KRISHNAMURTI: How can you see the ultimate thing if you have got many barriers between you and that? You must remove the barriers. To have fresh air you must open the window. You cannot say, "Let me sit down and see what the fresh air is like." You must open the windows. Similarly, you must see all the barriers, the limitations, the conditions; and seeing them all, you must put them aside; then you will find out. But to sit on this side and say, "I must find out" means nothing.

December 17, 1952

Eighth Talk at Rajghat

As you know, we have been talking a great deal about fear because it is a very strong element in our lives. Let us now for a while talk about what is love, what it means, and whether behind this word which to us has so much meaning, so much significance, whether behind this word and feeling there is also that peculiar quality of apprehension, of anxiety, of the thing which grown-up people know as loneliness. So, let us talk about the word or the feeling that we call *love*.

Do you know what love is? Do you know how to find it? Do you love your parents? Do you know how to love your father, your mother, your guardian, your teacher, your aunt, your husband, or your wife? Do you know what it means? When I say I love my parents, what does it mean? You feel safe with them, you are familiar with them? Find out as I talk whether this applies to you and to your love for your parents. You think your parents are protecting you; they are giving you money, shelter, clothes, and food; and you feel a sense of close relationship. Don't you? Also, you feel you can trust them. I do not know if you trust them, but you feel you can. You understand the difference. You feel you can, but you may not. Probably you do not talk to them as easily, as happily as to your own friends, and yet, you respect them—respect looking up to them, being guided by them and obeying them, feeling that you have a certain responsibility towards them, feeling that you have a duty to support them when you grow up, when they are old. They in turn love you, they want to protect you, they want to guide you, they want to help you—at least they say so. They want you to be married off so that you will lead a so-called moral life, so that you have no troubles, so that a man will look after you, or there is a wife to look after you, to cook, to look after your children. All this is called love, is it not?

We cannot find out if it is real love because love is something which cannot be so easily explained by words. It is not something that comes to you easily. It is much more complex and cannot be easily understood. Without it, life is very barren; without it, the trees, the birds, the smile of men and women, the bridge across the river, the boatmen, and the animals have no meaning. Without it, life becomes shallow. Do you know what "shallow" means? Like a pool. In a deep river many fish can live, there is richness. But the pool that is by the roadside, it soon dries up with the strong sun, and nothing remains except mud and dirt. For most of us, love is an extraordinarily difficult thing to understand. For most of us, it is very shallow. Behind that word there is a lurking fear. We want to be loved and also, we want to love. So, is it not very important for each one of us to find out what this extraordinary thing is? You can only find out if you know how you regard human beings, the trees, the birds, the animals, the stranger, the man who is hungry, and also how you regard your friends if you have any, how you regard your gurus if you have any, or how you regard your parents. When you say, "I love my father, my mother, my guardian, my teacher," what does it mean? When you look up to somebody, when you feel it is your duty that you ought to obey them, and when they feel that you must also have a duty towards them and that you must obey them, is that love? Do you understand what I am talking about? When you look up to somebody, when you respect him tremendously, is that love? When you look up to somebody, you also look down upon somebody else. Don't you? There is always that. Is it not so? Is that love? When you feel you must obey, you have a duty, is that love? Is love something which is apprehensive, in which there is the sense of looking up or looking down, in which there is the obeying of somebody?

When you say you love somebody, don't you depend on him? It is all right when you are young to be dependent on your father, on your mother, on your teacher, or on your guardian. Because you are young, you need to be looked after, you need clothes, you need shelter, you need security. While you are young, you need a sense of being held together, of somebody looking after you. But even as you grow older, this feeling of dependence remains, does it not? Have you not noticed it in older people, in your parents and your teachers? Have you not noticed how they depend on their wives, on their children, on their mothers? People when they grow up still want to hold on to somebody, still feel that they need to be dependent. Without looking to somebody, without being guided by somebody, without a feeling of comfort and security in somebody, they feel lonely, do they not? They feel lost. So, this dependency on another is called love, but if you watch it more closely, you will see dependency is fear; it is not love. Because they are afraid to be alone, because they are afraid to think things out for themselves, because they are afraid to feel, to watch, to find out the whole meaning of life, they feel they love God. So they depend on what they call God, but a thing created by the mind is not dependable; it is not God, the unknown. It is the same with an ideal or a belief. I believe in something, and that gives me great comfort; I love that ideal and I hold on to it, but remove the ideal, remove the belief and my dependency on it, and I am lost. It is the same thing with a guru. I depend, I want to receive, so there is a fear, an ache. It is the same when you depend on your parents or teachers. It is right that you should do so when you are young, but if you keep on depending when you have grown to maturity, that will make you incapable of thinking, of being free. Where there is dependence there is fear, and where there is fear there is authority; there is no love; when your parents say you must do this, you must obey; you must follow certain traditions; you must take certain jobs or do some work; in all these, there is no love. And when you depend on society and accept the structure of society as it is, it is not love because society is very rotten. You do not have to investigate it very deeply, for when you walk down the road, you see poverty, ugliness, squalor.

An ambitious man or woman does not know what love is, and we are ruled by people who are ambitious. Therefore, there is no happiness in the world. It is very important for you, as you grow up, to see all this and to find out if you can ever discover this thing called love. You may have a very rich house, a marvelous garden, a good position, many saris or clothes, a good job; you may be the great prime minister, but without love, all these things have no meaning.

So, what you have to do is to find out now—not when you grow old, you will never find out then—how you love your parents or your teacher or your guru; you have to find out what it all means, not to accept any word, but to go behind the word, to find out what lies behind the meaning of words and see if there is any reality behind them—the reality being that which you actually feel, not what you are supposed to feel—to feel the real when you are jealous, when you are angry. The moment you say, "I must not be jealous," that is a varying wish that has no meaning. If you can find out exactly, be very clear, be very honest with yourself to find out exactly what you feel, what the actual state is—not what the ideal state is, not how you should act or how you should feel at some future date but what you actually feel at the moment—then you can do something about it. But to say, "I must love my parents, I must love my guru, I must love my teacher," has no meaning, has it? Because, behind those words you are quite different; you say a lot of words and behind those words you hide. So, is it not intelligence to go beyond words, beyond the accepted meaning of words? Words like *duty, responsibility, God, love* have acquired a lot of traditional meaning, but an intelligent person, a really deeply educated person goes beyond the words. For instance, if I told you that I do not believe in God, how shocked you would be. Would you not? You would say, "Goodness, what an awful idea." You believe in God, don't you? At least you think you do. That has very little meaning—your belief or nonbelief.

What is important is to go behind the word, the word that you call love, and to see actually whether you do love your parents and whether the parents actually love you. Because if you really loved your parents or your parents actually loved you, the world would be entirely different. There would be no wars, there would be no starvation, there would be no class differences. There would be no rich and no poor. Without this thing called love, you try to arrange society economically, to adjust economically, to put right, but without love, you cannot bring about a social structure which is without conflict, without pain. So, you have to go into this very, very carefully, and perhaps then you will find out what love is.

Question: Why is there sorrow in the world?

KRISHNAMURTI: I wonder if that boy knows what that word means. Probably, he has seen the donkey carrying an overweight load with his legs almost breaking; probably he has seen some child crying; probably he has seen the mother beating the child, the father scolding the child. Probably, he has seen people quarreling or fighting each other. There is death, the body being carried to be burned; there is the beggar; there is disease; there is poverty, old age, not only outside but inside of us, so perhaps, he says, "Why is there sorrow?" Don't you want to know, too? Have you searched, not only outwardly, but inwardly, your own sorrow? What is it, why does it exist? Suppose I want something and I cannot get it, I feel miserable; I want a few more saris, I want to be a little more rich, a little more beautiful, and I cannot be that; without it I feel unhappy. I want to be friends with that boy or girl and I cannot be, and I feel unhappy. I want to love that person and that person does not love me, and I am miserable. My father dies, I am in sorrow. Why?

Why do you feel unhappy when you cannot get what you want? Why should you get what you want? We think we have a right to get what we want. If you want a sari, you say that you must have it. If you want a coat, you feel that you must have it. But you never ask why you should have it when millions have not got it. Why should you have what you want? And besides, why do you want it? There is your need for enough clothes, food, shelter, but you go beyond that and want some more. Suppose you have what clothes, what food, what shelter you need; you are not satisfied with that—you want more power, you want to be respected, you want to be loved, you want to be looked up to, you want to be powerful, you want to be poets, saints, you want to be prime ministers, presidents, good speakers. Why? Have you ever looked into it? Why do you want all this? This does not mean that you must be satisfied with what you are. I do not mean that. That would be ugly, silly. But this constant craving, the desire, the longing for more and more and more—why? This indicates that you are dissatisfied, discontented—but with what? Discontent, dissatisfaction with what you are? I am this, I do not like it, I want to be that. I think I look much more beautiful in a new coat or a new sari, so I want that. What does that mean? That means I am dissatisfied with what I am. I think I can escape from the discontent by having something more, more clothes or more power and so on. But the dissatisfaction is still there, is it not? I only cover it up with clothes, with power, with cars; I just cover it up.

So, until you find out how to understand what you are, to merely cover yourself with words, with power, with position, has no meaning. You will still be unhappy. Seeing this, the unhappy person, the person who is in sorrow, does not run away to gurus, to position, to power; he wants to know what is behind that word, what lies behind that sorrow. If you go behind it, you will find that it is yourself, yourself who is very small, yourself who is miserable, unhappy, struggling to achieve greatness. So, this struggle to be something is the cause of sorrow. But if you can understand the thing, that which you are, go deeper and deeper behind it, you will find something quite different.

Question: How can we wipe out sorrow?

KRISHNAMURTI: I have just explained it to you. You had better talk it over with your teachers afterwards. I just explained how sorrow comes into being and how it is possible to wipe it out.

Question: If a man is starving and I have a feeling that I can be useful to him, is it not with ambition that I am loving the man?

KRISHNAMURTI: It all depends with what motive you help him. The politician says he helps you and gets to New Delhi, living in a big house and speaking and showing himself off. He is helping the poor man, he says so. Is that love? Do you understand? Is that love?

Question: If I relieve him from starvation by my usefulness?

KRISHNAMURTI: He is starving, and you help him with food to relieve starvation. Is that love? Why do you want to help him? This means, have you no motive, have you no incentive, do you not get any benefit out of it? Think it out, do not say yes or no. If you get any benefit out of it, politically or inward benefit or outward benefit, then you do not love him. You feed him in order to become more popular or in order that your friends may help you to reach New Delhi. Then that is not love, is it? But if you love him, you feed him without any incentive, without any motive, without wanting anything in return. If you feed him and he is ungrateful, do you feel hurt? If so, you do not love him. If he says to you and to the villagers that you are a wonderful man, you will feel very flattered. Then it means you do not love him because you are thinking about yourself; surely that is not love. One has to be very careful to find out if one derives any kind of benefit and what the motive is that makes one feed him.

Question: Suppose I want to go home and the principal says, "no." If I disobey him, I will have to face the consequence. If I obey the principal, I break my heart. What am I to do?

KRISHNAMURTI: Do you mean to say that you cannot talk it over with the principal, that you cannot show him your problem, that you cannot take him into your confidence? If the principal is the right kind of principal, you can trust him, talk over your problem with him; and then if he is obstinate and says, "You must not go," then something is wrong with the principal, or he may have reasons which you must find out. So, it requires mutual confidence. That is, you must have confidence in the principal, and the principal must have confidence in you. Life is not just a one-sided relationship. You are a human being, so is the principal a human being. He may make a mistake. So, both of you must talk it over. You may say that you want to go, but that may not be quite enough; your parent may have written to the principal not to send you home. It must be a mutual thing, must it not, so that you do not get hurt, so that you do not feel that you are ill-treated, brutally pushed aside, and that can only happen when you have confidence in the teacher and he has confidence in you. That means real love, and that is what this school should be.

Question: Why should we not do puja?

KRISHNAMURTI: Have you found out why old people do puja? Because they are copying? The more immature you are, the more you want to copy. Have you noticed how you love uniforms? So, before you ask why you should not do puja, ask the old people why they do puja. They do it because, firstly, it is a tradition, their grandfathers did it. Then the repetition of words gives them a certain sense of peace. Do you understand that constantly repeated words dull your minds and that they give you a sense of quietness, if the words have significance? Especially, Sanskrit words have certain vibrations which make you very quiet. People also do puja because everybody is doing it, because their grandmother, their grandfathers, their aunts did it. For all these reasons, they do puja. You being very young, you copy them, and you say you must also do puja because your father, your mother, your guru, your teacher does it. Do you do puja because somebody tells you to do it or because you find a certain mesmeric, hypnotic effect in repeating certain words? Should you not find out why you do anything before you do it? It does not matter even if millions believe it to be so. Should you not find out without accepting anything, should you not use your mind to find the truth or the significance of puja?

You see that the mere repetition of Sanskrit words or of gestures will not really help you to find out what truth is, what God is. To find that out, you must know how to meditate. That is quite a different problem, quite different from doing puja. Millions of people have done puja, and has it brought about a happier world? Are people creative? By "creative," I do not mean the bearing of children. I mean "creative" in the sense of being full of initiative, of love, of kindness, of sympathy, of consideration. So, if you as a little boy do puja and repeat it, you will grow merely like a machine. But if you begin to question, if you begin to doubt, to inquire, to find out, then perhaps you will know how to meditate. Meditation is one of the greatest blessings if you know how to do it properly.

December 18, 1952

Ninth Talk at Rajghat

You remember yesterday morning we were discussing the complex problem of love. I do not think we shall understand it until we understand an equally complex problem which we call the mind. Have you noticed, when we are very young, how inquisitive we are? We want to know, we see many more things than older people. We observe, if we are at all awake, things that older people do not notice. The mind, when we are young, is much more alert, much more curious, and wanting to know. That is why when we are young we learn so easily mathematics, geography. As we grow older, our mind becomes more and more crystallized, more and more heavy, more and more bulky. Have you noticed in older people how prejudiced they are? Their minds are fixed, they are not open, they approach everything from a fixed point of view. You are young now, but if you are not very watchful, you will also become like that. Is it not then very important to understand the mind and to see whether you cannot be supple, be capable of instant adjustments, of extraordinary capacities in every department of life, of deep research and understanding, instead of gradually becoming dull? Should you not know the ways of the mind so as to understand the way of love? Because, it is the mind that destroys love. Clever people, people who are cunning, do not know what love is because their minds are so sharp, because they are so clever, because they are so superficial—which means to be on the surface, and love is not a thing that exists on the surface.

What is the mind? Do you understand what I am talking about? I am not talking about the brain, the physical construction of the brain about which any physiologist will tell you. The brain is something which reacts to various nervous responses. But you are going to find out what the mind is. What is the mind? The mind says, "I think; it is mine; it is yours; I am hurt; I am jealous; I love; I hate; I am an Indian; I am a Muslim; I believe in this; I do not believe in that; I know; you do not know; I respect; I despise; I want; I do not want." What is this thing?

Until you understand it, until you are familiar with the whole process of thinking which is the mind, until you are aware of that, you will gradually, as you grow older, become hard, crystallized, dull, fixed in a certain pattern of thinking.

What is this thing which you call the mind? It is the way of thinking, the way you think. I am talking of your mind—not somebody else's mind and the way it would think—the way you feel, the way you look at trees, at a fish, at the fishermen, the way you consider the villager. That mind gradually becomes warped or fixed in a certain pattern. When you want something, when you desire, when you crave, when you want to be something, then you set a pattern; that is, your mind creates a pattern and gets caught. Your desire crystallizes your mind. Say, for example, I want to be a very rich man. The desire of wanting to be a wealthy man creates a pattern, and my thinking then gets caught in it, and I can only think in those terms, and I cannot go beyond it. So, the mind gets caught in it, gets crystallized in it, gets hard, dull. Or, if I believe in something—in God, in communism, in a certain political system—the very belief begins to set the pattern because that belief is the outcome of my desire, and that desire strengthens the walls of the pattern. Gradually, my mind becomes dull, incapable of adjustment, of quickness, of sharpness, of clarity, because I am caught in the labyrinth of my own desires.

So, until I really investigate this process of my mind, the ways I think, the ways I regard love, until I am familiar with my own ways of thinking, I cannot possibly find what love is. There will be no love when my mind desires certain facts of love, certain actions of it, and when I then imagine what love should be. Then I give certain motives to love. So, gradually, I create the pattern of action with regard to love. But it is not love; it is merely my desire of what love should be. Say, for example, I possess you as a wife or as a husband. Do you understand "possess"? You possess your saris or your coats, don't you? If somebody took them away, you would be angry, you would be anxious, you would be irritated. Why? Because you regard your saris or your coat or kurta as yours, your property; you possess it because through possession you feel enriched. Don't you? Through having many saris, many kurtas, you feel rich, not only physically rich, but inwardly rich. So, when somebody takes your coat away, you feel irritated because inwardly you are being deprived of that feeling of being rich, that feeling of possession. Owning creates a barrier, does it not, with regard to love. If I own you, possess you, is that love? I possess you as I possess a car, a coat, a sari, because in possessing, I feel very rich; I depend on it; it is very important to me inwardly. This owning, this possessing, this depending, is what we call love. But if you examine it, you will see that behind it, the mind feels satisfied in possession. After all, when you possess a sari or many saris or a car or a house, inwardly it gives you a certain satisfaction, the feeling that it is yours.

So, the mind desiring, wanting, creates a pattern, and in that pattern it gets caught, and so the mind grows weary, dull, stupid, thoughtless. The mind is the center of that feeling of the 'mine', the feeling that I own something, that I am a big man, that I am a little man, that I am insulted, that I am flattered, that I am clever or that I am very beautiful or that I want to be ambitious or that I am the daughter of somebody or the son of somebody. That feeling of the 'me', the 'I', is the center of the mind, is the mind itself. So, the more the mind feels this is mine and builds walls round the feeling that "I am somebody," that "I must be great," that "I am a very clever man," or that "I am very stupid or a dull man," the more it creates a pattern, the more and more it becomes enclosed, dull. Then it suffers; then there is pain in that enclosure. Then it says, "What am I to do?" Then it struggles to find something else instead of removing the walls that are enclosing it. By thought, by careful awareness, by going into it, by understanding it, it wants to take something from outside and then to close itself again. So, gradually, the mind becomes a barrier to love. So, without the understanding of life, of what the mind is, of the way of thinking, of the way from which there is action, we cannot possibly find what love is.

Is not the mind also an instrument of comparison? You know what comparison is, to compare. You say this is better than that; you compare yourself with somebody who is more beautiful, who is more clever. There is comparison when you say, "I remember that particular river which I saw a year ago, and it was still more beautiful." You compare yourself with somebody, compare yourself with an example, with the ultimate ideal. Comparative judgment makes the mind dull; it does not sharpen the mind, it does not make the mind comprehensive, inclusive, because when you are all the time comparing, what has happened? You see the sunset, and you immediately compare that sunset with the previous sunset. You see a mountain and you see how beautiful it is. Then you say, "I saw a still more beautiful mountain two years ago." What happens when you are comparing is that you are really not looking at the sunset which is there, but you are looking at it in order to compare it with something else. So, comparison prevents you from looking fully. I look at you, you are nice, but I say, "I know a much nicer person, a much better person, a more noble person, a more stupid person"; when I do this, I am not looking at you, am I? Because my mind is occupied with something else, I am not looking at you at all. In the same way, I am not looking at the sunset at all. To really look at the sunset, there must be no comparison; to really look at you, I must not compare you with someone else. It is only when I look at you not with comparative judgment that I can understand you. But when I compare you with somebody else, then I judge you, and I say, "Oh! he is a very stupid man." So, stupidity arises when there is comparison; you understand? I compare you with somebody else, and that very comparison brings about a lack of human dignity. When I look at you without comparing, I am only concerned with you, not with someone else. The very concern about you, not comparatively, brings about human dignity.

So, as long as the mind is comparing, there is no love, and the mind is always judging, comparing, weighing, looking to find out where the weakness is. So, where there is comparison, there is no love. When the mother and father love their children, they do not compare them; they do not compare their child with another child; it is their child and they love their child. But you want to compare yourself with something better, with something nobler, with something richer, so you create in yourself a lack of love. You are all the time concerned with yourself in relationship to somebody else. So, as the mind becomes more and more comparative, more and more possessive, more and more depending, it creates a pattern in which it gets caught, so it cannot look at anything anew, afresh, and so it destroys that very thing, that very perfume of life, which is love.

Question: What should we ask God to give us?

KRISHNAMURTI: You are very interested in God. Are you not? Why? Because your mind is asking for something, wanting to find out.

So, it is constantly agitated. When I am asking something from you, my mind is agitated, is it not?

The boy wants to know what he should ask of God. He does not know what God is; he cannot possibly know what he wants. But there is a feeling of general apprehension, a general feeling, "I must find out, I must ask, I must be protected." The mind is always seeking, searching in every corner, and so the mind is never still; it is always wanting, grasping, watching, pushing, comparing, judging. You search your own mind and see what the mind is doing, how it tries to control itself, how it tries to dominate, to suppress, to find out, to search, to ask, to beg, to struggle, to compare. We call that mind very alert; is it alert? An alert mind is a still mind, not a mind that like a butterfly is chasing all over the place, not a mind that is constantly clinging, agitating, asking, begging, praying, petitioning—such a mind is never still. It is only a still mind that can understand what God is. A still mind can never ask of God. It is only an impoverished mind that can beg, that can ask. What it asks, it can never have, and what it wants is security, comfort, certainty. If you seek anything of God, you will never find God.

Question: What is real greatness and how can I be great?

KRISHNAMURTI: You see, the unfortunate thing is that we want to be great. We all want to be great. Why? We want to be Gandhis, prime ministers, we want to be great inventors, great writers. Why? You see, in education, in religion, in all the things of our life, we have examples. We have examples of the greatest poet, the greatest orator, the greatest writer, the greatest saint, the greatest hero. We have examples and we want to be like them.

When you want to be like another, you have already created a pattern of action, have you not? You have already set a limitation on your thought. You have already bound your thought within certain limits. So, your thought has already become crystallized, narrow, limited, suffocated. Why do you want to be great? Why are you not prepared to be what you are? You see, the moment you want to be something, there is misery, there is degradation, there is envy and sorrow. I want to be like the Buddha. What happens? I struggle everlastingly. I am stupid, I am ugly; I crave for something, and I wish to leave what I am and to go beyond that. I am ugly, I want to be beautiful, so I struggle everlastingly, until I die, to be beautiful or to deceive myself to think that I am beautiful. If I say to myself that I am ugly and I see it as a fact, then I can investigate, then I can go beyond. But if I am always trying to be something other than what I am, then my mind wears itself out.

If you say, "This is what I am, and I am going to understand this," then you will find that the understanding of what you are—not what you should be—brings great peace and contentment, great understanding, great love.

Question: Is there not an end of love? Is love based on attraction?

KRISHNAMURTI: Suppose you are attracted by a beautiful river, by a beautiful woman, or by a man. What is wrong with that? We are trying to find out. You see, when I am attracted to a woman, to a man or to a child or to truth or to a person, what happens? I want to be with it, I want to possess it, I want to call it my own; I say that it is mine and that it is not yours. I am attracted to that person, I must be near that person, my body must be near that person's body. So, what have I done? What generally happens? The fact is that I am attracted, and I want to be near that person; that is a fact, not an ideal. And also the fact is that when I am attracted and I want to possess, there is no love. My concern is with the fact and not with what I should be. Well, when I possess a person, I do not want that person to look at anybody else. When I consider that person as mine, is there love? Obviously not. The moment my mind creates a hedge round that person, as the 'mine', there is no love.

The fact is my mind is doing that all the time. That is what we are discussing, to see how the mind is working and perhaps, being aware of it, the mind itself will be quiet.

Question: Why has the earth been created and why are we on it?

KRISHNAMURTI: You know what the scientists say about how the earth has come into being. If you read biology, the beginning of life, they will tell you how the earth has been created, how human beings have grown upon it. That is the answer.

Question: Is that true?

KRISHNAMURTI: The girl wants to know if it is true? Who is going to tell you about what is true? You are here, are you not? There is the earth and you are here. Why speculate about something which you cannot possibly prove? I mean, the scientists, the biologists will tell you how the earth has been created, and some equally clever person will tell you how the earth has been created out of Brahma. He will tell you how you have been created, how you have evolved, and another will tell you how you have been created out of matter. Then, what will happen to you? Which are you going to choose? You will obviously choose something that will please you, you will choose according to your own conditioning. This is a useless process of speculating. It is a waste of time to speculate. But there is the earth to understand, and you have to find out why you are here, what you are thinking, what you are feeling, what your life is. Perhaps you feel you will be able to find out ultimately, but you must begin now to find out.

Question: Why does one feel the necessity of love?

KRISHNAMURTI: You mean why do we have to have love? Why should there be love? Can we do without it? What would happen if you did not have this so-called love? If your parents began to think out why they love you, you might not be here. They might throw you out. They think they love you; therefore, they want to protect you, they want to see you educated, they feel that they must give you every opportunity to be something. This feeling of protection, this feeling of wanting you to be educated, this feeling that you belong to them is what they generally call love. Without it, what would happen? What would happen if your parents did not love you? You would be neglected, you would be something inconvenient, you would be pushed out, they would hate you. So, fortunately, there is this feeling of love, perhaps clouded, perhaps besmirched and ugly, but there is still that feeling, fortunately for you and me; otherwise, you and I would not have been educated, would not exist.

Question: What is prayer? In daily life, what is its importance?

KRISHNAMURTI: I presume you put that question in all seriousness, and not just because you want to be clever; I presume you really put that question in earnestness. Let us find out. Do not listen, but find out.

Why do you pray and what is prayer? Most of your prayers are merely a petitioning, an asking. You indulge in this kind of prayer because you suffer, because you are alone, because you are depressed and in sorrow. You pray to God and ask for help; that is a petition, and that you call prayer. The content of prayer is generally the same although the intent behind it may vary. Prayer, with most people, is a petition, a begging, an asking. Are you doing that? Why are you praying? I am not saying you should or should not pray. But why do you pray? Is it for more knowledge, for more peace, for the world to be free from sorrow? Is there any other form of prayer than that? There is prayer which is really not a prayer but the sending out of good will, the sending out of love, the sending out of ideas. Which is it you are doing?

If your prayer is a supplication, a petition, then what happens? You are asking God or somebody to fill your empty bowl, are you not? You want that bowl to be filled according to your wishes. You want God to fill it according to your wishes, so you are asking God for that which you want. You are not satisfied with what happens, with what is given. So your prayer is merely a petition. It is a demand that you should be satisfied. You want to be satisfied; therefore, your prayer is not prayer at all. You just want to be gratified, so you say to God, "I am suffering; please gratify me; please give me my brother, my son. Please make me rich." So, you are perpetuating your own demands. That is not prayer.

The real thing is to understand yourself, to see why you are asking, and not for what you are asking, to see why there is this demand in you, this urge to beg. Then you will find out that the more you know about yourself physically as well as psychologically—the more you know what you are thinking, what you are feeling—the more you will find out the truth of *what is*. It is that truth that will help you to be free.

December 19, 1952

Tenth Talk at Rajghat

I think it is very important to know how to listen. If you know how to listen, you will get to the root of the matter immediately. If you listen to pure sound, you have immediate contact with the beauty of it. Similarly, if you knew how to listen to what another is saying or to what is being said, there would be an immediate transformation, an immediate change. After all, listening is the complete focusing of attention. You think that attention is a tiresome thing, that to learn to concentrate is a drawn out process, but if you know how to listen, then it is not so difficult because then you will see that you get to the heart of the matter immediately with an extraordinary understanding.

Most of us do not listen. We are distracted by noise, or we have so much prejudice, so much bias; we have a twist that prevents us from really listening to what is being said. This is so especially with older people because they have a series of achievements behind them, they are somebodies or nobodies in the world, and it is very difficult to penetrate through the layers of their formulations, their conceptions. The imagination, the achievements of older people will not allow the thing that is being said to penetrate. But if we knew how to listen without any barrier, just to listen as if to the sound of the bird in the morning, or to see the sunlight on the water, or to listen to what is being said without any interpretation, without any barrier, just to listen, then it is an extraordinary thing, especially when something true is being said. You may not like it, you may resist it, you may think it is enclosed, but if you really listen, you see the truth of it.

Really "listening" unburdens, it clears away the dross of many years of failure, of success, of longings. You know what propaganda is, don't you? It is to propagate, to sow, so that the constant repetition of an idea imprints on your mind what the propagandist, the politician, the religious leader wants you to believe. There is a listening there also because there is the constant repetition by some people of what you should do, what books you should read, whom you should follow, what kind of ideas are right, which guru is essential, which is not essential. This constant repetition of an idea, of a feeling over and over again, leaves a mark. Even if you do not listen to it, unconsciously it is leaving an imprint; that is the purpose of propaganda, the constant repetition. But you see propaganda does not bring that truth which you immediately understand when you are really listening, when you really pay attention without any effort.

You are now listening to me; you are not making any effort to pay attention; you are just listening, and if there is truth in what you hear, if what is being said is true, then you will find a remarkable change taking place in you, a change that is not wished for, a transformation, a complete revolution in which the truth alone is the master, and not your mind. So, if I may suggest, similarly listen to everything, not only to what I am saying, but to what other people are saying, to the birds, to the whistle of that engine, to the noise of the bus going by, and you will find that the more you listen, the greater is the silence, and that silence is not broken by noise. It is only when you are resisting, when you are putting up a barrier between yourselves, between listening and that to which you do not want to listen, then there is the struggle. So, if I may suggest, listen.

We were talking yesterday and the day before yesterday about what love is, and perhaps we can approach it from a different point of view, from a different angle. Is it not very important to be refined not only outwardly but inwardly? You know what refinement is? To have sensitivity to things about you, and also to thoughts, to beliefs, to ideas inside you—the refinement of clothes, of manners, of gestures, of the way you walk, the way you talk, the way you look at people. Now, refinement is essential, is it not? Otherwise, there is deterioration. You know what deterioration is? You know the meaning of the word *deterioration?* Do you know what it means, to deteriorate? To generate is to create, to build, to have initiative, to bring forward, to develop. To degenerate is the opposite, to destroy to pieces; to degenerate implies a slow decay, a withering away. That is what is happening in the world, in colleges, in universities, amongst nations, amongst people, in the individual; there is a slow decay, a slow withering away; the degenerating process is going on all the time. This is because there is no outward or inward refinement. You may have very fine clothes, nice houses, good food, cleanliness, but without the inner refinement, the mere outward perfection of form will have little meaning; the perfection of form without the inner refinement is merely another form of degeneration. To have a beautiful car and inwardly to be gross, to be concerned with oneself, with one's own achievements, with one's own grandeur or greatness or ambitions is the actual process of degeneration because then you are not creating inwardly.

The form, the beauty of form has meaning in poetry or in a person or when you see a beautiful tree only when there is the inward refinement, which is love. If there is love, there will be outward as well as inward refinement. The outward refinement is expressed in consideration, in how you treat not only your daughters, your parents, your servants if you have any, but also your neighbors, the coolie, the gardener. You may have a beautiful garden created by the gardener, but without that love of refinement, the garden has no meaning; it is merely an expression of your own vanity. So, it is essential to have outward and inward refinement. The way you eat matters a great deal; whether you make a noise while you are eating matters very much; the way you behave, your manners, the way you talk to your friends, the way you talk about others, all these matter because they are pointing to what you are inwardly, indicating whether in that inward state of being there is refinement. Where there is no refinement, it obviously expresses itself outwardly in a degeneration of form. But outward refinement or inward refinement has very little meaning if there is no love. We see that love is not a thing that we possess. It comes into being only when the mind has understood the complex problems which it creates. You and I are going to discuss these problems.

Question: Why do we feel a sense of pride when we succeed?

KRISHNAMURTI: Is there a sense of pride with success, and what is pride and what is success?

You understand those two words, success and pride? What is success? Have you ever considered what it is to be successful as a writer, as a poet, as a painter, as a businessman, as a politician? Inwardly to feel that you have achieved a certain control over yourself, inwardly to feel successful in achieving a certain thing, to feel that you have succeeded outwardly, what does all this indicate? To feel that you have achieved something, you are better than somebody else, you have achieved what you want, you have become a successful man, you are respected, you are looked upon as an example by others—what does all this indicate? Naturally, with that feeling comes pride—I have done something, I am very important. The feeling of 'I' is, in its very nature, a sense of being proud. So, with success, there always grows pride, the pride being that one is very important comparatively. This comparison with another, with your example, with your ideal, with your hope, gives you the strength, the purpose, the drive, which only gives importance to the 'I', to the feeling that you are much more important than anybody else; and that sense of feeling, of pleasure, is the beginning of pride. Pride is a thing that brings a great deal of egotistic vanity, an inflation. You watch the older people and you watch yourself. You pass an examination. When you are a little cleverer than another, a sense of pleasure comes in. It is the same when you outdo somebody in argument, or physically you are much stronger or more beautiful. Immediately, there is a sense of your importance. So, when there is that feeling of importance of the 'me', then you have conflict, the struggle, the pain to maintain that state all the time.

Question: How can we remove it, how can we be free from pride?

KRISHNAMURTI: I told you just now how to listen. If you had really listened to the answer to the last question, you would have understood how to be free from pride, and you would be free from pride, but you are concerned with the next question, you are concerned to find out how to put that question; you were not listening to the first question and to the answer. If you listen to what I say, you will find out the truth of it.

I am proud because I have achieved; I have been the principal; I have been to England, to America; I have done great things; I have appeared in the papers and so on and on. I am very proud, and I say to myself, "How am I to be free from pride?" Why do I want to be free? That is an important question, not how to be free. But why, what is the motive, what is the incentive? Does the incentive come into being because I find pride harmful to me, painful, spiritually not good? If that is the motive, then to try to free myself from pride is another form of pride, is it not? I am still concerned with achievement. If I find that pride is very painful, is spiritually ugly, I say I must be free of it. "I must be free" still contains the same motive as "I must be successful." I am still important. I must be free, I must be successful now. My struggle is to be free and I am still the center. So, what is important is not how to be free from pride but to understand the 'me'. The 'I' is so subtle, wanting this one year and wanting that another year; and when that is painful, then wanting something else. So, as long as this center of the 'me' exists, whether I have pride or whether I am humble is of very little importance. It is only a different coat to put on. When a coat appeals to me, I put it on; I put on another next year, depending on my fancies, on my desires.

What I have to understand is how this 'I' comes into being. The 'I' comes into being through various forms of achievements. This does not mean that you must not act, but the feeling that you are acting, the feeling that you are achieving, the feeling that you must be without pride has to be understood. You have to understand the structure of the 'me'. You have to sit, to watch, to be aware, to be conscious of your thinking, of the way you treat your servant, of the way you treat your mother, your father, the teacher, the coolie, those who are above you and those who are below you, those whom you respect and those whom you despise—all that indicates the ways of the 'I'. Then, when you know the ways, there is understanding, and then there is freedom from the 'I'. That is what is important, not how to be free from pride.

Question: How can a thing of beauty be a joy forever?

KRISHNAMURTI: Are you a student of the classics? Is that your original thought, or are you quoting from somebody? So, you want to find out if joy, if beauty is perishable, and also how there can be everlasting joy.

Question: Beauty comes in certain forms.

KRISHNAMURTI: Is beauty perishable? The tree, the leaf, the river, the woman, the man, those villagers carrying a weight on their head and walking beautifully.

Question: They walk, but they leave an impression.

KRISHNAMURTI: They walk and the memory of it remains. The memory remains of the tree, the leaf; the beauty and the memory of it remains. Now, is memory a living joy? When you see a beautiful thing, there is immediate joy; you see a sunset and there is an immediate reaction of joy. That joy, a few moments later, becomes a memory. That memory of the joy, is it a living thing? Is the memory of the sunset a living thing? No, it is a dead thing. So, with that dead imprint of a sunset, through that, you want to find joy. Memory has no joy; it is only the remembrance of something which created the joy. Memory in itself has no joy. There is joy, the immediate reaction to the beauty of a tree, and then memory comes in and destroys that joy. So, if there is constant perception of beauty without the accumulation of memories, then there is the possibility of joy everlasting. But it is not so easy to be free from memory. The moment you see something very pleasurable, you make it immediately into something to which you hold on. You see a beautiful thing, a beautiful child, a beautiful tree; and when you see it, there is immediate pleasure; then you want more of it. The 'more' of it is the reaction of memory. So, when you want more, you have already started the process of disintegration. In that there is no joy. Memory can never produce everlasting joy. There is everlasting joy only when there is the constant response to beauty, to ugliness, to everything—which means great inward and outward sensitivity, which means having real love.

Question: Why are the poor happy and the rich unhappy?

KRISHNAMURTI: Do you know that the poor are happy? Have you noticed the poor happy? Have you noticed the rich unhappy? Are the poor particularly happy? They may sing, they may have *bhajans,* they may dance, but are they happy? They have no food, they have no clothes, they are not clean, they have to work from morning until night, year after year. They may have occasional happiness, but they are not happy, are they? Are the rich unhappy? They have food, they have clothes, they have great position, they travel. They are unhappy when they are frustrated, when they are hindered and cannot get what they want.

What do you mean by happiness? Some will say happiness consists in getting what you want. You want a car, and you get it, and you are happy. I want a sari or clothes; I want to go to Europe, and if I can, I am happy. I want to be the biggest professor or the greatest politician, and if I get it, I am happy; if I cannot get it, I am unhappy. So, what you call happiness is getting what you want, achievement or success, becoming noble, getting anything that you want. As long as you want something and you can get it, you feel perfectly happy; you are not frustrated, but if you cannot get what you want, then unhappiness begins. All of us are concerned with this, not only the rich and the poor. The rich and the poor all want to get something for themselves, for their family, for society; and if they are prevented, stopped, they will be unhappy. We are not discussing, we are not saying that the poor should not have what they want. That is not the problem. We are trying to find out what is happiness and whether happiness is something of which you are conscious. The moment you are conscious that you are happy, that you have much, is that happiness? The moment you are conscious that you are happy, it is not happiness, is it? So you cannot go after happiness. The moment you are conscious that you are humble, you are not humble. So happiness is not a thing to be pursued; it comes. But if you seek it, it will evade you.

Question: Though there is progress in different directions, though people are making progress in different directions, why is there no brotherhood?

KRISHNAMURTI: What do you mean by "progress"?

Question: Scientific progress.

KRISHNAMURTI: As from the bullock cart to the jet plane? That is progress, is it not? Centuries ago, there was only the bullock cart, but gradually, through time, we have developed the jet plane; this is called scientific progress. Now, through sanitation, through great medical care, there has been progress. The means of transport in ancient times was very slow, and now it is very rapid; within twenty-four hours, you can be in London. All these things we call progress, and yet you see that although in one direction we are making progress, we are not developing or progressing equally in brotherhood.

Now, is brotherhood a matter of progress? We know what we mean by "progress." Through time, achieving something, evolution. You understand? The scientists say that we have evolved from the monkey; they say that, through centuries, through millions of years, we have progressed from the lowest animal to the highest, which is man. But is brotherhood a matter of progress? Is it something which can be evolved through time? There is the unity of the family, of the society, of the nation—from the nation to the international and then to the one-world. The one-world state is what we call brotherhood. Is brotherly feeling a matter of time? Is the feeling of brotherhood to be cultivated through time, through the stages of family, community, nation, society, international, one world? Is the feeling of brotherliness, which is love, to be cultivated step by step? Is love a matter of time? You understand what I am talking about? If I say that in ten years, in thirty years, in a hundred years there will be brotherhood, what does that indicate? It indicates that I do not love, I do not feel brotherhood. I wonder if you understand what I am talking about? If I say, "I will be brotherly, I will love," the actual fact is that I do not love, I do not have brotherliness. When I think "I will be," I am not. So, if I can remove this conception of "I will be," I will be brotherly in a hundred years, then I can begin to find out what I am—that I am not brotherly—and I can then begin to work.

Which is important, what I am or what I will be? Surely what is important is what I am because then I can deal with it. But, what I will be is something in the future, and that is unpredictable. The fact is I have no brotherly feeling, I do not love; that is a fact; with that fact I begin and immediately do something about it. But if I say, "I will be something," then it is too vague, then that is idealism. The man with ideals is an individual who is escaping from *what is.* All idealists are people who escape, who run away from the fact which can be altered.

December 21, 1952

Eleventh Talk at Rajghat

You remember that we have been talking about fear. Now, is not fear also responsible for the accumulation of knowledge? This is a difficult subject, and so let us see whether we can go into it very carefully and consider it. As I said just now, fear takes the form of knowledge, and that is why human beings accumulate knowledge and worship knowledge. They think that knowledge is so important in life—knowledge of what has happened, knowledge of what is going to happen, knowledge not only scientific but so-called spiritual knowledge. The whole process of accumulating information gradually becomes a thing which we worship as knowledge. Is that not also from the background of fear? We feel that if we do not know, we would be lost, we would not know how to conduct ourselves, we would not know how to behave. So, gradually through other people's beliefs and experiences, through our own experiences, through book knowledge, through what the sages have said, we gradually build up knowledge which becomes tradition, and behind that tradition, behind that knowledge, we take refuge. We think this knowledge is essential; we feel that without this knowledge, we shall be lost, we shall not know what to do.

Now, when we talk about knowledge, what do we mean by knowledge? What do we know? What do you know when you really consider the knowledge that you have accumulated? What is it? At some level, knowledge is important, such as science, engineering, but beyond that, what is it that we know? Have you ever considered this process of accumulating knowledge? Why is it that you pass examinations, why is it that you study? It is necessary, is it not, at certain levels because without knowledge of mathematics, geography, history, how can one be an engineer or be a scientist? All social contact is built upon such knowledge, and we would not be able to keep on earning a livelihood without it, so that kind of knowledge is essential. Beyond that, what do we know?

As I was saying, knowledge is essential at certain levels of our life in order to live. But beyond that, what is the nature of knowledge? What do we mean when we say that knowledge is necessary to find God, or that knowledge is necessary to know oneself, or that knowledge is essential to find a way through all the turmoils of life? Here, we mean knowledge as experience. What is it that we experience? What is it that we know? Is not this knowledge used by the ego, by the 'me', to strengthen itself? Say, for instance, I have achieved a certain social standing. That experience, the success of it, the prestige of it, the power of it, gives me a certain sense of assurance, of comfort; and so, the knowledge of my success, the knowledge of my being, of having power, my position, the knowledge that I am somebody strengthens the 'me', does it not? So, we use knowledge as a means of strengthening the ego, the 'me'. Have you not noticed the pundits of your father or mother or teacher, how knowledge-puffed they are? How knowledge gives the sense of the expansion of the 'me', the "I know and you do not know; I have experienced more and you have not." So gradually, knowledge, which is merely information, is used for vanity and becomes the sustenance, the food, the nourishment for the ego, for the 'me'. For the ego cannot be without some form of parasitical dependence. The scientist uses his knowledge to feed his vanity, to feel that he is somebody; so does the pundit; so does the teacher; so do the parents; so do the gurus—they all want to be somebody in this world. So, they use knowledge as a means to that, to fulfill that desire, and when you examine, go behind their words, what is there? What is it that they know? They know only what the books contain, or they know what they have experienced, the experiences depending on the background of their conditioning. So, most of us are filled with words, with information which we call knowledge, and without that, we are lost. So, there is fear lurking right behind the screen of words, the screen of information; and this we transform into knowledge as a means of our vocation in life.

So, where there is fear, there is no love, and knowledge without love destroys one. That is what is happening in the world at the present time. For example, people have knowledge of how to feed human beings throughout the world, but they are not doing it. They know how to feed them, clothe them, shelter them, but they are not doing it because each group of people is divided by its nationalistic, egotistic pursuits. If they really had the desire to stop war, they could do so, but they are not doing it for the same reason. So, knowledge without love has no meaning. It is only a means of destruction. Until we understand this, merely to pass examinations or to have a position or prestige or power leads to degeneration, leads to corruption, leads to the slow withering away of human dignity. So, what is important is not only to have knowledge at certain levels—which is essential—but to cultivate this feeling, to see how knowledge is used for egotism, for selfish purposes. Watch how experience is employed as a means of self-expansion, as a means for power, for prestige for oneself. You watch, and you will see how grown-up people in positions cling to their success, cling to their position. They want to build a nest for themselves so that they are powerful, so that they have prestige, position, and authority; and they survive because each one of us wants to do the same, wants to be somebody. You do not want to be yourself, whatever you are, but you want to be somebody.

There is a difference between being and wanting to be. The desire "to be" continues through knowledge which is used for self-aggrandizement, for power, position, prestige. So, what is important is for all of us, for you and me as we are maturing, to see all these problems and to go into them, to see that we do not merely respect a person because he has a title, a name, a position. We know very little. We may have plenty of knowledge of books, but very few have direct experience of anything. It is the direct experiencing of reality, of God, that is of vital importance. And for that, there must be love.

December 22, 1952

Twelfth Talk at Rajghat

Is it not very important, while we are young, to be loved and to love? It seems to me that most of us neither love nor are loved. And I think it is essential, while we are young, to understand this problem very seriously because it may be that while we are young, we can be sensitive enough to feel it, to know its quality, to know its perfume and perhaps, when we grow older, it will not be entirely destroyed. So, let us consider the question—that is, not that you should not be loved, but that you should love. What does it mean? Is it an ideal? Is it something far away, unattainable? Or is it something that can be felt by each one at odd moments of the day? To feel it, to be aware, to know the quality of sympathy, the quality of understanding, to help naturally, to aid another without any motive, to be kind, to be generous, to have sympathy, to care for something, to care for a dog, to be sympathetic to the villager, to be generous to your friend, to be forgiving, is that what we mean by love? Or is love something in which there is no sense of resentment, something which is everlasting forgiveness? And is it not possible while we are young, to feel it? Most of us, while we are young, do feel it—a sense of outward agony, sympathy to the villager, to a dog, to those who are little. And should it not be constantly tended? Should you not always have some part of the day when you are helping another or tending a tree or garden or helping in the house or in the hostel so that as you grow into maturity, you will know what it is to be considerate naturally—not with an enforced considerateness, not with considerateness that is merely a negative word for one's own happiness, but with that considerateness that is without motive. So, should you not, when you are young, know this quality of real affection? It cannot be brought into being; you have to have it, and those who are in charge of you, like your guardian, your parents, your teachers, must also have it. Most people have not got it. They are concerned with their achievements, with their longings, with their success, with their knowledge, and with what they have done. They have built up their past into such colossal importance that it ultimately destroys them.

So, should you not, while you are young, know what it is to take care of the rooms, to care for a number of trees that you yourself dig and plant so that there is a feeling, a subtle feeling of sympathy, of care, of generosity, the actual generosity—not the generosity of the mere mind—that means, you give to somebody the little that you may have? If that is not so, if you do not feel that while you are young, it will be very difficult to feel that when you are old. So, if you have that feeling of love, of generosity, of kindness, of gentleness, then perhaps you can awaken that in others. And that implies, does it not, that sympathy and affection are not the result of fear. But, you see, it is very difficult to grow in this world without fear, without having some personal motive in action. The older generation have never thought about the problem of fear, or if they have thought about it abstractly, generally, they have never applied it actually in daily existence, they have never gone into the problem. If you who are still watching, growing, inquiring, if you do not know what causes fear, you will grow up like them; then, like the weed that is hidden, fear will grow and grow and multiply and twist your mind.

So, what is important is that you should be sensitive to things that are happening around you—how the teachers talk, how your parents behave, and how you behave yourself—so that this question of fear is seen and understood.

You see, most grown-up people think that some kind of discipline is necessary. You know what discipline is? It is the process, the way of making you do something which you do not want to do, a way which you yourself have developed and through which, therefore, you want to achieve a result. Say, for instance, you are in the habit of smoking or chewing pan. What is the way to put an end to it? The way to put an end to the habit is generally called the disciplining of the mind to resist that particular action. That is, I smoke; what is the way of putting an end to it? Or, I chew pan, what is the way by which chewing pan may come to an end? The idea does exist that you must resist chewing pan or you must resist smoking. The resistance creates fear, and because you are afraid, you develop this process of resisting everything. Whereas, if you understood why you smoke, if you went into it, if you thought about it, if you talked about it, if you were aware of it or were helped to be conscious of it, you would see that by constantly watching it, you would not develop fear against this resistance. So discipline is not the way of love.

Where there is discipline, there is fear. And in a place like this, discipline at all costs should be avoided—discipline being coercion, resistance, persuasion, compulsion, the offering to you of a reward, or making you do something which you really do not understand. If you do not understand something, do not do it; do not be compelled to do it. Ask for an explanation; do not be obstinate; try to find out so that your mind becomes very pliable, very subtle, so that there is no fear involved in it. But if you are compelled by grown-up people, by authority, by parents, then you suppress your mind, and fear comes into being, and that fear pursues you like your shadow throughout life. So, do not be disciplined to a particular type of thought or to a particular pattern of action. Older people can only think in those terms. They make you do something for your good. The very making you do something for your good destroys your sensitivity, your capacity to understand, and therefore your love. All this is very difficult because the world about us is so strong; we do things thoughtlessly and we fall into a habit, and then it is very difficult for us to break away from it.

Should you, in a place like this, have authority? Or should you go to your teachers, discuss these problems, go into them, understand them, so that as you grow up and leave this place, you do so as an intelligent human being who is capable of meeting the world's problems? You cannot have that intelligence if there is any kind of fear. Fear only makes you obstinate, fear curbs you, fear destroys that thing which we call sympathy, generosity, affection, love. So, be very careful not to be disciplined into a pattern of action but find out—which means, you must have the time, and the teacher must have the time; if there is no time, then time must be made because fear is more important than any examination or any degree, because fear is a source of corruption and is the beginning of degeneration.

Question: What is love in its own self?

KRISHNAMURTI: What is intrinsic love? What do you mean? What is love without motive, without an incentive? Listen carefully, you will find out. We are examining the question, but not to find out the answer. You know, in your studies in mathematics or in putting a question, most of you want an answer. You are mostly concerned with the answer, not with the problem. If you understand the problem, if you study it, look into it, examine it, analyze it, the answer is in the problem. So, we are going to find out what the answer is in understanding what the problem is, not in looking for an answer at the end of the book or looking for an answer in the Bhagavad-Gita or in the Bible or in the Koran or in some sacred book or from some professor or lecturer. If we look at the problem, the answer will come out of it. A fruit cannot come into being without the tree, but what we do generally is to look for the fruit of the tree without understanding the whole structure of the tree, without understanding how the tree grows. The fruit is a part of the tree; they are not two separate things. Similarly, in the problem is the answer; the answer is not separate from the problem. Do not merely wait for an answer. The answers to your mathematical problems are in your personal effort, in your inquiry, in your search to understand the problems. In your looking at the problem, you will find out the right answer.

The problem now is: What is love without motive? Can there be love without any incentive, without taking something for oneself out of love? Can there be love in which there is no hurt, in which there is no sense of being wounded when love is not returned? Can there be love when you give and do not receive? When you give, are you not hurt when the person does not return? When I offer you my friendship, you turn away and then I am hurt; is that hurt the outcome of my friendship, the outcome of my generosity, the outcome of my sympathy? So, as long as there is hurt, as long as there is fear, as long as I am doing something in order to help you, in order that you may help me—which is called service—then you will see that the motive is not love. If you understand this, the answer is there.

Question: What is religion?

KRISHNAMURTI: Do you want to find out an answer from me, or do you want to find out the truth of what religion is? Are you looking for an answer from somebody, however great, however stupid? Or, are you trying to find out the truth of what true religion is?

If you try to find out what true religion is, then what have you to do? You must push away everything. If I have many colored windows, dirty windows, and I want to see the clear sunshine, if I want to know what real light is, I must clean the windows, or I must open the windows and go outside. Similarly, you want to find out what true religion is. Then you must find out what it is not. To find out or discover what it is not, you have to approach it in negation—that is, like opening the window. You must first find out what it is not, and then put that aside. Then, you can find out; then, you are in direct perception.

We are going to find out what true religion is, so let us find out first what it is not. Is ritual, puja, religion? You repeat over and over again a certain ritual, a certain mantram in front of an idol. It may give you a sense of pleasure, a sense of satisfaction; is that religion? Is putting on the sacred thread religion? Obviously, it cannot be. So, we have to find out whether calling yourself a Buddhist, a Christian, a Hindu, and accepting a certain tradition, dogma, ritual, is religion. Obviously it is not. So, religion must be something which can only be found when the mind has understood and put aside all this. Religion is not the outcome of separation, is it? You are a Muslim, I am a Christian, I believe in something, you do not believe in it. Your belief has nothing to do with religion, as such. Whether you believe in God or I do not believe in God has nothing to do with it because your belief is conditioned by your society, is it not? The society round you imprints your beliefs, your fears, and appeals to your mind to believe in certain things. The belief has nothing to do with religion. You believe in one way and I in another way because I happen to be born in England, Russia or America. Belief is only the result of conditioning. Therefore, it has nothing to do with religion.

Is the pursuit of personal salvation religion? I want to be safe; I want to reach nirvana or *moksha* or salvation; I must find a place next to Jesus, next to Buddha, next to a particular God. Your religion is not a thing that gives me deep satisfaction or comfort, so I have my religion. Your mind must be free from all these things, and then only will you find out what true religion is.

Is religion merely doing good or doing service or helping another? Or is it something more—which does not mean that we must not be generous or kind. But is that all? Is it something much greater, much cleaner, vaster, more expansive than any mere conception of the mind? To understand what is true religion, you must know all these things. It is like going out into the sunshine; then, I will not ask what is true religion; then, I will know; then there will be the direct experience of that which is true.

Question: Suppose somebody is unhappy and wants to become happy. Is it ambition?

KRISHNAMURTI: Did you listen to what was being said before? You do not listen. If you knew how to listen, really, to what was being said, you would have found what is true religion immediately. It is like somebody saying to you, "Go and open the door, and you will know what is sunshine." Sitting in the room and being lazy, you do not want to move, so you say, "Please tell me what the sunshine is, and I shall listen very carefully." But, I say, "Go to the door and open it, you will know without asking." If you have really listened to that, you will have gone to the door and seen the sunshine. That is the beauty of listening so completely that you have already opened the door and are in the sunshine.

The lady asks, "If I want to help somebody who is in sorrow, is that ambition?" If somebody is unhappy and he wants to become happy, is that ambition? Is truth ambition? I am unhappy, my father or my son is dead, I am starving, I am unhappy. To be in sorrow, to have pain, to have physical pain, to have emotional pain, inward pain or outward pain, the loss of somebody whom I think I love—all this we know. What is the process of becoming happy? Do you understand? Can I ever know when I am happy? I can only know when I have been happy. I can never know the moment in which I am happy. I can only know happiness when it is finished, like pleasure. At the moment of pleasure, you are not aware of it. Only a second after, you say, "How happy, pleasurable it was." You say, "I am suffering, I want to end my suffering." Is that ambition? That is a natural instinct of every person; that is not ambition. So, is it not the natural instinct of all of us not to have fear, not to have pain physically or emotionally? But life is such that you are constantly receiving pain. I eat something and it does not suit me, I have a tummy ache. Somebody says something to me and I get hurt. I want to do something which somebody prevents, and I feel frustrated, I feel miserable. So, life is constantly acting upon me, whether I like it or not—which is hurting, which is frustrating, which is reacting as pain. Is it not so? So what I have to do is to understand it. But I run away from it.

You see, what happens is: I suffer inwardly, I go to somebody, I run away from my feeling of suffering—I read a book, or turn on the radio, or I go and do puja. All these are indications of my running away from suffering. If you run away from something, obviously you do not understand it. In looking at it, you begin to understand the problem involved in it, and the search for the understanding of the problem is not ambition. But it will become ambition when you want to run away from it, when you cling to it, when you fight it out, when round it you gradually build theories and hopes. So, in a more subtle way, the thing to which you begin to run becomes important. The very thing becoming important is the self-identification with it, the identification of yourself with it, yourself with your country, with your position, with your God; and this is a form of ambition.

December 23, 1952

Thirteenth Talk at Rajghat

Perhaps, what we have been discussing for the last two weeks may be approached from a different point of view. You know what I am saying is not a thing to be remembered. You know what "remembering" is? It is to try to store in your mind what you have heard or what you have seen or what you have read to be recollected, and either to be thought of or to be followed. But we are not doing that here. You are not trying to remember what I was telling you. If you remember what I was telling you, it will be merely memory; it won't be a living thing. This is not like a class where you take notes while you listen. That is only to make you remember what you have heard; and what you have heard, if you remember it merely, is not something that you understand. It is the understanding that matters, not remembrance. I hope you see the difference between remembering and understanding. Understanding is something immediate, direct, something which you experience intensively. But if you merely remember what you have heard during these mornings, it will act as a guide, something to be compared, something to be followed, a slogan, the remembrance of an idea which should be followed, which should be imitated, which should act as a guide, as an example, something on which to base your lives. But understanding is something which you do not remember. It is a continuous, constant pressure.

So, if you understand what I have been talking about—understand, not remember—then you will see that your action, what you are doing, is in relation with your understanding. If you remember, you will try to compare your action or modify it or adjust your action to what you remember. But if you understand, that very understanding is bringing about action, and you do not have to act according to your remembrance. That is why it is very important to listen, not to remember, but to understand immediately.

If you remember certain sentences, certain feelings that are awakened here, certain phrases, certain words, you will try to compare your action with what you remember. So, there will always be a gap between what you remember and your action. But if you understand, there is no copying. So, it is very important, vitally important, to see that you really understand. Any fool can remember; anybody with certain capacities can pass an examination because he remembers, but if you understand the things involved in what you see, in what you hear, in what you feel, that very understanding brings about action which you have not got to guide, shape, control. If you remember, you will always be comparing, and comparison breeds envy. Our whole society is based on that structure of envy and acquisitiveness. So, mere comparison with what you remember will not help to bring about understanding. In understanding there is love. This is not mere intellectualization which is a mental thought, a mental process in which you are comparing, in which you are imitating, in which you follow, in which there is always the danger of the leader and the led. Do you understand that?

In this world, the structure of society is based on the leader and the led, the example and the one who follows the example, the hero and the worshipper of the hero. If you go behind this process of following and being the led, you will see that where you follow, there is no initiative, there is no freedom for you or for the leader because you shape the leader, you control the leader as the leader controls you. If you are following examples—examples of self-sacrifice, examples of greatness, examples of success, examples of love—then those examples become the ideals which are to be remembered and followed, so you have, between the ideal and the action, a gap, a division. A man who really understands this has no ideal, he has no example, he is not following anybody; for him, there is no guru, no mahatma, no historical leaders because he is constantly understanding what he hears, whether it is from the father or mother or from the teacher or from a person like myself who comes into his life occasionally.

You are now listening; you are understanding and not following. You are not imitating here; therefore, there is no fear, and so there is love.

So, it is very important to see this very clearly for yourselves so that you are not bewitched, mesmerized by heroes, by examples, by ideals. Examples, heroes, ideals, and the things that are remembered are soon forgotten. Therefore, there has to be a constant reminder by a picture, by an ideal, by a slogan. If you have an ideal, an example, then you are following; that is merely remembering. In that remembrance, there is no understanding. It is only comparing 'what you are' to 'what you want to be'. That very comparison breeds envy and fear; and that comparison breeds authority in which there is no love. Please understand all this, hear all this very carefully so that you have no leaders, no examples, no ideals to imitate, to follow, to copy, so that you are a free human being with dignity. You cannot be free if you are everlastingly comparing yourself with the ideal, with what you should be. If you understand what you are, however ugly, however beautiful, however frightened, actually what you are, that does not demand remembrance; remembrance is merely recollection. But, to watch, to be aware, to be conscious of what you actually are, is the process of understanding, and this is not a process of recollection, it is not a way of remembrance.

If you really understood what I am talking about, listened to it completely, then you would be free of all the things that past generations have created which are utterly false and have no significance; you will have no recollection which only cripples the mind and the heart, which breeds fear and envy. If you really understand what I am talking about, you will listen. Unconsciously, you may be listening very deeply; I hope you are. Then you will see what an extraordinary power it brings, that comes with listening, with freedom from remembrance.

Question: Is beauty a subjective quality or objective?

KRISHNAMURTI: Why do you ask that question? To write an essay on it? You know, in school and at college you are asked to write essays, and so, what do you do? You collect, you read books and, like squirrels, collect ideas from books, from other people and put all these ideas together and put them on paper and pass it on to the examiner. Is that why you are asking? Please listen. Or, do you really want to know whether beauty is subjective or objective? Do you really want to understand, to find out, not to remember and say, "Yes, that is what he said," or "It is true or wrong?" If you really want to understand it, not merely remember it, then, let us proceed.

You see something beautiful, the river from the veranda; if you are not sensitive, then you pass it by. You see a child in tatters, crying; if you do not appreciate things about you, if you are not aware of things around you, then that is of very little value. There is a woman carrying a weight on her head with dirty clothes, starving, tired; do you see the beauty of her walk or feel the sensitivity of her state, the color of her sari, however dirty it is? There are objective influences that are all about you; if you have not that sensitivity, you will never appreciate them, will you? If you are sensitive, you are aware not only of the things which you call beautiful but also of the things called ugly—to see the river, the green field and the trees from the distance, the clouds of the evening, or to observe the dirty villagers, the half starved people with very little thought, very little feeling, with dirty clothes. The one we call beautiful and the other we call ugly. If you are listening, you will see that what is important in this is that you cling to the beautiful, to the everlasting, you watch the beautiful, but you shut yourself away from the ugly. Is it not important to be sensitive to both, to what you call beautiful and to what you call ugly? It is the lack of that sensitivity that divides life into the ugly and the beautiful. But if you are sensitive, receptive, capable of appreciating both what is called ugly and what is beautiful, then you will find their significance—that they are full of meaning, that they give enrichment to life.

So, is beauty subjective or objective? If you were blind, if you were deaf, if you did not hear any music, would you miss beauty? Or, is beauty something inward? You may not see, you may not hear, but the feeling, that extraordinary feeling of being open, of appreciating everything even though you do not hear or you do not see, to be aware inwardly of all the things that are happening inside you, to every thought, to every feeling—is that not also beauty, is that not also subjective? But you see, we think beauty is something outside. That is why we buy pictures, hang them up on the wall. We want beautiful saris, beautiful trousers, coats, turbans; we want to have everything outside of us, for we are afraid that without a reminder, we shall lose something inwardly. Can you divide life, the whole process of existence, of living, as subjective or objective? Is it not a wrong thing to divide life into the subjective and the objective? It is a double process, is it not? It is a complete process; without the outside, there is no inside; without the inside, there is no outside.

Question: Why is it that a strong man suppresses the weak?

KRISHNAMURTI: Do you suppress? Find out. Why do you, in argument, in physical strength, push away your brother younger than yourself, the smaller one? Why? Because you want to assert yourself, because you want to show your strength, you begin to assert, you begin to dominate, you begin to push the little child away; you begin to throw your weight about because you want to show how much stronger, how much better, how much more powerful you are. It is the same thing with older people; they know a few more details from books, they have positions, they have money, they have got authority; and so they suppress, they push you aside, and you accept being pushed aside because you also want to suppress somebody below you. So, the top people suppress you, and you suppress those who are below you. Each one wants to assert, to dominate, to show power over others. The very showing of power gives you satisfaction, the feeling that you are somebody, because most of you do not want to be nothing, you want to be somebody.

Question: Then, why do the bigger fish want to swallow the smaller fish?

KRISHNAMURTI: Because, they want to live. The little fish live on the tiny fish, and the little fish are lived on by bigger fish. In the animal world, it may be perhaps natural. It may be you cannot alter it—the big fish living on the small fish. But the human big fish need not live on the human little fish. If you know how to use your intelligence, you can avoid living on each other, not only for physical, but also for psychological reasons, for inward reasons. If you see this problem, if you understand it, which is, to have intelligence, then you will not live on another. But you want to live on another, so you live on somebody who is weaker than you. Freedom does not mean that you are free to do anything you like. Freedom can only be where there is intelligence, and intelligence can only come through the understanding of the relationship of you and me and all of us together with somebody else.

Question: Is it true that scientific discoveries make our lives easy to live?

KRISHNAMURTI: Have they not made life easier? You have electricity, have you not? You use the switch and you have light. There is a telephone in that room, and you can listen, if you want, to New York or to your friend in Banaras; is that not easy? Or, you can get into a plane and go to Delhi or New York. These are all scientific discoveries and they have made life easier. Science has also given you the atom bomb which can destroy human beings. Science has not only helped to destroy human beings, but it has also helped to cure diseases. But if we do not use scientific knowledge with intelligence, with love, we are going to destroy ourselves because science is now discovering more and more, and there are atomic bombs which will destroy human beings. That is, using knowledge without love, we destroy each other, though science helps to make life easy.

Question: What is death?

KRISHNAMURTI: What is death? This question from a little girl! You know, you see dead bodies being carried to the river; you have seen dead birds, dead leaves, dead trees, fruits that wither away, decay. Have you not seen the birds that are full of life, chattering away in the morning, calling to each other in the morning? In the evening, they may not be; they wither, they die. The person who lives in the morning may be carried away by disaster and be dead in the evening. We have seen all this. Death is common to all of us. We will all end that way. You may live for thirty or forty years crying, suffering, fearful, and at the end of forty or fifty years, you are no more.

What is death and what is living? It is really a complex problem, and I do not know if you want to go into it. What is it we call living, and what is it that we call death? If I know, if I can understand what living is, then I can understand what death is. Either one is frightened or one does not understand it. Or, one has lost somebody whom one loves and feels bereft, lonely; and therefore that has nothing to do with living. You separate death from living. Is death separate from life? Is not living a process of dying?

For most of us, living means what? It means accumulating, choosing, suffering, laughing. At the background of it all, behind all pleasure and pain, there is fear—the fear of coming to an end, the fear of what is going to happen tomorrow. Please listen, ask your teachers afterwards what I am talking about, question them, find out. So, behind this, there is fear—fear of not being with name and fame, with property, with position which you want to continue. So, you say what happens after death? What is death, and what is it that comes to an end? Life?

What is life? Is life merely breathing in oxygen and expelling it, is that life? Feeding, hating, loving, possessing, acquiring, being envious, comparing—that is what we know of life. For most of us, life is the constant battle that we have of pain and pleasure and suffering. Can that come to an end? Should we not die? In the autumn, the leaves on trees fall; in the cold weather the leaves drop and they reappear in the spring. So also should we not die to everything of yesterday, to all the accumulations, to all the hopes, to all the successes that we have gathered? Should we not die to all that and relive again tomorrow so that we are fresh, like a new leaf, tender and sensitive? To such a man who is constantly dying, there is no death. But to a man who says, "I am somebody, I must continue," to him there is always death and the burning ghat; that man knows no love.

December 24, 1952

Fourteenth Talk at Rajghat

Perhaps what I am going to talk about this morning may be rather difficult, and if you do not understand all the implications in it, perhaps you would, if you are inclined, discuss it with your teachers and get more out of it by talking it over together.

There are various factors, various feelings, various ways in which human beings deteriorate. You know what it is to deteriorate, to disintegrate? What does it mean to integrate? To bring together, to be complete—that is, to be integrated so that your feelings, your body, are entirely one, in one direction, not in contradiction with each other, so that you are a whole human being without conflict. That is what is implied by integration. To disintegrate is the opposite—that is, to go to pieces, to scatter away that which has been put together, to tear asunder. There are many ways in which human beings destroy themselves, disintegrate, go to pieces. I think one of the major factors is the feeling of envy, which is so subtle, which is regarded under different names—as something worthwhile, something beneficial, something which is creditable in human endeavor.

You know what envy is? It begins when you are very small—to be envious of your friend who looks better than you, who has better things than you, who has a better position than you; to be jealous if he is better than you in class, if he has got more marks, if he has better parents, if he belongs to a more distinguished family. So, jealousy begins at a very tender age and gradually takes on the form of competition—to get better marks, to be a better athlete, to do something distinguished, to be more significant, more worthwhile, to outdo, to outshine others. It begins when you are very young at school, and as you grow older, it gets stronger and stronger—the envy of the rich to be richer, the envy of the poor to be rich, the envy of those who have had experience and who want more experience, the envy of those who write and want to write still better. The very desire to be better, to be more, to be something worthwhile, to have more experience is the process of acquisitiveness—to acquire, to gather, to hold. If you notice, the instinct in most of us is to acquire in order to get more and more saris, more and more clothes, more and more houses, more and more property. If it is not that, as you grow older, you want more experience, to have more knowledge, to feel that you know more than anybody else, that you have read much more than another, or that you are nearer to some big official higher up in government; or spiritually, inwardly, to know that you have greater experience than another, to inwardly be conscious that you are humble, that you are virtuous, that you can explain and others cannot. So, the more you acquire, the greater the disintegration. The more lands, the more property you acquire, the more fame, the more experience, the more knowledge you gather, the greater the disintegration. You desire to acquire more; from this springs the universal disease of jealousy, of envy. Have you not noticed this not only in yourself but in the older people about you—how the teacher wants to be a professor, how the professor wants to be the principal, or how your own father and mother want to have more property, a bigger name? In the process of struggle in acquiring, you become cruel. In that acquisition, there is no love; in that way of life, you are in constant battle with your neighbor, with society. There is constant fear, and this is justified. So, we accept it as inevitable that we must be jealous, that we must acquire—though we give it a different name, a better sounding name than just acquisition or creating envy. We call it evolution, growing, struggling; and we say that it is essential. But, you see, most of us are unconscious of all this; most of us are unaware that we are greedy, that we are acquisitive, that our hearts are being eaten away by envy, that our minds are deteriorating. When we do become aware of it, we justify it or say that is wrong or try to run away.

So, envy is a very difficult thing to uncover or to discover because the mind is the center of that envy. The mind is envious. The structure of the mind is built on acquisition and envy. Look at your thoughts, for example, at the way you are thinking. The way of thinking is generally the way of mere comparison—"I can explain better, I have greater memories." The 'more' is the working of the mind. You understand, that is its way of existence. Cut it off and you will see what happens to the mind. If you cannot think in terms of the 'more', you will find it extremely difficult to think. So, the 'more' is the comparative process of thought which creates time—time to become, to be somebody. So, this is the process of envy, of acquisition—the thinking comparatively: "I am this and I would be, some day, that; I am ugly, but I am going to be beautiful some day." So, acquisitiveness, envy, comparative thinking produces discontent, restlessness. In contrast to that, we say we must be contented, we must be content with what we have; that is what people say who are on the top of the ladder. Universal religions preach contentment.

Contentment is not a contrast, the opposite of acquisitiveness, as it is generally understood. Contentment is something which is much vaster and much more significant than the opposite of acquisitiveness, than the opposite of envy—which is to become a vegetable, a dead entity, as most people are. Most people are very quiet, but inwardly they are dead, and because they have cultivated this feeling of the opposite, the opposite to everything that they are, they say, "I am envious and I must not be envious." In contrast to the everlasting struggle of envy, you may deny all that you are, you may say you are not going to acquire, you may say you are going to wear a loincloth. But this very desire to be good, this very desire to pursue the opposite is still in time, in the vision of envy, in the feeling of envy; you still want to be something. But contentment is not that. Contentment is something much more creative, something more profound. Contentment is not when you choose to be content; contentment does not come that way. Contentment comes when you understand what you are, what you actually are, and not what you should be.

You think contentment comes when you achieve all that you want. You want to be a collector or the greatest saint, and you think you will have contentment by that. So, through the process of envy, you hope to arrive at contentment. That is, through a wrong process, you want to achieve the right result. Contentment is not that. Contentment is something very vital. It is a state of creativeness in which the understanding of what actually is, exists. If you understand what you are actually, from moment to moment, from day to day, then, if you pursue that, if you understand that, you will see that out of it comes an extraordinary feeling of vastness, of limitless comprehension. That is, if I am greedy, I want to understand that, not how to become nongreedy; the very desire to become nongreedy is still greed.

Our religious structure, our ways of thinking, our social life, everything, is based on acquisitiveness, on an envious system; and for centuries, we have been brought up like that. We are so conditioned that we cannot think apart from the 'better', the 'more'. Because we cannot think apart from that, we make envy into a virtue; we do not call it envy; we call it by a different name, but if you go behind the words and look at it, you will see this extraordinary feeling is egotistic, which is self-inclusive, which is limiting thought.

The mind that is limited by envy, by the 'me', by acquisitiveness of things or of virtue, such a mind can never be a truly religious mind. The religious mind is not a comparative mind. The religious mind sees *what is* and understands the full significance behind it. That is why it is very important to understand yourself, to understand the workings of your mind, the motives, the intentions, the longings, the desires, the constant pressures of pursuance, which create envy, acquisitiveness, the comparative mind. It is only when all these come to an end that you really understand *what is;* then, you will know true religion, what God is.

Question: Is truth relative or absolute?

KRISHNAMURTI: First of all, let us look behind the meaning and significance of that question. We want something absolute, don't we, something permanent, fixed, immovable, eternal, something definite. The human craving is for something permanent, something that is not decaying, that has no death, so that the mind can cling to an idea or to a feeling that is everlasting. Or the mind seeks the absolute, something that does not die, that does not decay as thought does, as feeling does. Or the mind says, "Is there something permanent?" First, we must understand all this before we can understand this question and answer it rightly.

The mind, the human mind, wants something permanent in everything—in relationship, in my father, in my wife, in my husband, in my property, in virtue—something which cannot be destroyed, and so we say God is permanent, or truth is absolute. What is truth? Is truth something extraordinary, something beyond, outside, unimaginable, abstract? Or, is truth something which you discover from moment to moment, from day to day? If it is something to be accumulated, to be gathered through your experiences, then it is not truth because the same spirit of acquisitiveness lies behind this gathering. Is truth something which lies beyond, which can only be found through profound meditation? Then there is a process of acquisitiveness and also, at the same time, a process of denial, of sacrifice.

Truth is something to be understood, to be discovered in every action, in every thought, in every feeling, however trivial, however transient; truth is something to be looked at, to be listened to—as to what the husband says or what the wife says or what the gardener says or what your friends say or what your own thinking is. To discover the truth of what you think—because your thoughts may be false or your thoughts may be conditioned—to discover that your thought is conditioned is truth. To discover that your thought is limited is truth; that very discovery sets your mind free from limitation. If I discover that I am greedy—discover it, not be told by you that I am greedy—that very discovery is truth; that very truth has an action upon my greed. Truth is not something which is gathered, accumulated, stored up, upon which you can rely as a guide. If you do, it is only another form of the same thing, another form of possession. It is very difficult for the mind not to acquire, not to store. When you realize this, you will find out what an extraordinary thing truth is. It is timeless because the moment you capture it, it is not truth—as when you say, "It is mine," "I have found it," "It is so," "It is not so."

So, it depends on the mind whether truth is absolute or timeless. Because, the absolute is unchangeable, and the mind that says, "I want the absolute, that which has no death, that which is never decaying," such a mind wants something permanent and creates the permanent. But a mind that is being aware of everything that is happening inwardly and sees the truth of it, such a mind is timeless; such a mind only can know what is beyond words, beyond names, beyond the permanent and the impermanent.

Question: What is external awareness?

KRISHNAMURTI: Are you not aware that you are sitting in this hall? Are you not aware of the trees, of the sunshine? Are you not aware that the crow is cawing, the birds are calling, the dog is barking? Do you not see the color of the flowers, the movement of the leaves, the people walking? That is external awareness. The stars at night, the moonlight on the water, the sunset, the birds, all that is external awareness, is it not? And if you are thus externally aware, you are also inwardly aware of your thoughts, inwardly aware of your feelings, of your motives, of your urges, your prejudices, envies, greed, pride, and so on. Are you not aware inwardly? The inward awareness begins to awaken, to become more and more conscious, through reaction—the reaction to what people say, the reaction to what you read. The reaction, the response of your relationship with other people, may be external, but that response is the outcome of an inward suspense, an inward anxiety, an inward fear. The outward awareness and the inward awareness bring about a total integration of human understanding.

Question: What is real and eternal happiness?

KRISHNAMURTI: As I said the other day, when you are conscious of anything, conscious that it is so, what happens? Let me put it differently. When are you conscious? When are you aware of something? When are you conscious that you are ill, that you have a tummy ache? When you are completely healthy, you are totally unconscious of your body. It is only when there is disease, when there is friction, when there is trouble, that you become conscious of it. If you have a perfectly healthy body, are you aware of it? It is only when you have some kind of pain that you are conscious that you have a body. When you are really free to think completely, then there is no consciousness of thinking. It is only when there is friction, when there is a blockage, a limit, that you begin to feel, that you become conscious. Is happiness something of which you are aware? When you are healthy, are you aware that you are healthy? When you are joyous, are you aware that you are joyous? It is only when you are unhappy that you want happiness. Therefore, the question arises, what is permanent and eternal happiness?

You see how the mind plays tricks. Because you are unhappy, miserable, because you are in poor circumstances and so on, you want something which is eternal, some permanent happiness. Is there such a thing? Instead of asking the question whether there is permanent happiness, find out how to be free from the diseases which are gnawing at you, how to be free from pain, not only the physical, but the inward. When you are free, there is no problem of whether there is eternal happiness or what that happiness is. It is like a man who is in prison. He wants to know what freedom is, and lazy, foolish people tell him what freedom is, and to the man in prison, it is mere speculation. If he knew how to get out of that prison, he would not ask what freedom is; it would be there. Similarly, is it not important to find out why it is that we are unhappy, and in what is happiness? Why is it our minds are so crippled? Why is it that our thoughts are so limited, so small, so petty? If you can understand that, see the truth of that, then there is liberation, and that liberation is the discovery of the limited thought, and that discovery is the truth and that truth liberates.

Question: Why do people want things?

KRISHNAMURTI: Don't you want food when you are hungry? Don't you want clothes, don't you want a house to shelter you? Those are normal wants, are they not? Healthy people naturally have wants. It is only the diseased man that says, "I do not want food." It is a perverted mind that either must have many houses or no house to live in.

Your body is hungry because you are using energy, so it wants more food; that is normal. But if you say, "I must have the tastiest food, I must have the food that I like, that my tongue takes pleasure in," then there is perversion taking place. We all must have—not only the rich, but everybody in the world must have—food, shelter, and clothing; but if shelter, food, and clothing are limited, controlled and divided among the few, then there is perversion, and there is the unnatural process set going. At the physical level, we must have food, clothing, and shelter, not only for you, but for the villager; but if you say, "I must accumulate, I must have everything," then you are depriving others of that which is essential for their daily needs. But you see it is not so simple as that because we want other things than those which are essential for our daily needs. I may not want too many clothes; I may be satisfied with a few clothes, with a small room, though you may want to live in a house and not in a small room, but I want something more—I want to be a well-known person, I want to have an enormous amount of money, I want to be nearest to God, I want my friends to think well of me, I want to be well-known, I want to be a poet, I want money, many things other than merely the physical necessities. Inward wants prevent outward interests in every human being. It is a little difficult because the inward wants and the feeling that "I am the richest man," "I am the most powerful man," "I want to be somebody," and so on are made dependent on things, on food, clothes, shelter; I lean on those things in order to become inwardly rich; therefore, so long as I am in this state, it is not possible for me to be inwardly rich, to be utterly simple inwardly.

December 25, 1952

Fifteenth Talk at Rajghat

Perhaps, some of you were interested in what I was saying yesterday about envy. I am not using the word *remember* because as I have explained, remembrance, remembering the word or phrases only, makes the mind dull, lethargic, heavy, slow, and so very uncreative. It is very destructive merely to remember things. But what is very important while we are young, in spite of modern education, is to understand and not to cultivate memory because understanding frees, understanding brings the critical faculty of analysis; you see the fact and then perhaps rationalize it. But merely remembering certain phrases and sentences or certain ideas prevents you from looking at the fact of jealousy, at the fact of envy. If you understand envy—which lurks behind good works, behind philanthropy, behind religion, behind your pursuit to be great, to be saintly—if you really understand that, then you will see that there is an extraordinary freedom from jealousy.

As I was saying, it is important, really important, to understand because remembrance is a dead thing, and perhaps also that is one of the major causes of our deterioration, especially in this country where we imitate, copy, follow, create ideals, heroes, so that gradually the picture, the symbol, the word remains, the phrase remains, without anything behind it. This is especially so in modern education which merely prepares you to pass certain examinations—which is, merely to memorize. This is not creative; this is not understanding but merely remembering things that you have read in books, that you have been taught, and so throughout life, gradually memory is cultivated and real understanding is destroyed. Please listen to this very carefully because it is very important to understand this. Understanding is creative, not memory, not remembrance. Understanding is the liberating factor, not memory of the things that you have stored up. Understanding is not something in the future. The cultivation of memory brings to you the idea of the future, but if you understand directly, that is, if you see something very clearly, then there is no problem; the problem exists only when we do not see clearly.

As I was saying, what is important in life is not what you know, what you have gathered, how much knowledge or how much experience you have. What is really important is to understand, to see things as they are, and to see them immediately because comprehension is immediate. That is why experience and knowledge become deteriorating factors in life. For most of us, experience is very important; for most of us, knowledge is very significant, but when you really go behind the words and see the significance, the meaning of knowledge, the meaning of experience, you will find it is one of the major facts of deterioration. This does not mean that it is not right at certain levels of life, at certain levels of existence—to know how to grow a tree, to know what kind of nourishment it should have, how to feed the chickens, how to raise the family properly, how to build a bridge. There is an enormous amount of knowledge with regard to science which is right; for example, it is right that we should know how to run a dynamo or a motor, but when knowledge is merely memory, it is destructive; you will find experience also becomes a very destructive thing because experience brings memory.

I do not know if you have noticed how certain grown-up people think merely bureaucratically as officials. They are teachers and their only function is to be teachers, not to be human beings pulsating with life; they know certain rules of grammar or mathematics or history, and because of their memory, their experience, that knowledge is destroying them. Life is not a thing that you learn from somebody. Life is a thing that you listen to, that you understand from moment to moment without accumulating experience. Because, after all, what have you got when you have experience, when you say, "I have had an enormous amount of experience," when you say, "I know the meaning of those words"? Memory, is it not? You have had certain experiences, how to run an office, how to put up a building or bridge, and according to them, you have further experience. So, you cultivate experience and that experience is memory; and with that memory you meet life.

Life is like the river—running, swift, volatile, never still. You meet life with the heavy burden of memory, of experience; naturally, you never contact life. You are only meeting your own experience which only strengthens your knowledge, and gradually, knowledge and experience become the most destructive factors in life.

I hope you understand this very deeply because what I am saying is very true, and if you understand it, you will use knowledge at its proper level. But when you merely accumulate knowledge and experience as a means to understand life, as a means to strengthen your position in the world, then it becomes most destructive, it destroys your initiative, your creativeness. In this world, especially here, most of us are so burdened with authority or with what people have said or with the Bhagavad-Gita or with ideals, that our lives have become very dull. But these are all memories, remembrances; they are not things that are understood, that are living; there is no new thing in being burdened with those memories, and as life is everlastingly new, we cannot understand it, and therefore living becomes a burdensome thing; we are lethargic; we grow mentally and physically fat and ugly. It is very important to understand this.

Simplicity is the freedom of the mind from experience, from remembering, from memory. We think simplicity is to have a few clothes, a begging bowl; we think that a simple life is externally to have very little. That may be all right, but real simplicity is the freedom from knowledge, from remembering that knowledge, or from accumulating experience. Have you not noticed people who have very little, those people who say they are very simple? Though they may have only a loincloth and a staff, they are all full of ideals. Have you listened to them? Have you heard them? They are very complex inwardly, struggling, battling against their own projections, their own beliefs. They believe; they have many beliefs. Inwardly, they are very complex, they are not simple; they are full of books, they are full of ideals, dogmas, fears. But outwardly, they have only a staff and a few clothes. The simplicity of real life is to be inwardly completely empty, to be innocent inwardly without the accumulation of knowledge, without belief, without dogmas, without the fear of authority; and that can only take place if you really understand every experience. If you have understood an experience, then that experience is over, but because we do not understand it, because we remember the pleasure or the pain of it, we are never inwardly simple. So those who are religiously inclined pursue the things that make for outward simplicity, but inwardly, they are chaotic, confused, burdened with innumerable longings, desires, knowledge; they are frightened of living, of experiencing.

When you look at all this, you will see that envy is a very deep-rooted form of remembering, it is a very destructive factor, it is a very deteriorating thing; so likewise, is experience. The man who is full of experience is not a wise man. Please listen. The man who has experience and clings to that experience is not a wise man; he is like any schoolboy who reads, who has accumulated information from books; such a man is not a wise man. A wise man is innocent, inwardly free of experience; such a man is a simple man inwardly, though he may have all the things of the earth or very little.

Question: Does intelligence build up character?

KRISHNAMURTI: What do you mean by "character"? Please listen very carefully to everything that is being said, both to the question and to the answer.

What do we mean by "character"? What do we mean by "intelligence"? Let us find out what we mean by these two words. We use these words very freely. Every politician from Delhi or your own local tub-thumper uses them—character, ideal, intelligence, religion, God. These are words and we listen to them with rapt attention because they seem very important. We live on words, and the more elaborate, the more exquisite the words we use, the more we are satisfied. Let us find out what we mean by intelligence and what we mean by character. Do not say I am not answering you definitely. That is one of the tricks of the mind; that means, you are definitely not understanding and you just want to follow words.

What is intelligence? Is a man who is frightened, anxious, envious, greedy; whose mind is copying, imitating, filled with other people's experiences and knowledge; whose mind is limited, controlled, shaped by society, by environment—is such a man an intelligent man? You call him an intelligent man, but he is not, is he? Can such a man who is frightened, who is not intelligent, have character—character being something original, not the mere repeating of traditional do's and don't's? Is character respectability? Do you understand what respectability means? To be respected by the majority, to be respected by the people about you. What do the people of the family respect, what do the people of the mass respect? They respect the things which they themselves project, which they themselves want, which they themselves see in contrast. That is, you are respected because you are rich or powerful or big, because you are well-known politically, because you have written books; you may talk utter nonsense, but when you have talked, people say you are a big man. As you know people, as you win the respect of the many, the following of the multitude gives you a sense of respectability which is the 'being safe'. The sinner is nearer to God than the respectable man because the respectable man is enclosed by hypocrisy.

Is character the outcome of imitation, the outcome of what people will say or won't say? Is character the result of the mere strengthening of one's own prejudiced tendencies, the following of the tradition of India or of Europe or of America? That is generally called character—to be a strong man, to be respected. But when you are imitating, when you are frightened, is there intelligence, is there character? When you are imitating, following, worshipping, when you have ideals which you are following, that way leads to respectability, but not to understanding. A man of ideals is a respectable man, but he will never be near God, he will never know what it is to love. Ideals are a means to cover up his fear, his imitations, his loneliness.

So, without understanding yourself—how you think, whether you are copying, whether you are imitating, whether you are frightened, whether you are envious, whether you are seeking power—without understanding all this which is operating in you, which is your mind, there cannot be intelligence; and it is intelligence that creates character, not hero worship, not the ideal, not the picture. The understanding of oneself, of one's own extraordinarily complicated self, is the beginning of intelligence which brings character.

Question: Why does a man feel disturbed when a person looks at him attentively?

KRISHNAMURTI: Do you feel nervous when somebody looks at you? Do you feel nervous when somebody whom you consider inferior, a servant, a villager, looks at you? You do not even know that he is looking at you, you just pass him by; you don't even know that he is there, you have no regard for him. But when your father, your mother, your daughter looks at you, you feel anxious because you feel that they know a little more than you do, that they may find out things about you; you are anxious. If you go a little higher, if a government official or a priest or somebody looks at you, you are pleased; you hope to get something from him, a job or some reward. But if a man looks at you who does not want anything from you—neither your flattery nor your insult—who is quite indifferent to you, then you will find out why he is looking at you. You should not be nervous but you should find out what is operating in your own mind when such a person looks at you because looks mean a great deal, because a smile means something.

You see, unfortunately, most of you are utterly unaware of all these things. You never notice the beggar; you never notice the villager carrying his heavy burden or the parrot that flies. You are so occupied with your own sorrows, with your longings, with your fears, with your rituals that you are never aware of the things of life, and so if anyone looks at you, you are apprehensive.

Question: Cannot we cultivate understanding? Is understanding experience? When we try to understand constantly, does it not mean that we want to experience understanding?

KRISHNAMURTI: Is understanding cultivable? Is understanding to be practiced? You practice tennis, you practice the piano or singing or dancing, or you read a book over and over again until you are familiar with it. Now, is understanding the same thing, something to be practiced—which means repeating, which means really, cultivating remembrance? If I can remember constantly all the time, is that understanding? Is not understanding something from moment to moment, something that cannot be practiced?

When do you understand? What is the state of your mind or your heart when there is understanding? When I say that experience and the memory of experience are destructive, are deteriorating, what is the state of your mind when it hears that? When you hear me say that jealousy is destructive, that envy is one of the major factors which destroys relationship, how do you react to it? What happens to you? Do you say, "It is perfectly true, I understand it"? Or do you say, "What would happen if I am jealous?"—which is to rationalize it. When you hear something very true about jealousy, do you see the truth of it immediately, or do you begin to think about it, talk about it, discuss it, analyze it, see what it all means and then see if you can be free from jealousy? Is understanding a process of slow rationalization, of slow analysis? When you hear the truth of something—like "envy is destructive"—do you immediately understand that it is so? Do you follow?

Can understanding be cultivated as you cultivate your garden to produce fruits or flowers? Can you cultivate understanding, which is really to see something without any barrier of words or of prejudices or of motives, to see something direct?

Question: Is the power of understanding the same in all persons?

KRISHNAMURTI: You see very quickly, you understand immediately because the thing is presented to you and you have no barriers. I have many barriers, many prejudices; I am jealous; my conflicts have been built upon envy, upon my importance. You are not full of your own importance, so you see immediately. You are eager to find out, but I have done many things in life, and I do not want to see. You have no barriers, and you see immediately; I have innumerable barriers; I do not want to see, and so I do not see. Therefore, I do not understand and you understand.

Question: I can remove the barriers slowly by constantly trying to question.

KRISHNAMURTI: No. I can only remove the barriers, not try to understand.

You hear someone say that envy is destructive. You listen and understand the significance and the truth of it, and you say, "Yes"; you are free from that feeling of jealousy and envy.

I do not want to see it because if I listen to the truth of it, it would destroy my whole structure of life. What am I to do? Am I to remove the structure or the barrier? I can only remove the barrier when I really feel the importance of not having the barriers, which means that I must feel the barriers.

Question: I feel the necessity.

KRISHNAMURTI: When do you feel that? Will you remove the barriers because of circumstances or because somebody tells you? Or will you remove it when you yourself feel inwardly that to have any barriers creates a mind in which slow decay is taking place—that is, when you yourself see the importance of removing the barriers. And when do you see it? When you suffer? But suffering does not necessarily awaken you to remove these barriers; on the contrary, suffering helps you to create more barriers. You remove those barriers when you yourself are beginning to listen, to find out. There is no reason for removing, no outside reason or inward reason; the moment you bring in a reason, you are not removing the barriers. So, that is the great miracle, that is the greatest blessing, to give the inward something an opportunity to remove the barrier. But, you see, when we want to remove it, when we practice to remove it, when we say it must be removed, all that is the work of the mind, and the mind cannot remove the barrier. No rituals, no compulsions, no fears can remove the barrier. But when you see that nothing will remove it, that no attempt on your part will remove it, then the mind becomes very quiet, the mind becomes very still, and in that stillness, you find that which is true.

December 26, 1952

Sixteenth Talk at Rajghat

You may remember that we have been talking about the deteriorating factors in human existence. We said fear was one of the fundamental causes of this deterioration. We also said that the following of authority in any form, whether self-imposed or established from outside, is destruction to incentive, to creativeness. We were saying that any form of imitation, copying, following, is destructive to the creative discovery of what is true. We said that truth is not something that can be followed; truth has to be discovered; you cannot find it through any book, through any particular accumulated experience. Experience itself, as we discussed the other day, becomes a remembrance, and the remembrance is the destruction of creative understanding. Any form of malice, envy, however small it be—which is really comparative thinking—is also destructive to this creative life, without which there is no happiness. Happiness is not something to be bought; it is not something that comes when you go after it; it is there when there is no conflict. Is it not very important not only to listen to all these discussions, these talks in the mornings, but to actually find out for yourself—not only when you are young, but also as you grow older into maturity—all the complications of maturity?

But before we go into that, should we not, while we are in school, try to find out the significance of words? The symbol has become an extraordinarily destructive thing for most of us, and of this we are unaware. You know what I mean by "symbol"? The shadow of a truth. The shadow is the symbol of truth. The gramophone record is not the real voice, but the voice, the sound, has been put on record and to that you listen. The image is the symbol, the idea of what the original thing is. The word, the symbol, the image and the worship of the image, the reverence to the symbol, the following, the giving significance to words—all this is very destructive because then the word, the symbol, the image, becomes all-important. That is how temples, stupas, churches become very important organizations, and the symbols, ideas, dogmas become the factors which prevent the mind from going beyond and discovering what the truth is. So, do not be caught up in words, in symbols, which automatically cultivate habit. Habit is the most destructive factor when you want to think creatively; habit comes in the way. Perhaps, you do not understand the whole significance of what I am saying, but you will if you think about it. Go out for a walk yourself occasionally and think out these things. Find out what words like life and God mean, and also what is meant by those extraordinary words, like duty and cooperation, which we use freely.

What does *duty* mean? Duty to what?—to the aged, to what tradition says, to sacrifice yourself for your parents, for your country, for your gods? That word duty becomes extraordinarily significant to us. It is pregnant with a lot of meaning which is imposed upon us. What is much more important than duty to anything—to your country, to your gods, to your neighbor—what is much more important than the word is to find out for yourself what truth is—not what you want, not what you would like, not what gives you pleasure, not what gives you pain. But, to find out what truth is, the word duty has very little meaning because parents or society use that as a means of molding you, of shaping you to their particular idiosyncracies, to their habits of thought, to their liking, to their safety. So, find out for yourself, take time, be patient, analyze, go into it; do not accept the word duty because where there is duty, there is no love.

Similarly, the word *cooperation*. The state wants you to cooperate with it. Cooperation with something is not what is true. You merely imitate when you copy. If you understand, if you find out what the truth of something is, then you are living with it, you are going with it; it is part of you. It is very significant to be aware, it is very necessary to be aware of all the words, the symbols, the images which cripple your thinking. To be aware of them and to see whether you can go beyond them is essential if you are to live creatively without disintegration. You know, we use the word duty to kill us. Duty—the duty to the country, the duty to parents, the duty to relations—sacrifices you. It makes you go out, fight and kill and be maimed because the politician, the leader says it is your duty to protect the country, it is your duty to your community to destroy others. So, killing another for the sake of your country becomes part of your duty, and gradually, you are drawn into the military spirit, the spirit which makes you obedient, which makes you physically very disciplined; but inwardly, your mind gets destroyed because you are imitating, following, copying; and so, gradually, you become a tool to the older people, to the politician, to propaganda. So you gradually learn to kill, and you accept killing in order to protect your country as inevitable because somebody says so. It does not matter who says so; think it out for yourself very clearly.

To kill is obviously the most destructive and most corrupt action in life, especially to kill another human being because when you kill, you are full of hatred, you create antagonism in others. You can kill with a word, with an action; killing another human being has never solved any of our problems. War has never solved any of our economic, social, human relationships, and yet the whole world is preparing for war everlastingly because there are many reasons why they want to kill people. But do not be swept away by reason; because you may have one reason and I may have another reason, your reason may be stronger than my reason. But no reason is necessary. First get to the truth of it, to the feeling of it, how necessary it is not to kill. It does not matter who says so, from the highest authority to the lowest; inwardly find out the truth of it in general principles; when you are clear of that inwardly, then the details can be gone into later, then you can reason them out, but do not start by reasoning because every reason can be countered; there can be a counter reason for every reason, and you are caught in reasoning. It is necessary to know for yourselves what the truth is; then you can begin to use reason. When you know for yourself what is true, when you know that killing of another is not love, when you feel inwardly the truth of "there must be no enmity," when you really feel that inwardly, then no amount of reason can destroy it. Then no politician, no priest, no parent, can sacrifice you for an idea or for their safety.

Always, the old sacrifice the young, and you in your turn, as you grow older, will sacrifice the young. But you have to prevent this because it is the most destructive way of living and is one of the greatest factors of human deterioration. In order to prevent this degeneration, to put an end to it, you have to find out the truth for yourself. You, as an individual, not belonging to any group, to any organization, have to find out the truth of not killing, the feeling of love, the feeling that there must be no enmity. Then, no amount of words, no reasons can ever persuade you. So, it is very important, while you are young, especially in a school of this kind, to think out these things, to feel them out and to establish and lay the foundations for the discovery of truth.

We are going to make something out of this school though it is not what it should be; you and I, you the students and teachers, all of us together, are going to make something out of it; all of us are going to build this thing—a school where you are taught not merely information but also to discover what is truth—so that throughout life, as you grow, you know how to find out for yourself without any authority, without any following, that which is real. Otherwise, you will become one of the factors of destruction and deterioration, and there is no greater corruption. Listen to all this carefully. If there is the right foundation now, then as you grow older, you will know how to act.

Question: What is the purpose of creation?

KRISHNAMURTI: Are you really interested in it? What do you mean by "creation"? What is the purpose of living? What do we mean by "living"? What is the purpose of your existence, of your reading, studying, passing examinations? What is the purpose of the relationship of parents, wife, children? What is life? Is that what you mean? What is the purpose of creation? When do you ask that question? When you do not see clearly, when you are confused, when you are in the dark, when you are blind, when you do not know, when you do not feel it for yourselves, then you want to know what the purpose of existence is. When inwardly there is no clarity, when there is misery, then you ask, "What is the purpose of life?"

There are many people who will give you the purpose of life; they will tell you what the sacred books say. Clever people will go on inventing what the purpose of life is. The political group will have one purpose, the religious group will have another purpose, and so on and on. So, what is the purpose of life when you yourself are confused? When I am confused, I ask you this question, "What is the purpose of life?" because I hope that through this confusion, I shall find an answer. How can I find a true answer when I am confused? Do you understand? If I am confused, I can only receive an answer which is also confused. If my mind is confused, if my mind is disturbed, if my mind is not beautiful, quiet, whatever answer I receive will be through this screen of confusion, anxiety, and fear; therefore, the answer will be perverted. So, what is important is not to ask, "What is the purpose of life, of existence?" but to clear the confusion that is within you. It is like a blind man who asks, "What is light?" If I tell him what light is, he will listen according to his blindness, according to his darkness; but suppose he is able to see, then, he will never ask the question "What is light?" It is there.

Similarly, if you can clarify the confusion within yourself, then you will find what the purpose of life is; you will not have to ask, you will not have to look for it; all that you have to do is to be free from those causes which bring about confusion. The causes of confusion are very clear; they are in the 'me', in the 'I', that is constantly wanting to expand itself through envy, through jealousy, through hatred, through imitation; and the symptoms are jealously, envy, greed, fear, the wanting to copy, and so on. As long as inwardly that is so, there is confusion. You are always seeking for outward answers, but it is only when the confusion is cleared that you will know the significance of existence.

Question: What is karma?

KRISHNAMURTI: Are you all interested in that? Why do you ask such a question? Yet that is one of the peculiar words we use, one of the words in which our thought is caught. The poor man says, "My karma." He has to accept life as a theory; he has to accept misery, starvation, squalor, dirt. He has to accept it because he has no energy, he has not enough food, he does not break away from it and create a revolution. He has to accept what life gives, and so he says, "It is my karma to be like this"; and the politicians, the big ones, encourage him to accept life with its squalor, with its misery, with its dirt and starvation. You do not want to revolt against all this, do you? When you pay the poor so little and you have so much, what is going to happen? So, you gradually invent that word *karma*, the passive acceptance of the misery of life. The man on the top, who has achieved, who has inherited, who has been educated, who has come to the top of things, says, "It is also my karma; I have done well in my past life, and so it is my karma to reap the reward of my past action"; he wants to go to the top of things, to have many houses, power, position, and the means of corruption. Is that karma, to accept things as they are? Do you understand? Is it karma to have the spirit of acceptance of things as they are—which many of the teachers and you have—without a spark of revolt, to be ready to accept, to obey? So, you see how easily, because we are not alive, words become nets in which we are caught.

But there is a bigger significance to that word karma, which has to be understood not as a theory, which cannot be understood if you say, "That is what the Bhagavad-Gita says." You know, the comparative mind is the most stupid mind because it does not think; it says, "I have read that book and what you say is like it." When you have such a mind, it means you have stopped thinking, you have stopped investigating to find out what is true, irrespective of what any book or any particular guru has said. When you compare, has not your mind ceased to think, ceased to discover what is true? When you read Shakespeare or Buddha or when you listen to your guru, suppose you compare them; what happens to your mind? Your mind has not found out, has not discovered; it does not throw off all authorities and investigate. So, what is important is to find out and not to compare. Comparison, as I pointed out to you, is authority, is imitation, is thoughtlessness; and it is the very nature of our mind not to be awake to discover what is true. You say, "That is what has been said by the Buddha; that is so," and you think that thereby you have solved your problems. But to discover the truth of anything, you have to be extremely active, vigorous, self-reliant; and you cannot have self-reliance if you are thinking comparatively. Please listen to all this. If there is no self-reliance, you lose all power to investigate and to find out what is true. Self-reliance brings a certain freedom in which you discover, and that freedom is denied to you when you are comparing.

So really the problem of karma is quite complex, and I do not know if we should go into it here. This may not be the right place because we are not dealing with the problems of the old and their extraordinarily complex minds. What we are dealing with here are the problems of the young in relation to their teachers, in their relationship to their parents, and in their relationship to society.

Question: Is there an element of fear in respect, or not?

KRISHNAMURTI: What do you say when you show respect to your teacher, to your parents, to your guru, and disrespect to your servants? You kick those people who are not important, and you lick the boots of those who are above you, the officials, the politician, the big ones. Is there not an element of fear in that? Because, from the big ones you want something; from the teacher, from the examiner, from the professor, from the parents, from the politician, from the bank manager, you want something. What can the poor people give you? So, you disregard them, you treat them with contempt, you do not even know that they pass you by. You do not even look at them, you do not even know that they shiver in the cold, that they are dirty and hungry, but you will give to the big ones, the great ones of the land, the little that you have in order to receive more of their favors. So in that, there is definitely, is there not, an element of fear; there is no love. If you had love, then you would show love to those who have nothing and also to those who have everything; then, you would not be afraid of those who have, and you would not disregard those who have not. So respect in that sense is the outcome of fear. Love is not the outcome of fear; in love, there is no fear.

December 28, 1952

Seventeenth Talk at Rajghat

We have been trying to point out the various factors that bring about human deterioration in our existence, in our lives, in our activities, in our thoughts; and we said that it is conflict that is one of the major factors of this deterioration. Is not peace also, as it is generally understood, a destructive factor? Can peace come about by the mind? If we have peace of mind, does not that also lead to corruption, deterioration? If we are not very observant, we will narrow down the window of that word, through which we can look at the world and understand. We can make the word *peace* such a narrow phrase that we will see only part of the sky and not the whole. It is only when we can perceive the whole vastness, the enormity, the magnificence of the sky, then only is there the possibility of having peace—not by merely pursuing peace, which is the inevitable process of thought, of mind. Perhaps it may be a little difficult to understand this. I am going to try to make it as simple and clear as it is possible.

I think if we can understand this, what it means to be peaceful, what is peace, then perhaps we shall understand the real significance of love. We think peace is something to be got through the mind, through reason, but can peace ever come through any quieting, through any control, through any domination of thought? We all want peace. For most of us, peace means to be left alone, not to be interfered with, to build a wall round our own mind by means of ideas. This is very important in your lives, for as you grow older, you will be faced with these problems of war and peace. Is peace something to be pursued after and got and tamed by the mind? For most of us, peace means a slow decay; wherever we are, stagnation comes; we think by clinging to an idea, by building walls of security, of safety, of ideas, of habits, of beliefs, by pursuing a principle, a particular tendency, a particular fancy, a particular wish, we will find peace. That is what most of us want, not to make effort, but to live without an effort in some kind of stagnation. When we find we cannot have that kind of peace, we make tremendous efforts to have peace, to find some corner in the universe, in our being, where we can crawl and in the darkness of self-enclosure, live. That is what most of us want in our relationship with the husband, with the wife, with parents, with friends. Unconsciously we want peace at any price, and so we pursue.

Can the mind ever find peace? Is not the mind itself a source of disturbance? The mind can only gather, accumulate, deny, assert, remember, and pursue. Is peace—which is so essential because without peace you cannot live, you cannot create—something to be realized through the struggles, through the denials, through the sacrifices of the mind? Do you understand what I am talking about? As we grow older, unless we are very wise and watchful, though we may be discontented while we are young, that discontent will be canalized into some form of peaceful resignation to life. The mind is everlastingly seeking somewhere to create a secluded habit, belief, desire, in which it can live and be peaceful with the world. But the mind cannot find peace because the mind can only think in terms of time—as the past, the present, and the future, what it has been, what it is, and what it will be—condemning, judging, weighing, pursuing its own vanities, habits, beliefs. The mind can never be peaceful though it can delude itself into some kind of peace, but that is not peace. It can mesmerize itself with words, by the repetition of phrases, by merely following somebody, by knowledge, but such a mind is not a peaceful mind because the mind is itself the center of attraction; the mind is by its very nature the essence of time. So, the mind with which you think, with which you calculate, with which you contrive, with which you compare, such a mind is incapable of finding peace.

Peace is not the outcome of reason, and yet when you observe the organized religions that you know, you see that they are caught in the pursuit of the peace of the mind. But peace is something which is as creative as war is destructive, something which is as pure as war is destructive, and to find that peace, one must understand beauty. That is why it is very important, while we are very young, to have beauty about us—the beauty of buildings, of proper proportions, of true appreciation, of cleanliness, of quiet talk among the elders—so that in understanding what beauty is, we shall know what love is, how beauty of the heart is the peace of the heart.

Peace is of the heart, not of the mind. So, you have to find out what beauty is. It matters very much the way you talk, for you will discover through the words you use, the gestures you make, what the refinement of your heart is. For, beauty is something that cannot be defined, that cannot be explained through words. It can only be called or understood when the mind is very quiet.

So, while you are young and sensitive, it is essential for you as well as for those who are responsible for the young, for students, to create this atmosphere of beauty. The way you dress, the way you sit, the way you talk and eat, and the things about you are very important. For, as you grow, you will meet all the ugly things of life—ugly buildings, ugly people, malice, envy, ambition, cruelty—and if in your hearts there is no perception of beauty founded and established in yourself, you can easily be swept away by the enormous current of the world, and then you will be caught in the struggle to find peace of the mind. The mind creates the idea of what peace is and tries to pursue it and then gets caught in the net of words, of fancies, of illusions.

So, peace can only come when you understand what love is. Because, if you have peace merely through security, financial or otherwise—through money, or through certain dogmas, rituals and repetitions—there is no creativeness; there is no urgency to bring about a fundamental, radical revolution in the world. Because, peace then only leads to contentment and resignation. But when you understand the peace in which there is love and beauty, the extraordinary strangeness of it, then you will find peace—the peace that is not understood by the mind. It is this peace that is creative, that brings order within oneself, that removes confusion. But this does not come through any effort. It comes when you are constantly watching and being sensitive both to the ugly and to the beautiful, to the good and to the bad, to all the fluctuations of life because peace is something enormously great, extensive, not something petty, not created by the mind. That can only be understood when the heart is full.

Question: Why do we feel inferior before our superiors?

KRISHNAMURTI: Who are your superiors? Who are the people whom you consider your superiors? Those who know? Those who have titles, degrees, or those from whom you want some kind of reward, some kind of position, from whom you are asking something? Whom do you call your superiors? The moment you regard somebody as superior, do you not regard others as inferior?

Why do we have this division, the superior and the inferior? That exists only when we want something. I may be less intelligent than you, I may not have as much as you have, I may not be as happy inwardly as you are, or I am asking something from you, so I feel inferior to you. You may be more intelligent; you may be more clever; you may have a gift, a capacity, and I might not have it. But when I am trying to imitate, when I want something from you, I immediately become your inferior because I have put you on a pedestal, I have given you a certain value. So, I create the superior and I create the inferior; psychologically, inwardly, I create this difference of those who have and those who have not.

Is it possible to bring about a world in which the haves and have nots do not exist? You understand the problem? That is, the world is divided into those who are rich, who are powerful, who have everything, position, prestige, and those who have not. In the world, there is enormous inequality of capacity—the man who invents the jet plane and the man who drives the plow. There is vast contrast in capacity—intellectual, verbal, physical. We give enormous values and significance to certain functions. We consider the governor, the prime minister, the inventor, the scientist, as something enormously significant. We have given function great importance, and so function assumes status and position. So long as we give status to functions, that gives rise to such inequality that the difference between those that are incapable and those that are capable becomes unbridgeable. But if we can keep function stripped of status, which gives position, prestige, power, money, wealth, and pleasure, then there is the possibility of bringing about a sense of equality. Even then, equality is not possible if there is no love. It is love that destroys the sense of the unequal, of the superior.

You see, what is happening in the world is this: politicians, economists see this breach, this gulf between the man of capacities and the man who has no capacities, and they try to approach this problem through economic and social reformation; they may be right, but that approach can never take place as long as we have not love, as long as we do not understand the whole process of antagonism, envy, malice. That can only come to an end when there is love in our heart.

Question: Can there be peace in our life when, every moment, we are struggling against our environment?

KRISHNAMURTI: What do we call environment and what is environment? We say environment is society—the economic, the religious, the national, the class environment, the climate. We are struggling either to fit into it or to move away from it. Most of us are struggling to fit, to adjust ourselves, as individuals, into the environment. From the environment we hope to have a job, we hope to be able to accept all the benefits of that particular society, so we are struggling to fit or to adjust ourselves into that society. What is that society made up of? Have you ever thought about it? Have you looked at the society in which you are living, to which you are trying to adjust yourselves? That society is based on what you call religion, is it not, a set of traditions, certain economic values; you are part of that society and you are trying to live with it. Can you live with a society which is based on acquisitiveness, which is the outcome of envy, fear, greed, possessive pursuits with occasional flashes of love? Can you? If you try to be intelligent, fearless, nonacquisitive, can you adjust yourself with that society? So why struggle with that society?

You have to create your own new society—which means, you have to be free from acquisitiveness, from envy, from greed, from any religious narrowing down of thought, from nationalism, from patriotism; then only is it possible for you not to struggle but to create something anew, a new society. But as long as you are trying to adjust, trying to make an effort to adjust yourself to the present society, you are merely following a pattern created of envy, of prestige, of those beliefs which are corruptive.

So, is it not important, while you are young, while you are in this place, to understand all these problems and to bring about a freedom in yourselves so that you may create a new world, a new society, a new relationship between man and man? Surely that is the function of education.

Question: Why do human beings suffer, and why cannot one be free from certain types of suffering such as death, sorrow, and disaster?

KRISHNAMURTI: Why do we suffer and is it possible to be free from death and disaster?

Medical science is trying to free humanity from diseases through sanitation, through clean living, and clean food. Through various forms of surgery, they are trying to find a cure for incurable diseases like cancer. A capable, efficient doctor does relieve, does try to eliminate diseases.

Is death conquerable? It is a most extraordinary thing that you are so much interested in death. Is it because you see so much death about you, the burning ghats, the body being carried to the river? Why are you so preoccupied with it? You know, a man who has no urge, no creative thing in him, suffers; he is concerned with that, his concern is about his suffering. So, similarly, you are concerned with death because you are so familiar with it. It is so constantly with you, and there is fear of death.

I explained this question the other day. You do not listen. I can answer it in a different way. But if you do not listen, if you do not really find out, if you do not really understand what the implications of death are, you will go from one preacher to another preacher, from one hope to another hope, from one belief to another, trying to find a solution to this problem of death. Do you understand? I answered it last week, and if you are interested, read what we have discussed when printed on paper. Read it; do not keep on asking but try to find out. You can ask innumerable questions; that is the shallow characteristic of a petty mind—to always question, but never try to find out and discover.

You see, death is possible only when we cling to life. When you understand the whole process of living and dying, then there is the possibility of understanding the significance of death. Death is merely the extinction of continuity and the fear of not being able to continue. But, as you see, that which continues can never be creative. It is only that which can come to an end voluntarily that is creative. You think it out. You will find for yourself what is true, and it is truth that liberates you from death, not your mere reading, not your believing in reincarnation. Discover for yourself by understanding the whole process of life; then you will find there is nothing beyond that which is perishable.

December 29, 1952

Eighteenth Talk at Rajghat

Fortunately, while one is quite young, the main conflicts of life, the worries, the passing joys, the physical disasters, death, and the mental twists do not affect us. Fortunately, most of us, while we are young, are out of the battlefield of life, but as we grow older the pains, the disasters, the questionings, the doubts, the economic and inward struggles crowd in on us, and we want to find the significance of life, we want to know what it is all about. We are not easily satisfied by economic explanations or by any particular definitions. We want to know all about the struggles, the pains, the poverty, the disasters; why some are well-placed and others are not; why one is a healthy, intelligent human being, gifted, capable, while another is not. We want to know why, and we soon are caught in a hypothesis, in a theory, in a belief because we must find an answer. It is never the true answer, but we invent it; we have a theory, a belief about it. So, we start out with an inquiry, and not having enough self-reliance, vigor, intelligence, and innocence, we are soon caught in theories, in beliefs.

We realize that life is ugly, painful, sorrowful; we want some kind of theory, some kind of speculation or satisfaction, some kind of doctrine which will explain all this, and so we are caught in explanation, in words, in theories, and gradually, beliefs become deeply rooted and unshakable because behind those beliefs, behind those dogmas, there is the constant fear of the unknown. But we never look at that fear; we turn away from it. The stronger the beliefs, the stronger the dogmas. And when we examine these beliefs—the Christian, the Hindu, the Buddhist—we find that they divide people. Each dogma, each belief, has a series of rituals, a series of compulsions which bind man and separate man. So, we start with an inquiry to find out what is true, what the significance is of this misery, this struggle, this pain; and we are soon caught up in beliefs, in rituals, in theories. We have not the self-reliance nor the vigor nor the innocence to push all aside and inquire. So, belief begins to act as a deteriorating factor.

Belief is corruption because behind belief and morality lurks the 'mine', the self—the self growing big, powerful, and strong. We consider belief in God, the belief in something, as religion. We consider that to believe is to be religious. You understand? If you do not believe, you will be considered an atheist, you will be condemned by society. One society will condemn those who believe in God, and another society will condemn those who do not. They are both the same. So, religion becomes a matter of belief, and belief acts and has a corresponding influence on the mind; the mind then can never be free. But it is only in freedom that you can find out what is true, what is God, not through any belief because your very belief projects what you think ought to be God, what you think ought to be true. You understand? If you believe God is love, God is good, God is this or that, that very belief prevents you from understanding what is God, what is true. But, you see, you want to forget yourselves; you want to sacrifice yourselves; you want to emulate, to abandon this constant struggle that is going on within you; you want to pursue virtue.

There is constant struggle, there is pain, there is suffering, there is ambition; in all that, there is constant pain and transient pleasure, pleasure that comes and goes, but your mind wants something enormous to cling to, something beyond itself, something with which you can identify yourself. So, that thing which it wants beyond itself, it calls God, it calls truth, and so it identifies itself with it through belief, through convictions, through rationalization, through various forms of discipline and moralities. But this identifying—that is, the recognition of the thought as something vast, which the mind invents and which creates speculation—is still part of the 'me', is still part of the struggle, is still projected by the mind in its desire to escape from the turmoils of life. You identify yourself with a country—India or England or Germany or Russia or America—you identify yourself as a Hindu. Why? Have you ever looked at it, gone behind the meaning of the word, behind the words that have captured your mind? Why do you identify yourself with India? Because you are living in a small town, leading a miserable life with your struggles, with your family quarrels, because you are dissatisfied, discontented, miserable, you want to identify yourself with a thing called India. This gives you a sense of vastness, a bigness, a psychological satisfaction, so you say, "I am an Indian," and for this, you are willing to die, to kill and to be maimed. In the same way, because you are very small, because you are in constant battle with yourself, because you are confused, miserable, uncertain, because you search and know there is death, you want to identify yourself with something beyond, something vast, significant, full of meaning, which you call God. So, you say that is God, and you identify yourself with that; this gives you an enormous importance and significance, and you feel happy. So with the identifying process comes the self-expansive process; that is still the 'me', that is still the self, struggling.

So, religion, as we generally know it or acknowledge it, is a series of beliefs, of dogmas, of rituals, of superstitions, of worship of idols, of charms, and gurus that will lead you to what you want as an ultimate goal. The ultimate truth is your projection, that is what you want, which will make you happy, which will give you a certainty of the deathless state. So, the mind caught in all this creates a religion—a religion of dogmas, of priest craft, of superstitions, and idol-worship—and in that, you are caught, and the mind stagnates. Is that religion? Is religion a matter of belief, a matter of knowledge of other people's experiences and assertions? Or is religion merely the following of morality? You know it is comparatively easy to be moral—to do this and not to do that. Because it is easy, you can imitate a moral system. Behind that morality lurks the self, growing, expanding, aggressive, dominating. But is that religion?

You have to find out what truth is because that is the only thing that matters, not whether you are rich or poor, not whether you are happily married and have children, because they all come to an end, there is always death. So, without any form of belief, you must find out; you must have the vigor, the self-reliance, the initiative, so that for yourself you know what truth is, what God is. Belief will not give you anything; belief only corrupts, binds, darkens. The mind can only be free through vigor, through self-reliance. Surely, it is the function of education, especially here, to create such individuals who are not bound by any form of belief, of morality, of respectability. For, behind it lurks the 'me' that is so important and that seeks to become respectable. Surely it is the function of an educational center of this kind to make individuals truly religious—that is, the religion of discovery, of direct experiencing of what God is, what truth is. That experiencing is not possible, is never possible, through any form of belief, of rituals, of following another, of worshipping another. That religion is free from all gurus. You as an individual can, as you grow through life, discover the truth from moment to moment; you are capable of being free.

You think that to be free from the material things of the world is the first step towards religion. It is not. That is one of the easiest things to do. The first thing is to be free to think fully, completely, and independently—not to be crushed by any belief, by circumstances, by environment—so that you are an integrated human being, capable, vigorous, self-reliant, so that your mind being free, unbiased, unconditioned, can find out what God is, what truth is. Surely, it is for that purpose that this center exists, to help each individual that comes here to be free to discover reality, not to follow any system nor any belief nor any ritual, nor any guru; the individual has to awaken his intelligence through freedom, not through any form of discipline—which means resistance, compulsion, coercion—so that through that intelligence, through that freedom, the individual can find out that which is beyond the mind. Because, it is only when directly experienced that the immensity of the thing will be known—the thing that is not nameable, the thing that is not measurable by words, that is limitless, in which there is that love which is not of the mind. The mind cannot conceive all that, and as it cannot conceive it, the mind must be very quiet, astonishingly still, without any demand or any desire. Then only is it possible for that extraordinary thing, what we call God or reality, to come into being.

Question: What is obedience? Is it at all possible to obey without understanding the order?

KRISHNAMURTI: Is it possible to obey the order without understanding the order? Is it not what most of us do? Parents, teachers, the older people say, "Do this." They say it either politely or with a stick, and we are afraid and obey. That is what governments do. That is what the military people do. We are trained from childhood, not knowing what it is all about. The more tyrannical the government, the more totalitarian, the more authoritarian, the more we are compelled, shaped from childhood; not knowing why, we should obey. We are told what to think. Our mind is purged of any thought which is not of the state, of the authority. We are never taught or helped to find out how to think, but we must obey. The priest says so, the religious books says so; our own fear inwardly compels us to obey because if we do not obey, we will be lost, we will be confused.

So, we obey. Why do we obey? Do you understand? The social structure, the religious state, forces us to blindly follow the pattern created by another in the hope of some reward or happiness. Why do we obey? Must we obey? We are very thoughtless. To think is very painful; to think, we have to question; we have to inquire; we have to find out how the older people do not want us to find out that they have not the patience, that they are too busy with their quarrels, with their ambitions, with their prejudices, with their do's and don'ts of morality and respectability. So, the older people have not the patience, and we are young; we are afraid to go wrong because we also want to be respectable. Don't we all want to put on the same uniform, to look alike? We do not want to do anything different. To think separately, to be apart, is very painful, so we join the gang.

Why do we do all this—obey, follow, copy? Why? Because, we are frightened inwardly to be uncertain. We want to be certain—we want to be certain financially, we want to be certain morally—we want to be approved, we want to be in a safe position, we want never to be confronted with trouble, pain, suffering, we want to be enclosed. So fear, consciously or unconsciously, makes us obey the master, the leader, the priest, the government. Fear also controls us from doing something which may be harmful to others because we will be punished. So behind all these actions, greeds, pursuits, lurks this desire for certainty, this desire to be assured. So, without resolving fear, without being free from fear, merely to obey or to be obeyed has little significance; what has meaning is to understand this fear from day to day and how fear shows itself in different ways. It is only when there is freedom from fear that there is that inward quality of understanding, that aloneness in which there is no accumulation of knowledge or of experience, and it is that alone which gives extraordinary clarity in the pursuit of the real.

December 30, 1952

Nineteenth Talk at Rajghat

As we grow older and go out of this institution after receiving education, so-called education, we have to face many problems. What profession are we to choose so that in that profession, we can fulfill ourselves, we can be happy; so that in that profession or vocation or job, we are satisfied and are not exploiting others, we are not being cruel to others? We have to face death, suffering, disasters. We have to understand starvation, overpopulation, sex, pain, pleasure, the many confusing and conflicting and contradictory things in life, the wrangles, the conflicts between man and man or between woman and man, the conflicts within, the struggles within and the struggles without, wars, the military spirit, ambition, and that extraordinary thing called peace, which is much more vital than we realize. We have to understand the significance of religion, not the mere worship of images, nor the mere speculations which we think give us the right to assume the religious feeling, but also that very complex and strange thing called love. We have to understand all this, and not merely be educated to pass examinations; we have to know the beauty of life—to watch a bird in flight, to see the beggars, the disasters, the squalor, the hideous buildings that people put up, the foul road, the still fouler temples—we have to face all these problems. We have also to face whom to follow, whom not to follow, and whether we should follow anybody at all.

Most of us are concerned with doing a little bit of change here and there, and we are satisfied with that. As we grow older, we do not want any deep fundamental change because we are afraid. We do not think in terms of transformation; we only think in terms of change, and you will find when you look into that change that it is only a modified change, which is not a radical revolution, not a transformation. You have to face all these things, from your own happiness to the happiness of the many, from your own self-seeking pursuits and ambitions to the ambitions and the motives and the pursuits of others; you have to face competition, the corruption in oneself and in others, the deterioration of the mind, the emptiness of the heart. You have to know all this, you have to face all this, but you are not prepared for it. What do we know when we go out from here? We are as dull, empty, shallow as when we came here, and our studies, our living in school, our contacts with our teachers and their contact with us have not helped us to understand this very, very complex problem of life. The teachers are dull, and we become dull like them. They are afraid and we are afraid. So, it is our problem, it is your problem as well as the teachers' problem to see that you go out with maturity, with thought, without fear, so that you will be able to face life intelligently. So, it appears very important to find an answer to all these problems, but there is no answer. All you can do is to meet these very complex problems intelligently as they arise. Please follow this. Please understand this. You want an answer. You think that by reading, by following somebody, by studying some book, you will find an answer to all these very complex and very subtle problems. But you will not find answers because these problems have been created by human beings who may have been like you. The starvation, the cruelty, the hideousness, the squalor, the appalling callousness, the cruelty—all this has been created by human beings. So, you have to understand the human heart, the human mind, which is yourself. Merely to look for an answer in a book, or to go to a school to find out, or to follow an economic system however much it may promise, or to follow some religious absurdity and superstition, to follow a guru, to do puja, in no way will help you to understand these problems because they are created by you and others like you. As they are created by you, you cannot understand them without understanding yourself, and to understand yourself as you live, from moment to moment, from day to day, year in and year out, you need intelligence, a great deal of insight, love, patience.

So, you must find out, surely, what is intelligence, must you not? You all use that word very freely, and by repetition of that word, you think you become intelligent. The politicians keep on repeating certain words like *integration, a new culture, you must be intelligent, you must create a new world,* but they are all empty words without much meaning. So do not use words without really understanding them. We are trying to find out what intelligence is because if we know what it is and if we can have the feeling of it—not merely a definition of it because any dictionary will give that—the knowing of it, the understanding of it, it will help each one of us, as we grow, to meet the enormous problems in our life; if we have it, then we shall find out how to deal with these problems. Without that intelligence, do what you will—read, study, accumulate knowledge, fight, quarrel, change, bring about little changes here and there in the pattern of society—you will never alter, there will be no transformation, there will be no happiness. So, is it not necessary to question what it is we mean by intelligence? What is intelligence, not the definition of the word, but what does it mean? I am going to find out what it means, and perhaps for some of you, it is going to be difficult, but do not bother with trying to understand it, with trying to follow the words, but try to feel what I am talking about. Try to feel the thing, the quality of it, and then you will, as you grow older, begin to see the significance of what I have been saying. So, listen not to the word but rather to the inward content of that word.

Most of us think that intelligence can be gathered or cultivated through acquiring more knowledge, more information, more experience, by having knowledge to utilize that knowledge, by having experience to meet life with that experience. But life is an extraordinary thing; it is never stationary; it is like a river, a lively thing that moves, that is never still. We think that by having more experience, more knowledge, more virtue, more wealth, more possessions, more and more, we shall find out what intelligence is. This is why we respect people who have knowledge, the scholars, the people who have had rich, full experiences. Is intelligence the outcome of the 'more'? What is this process of the 'more'—having more, wanting more? What is behind it? We are concerned, are we not, with accumulating, and so we say, "If I know, I shall be able to meet life," "If I can understand what the purpose of life is, then I can follow along that path," "If I have more experience, then I shall meet the very complex problems of life." So, we are very concerned, from childhood up to old age, with the problems of the 'more', having more, more, and more.

Now, what happens when you have accumulated knowledge, experience, position? Whatever experience you may have, it is translated into the terms of the 'more' so that you are never experiencing, you are always gathering, and this gathering is the process of the mind. The mind is the center of this 'more'. So, as it gathers, there is the more and more accumulating; and the 'more' is the 'me', the self, the ego, the self-enclosed entity, which is only concerned with the 'more', either negatively or positively. So, with that mind, with the accumulated experience of the 'more', it meets life. So, in meeting life in which there is experience, it is only concerned with the 'more' and so it never experiences; it only gathers, so the mind becomes merely the instrument of gathering; there is no real experiencing. How can you experience when you are thinking always of getting something out of that experience, something more? So, the man who is accumulating, the man who is gathering, the man who is desiring more, is never experiencing life. It is only when the mind is not concerned with the 'more', with the accumulating, that there is a possibility for that mind to be intelligent. When the mind is concerned with the 'more', every experience strengthens that self which is self-enclosing, the 'me' which is the center of all conflict; every experience only strengthens the egocentric process of life. Please follow this. You think experience is the freeing process. But it is not, for as long as the mind is concerned with accumulation, with the 'more', the more experiences you have, the more strengthened you are in your egotism, in your selfishness, in your self-enclosing process of thought.

Intelligence is only possible when there is really freedom from the self, from the 'me', when the mind is not the center of the demand for the 'more', the center of the longing for greater, wider, more expansive regions of thought. So, intelligence is, is it not, the freedom from the pressure of time, for the 'more' implies time; the mind is the result of time. So, the cultivation of the mind is not intelligence. The understanding of this whole process of the mind is self-knowledge, to know oneself as one is, in which there is no accumulating center. Then, out of that comes that intelligence which can meet life, and that intelligence is creative.

Look at your lives—how dull, how stupid, how narrow and silly they are because you are not creative! You may have children, but that is not to be creative. You may be a bureaucrat, but that is not to be creative; in it there is no vitality; it is dead routine, a boredom. Your life is hedged about by fear, and so there is authority and imitation, so you do not know what it is to be creative—I do not mean to paint pictures, to write poems or to be able to sing a song, but I mean the deeper nature of creativeness which, when once it has been discovered, is an eternal source, an undying current—and it can only be found through intelligence because that is the source, that is the timeless thing. But the mind cannot find it, for the mind is the center of the 'me', the self, the constant thoughts everlastingly asking for the 'more'. When you understand all this, not only verbally, but deep down, then you will find that with that intelligence there comes that creativeness which is reality, which is God, which is not to be speculated about or meditated upon. You won't get it through your meditation, through prayer for the 'more', or by the escape from the 'more'. That thing can only come when you understand, from moment to moment every day, the complex reactions, the state of mind as you meet malice, envy. Knowing all that, there comes that thing which we call love; that love is intelligence, and with that intelligence there comes that creative state which is timeless.

Question: The formation of society is based on interdependence. The doctor has to depend on the farmer and the farmer on the doctor. Then, how can a man be completely independent?

KRISHNAMURTI: Life is relationship. You cannot live without having some kind of relationship. Even the sannyasi has relationship; he may renounce the world, but he is still related to the world. So life is the process of relationship. You cannot escape from relationship, and because relationship causes conflict, because in relationship there is fear, you depend either on the husband or on the parent or on the wife or on society. As long as we do not understand relationship—you understand what I mean by relationship, not only the relationship of the parent to the child, but the relationship of the teacher, the cook, the servant, the governor, the commander, the whole of society, which after all is the extension of the relationship of the one with the other—as long as we do not understand that relationship, there is no freedom from the dependency which is brought about through fear, through exploitation. Freedom comes only through intelligence, and only intelligence can meet relationship. Without intelligence, merely to seek freedom or independence from relationship is to pursue an illusion which has no meaning.

So, what is important is to understand relationship which causes conflict, misery, pain, fear. It is in exposing a great many things of the heart, of the mind, of loneliness that there is understanding, and as we understand, there is freedom not from relationship but from the conflicts that cause misery.

Question: Why is truth unpalatable?

KRISHNAMURTI: If I think I am very beautiful and you tell me I am not, which may be a fact, do I like it? If I think I am very intelligent, very clever, and you point out that I am rather a silly person, do I like it? It is very unpalatable to me, but you are pointing it out because it gives you pleasure, does it not? Your pointing out my stupidity gives you a sense of pleasure, a sense of vanity; it shows how clever you are. You take pleasure in pointing out my stupidity, but when it concerns your own stupidity, you do not want to find out what you are, you want to run away from yourself, you want to hide, you want to cover your own emptiness, your own loneliness, your own stupidity. So, you have friends who will never tell you what you are. You want to show to others what you are not, but if others point out your mistake and show you what you are, you do not like it. So, you avoid knowing that which exposes your own inner nature.

Question: Up to now, our teachers have been very certain and have taught us as usual. But having listened to what has been said, following all the discussions, the teachers have become very uncertain. An intelligent student will know how to deal with the problem, but what will happen to those who are not intelligent?

KRISHNAMURTI: Who are the teachers that are uncertain? What are they uncertain about? Not what to teach, because they can carry on with what they teach, with mathematics, with geography, the usual curriculum. That is not what they are uncertain about, are they? They are uncertain how to deal with the student, their relationship with the student. Is it not? They are uncertain of their relationship because up to now, they were never concerned with the student; they just came to the class, taught, and went out. Now, they are concerned about their relationship with the student, whether they are creating fear, whether they are exercising their authority to make the student obey, and so destroying his initiative. They are concerned whether they are repressing the student, or whether they are helping him to find out his true vocation, or whether they are encouraging initiative, or whether they are compelling him to obey. They are concerned with themselves and with their relationships with students. Naturally, it has made them uncertain. But surely, the teacher, like the student, has also to be uncertain, to inquire, to search.

That is the whole process of life from the beginning to the end, is it not—never to stop in a certain place and say, "I know it is so."

An intelligent man is never static, never says, "I know." He is always inquiring, always uncertain, always searching, looking, finding. The moment he says, "I know," he is already dead; and most of us—whether we are young or old, because of tradition or compulsion or the absurdities of our religion, or fear or bureaucracy—are almost dead, with no vitality, with no vigor, with no self-reliance. So, the teacher has also to find out. He has to discover for himself his own bureaucratic tendencies so as not to corrupt the mind of others, and that is a very difficult process; that requires a great deal of understanding.

So, the intelligent student has to help the teacher, and the teacher has to help the student. That is relationship. What happens to the dull boy or girl who is not very intelligent? Surely no boy or girl is so dull as not to be able to feel, not to be able to understand this difficulty, because when the teacher is uncertain, he is more tolerant, he is more hesitant with the dull boy, he is more patient, more affectionate; and therefore perhaps he may be able to help.

Question: The farmer has to depend on the doctor for the cure of physical pain. Is this also governed by dependent action?

KRISHNAMURTI: In it there is an element of fear. As I have explained already, it is a problem of relationship. If my relationship with you is based on fear, I depend on you economically, socially, or psychologically. Inwardly, as long as fear exists, there is no independence, and the problem of freeing the mind from fear is quite a complex problem, which we have discussed.

You see, what is important in all these questions and answers is not what one says or answers but to find out in oneself the truth of the matter by constant inquiry, searching, looking, by not being caught in any particular system because it is the searching that creates initiative, that brings about intelligence. But to be merely satisfied by an answer dulls the mind. So, it is very important for you, while you are at this school, not to accept but to constantly inquire, to apprehend, to discover freely for yourself the whole meaning of life.

December 31, 1952

Poona, India, 1953

First Talk in Poona

As there are going to be only four talks, I think it is important to establish the relationship between the speaker and yourselves. The attitude an audience generally has towards a speaker is: the audience listening to certain ideas of the speaker, and the speaker carrying on with his ideas which he wants to translate to the audience. But unfortunately, that is not so where I am concerned. I am not a lecturer. I am not giving you a speech for you to either confirm or to contradict.

What we are going to try today is to think out the problems together, if we can, because it is your problem as well as mine; and if you merely listen either to criticize or to accept or to deny, it will be utterly futile because that is not my intention. What we shall do during these four talks is to find out the truth of the problem together. You are not going to listen to the truth of what I say, from me, but we are going to discover it together. We, you and I, shall discuss, shall talk it over, shall think out the problems together. I think it is very important to bear this in mind; otherwise, there will be a discussion only on the verbal level.

So, if I may suggest, please listen, not in order to confute or to conform, but really to go into the problems that confront us and which are multiplied everyday. Together we shall find out the true answer. Please bear this in mind—together. It is your problem as well as mine. We are going to discuss, to fathom the truth of the problem. So with that intention, please listen.

It is important to know how to listen, not only to me particularly, but to anybody. It is important to know how to listen because if we know how to listen truly, something extraordinary happens to us, because then without any bias, without any prejudice, we can go to the root of the matter immediately. But if we throw up a lot of arguments, concoct devices or contradictions to see who is correct and who is not correct and carry on with our own particular idiosyncrasies and ideas, then we will not discover the truth of the matter at all. We shall only be concerned with our own particular conclusions, with our own point of view. So if I may suggest, it is important that we should listen truly because if we can know how to listen, the truth will reveal itself. We do not have to explore the problem, but if we know how to listen to the song of a bird, to the voice of another, if we can listen as to music without any interpretation or translation, it definitely clarifies the mind; so similarly, if it is possible, let us listen with that intention—not to confute or to conform, but to directly find out the truth for ourselves.

We see about us in the world innumerable problems created by society, by individuals, and in the solution of a particular problem, we seem to find an increase of the problem; we introduce new problems. Immediately we solve any one particular problem like starvation or any other problem—economic or social or spiritual—we awaken, do we not, to other innumerable problems. As we find that in the solution of one problem other problems come into being, the mind gets more and more involved in problems. There is never a solution, definite or final, of any particular problem but always the multiplication of problems. I do not know if you have noticed this in your daily life. You think you have solved something, but in its very solution, you find half a dozen problems have come into being.

Now, is it possible to solve any particular problem totally without increasing it and introducing other problems? That is one of our main concerns in life because we have got so many problems in the world—economic, social, religious—the destructive wars, the relationship of people with one another, the way of thought, whether there is God or not, and so on.

We want to be loved, and also we want to love; we want to have the capacity to discover, to find out what is truth—truth which is not merely the hearsay of another, which is not learned from the book, whatever the book may be. We want to know truth ourselves, to directly experience truth without interpretation.

We have got many, many problems; the whole day is full of problems—what kind of action we should do, what kind of job we should have, the desire for fulfillment and, without knowing it, the continuous chain of frustration. To solve these problems, we generally turn to somebody—to a book, to a system, to a leader, to a guru, or to some direct experience which we have accumulated ourselves. The desire to find an answer through someone—through a guru, through a book, through a political panacea, through following another—only leads us, if we observe carefully, to frustration. Is that not so in the lives of most of us? Politically, you have followed, you have been to prison, you have been carried away by the enthusiasm of freedom or nationalism or what you will; at the end of it all, what have you? You have the word *freedom,* but the word is not freedom.

You have religious books, guides, philosophers; you do many rituals, and through all this there is fear, there is frustration, there is the hope that can never be fulfilled, there is bitterness, there is anxiety. This is the lot of all of us.

And as we grow older with more and more experience, more and more living a life of frustration, we find, do we not, that we are losing the essential thing in us, which is faith. What I mean by faith is not what you have been used to, namely, the faith in the leader, faith in the guru, faith in the book, faith in your own particular experience. You may not believe in anything, and it is quite right not to believe; if you do not believe, there is a possibility of discovering. But unfortunately, to be without faith leads to cynicism, leads to skepticism, to a life of superficial enjoyment, superficial activities, to doing good superficially. If we do not turn into cynics, we are active, doing good, but that fire which is so essential for creative thinking is denied, is destroyed. I think it is that thing, that fire, that we must find—not the answer to any particular problem because answers to problems are comparatively easy.

If you are intelligent, if you have the capacity, if you have energy, then it is comparatively simple to study the problem. The perfect studying of the problem is the answer itself; the answer is not away from the problem. But to study, to find out the truth of the problem, you need energy, you need vitality, and that vitality and that energy is destroyed when you are following somebody, when you are following your guru, when you are following your political leader or an economic system. All your creative energy is gone in following something, in disciplining your mind to a particular pattern of action. When the leader fails, when the leader dies, when something happens, you are left alone.

So is it possible to have that creative faith, if I can use that word, without identifying it with a particular pattern of thought? I am not referring here to the faith in a guru, in a book, or in your experience, but to that faith that comes, that confidence which you have through your own direct experiencing—not the experience of tradition, not the experience of your teachers, but your own direct understanding of the problem, your dealing with the problem energetically, and therefore having that extraordinary confidence, that capacity to discover the truth of a particular problem. Surely that is the answer, is it not? Because without that we are not creative human beings. And that is what is necessary in the world at the present time—not leaders, not systems, not innumerable multiplication of gurus, but the capacity on the part of the individual to discover what is truth for himself.

Truth is not yours or mine. It is not personal. It is something that comes into being when the mind is very clear, simple, direct, and silent. It can only come in that state. You cannot pursue it. You try to pursue it when you are crippled with the anxiety to find an answer to a particular problem.

So, what we now need is the confidence or the faith in the discovery of what is truth. We cannot discover what is truth if our minds are conditioned. After all, the window through which we look at life is conditioned. We are conditioned as a Hindu, as a Muslim, as a Christian, as a Buddhist—that is, we are conditioned to think in a particular way. The behavior, the pattern of action, is already inculcated in us from childhood. So when we grow up, as we begin to experience, we experience through that screen of conditioning; this is an obvious psychological effect whether we like it or not.

We are never free to discover. We have so far tried one particular form of conditioning—capitalist or socialist. We now say, "That form is foolish; therefore, let us become communists." Becoming communists is also another conditioning. Through any conditioning will you ever solve the problem? On the contrary, to solve any problem you must be free to think out, to experience directly that problem. And because we are so conditioned religiously, economically, climatically, in every way, we are not free to look, to observe, to discover. We are bound, especially here in this country; we are incapable of thinking independently, freely for ourselves without guides, books, leaders. Do please think about this because that is what the problem is. Because we are image worshipers, we have so many examples, so many heroes. Our minds are so crippled with imitation that we are incapable of putting aside all books and leaders and of thinking out every problem for ourselves and discovering the truth.

In discovering the truth of anything, there is the feeling of thinking together. Do you understand the implication of that? So far, we have followed someone and in the very following, we have created division. It is no use saying we are together in following some leader because basically we are separated, and therefore there is never a creative feeling of building together—that this is our earth, that you cannot live without me and I cannot live without you. That is the feeling that we have to build together, and not that one political or religious leader or one dynamic personality has to lay down the plan—the feeling that this is our earth, the feeling that this crumbled civilization can be brought together, rebuilt, the feeling that you and I together are building this civilization anew.

This feeling of 'ourness' cannot come into being if you and I are not free to discover the truth—the truth being not yours or mine. It is only in the discovery of what is truth that there is a possibility of the feeling that we are creating together, that we are living together, that we beautify the earth together. Please think about what I am saying. Don't just discard it, thinking that this is also one of those speeches we hear occasionally. Don't brush this aside because this is the vital necessity at the present time.

We are in a tremendous crisis, whether we know of it or not. And in this crisis you cannot follow the old-fashioned book or leader; you have to find the truth in your own heart, and you can only find it when your mind is unconditioned. As long as there is conditioning that makes you pursue, follow, create ideologies, worship, as long as there is the conditioning of the mind either as a Hindu, a communist, a socialist, or a capitalist, or what you will, you cannot find the truth of any problem. And it is only when you and I discover the truth which is not personal or individual that there is a possibility of bringing about a revolution which is not a revolution of ideas but of truth. That is what is needed in the present times.

It is also important to find out what your relationship is to that creative reality, God, or what you will—names are of no importance. You cannot find that creative reality if your mind is clotted with ideas, with words that have no meaning. You cannot find it or discover it if your mind is incapable of pulling itself away from traditional thought.

Truth is not something made up of the mind. The mind cannot perceive truth. Truth is not a product of the mind; on the contrary, as long as the mind is active, is trying to scheme out, to discover, to dig out, it will not find truth. It can only find it when there is understanding that frees the mind, when only there is a possibility of the mind being very silent. A silent mind is essential, a mind that is very still, with a stillness that is not brought about by discipline, by coercion, by persuasion. A mind that is disciplined is not a free mind, it is a narrow mind, it is a conditioned mind; therefore, it is incapable of finding out what is truth. But a mind that understands, that penetrates, that is capable of directly experiencing in action, in relationship, in everyday living, such a mind is capable of discovering the truth, and it is that truth that sets us free from our problems.

Here are some questions and I shall try to answer them. In answering them, I am not concerned with the problem nor to find an answer to the problem. While listening to me, if you are looking for an answer, you will never find an answer. But if you know how to study the problem, how to look at the problem, then you will find the answer in the problem itself, not away from it.

Most of you, unfortunately, have got a schoolboy mentality, which is to find an answer. You are only concerned in finding the answer which is at the end of the book, or the answer from a teacher, from a guru, or from a system, from a newspaper, through a book; that is, you want to find an answer away from the problem, in a panacea, in a word, in a name, and you think you have solved the problem. So, in answering these questions, please bear in mind that we are not trying to find an answer. We are trying to understand the problem, and in the very understanding of the problem, we shall find an answer. Then the answer is not separate from the problem. Then you do not have the answer which you are trying to live up to. Then the answer is in your hands, to make what you like with it or to destroy it. Please follow this point carefully; otherwise, you will miss what I am talking about.

Our mentality is, especially at meetings of this kind, to wait for an answer. But what we are going to do is to think out the problem together, to see the truth of the problem together, because there is no answer to a problem. Problems are created by our thinking, by our life, by our actions, and we want an answer outside our thoughts, our daily activity, our daily relationship; and so we are everlastingly waiting for somebody to tell us what to do. And as people are only too willing to tell us what to do, we call them leaders. At the end of our search, there is frustration, there is despair, there is bitterness; all our life is wasted; then disintegration takes place in our very being. So it is only in studying the problem that it is possible to find a true answer.

Question: In an underdeveloped and economically backward country like India which has just attained political freedom, problems of material reconstruction are obviously primary. What is your contribution to the creation of a new social order here?

KRISHNAMURTI: Now, what is the problem involved here? We want an economic way of life, a new pattern of action, a new relationship between human beings in the economic field—especially in a country which has recently attained freedom, in a so-called underdeveloped country where there is overpopulation, where there is not enough food for the whole of the people, where there is a superficial revolution but not a fundamental revolution, where there is merely an exchange, or rather substitution, of leadership and not fundamental radical revolution in the ways of life or in the outlook. We say we want to create a new social order, a new economic order, without radically transforming ourselves; we want a radical answer. Do you follow?

The questioner asks what my contribution is to this. He wants an answer, an economic panacea, a system for this country. Now, can you, as human beings living in this world of reality, be ideologically free and independent of any other country? Are not your economic relationships based on and related to other countries? So, there is no answer to the economic problem independently, apart from other countries.

So, the first fallacy is to want economic freedom, an economic solution for the people living in this country apart from other countries. The problem is rather confused; it is much deeper than the economic solution or reconstruction of this country. It is the problem of all human beings living together on this earth. Sirs, don't nod at me; that means absolutely nothing. What we need is a revolution—not an economic revolution, not a new economic order, not a revolution of ideas nor that of substituting one system for another, but a fundamental revolution in our thinking.

The questioner wants to know what contribution I have to solve the problem of food, as food is the primary, important thing. Now, at which level, from what point of view are we, you and I, approaching the problem? We all admit that food is the primarily important thing; without food, you and I cannot sit here. The problem of food is primary and it must be tackled immediately. But, let us study and understand this problem. We said that food is of primary importance. But is it really the primary necessity for the individual? Is there not something else much deeper?

You may have food, but have you solved the problem of human relationship, which is of primary importance? That is, you may have food, you may organize economic safety for every individual, but in bringing that about, you may lose yourself, you may no longer be free. That is what is happening in the world, sirs.

In considering food as the primary important thing, you hand over to a person or to a system your freedom, your capacity to think freely and independently and to discover what is truth; and in that very process, you become slaves, and the capacity of creative being is destroyed. To put it differently, the primary necessity is not food. The primary necessity is for each individual to be creative. If the mind is assured of being creative, then nothing else very much matters. Then our emphasis is not on food, not on an economic plan or system, but on something else which will bring about the economic security of mankind.

Each one of us is ambitious. You want to be something in this world. If you are a clerk, you want to be the manager, the chief executive, the director; if you are a clerk in a court of law, you want to become the judge. You want to keep on climbing and climbing. So, as long as there is ambition, the desire to be somebody in this world, you are going to destroy any economic plan for the security of mankind. Therefore, so long as the urge to be somebody—to be great, to fulfill, to have a name, position, prestige, power—is the drive, then the primary necessity which is food will not come into being. Sirs, this is proved over and over again; it is not my own invention. When you observe this fact, you do not lay emphasis on food as the primary necessity, but you realize that there must be a fundamental revolution in our thinking for this necessity to come into being. You must do away with your communal divisions, castes, and all the narrow petty-mindedness of human beings; there must be no nationalism, no artificial distinction; it is only then that there is a possibility of the primary necessity of mankind being fulfilled.

Therefore, the revolution for economic well-being must be inward and not outward. Do you agree to all this? Yes? But you say you cannot have fundamental inward revolution because you have not the vigor, you have not the self-reliance; because you are exhausted; because you have done so many foolish things in your lives, followed so many leaders, teachers; because mentally you say you are exhausted. This inward revolution in which the mind is not seeking fulfillment through any ambition requires a great deal of inside research, inward understanding. This means the setting aside of any particular ambition to discover and to solve this primarily important issue—which is, that everyone on the earth can have food, clothing, and shelter. That is only possible when there is a feeling that this is our earth, that we are responsible for the whole of mankind. That is only possible when everyone of us is not struggling, achieving to be someone. Sirs, this is the fundamental revolution which will produce your new social order.

Question: Scientific inventions have turned from a blessing to a curse for humanity. Can you not help mankind to escape from the criminal folly of its cleverest and most powerful men?

KRISHNAMURTI: Sir, it is your responsibility, is it not? We know the world; if we are not very wise, it is going to destroy itself. There is a super-hydrogen bomb which has been recently exploded and which, in its explosion, totally vaporized. Probably you have read about that terrible invention. War seems to be the perpetual occupation of civilized man. Now, how are we going to solve this? Inventions are necessary. Atomic energy may be used for producing the necessities of mankind; it may be the cheapest power and so on. But we must find out why men want to destroy each other; why we want to kill somebody else; that is the problem, not scientific inventions. Because the more we can discover about the scientific use of nature, the more we shall be free to enjoy, to look at the trees, the sky, the birds, the running waters, the sunset.

So it is not the fault of science. We must see why it is that you and I want to kill our next door neighbor—the Russian, the American, the English, or the Muslim. Why? That is our problem. Why do we hate, why do we create enmity, why have we no love? If we can really go into it, if we find out what it means to love someone, then probably we shall prevent wars.

One of the fundamental causes of war, we are told, is economic. But, much more than that, the fundamental cause is the belief in something. When I believe in something, I want to convert you to my ideas, and if you do not agree with me, I am going to liquidate you. You have a panacea, you have a system, you have the Bible or a book of Marx with truths, high dogmas, disciplines; and if I do not agree with your way of thinking, if I do not believe in God as you believe, then you destroy me. It is that thing that we must understand, why we create enmity between each other.

Is not so called religion one of the causes of enmity? Please do consider it. Do not brush it aside. You believe that you are a Hindu, and I am told from childhood that I am a Muslim. I do certain rituals and you don't do certain rituals. So belief, rituals, divide us, do they not? You are a Brahmin and I am not. You believe in the only savior—in Marx or in Jesus or in Buddha; if I disagree with you, you are going to push me aside.

So you see, fundamentally, one of the causes of enmity between men is belief, and belief projects. I want some kind of security in life; I have money, I have position, but I want deeper security. So I project out of my mind the desire, the urge which compels me to find security in some super-idea, some superman, some super-convictions, or super-conclusions. So out of my very desire, I create belief, the idea of security, the idea of there being God or no God; and to that my mind clings. So it is my belief which gives me a sense of security, of certainty; and I say that it is my urge, that it is mine, because you are isolated from me by your belief. Gradually out of all this, division or antagonism comes into being; you are an Englishman and I am a Negro; you are a capitalist, I am a communist. So belief, the desire of the mind to be secure in some conclusion, in some conviction, is one of the causes of enmity.

Love is not a thing of the mind. I wonder if you love your children? I doubt it very much because if you did, there would be no war; because if you love, you would not create in the mind the division of Hindu and Muslim; if you love, you would have no division of clerks and managers and so on. If you love the child, you would help him to grow into an intelligent human being without any conditioning so that his intelligence can pierce through all the conditioning of life.

So the cause of war is not outside of us but in us. We preach nonviolence; we have ideals of brotherhood; we use so many words without much significance. The idealist is the worst warmonger. (Laughter) Sirs, please don't laugh. The man who preaches brotherhood is not brotherly; that is why he preaches brotherhood; the man who is brotherly does not talk of brotherhood. When a man has the ideal of brotherhood, it means he is not brotherly and he is going to be, some day, brotherly. We have developed a philosophy of postponement and an ideal; and the man who preaches an ideal obviously is not that which he thinks he should be. It is only when we understand what we are in actual fact, not theoretically, but actually, that there is a possibility of freeing ourselves from enmity.

We have to see the truth—how mankind is dividing itself by various theories, dogmas, principles, philosophies, beliefs; how each one is trying to fulfill, trying to become something in this world; and how this is the real cause of war, of destruction, of degeneration. But we do not want to face that; we want economic safety; we want outside conditions to be altered without radically, fundamentally bringing about a transformation in our own thinking, in our own feelings. It is only when we see this truth that there is a possibility of stopping wars, of seeing that the inventions which can be the means of appalling destruction do not bring greater misery and havoc to mankind.

Question: Your denunciation of all discipline would only lead young people to the already rampant cult of body worship. Until all desire is sublimated, is not some form of self-control absolutely essential?

KRISHNAMURTI: Sir, let us go into this problem very carefully and see the truth of the matter. First, we must take things as they are: that the world has gone crazy about sensate values, that this so-called body worship, the cinemas, and so on is cultivated. And knowing that, you say we must discipline ourselves, we must control ourselves.

Now, what is meant by *discipline?* First let us understand the word, the implication of that word, and then we can approach the problem. What do we mean by discipline? Obviously, it is a process of resistance, is it not, a process of controlling one desire by another desire, a process of conformity.

I think this is the only way and I must conform to it—to the social pattern or to my elders, or to the guru or to the political party. I must suppress what I think or what I feel, and I must conform to the system, to the plan laid down by the party. I must not deviate, I must not think differently because what the system says is the absolute; the system may be changed by the leader tomorrow, but in the meantime I must conform to it. This is one attitude, which is conformity, resistance, either sublimation or substitution. We mean all these things when we talk about discipline.

What happens when we have disciplined? What has happened to you when you have followed a guru and disciplined your mind and heart to a pattern laid down by him? What has happened to your mind? You are no longer a living, vital entity, but you have a mind that is completely disciplined, controlled, molded; and behind that molding, there is fear—fear of what the public will say, fear of not following the party, the leader, fear that you might lose your job, fear of going wrong. At the back of discipline, which is to resist, to conform, there is fear—fear of what your parents will say, what your wife or husband or guru will say, what will happen. So the basis of discipline is conformity, resistance, or substitution; and behind that, there is fear.

Now, how can the mind understand the problem of conformity, which is imitation, as long as the urge is fear? Do you understand? What is vital is the understanding of the process of fear and thereby being intelligent—which does not mean to either conform, resist, or find a substitute. It is an obvious fact that discipline destroys intelligence. Every teacher in a school disciplines. Because he has so many children to deal with, he must discipline, he must frighten them, and so he begins to discipline, to control, and thereby, he destroys intelligence—intelligence being the freedom to discover what is truth in every part of our life, from childhood upwards.

So discipline does not bring intelligence. You can only have intelligence when there is freedom, not fear. And a mind that is disciplined can never discover what is truth—

which means, a mind that is the outcome of fear can never find what is love. Please understand this, please see the truth of it.

Do not say, "What will happen to me if I do not discipline myself?" What has happened to you up until now? You are supposed to have disciplined yourself until now—at least you say you are disciplining yourself. Where are you? You are everlastingly struggling with what you should be and with what you are.

Why not put aside the ideological theory as to what you should be, which is not a fact, which has no truth in it. The fact is what you are now. Why not understand what you are? The understanding of what you are does not demand discipline; on the contrary, you can investigate, go into it, search out the truth of it. But you see, most of us do not want to understand what we are; we are always seeking what we are not; we are always running after what we should be, hoping thereby to escape from what we are. The understanding of what we are is the only fact, the only reality, and in that understanding you will find out the infinite truth that *what is* is, and that *what is* is never static. But that requires a mind which is not burdened by fear, which is not crippled by ideas of discipline or with what my father will say, what my mother, my guru, society is going to say.

Discipline prevents intelligence. Intelligence is the outcome of freedom from fear. But you see, you think you should not be free from fear. You think that fear keeps man on the true path and that therefore you must discipline your child not to rebel against you, and you teach him what you think is truth. So you begin to condition him through fear; you want him to conform to the social pattern of your society. So gradually you instill fear in him and thereby destroy his intelligence. That is what is happening to most of us, is that not so? Cleverness, erudition, being capable of argument, of quoting—those are not the signs of intelligence. A man who is intelligent is without fear. Fear is not to be dispelled by any compulsion or by any conformity. Fear is a venom that slowly works in your system, destroying clearness and clarity of perception.

So when you look at the problem of discipline, you will find that discipline is not important, and that what is important is to understand the process of the mind, the process of behavior not only in yourself but all about you. The understanding of yourself is essential. The understanding of yourself is not the withdrawal from life, to become a hermit or a monk. You cannot understand yourself in isolation; you can only understand yourself in relationship with another because to live is to be related, and to understand yourself, you have to use the mirror of relationship, and that requires an enormous competence, not fear, not the mind which says, "This is wrong," or "That is correct"—that is a schoolboy mentality; it is immature thought that is always condemning, justifying.

So what is important in this question is what we mean by discipline. An intelligent mind does not need discipline; it is disciplining itself all the time—that is, it is observing, adjusting; it is never in the rigid frame of what you call discipline. Sir, a creative mind is the most disciplined mind—not with the discipline which is the outcome of fear but that discipline which comes with the mind that understands, that is constantly aware of its actions and of the movements of its own desires. Such an awareness does not demand discipline. It is only the lazy, crippled, disintegrated mind that is afraid to grow; therefore, it says, "I must discipline, control; I must be this and I must be that or I must not be that"; such a mind can never discover what is truth. A disciplined mind can never discover what is truth.

A disciplined mind can never know what is love. So we never know what love is. We only know the sensation of sex or of the vanity of being loved or of loving. We do not know what love is. Love is not a thing of mind. Love is not the outcome of a cunning device which believes, which limits itself, or which is afraid. Love comes into being only when the mind understands the ways of envy. When it understands the ways of its own fulfillment, when it understands its desire and the fear of frustration, when all these have ceased, then only that thing which is not merely a sensation but is the quality of love which will solve all our problems, comes into being.

January 24, 1953

Second Talk at Poona

Perhaps in considering the problem of suffering and pain, we shall be able to find out directly for ourselves the full problem of a conditioned mind. We are not discussing merely the various forms of suffering—physical, psychological, or psychosomatic—but the problem of suffering, which is surely linked to the question of the conditioned mind—the mind that is incapable of comprehending the whole, the total, the mind that is only concerned with the particular, with the limited, with the part. Perhaps if we can understand that, not merely speculate on what the whole is and thereby project in words, but perhaps if we understand the whole, the total, there is a possibility of overcoming sorrow, of being free from sorrow.

Our outlook, our approach generally is through the part to the whole, and we hope to understand the all through the part; that is, we hope that through the part—the part being the 'me'—we can comprehend our suffering, our relationship to the world, our attitude, our pain, our frustration; through the part, the 'me', we hope to comprehend the whole complex problem of living. After all, the 'me', the mind, is the only instrument you and I have; and that mind is so conditioned, so specialized, that it is capable of only thinking in conditioned values, outlooks, actions; and we hope that through the understanding of the part, of the 'me', we shall comprehend the whole. The whole is not a theory, not a speculation, not what some teacher says, not some idea of a state, not some idea of God or of a state of being. But the direct experiencing of the whole, not speculatively, but actually, may be the ultimate release from man's suffering.

Because we, you and I, are conditioned, totally conditioned by our thinking, our mind is incapable of comprehending the 'whole' of which we do not know. All thinking is conditioned; thought, at whatever level you may place it, is conditioned. You do not want to admit that. You think there is a part within you which is not conditioned, which is above all the influences that bring about conditioning—the climatic, the religious, the social influences, the education, the memory, the experience. You think that that something is beyond all conditioning, and that it is not the 'me'. But, when you think of that state which you say is unconditioned, that very thinking conditions, and also that thing which is beyond all conditioning is still conditioned if it is related to thought. This is not merely a speculation, a cunning argument.

If you can go into this question of the conditioned mind, you will find out that there is no part of thought which is not controlled, conditioned. Perhaps that very conditioning is the source from which all suffering begins and ends. Perhaps if we can go into it, if we do not remain at the verbal level—you know what I mean by the verbal level: the mere thinking about it, the mere speculating whether the mind can ever be unconditioned—if we can understand it, then in that understanding, we shall discover a great many things.

First, if we are at all aware, if we are observant of the state of our own mind, we realize that thought is conditioned, that there is no thinking apart from conditioning. If we admit that, if we realize that, then there are different ways of approaching the problem. That is, I admit that I am conditioned and that there is no possibility of unconditioning the mind at all; then I attempt to modify the conditioning, to change the condition by being no longer a believer of certain ideas or ideals, but in this process, I get conditioned to accept other ideas or ideals. So there is a progress in conditioning, and that is what most of us are concerned with. We want to progress socially, economically, or religiously, or in our relationship with one another, in being conditioned or better conditioned; and thereby, we admit that all suffering can never come to an end, and that there can only be a modification of suffering, various forms of escapes from suffering.

But when we know, when we are completely, totally aware that our whole thought is conditioned and there is no part of it unconditioned, then there is a possibility of finding out if there is anything beyond the mind, beyond the projections, beyond the fabrications of the mind. I think this is a very important point; if you can really go into this, if we can really, actually experience it as we talk, then there may be a real solution to all the innumerable problems that we may have, the chief of which is sorrow, pain—not only bodily pain, but the greater involvements of psychological pain, the inward struggle, the conflicts, the frustrations, the despair, the hope.

So what is important is to find out, to actually experience—if there is a state which is not conditioned—the total, the 'whole' which is not conditioned, which is not controllable by the mind or projected by the mind. All our answers—social, economic, or religious—are sought by a mind that is conditioned and therefore, whatever it is, the answer will be progressively conditioned, never beyond conditioning. That is, instead of worshipping the word *God*, we now worship the word *state*, and by using the word *state*, we think we have made tremendous progress. Or if we do not like the word *state*, we take the word *science* or the word *dialectical materialism* as though that is going to solve all our problems. That is, we are always approaching the solution of all our problems with a conditioned thought.

Thought is always conditioned, there is no thought which is not conditioned. As I said, you may comprehend the highest self sublimely and at the highest level, but it is still conditioned. When once we realize it, not theoretically, but actually, when we watch the operations of the mind, we see how the mind is constantly thinking, always with the background, and how there is no thought without memory; there is no experience without memory, without the process of recognition and therefore the contradiction of that. That is the state we know, and we approach our problems from that point of view. But, I do not think our problems can ever be solved in this way, by merely approaching the problem from a particular point of view. The problem can only be solved when we comprehend the 'whole', and the comprehension of the 'whole' is not possible as long as thought, the idea, is functioning. Do please think about this, not when you go home, but actually as I am talking to you.

The difficulty is that most of us translate or interpret or compare what we hear. Do you follow? You say that is what the Upanishads said, that is what that phrase in the Bhagavad-Gita meant, so you are interpreting, you are not understanding; so, your knowledge becomes a hindrance to direct experience. Therefore, there must be suppression of knowledge, the putting aside of all knowledge—I am not talking of the knowledge of how to build a bridge, which is essential; I am not talking of becoming primitive, which would be absurd—the putting aside of all knowledge which is comparative, the knowledge that interprets what others say. This interpretation, this translation, indicates a form of self-fulfillment, the desire to be always sure, always certain; therefore, the mind is always comparing, saying, "That is what the book says," and the very statement, the very translation has put an end to further experimentation, further study.

The mind must surely be in a state of complete uncertainty—that means, in a state of complete inaction, of not knowing, a mind which is not saying, "I know," "I have experience," "It is so." A mind which says, "I know," is incapable of solving any complex problem of living because life is moving, because life is not stagnant. You may translate life, you may interpret it as a socialist, as a communist, as a dialectical materialist, or what you will; you may translate it and thereby hold it in the words of explanation, but the reality is a living thing, and that living thing cannot be approached through the particular, which is thought. Please do see this, and reality will reveal itself to you. If you are really listening to it, you will do an extraordinary thing: it will break down immediately the conditioning of the mind, and then the mind will be capable of being so alert, so watchful that the 'whole' is then not something miraculous, not something beyond the mind. That 'whole', that totality, will be experienced only when this whole process of conditioning is understood, and when you actually realize that through a conditioned thought there is no solution to any of our problems. When you have an experience of that kind, when you have the perception or the experience of the 'whole', then there is a tremendous inward revolution, which is the only revolution—not the economic revolution, which is merely progressive thought, conditioned action.

And so we have to approach all our problems realizing that our thought is conditioned. Do what you will, gather psychological knowledge, read all the sacred books of the world; if with that knowledge you approach the problem of life, which is ever living, never static, you will never find an answer. But if there is the experiencing of the 'whole', with the comprehension of the 'whole', where the conditioned mind is realized, then with that understanding of the 'whole', every problem can be solved not in terms of progressive conditioning but in the complete cessation of that particular problem.

As I said yesterday, there is in this world of so-called progress more and more sorrow, more and more destruction, misery, suffocation, frustration. You may not be aware of it because your nose is accustomed to the grinding stone of everyday routine, but if you are at all aware, you will see that this is the process of existence—everlasting frustration without any end, and the more you seek fulfillment, the more there is frustration. In self-fulfillment, in the desire to fulfill, there is further desire, further misery, because the source of your action, the impetus of your action, is self-fulfillment—fulfillment in your son, in your family, in the nation, or in the society—the desire to fulfill and the resulting action bring about frustration. When there is frustration, there is despair. So the mind is seeking a way of hope through the state, through God, or something else through which it can fulfill, and so we are caught in that chain again.

So if there is to be an action which is not of a particular system, of a particular theory, if there has to be the action of togetherness, of you and me, which is not the action of fulfillment, there must be the understanding of how the mind is conditioned. The liberation of the mind from its conditioning is essential; then there is cooperation and there is action of 'ourness', not of yours or mine. That is truth. All this requires, naturally, a great deal of observation. This you cannot buy in books. This is real meditation—not the meditation of controlled thoughts, not the meditation that is only the narrowing down of thought but the meditation of extensive awareness. Extensive awareness is the awareness of all the processes of thinking—being aware of how the mind is operating, of every reaction, every experience, every infringement of life, being aware of how the mind works at every moment, being aware of every response without shaping it, controlling it, guiding it, disciplining it. In that state of extensive awareness, the mind becomes astonishingly still, the mind is no longer concerned with achievement, with self-fulfillment, with being or not being. That state of stillness is not compelled or disciplined. It is the state of being which is not of the mind, and therefore the mind is quiet, still, and in that stillness, that which is the 'whole' is comprehended.

Question: Common men and women like me are mostly concerned with their immediate problems of famine, unemployment, illness, and conflicts; how can I give my real attention to the deeper issues of life? All I seem to be seeking is relief from the immediate calamities.

KRISHNAMURTI: We all want immediate relief from our calamities. We are all common people, however high we may be placed—bureaucratically, socially, or religiously. There are these little calamities of everyday life, the jealousy, the anger, the anguish of not being loved, and the great ecstasy of being loved; if you can understand these little things of life, you can see in them the workings of your mind; it does not matter if you are a housewife, cooking three meals everlastingly through the rest of your life, being the slave to the husband, or if you are the husband, being a slave to the wife. In that relationship of pain, of pleasure, of calamities, of despair, of hope, at the very, very superficial level, if you begin at that, then you will find—if you can observe, watch, wait, be aware, without condemning, without judging—that the mind goes deeper and deeper with the problems, but if you are only concerned with the aspect of getting away from the particular problem, then your mind remains at a superficial level.

Let us consider the problem of envy because our society is based on envy. Envy is acquisitiveness, greed. You have, I have not; you are somebody, I am nobody, and I am going to compete with you to become somebody; you have more knowledge, more money, more experience, I have not. There is this everlasting struggle: you always going on and on and I always falling back; you are the guru, I am the disciple or the follower, and there is the vast gulf between us—you always ahead, I always behind. If we can see, there are immense implications in all these struggles, in all these efforts, in these sufferings, in the little illnesses, and other little things of everyday life. You do not need to read all the Vedas, all the books; you can put all of them aside, they have no importance; what is important is to see actually and directly in these little things of life, things that are implied differently. After all, when you observe the beauty of a tree, the bird flying, the sunset on water, they tell you a great deal, and also when you see the ugly things of life—dirt, squalor, the despair, the oppression, the fear—they also reveal a fundamental process of thought. But we cannot be aware of all that if the mind is merely concerned with escapes, with a panacea, with avoiding the discovery which exists in all relationships.

Unfortunately, we have not the patience; we want an immediate answer; our mind is so impatient with the problem. But if the mind is capable of observing the problem—not running away from it, but living with it—then that very problem begins to reveal its extraordinary quality. The mind gets to the depth of the problem, and so the mind becomes not a thing pushed around by circumstances, by calamities. Then the mind is like a pool, like rich water, quiet; and it is only such a mind that is capable of stillness, of calmness, of peace.

Question: Faith in dialectical materialism has released a flood of creativity in New China. Faith in religion seems to make men smug and otherworldly. Can the kindliness of a spiritual way be combined with the dynamic action of the materialists?

KRISHNAMURTI: It is comparatively easy, as you must have noticed, to create enthusiasm for the state, for freedom, for peace, or for war, and to identify ourselves with the state, with God, with an idea. That is, to forget oneself—through the idea of the state, of God, or material dialecticism—or rather to fulfill oneself, is comparatively easy; that gives you an astonishing enthusiasm, a capacity.

How do you think wars are fought—the wars that demand ruthless murder, that encourage enmity, endurance, sacrifice, the putting aside of all one's responsibility and going out to the front to kill? For that, you must have astonishing enthusiasm, energy, drive, hatred, and the so-called love of the country which makes one fulfill in that particular action. Therefore, there is no problem for such a man. He is living. Similarly, the identification with what we call God, the state, the identification with the idea which is considered bigger than the 'me' obviously gives one an astonishing energy and creativeness. And the same is the case with religion; if I am at all so-called religious, it also gives me great faith, capacity, drive. You have it all in this country. When you were struggling, fighting for freedom, you could do anything.

The struggle for freedom is self-fulfillment; the country with which you identify yourself is the means of escaping from yourself. The struggle, pain, suffering to create a new world, a new India, is an artificial means of self-forgetfulness. They are all fulfillment, in various ways, of the 'me'. And they all give extraordinary temporary energy, a release of enthusiasm. But behind it, there is always the 'me', the 'I', seeking everlastingly to fulfill; and the fulfillment, the desire to fulfill, brings conflict.

Religion, as you know it, as you practice it, is a dull routine, a dead thing, because it is bound by tradition, by what Shankara or Buddha said. So the mind creates what Shankara meant, what the Bhagavad-Gita meant, and that meaning is the way through which you fulfill. So your interpretation, your commentaries, become extraordinarily important. There is a false creativity which comes into being when you are fulfilling, but that is not creative; that is merely progression in calamity, progression in conditioned thinking. But there is an activity which is far beyond and above this urge of self-fulfillment, and that activity comes only when the desire to fulfill in different ways has come to an end.

Do think about all this, sirs. Don't just agree or disagree. The actual listening to experience is an essential thing. That will give you an untold energy, a life in which there is no hurt, in which there is no enforcement, no enforced slavery. That gives rise to a creativity in which there is not the 'me' that is fulfilling.

The 'me' identifying with the state or with a particular system brings calamity; that brings position, that brings enmity, that brings hatred.

If you identify yourself with a particular caste, won't you feel astonishingly enthusiastic to maintain that caste and struggle and fight to destroy other castes? So, similarly, mere identification with the larger is not the problem, nor is it the solution to the problem. See how, again, our mind moves, hoping to understand the 'whole' through the part. We think the 'whole' is the state, the community, the nation, or an ideal. The 'whole' is none of these things because they are projections of thought, and thought is always conditioned. That is why through religion or books, you cannot see the 'whole'.

The discovery of the experience of the 'whole' can only be understood and experienced when the mind is completely assured that it is conditioned. Then the mind which is the center of the 'me', everlastingly seeking fulfillment and therefore escaping through enthusiasm, realizes that it is incapable of movement in any direction and becomes still; then in that stillness there is an activity which is not merely producing, inventing, but which is creative. That creativity is essential in each of us to break the source of mischief, of misery, and destructivity. You and I are ordinary human beings, but if we discover this creativity, then this world will be our world, you and I building it together, you and I acting together, creating a world in which sorrow, pain, and starvation have come to an end. But without that creative reality, all other creation is merely progression in misery, progression of conditioned thought.

Question: As a man thinks, so he becomes. Is it not essential to know how not to be at the mercy of one's own evil and wayward thoughts?

KRISHNAMURTI: First, the questioner begins with the quotation, "As a man thinks, so he becomes." Is it not very odd that we cannot think of any problem directly? We have innumerable quotations to support our theories—what the Bhagavad-Gita, Marx, Shankara, Churchill, or Mao Tse-tung have said. Our mind is incapable of looking at anything directly and experiencing a thing directly. Quotation-knowledge has destroyed our capacity to find out the truth for ourselves. (Laughter) Yes, sirs, you laugh and you don't know the misery behind that laugh.

Now, your mind is crippled, and the mind that is crippled is not capable of being free. It is only free when it realizes it is crippled; then there is a possibility of doing something. A mind saying "I am not crippled," "I am full of knowledge," "I am full of quotations of other peoples' ideas," is incapable of the discovery of what is real. The man with such a mind is living at a level of "second-hand."

Now the next part of the question is, "Is it not essential to know how not to be at the mercy of one's own crazy, evil, and wayward thoughts?" In this question, there are two things involved. He says, "How can I remain free from evil thoughts, evil and wayward thoughts?" Please follow this closely because it is very important, because if we can really see the significance of it, go behind the words, you will discover something. Don't follow me merely verbally—which is, don't merely listen to the words and the vibrations of the words—but go into it.

Is there the thinker, the one apart from thought, apart from the evil, wayward thoughts? Please watch your own mind. We say, "There is the 'I' who wants to remain apart from the evil, apart from thoughts which are vagrant, wandering." That is to say, there is the 'I', the 'me' which says, "This is a wayward thought," "This is an evil action," "This is good," "This is bad," "I must control this thought," "I must keep to this thought." That is what we know. Is the one, the 'I', the thinker, the judger, the one that judges, the censor, different from all this? Is the 'I' different from thought, different from envy, different from evil? The 'I' which says that it is different from this evil is everlastingly trying to overcome me, trying to push me away, trying to become something. So you have this struggle, the effort to put away thoughts, not to be wayward.

We have, in the very process of thinking, created this problem of effort. Do you follow? Then you give birth to discipline, controlling thought—the 'I' controlling the thought which is not good, the 'I' which is trying to become nonenvious, nonviolent, to be this and to be that. So you have brought into being the very process of effort when there is the 'I' and the thing which it is controlling. That is the actual fact of our everyday existence.

Now, is the 'I' who is observing—the observer, the thinker, the actor—different from the action, from the thought, from the thing which it observes? We have so far said that the 'I' is different from thought. So let us keep to one thing—that is, the thinker is different from thought. The thinker says, "My thoughts are vagrant, evil; therefore, I must control them, shape them, discipline them." In that process that has been brought into being—this whole problem of effort and the negative form 'not to be'. Please listen to what I am saying and don't interpret; if you will listen carefully, you will see something extraordinary coming out. As I said, you have brought into being the effort in different forms, the negation and assertion; that is our daily life.

But is there a difference between the thinker and the thought? Please find out. Is there? That is, if you didn't think, would there be an 'I'? If there were no thought, no idea, no memory, no experience, would there be the 'I'? You say 'I' is the higher self, the thing which is beyond thought, which is guiding you, which is controlling you. Now, if you say that, again examine it; don't accept it. If you say that, then the very entity that thinks about the atma is still within the field of thought. The thing that is capable of being thought about is still within thought. That is, when I think about you—the particular name I know—when I recognize, you are already within the field of thought. Aren't you? So, my thinking is related to you. So the atma or the higher self or whatever word you use, is still within the field of thought. So there is always a relationship between the thinker and the thought; they are not two separate states, they are one unitary process.

So there is only the thought, which divides itself into the thinker and the thought and brings the thinker into prominence. That thought creates the 'I' which becomes permanent because, after all, that is what it is seeking—security, permanency, certainty in my relationship with my wife, with my children, with my society; always the desire to be ever certain. Thought is desire; so thought, the desire seeking certainty, creates the 'I'. Then the 'I' is enclosed in permanency. Then that says, "I must control my thoughts, I must push away this thought and take on that thought," as though that 'I' is separate. If you observe, the 'I' is not separate from thought. That is where the importance comes of really experiencing this thing, in which the thinker is the thought. That is real meditation—to find out how the mind is everlastingly operating in dividing the thinker and the thought.

The whole total process of thinking is what we are concerned with, not the 'I' which wants to look, which is creating, dominating, subjecting, sublimating thought. There is only one process which is thinking. The thinking which says, "That is my house," has behind it the desire for security in that house. Similarly when you say "my wife," in that thought there is security. So the 'I' is given prominence in certainty. There is only a process of thinking and not the 'I' separate from thought.

So when you realize that, when this realization, this understanding comes, what happens to the thoughts which are vagrant, wandering, going all over the place like a butterfly, like a monkey? When there is no censor any more, when there is no entity which says, "I must control thought," then what happens? Please follow this, sirs. Then, is there such a thing as a wandering thought? Do you follow? There is no entity which is operating, which is judging; therefore, every thought is a thought in itself, not to be compared as good and bad. So, there is no wandering or wavering.

The wandering thought exists when thought says, "I am wandering, I must not do that, I must do this." When there is no thinker—the entity which says that it will control thought—then we are only concerned with thought as it is, not as it should be. And then you will find the beauty of really observing every thought and its significance because then there is no such thing as a wandering thought. You cut away the whole problem of effort because you cannot come to reality through effort; effort must come to an end for reality to come. You must be capable of receiving. It is not a reward or a punishment. It is not a reward for good deeds. Society is concerned with your respectability, but truth is not.

For truth to be, thought must be silent. Thought must not seek reward or punishment; it must not be concerned. Only in that state of mind in which there is no seeking, does truth come into being. Truth that is seeking is not truth at all; it is only the self-projected voice of self-fulfillment. So, when you see all this, when you see this whole picture of how the mind operates, then there is no thought to be controlled, to be disciplined; then that very thought has significance; there is an observation of the thought as the observer watching thought, which is very difficult to experience, very arduous because that requires extraordinary perception and peace of mind. Every thought is the result of memory—memory which is but a name. After all, you think in words; your thought is the outcome of memory; memory is formed of images, symbols, words. So long as there is the "projection," there must be thought. So a man who is concerned with the understanding of thought understands the whole process of naming, terming, remembering, recognizing. Then only is there a possibility of the mind becoming thoroughly still. This stillness comes with understanding. Then truth may bless that individual, may come to him, may set him free from all problems; and then only is there the creative being, not the man who paints, writes a poem, or works ten hours a day.

Question: Nāma-japam *is the most effective means of quieting the incessant wanderings of the mind. Why do you object to these preliminary exercises which help the seeker to turn away from the fleeting shadows of existence?*

KRISHNAMURTI: What most of us want to be is to be hypnotized by words, by sound. We want to be quiet, and so we invent words or take a drug that will temporarily quiet the nerves.

If you are only concerned with the superficial quieting of the mind, *nāma-japam* does quiet the mind, the nerves, by the repetition of words. Instead of repeating *nāma-japam*, just repeat "two and two make four" several times, and your mind becomes very quiet. (Laughter)

Please follow this. The mind wants a vocation in which it cannot be disturbed. After all, that is what most of you want—you do not want to be disturbed in your job, in your relationship with your wife, with your neighbor; you want to be assured of your income; you want to be assured of your life; you want rest; you do not want to be disturbed politically, religiously. Only if you are hungry, if you are starving, then there is disturbance. The man who starves will somehow acquire a state of nondisturbance. After all, tyrannies and concentration camps are filled with those people who are disturbed. So doubt becomes a hindrance to a man who is seeking. That is what your religion says; that is what your politicians, your leaders assert. So the mind does not want to be disturbed, and so it turns to various resorts to quiet the mind.

After all, contentment is the thing essential for quietness. There must be the watching of mind and heart, of what is truth—not the ultimate truth, but truth in the everyday movement of life, the truth of thinking. It is necessary to be watchful, not just go to sleep by some repetition of words. Truth is not something ultimate; it is to be found every minute of the day. Truth is not something which is accumulative, which is tied up and thereby becomes time. That which is caught up in time is not the truth; it is memory, and that memory says, "I must not be disturbed," "I had a most beautiful experience of reality, of God, of the sunset," or "the joy of fulfillment," "I had a certain desire," "I must not be disturbed."

So the mind is everlastingly seeking a way in which it can remain quiet, in which it can function in a habitual manner. After all, all your experiences are merely established habits, and in that habit the mind is quiet, and so you create *nāma-japam* and repeat certain words, and your superficial mind is made quiet. But there is an urge going on inside, the becoming something, the urge for fulfillment, thoughts which are ambitious, struggling, striving, thoughts that are to be understood, that are to be apprehended. They are revealed in your daily relationship with your wife, with your children, in the job you are doing.

So life is a process of relationship in which there is disturbance. There must be disturbance, and that disturbance is the mirror in which you discover; you discover the state of your mind, of your heart; you see how it moves, how it functions. But if you condemn it, then you put a hindrance to it. You cannot go beyond it. So again the entity that judges, that compares, that condemns is still thought—the thought that is trying to become something, the thought that is ambitious, and such a thought will never find reality. The ambitious man is the political man, and the political world will never solve the problem of human existence. No parliament, no political leader will understand and bring about an inward revolution in the world.

The world is you; your world is the world in which you live with your people. It is in the heart that there must be revolution. And that revolution does not come about by putting yourself to sleep; it comes through something which is creative, which is dynamic, which is the ultimate reality. That revolution is only possible when you understand the things of life. The understanding of the heart is the 'beginning to listen', and meditation is the understanding of the whole process of the mind.

January 25, 1953

Third Talk in Poona

Many of us must have considered the problem of disintegration. Almost everything that we touch soon disintegrates. There is no creative, worthwhile action which soon does not end in complexities, worries, miseries, and confusion. It must have occurred to many of us why this should be so, and why at different levels of our human existence there is a darkened withering away and deterioration. We must have noticed this and found some kind of answer. We accept it as inevitable and find some worthwhile or merely verbal explanation, and we are satisfied because whatever we do, we want some explanation, some satisfactory words that will soothe our active mind. So we will soon get lost in the jungle of explanations.

We are going to discuss this evening the question of "education." It seems to me that one of the major factors of deterioration everywhere is the so-called education. We are going into that presently as succinctly as possible. But before I go into that very complex problem, I think it is very necessary that you and I should not merely either accept or refute anything I am going to suggest. Perhaps it may be new or it may be very old, but the mere rejection or acceptance of it without really understanding the whole complex problem is utterly valueless. So, may I suggest that while you are listening, you do not say, "That is impossible," "It is not practical," "It is not worthwhile," "All that we know already." All that indicates merely, does it not, a very sluggish mind, a mind that does not want to penetrate and understand the problem. And our minds are dull, especially at the end of the day after doing some worthless action of a routine, stupid life; we come here generally for entertainment, for something to listen to or talk about afterwards. At this meeting, I suggest that we consider this problem of education and examine it together—but not that I am stating the problem and you are looking at it.

What do we mean by education? Why do we want to be educated? Why do you send your children to be educated? Is it the mere acquisition of some technical knowledge which will give you a certain capacity, with which to lead your life so that you can apply that technique and get a profitable job? Is that what we mean by education, to pass certain examinations and then to become a clerk, and from a clerk to climb up the ladder of managerial efficiency? Or, do we educate our children or educate ourselves in order to understand the whole complex problem of living? With what intention actually do we send our children to be educated or do we get educated ourselves? Obviously, taking it factually as things are, you get educated in order to get a job and with that you are satisfied; and that is all you are concerned with—to be able to earn a livelihood by some means. So you go to a college or to a university, you soon marry and you have to earn a livelihood, and before you know where you are, you are a grandfather for the rest of your life. That is what most of us are doing with education; that is the fact. With that, most of us are satisfied.

But is that education? Is that an integrating process in which there can be a comprehension of the whole, total process of life? That is, do you want to educate your children to understand the whole of life, and not merely a segment of life like the physical, emotional, mental, psychological, or spiritual; to have not the compartmental, divided outlook but a whole, total, integrated outlook on life in which, of course, there is the earning capacity? Now, which is it that we want—not theoretically but actually? What is our necessity? According to that, you will have universities, schools, examinations or no examinations. But to merely talk narrowly about linguistic divisions seems to me utterly infantile. What we will have to do as mature human beings—if there are such entities existing—is to go into this problem. Do you want your children to be educated to be glorified clerks, bureaucrats, leading utterly miserable, useless, futile lives, functioning as machines in a system? Or, do you want integrated human beings who are intelligent, capable, fearless? We will find out, probably, what we mean by "intelligence." The mere acquisition of knowledge is not intelligence, and it does not make an intelligent human being. You may have all the technique, but that does not necessarily mean that you are an intelligent, integrated human being.

So, what is this thing that brings about integration in life, that makes a human being intelligent? That is what we want; at least, that is what we intend to find out in our education, if we are at all intelligent and interested in education. That is what we are attempting to do, are we not? Does this subject interest you, sirs? You seem rather hesitant. Or do you want to discuss about the soul? Sirs, education is really one of our major problems, if not the most important problem in life because as I said, everything is deteriorating around us and in us. We are not creative human beings. We are merely technicians. And if we are creating a new world, a new culture, surely there must be a revolution in our outlook on life, and not merely the acceptance of things as they are or the changing of things as they are.

Now, is it possible through education, the right kind of education, to bring about this integrated human being—that is, a human being who is thinking in terms of the whole, and not merely of the part; who is thinking as a total entity, as a total process, and not indulging in divided, broken up, fractional thinking? Is it possible for a human being to be intelligent—that is, to be without fear—through education so that the mind is capable of thinking freely, not thinking in terms of a Hindu or a Muslim or a Christian or a Communist? You can think freely only when your mind is unconditioned—that is, not conditioned as a Catholic or a Communist and so on—so that you are capable of looking at all the influences of life which are constantly conditioning you; so that you are capable of examining, observing, and freeing yourself from these conditions and influences; so that you are an intelligent human being without fear.

Our problem is how to bring about, through education, a human being who is creative, who is capable, who possesses that intelligence which is not burdened and which is not shaped in any particular direction but is total, who is not belonging to any particular society, caste, or religion so that through that education and with that intelligence, he arrives at maturity and therefore is capable of making his life, not merely as a technician but as a human being.

Now, that is our problem, is it not? Because we see what is happening in the world and especially here in this industrially backward country, we are trying to catch up industrially with the rest of the world; we think it will take ourselves and our children to catch up with the rest of the world. So, we are concerned with that, and not with the whole, total problem of living in which there is suffering, pain, death, the problem of sex, the whole problem of thinking, to live happily and creatively; we brush all that aside and are only concerned with special capacities. But we have to create a different human being, so obviously, our whole educational system must undergo a revolution, which means, really, there must be the education of the educator. That is, the educator must himself obviously be free or attempt to be free from all those qualities which are destructive in him, which are narrowing him down.

We must create a different human being who is creative. That is important, is it not? And it is not possible to do this in a class where there are a hundred children or thirty or forty children and only one teacher—which means, really, every teacher must have very few children, which means again, the expense involved. So, seeing the complexities, the parents want to get their children educated somehow so that they may serve for the rest of their life in some office.

But if you, as parents, really love your children—which I really question—if you are really concerned with your children, if you are really interested in their education, obviously you must understand this problem of "what is education." It must present itself to you, must it not?

As things are at present, and with this educational system and the so-called passing of examinations, is it possible to bring about an integrated human being, a human being who understands life or who is struggling to understand life—life being earning a livelihood, marriage, and all the problems of relationship, love, kindliness? This is only possible where there is no ambition. Because, an ambitious man is not an intelligent man, he is a ruthless man; he may be ambitious spiritually, but he is equally ruthless. Is it possible to have a human being without ambition? Can there be the right education which will produce such a human being—which means, really, a spiritual human being? I rather hesitate to use the word because you will immediately translate it in terms of some religious pursuit, some superstition. But if you are really concerned with education, is not that our problem?

Your immediate reaction to that is: What is the method? You want to know what the method is, how this can be brought about. Now, is there a method? Do please listen to this; don't brush it aside. Is there a method—a system—for the educator which will bring about that state of integration in a human being? Or, is there no method at all? Our educator must be much concerned, very watchful, very alert with each individual. As each individual is a living entity, the educator has to observe him, study him, and encourage in him that extraordinary quality of intelligence which will help him to become free, intelligent, and fearless. Can there be a method to do that? Does not method imply immediately conditioning a student to a particular pattern which you, as educator, think is important? You think you are helping him to grow into an intelligent human being by inflicting on him a pattern which you already have of what an intelligent human being should be. And you call that education, and feel as though you have created a marvelous world, a world in which you are all kind, happy, creative.

We have not created a beautiful world, but perhaps, if we know how to help the child to grow intelligently, he might create a different world in which there will be no war, no antagonism between man and man. If you are interested in this, is it not the obvious responsibility of each grown-up individual to see that this kind of education does come about—which means, really, the educator can have only a very few students with him; there may be no examinations, but there will be the observation of each student and his capacities. This means, really, that there will be no so-called mass education, that is, educating thousands in two or three classes. That is not education.

So if you are interested in this, you will create a right kind of educator and help the child to be free to create a new world. It is not a one man job; it is the responsibility of the educator, of the parent, and of the student. It is not just the teacher alone that is responsible for creating a human being, intelligent and fearless, because the teacher may attempt it, but when the child goes back home, the people there will begin to corrupt him; they will begin to influence him; his grandmother will begin to condition his mind. So it is a constant struggle. And unless you as parents cooperate with the teacher and produce the right kind of education, obviously there is going to be greater and greater deterioration. That is what intelligent human beings are concerned with—how to approach this problem. But, most of you say you do not want to think of these problems at all;

you want to be told what to do, to follow certain systems and put other things aside. All that you are concerned with is the begetting of children and passing them on to teachers.

But if you were really concerned with the right type of education, surely, it is your responsibility as grown-up people to see that through education there is right livelihood, not any old livelihood. Right livelihood implies, obviously, not joining the army, not becoming a policeman, not becoming a lawyer. Obviously, those three professions are out if you are really concerned with the right kind of education. I know, sirs, you laugh at it because it is a joke to you, it is an amazing thing; but if you really take it seriously, you would not laugh. The world is destroying itself; more and more means of vast destruction of human beings are there; those who laugh are not really concerned with the shadow of death which is constantly accompanying man. Obviously, one of the deteriorating factors for man is the wrong kind of education as we have at present.

To create an intelligent human being, there must be a complete revolution in our thinking. An intelligent human being means a fearless human being who is not bound by tradition, which does not mean he is immoral. You have to help your child to be free to find out, to create a new society—not a society according to some pattern such as Marx, Catholic, or capitalist. That requires a great deal of thought, concern, and love—not mere discussions about love. If we really loved our children, we would see that there would be right education.

Question: Even after the end of the British rule, there is no radical change in the system of our education. The stress as well as the demand is for specialization—technical and professional training. How best can education become the means to the realization of true freedom?

KRISHNAMURTI: Sir, what do we mean by true freedom? Political freedom? Or is it freedom to think what you like? Can you think what you like? And does thinking bring about freedom? Is not all thinking conditioned thinking? So, what do we mean by true freedom?

So far as we know, education is conditioned thinking, is it not? All that we are concerned with is to acquire a job or use that knowledge for self-satisfaction, for self-aggrandizement, to get on in the world. Is it not important to see what we mean by true freedom? Perhaps if we understand that, then the training in some technique for professional specialization may have its value. But merely to cultivate technical capacity without understanding what is true freedom leads to destruction, to greater wars; and that is actually what is happening in the world now. So let us find out what we mean by true freedom.

Obviously the first necessity for freedom is that there should be no fear—not only the fear imposed by society, but also the psychological fear of insecurity. You may have a very good job and you may be climbing up the ladder of success, but if there is ambition, if there is the struggle to be somebody, does that not entail fear? And does that not imply that he who is very successful is not truly free? So fear imposed by tradition, by the so-called responsibility of the edicts of society, or your own fear of death, of insecurity, of disease—all this prevents the true freedom of being, does it not?

So freedom is not possible if there is any form of outward or inward compulsion. Compulsion comes into being when there is the urge to conform to the pattern of society or to the pattern which you have created for yourself as being good or not good. The pattern is created by thought which is the outcome of the past, of your tradition, of your education, of your whole experience based on the past. So, as long as there is any form of compulsion—governmental, religious, or your own pattern which you have created for yourself through your desire to fulfill, to become great—there will be no true freedom. It is not an easy thing to do nor an easy thing to understand what we mean by true freedom. But we can see that as long as there is fear in any form, we cannot know what true freedom is. Individually or collectively, if there is fear, compulsion, there can be no freedom. We may speculate about true freedom, but the actual freedom is different from the speculative ideas about freedom.

So, as long as the mind is seeking any form of security—and that is what most of us want—as long as the mind is seeking permanency in any form, there can be no freedom. As long as individually or collectively we seek security, there must be war, which is an obvious fact, and that is what is happening in the world today. So there can be true freedom only when the mind understands this whole process of the desire for security, for permanency. After all, that is what you want in your gods, in your gurus. In your social relationships, your governments, you want security, so you invest your God with the ultimate security, which is above you; you clothe that image with the idea that you as an entity are such a transient being, and that there, at least, you have permanency. So you begin with the desire to be religiously permanent; and all your political, religious, and social activities, whatever they are, are based on that desire for permanency—to be certain, to perpetuate yourselves through the family or through the nation or through an idea, through your son. How can such a mind which is seeking constantly—consciously or unconsciously—permanency, security, how can such a mind ever have freedom?

We really do not seek true freedom. We seek something different from freedom, we seek better conditions, a better state. We do not want freedom; we want better, superior, nobler conditions, and that we call education. Can this education produce peace in the world? Certainly, not. On the contrary, it is going to produce greater wars and misery. As long as you are a Hindu, Muslim, or God knows what else, you are going to create strife for yourself, for your neighbor, and nation. Do we realize this? Look at what is happening in India! I do not have to tell you because you already know it.

Instead of being integrated human beings, you are thinking separatively; your activities are fractioned, broken up, disintegrated—you're Maharashtra, you're Gujarat, you're Andhra, you're Tamil—you are all fighting; that is the result of this so-called freedom and so-called education. You say that you have unity religiously, but actually you are fighting, destroying each other, because you do not see the whole process of living, because you are only concerned with tomorrow or to have better jobs. You will go out after listening and do exactly the same thing. You will be a Maharashtrian forgetting the rest of the world. As long as you are thinking in those terms, you are going to have wars, miseries, destruction. You will never be safe, neither you nor your children, though you want to be safe, and therefore you are thinking in this narrow, regional way. As long as you have these ways, you have got to have wars.

Your present way of living indicates that you really do not want to have freedom; what you want is merely a better way of living, more safety, more contentment, to be assured of a job, to be assured of your position—religiously, politically. Such people cannot create a new world. They are not religious people. They are not intelligent people. They are thinking in terms of immediate results like all politicians. And you know that as long as you leave the world to politicians, you are going to have destruction, wars, misery. Sirs, please don't smile. It is your responsibility, not your leaders' responsibility; it is your own individual responsibility.

Freedom is something entirely different. Freedom comes into being; it cannot be sought after. It comes into being when there is no fear, when there is love in your heart. You cannot have love and think in terms of a Hindu, a Christian, a Muslim, a Parsee, or God knows what else. Freedom comes into being only when the mind is no longer seeking security for itself, either in tradition or in knowledge. A mind that is crippled with knowledge or burdened with knowledge is not a free mind. The mind is only free when it is capable of meeting life at every moment, meeting the reality which every incident, which every thought, which every experience reveals, and that revelation is not possible when the mind is crippled by the past.

It is the responsibility of the educator to create a new human being, to bring about a different human being, fearless, self-reliant, who will create his own society—a society totally unlike ours because ours is based on fear, envy, ambition, corruption. True freedom can only come when intelligence comes into being—that is, the understanding of the whole, total process of existence.

Question: Modern life has become abjectly dependent on highly trained persons; what are your views on university education? How can we prevent the misuse of higher technical knowledge?

KRISHNAMURTI: Sir, surely it all depends on for what you are being educated. If you are merely being educated to a particular specialized job through university education in which there is no consideration of the total process of existence—which is love, concern for your neighbor, the problem of what is truth, death, envy, the whole problem of life—if you are only concerned with the acquisition of a particular type of knowledge, and not with the problem of life, then obviously you are creating a world of confusion, of darkness, of misery; and then you ask how that can be prevented.

Now, how are you going to prevent it, sirs? How are you and I going to prevent it? Sirs, is it not your responsibility? Or do you say, "It is our karma, we do what we can to live, but life is too much for us," and leave it at that? Do you not feel this is your responsibility? As parents, do you not feel that the darkness is closing in, deterioration is setting in fast in every human being? Do you not feel that we have ceased to be really creative? Merely painting pictures or being trained to paint them or writing a poem occasionally is not what I mean by creativity. Creativity is something entirely different, and it comes into being when there is no concern or fear of oneself clothed in the form of virtue, or concern for oneself socially, economically, politically. When that concern, that fear ceases, there is creativity.

The understanding of the whole process of thought which builds the 'I', the 'me', and the dissolution of that—is not that true education? And if it is, should not universities help towards that end and at the same time give students the right opportunity to cultivate capacities? But now, we are concerned with the cultivation of capacities, gifts, tendencies to become more and more efficient, and we deny the whole of life which is much deeper, truer, more complex. So it is your responsibility, is it not? Sirs, the individual problem is the world problem. Your problem is the problem of the world. Those problems are not separate from your daily problems.

How you live, how you think, what you do will create the world or destroy the world. We do not realize this. We do not see this responsibility, and so we say, "Technical knowledge is bringing about the destruction of man; how can that be prevented?" I will give you the explanation, the manner of doing it, and you will listen and go away, and carry on as usual. So explanations no longer matter; descriptions of theories have no value any more; what is of importance now is that you, as an individual, understand and become responsible for your actions. You are responsible. You and others can, with equal enthusiasm and interest, create a new world. You are to think of the problem anew, not create a new pattern—communist or another religious form.

Real revolution does not come merely at the superficial level, at the economic level. Real revolution lies in our hearts and minds, and it can only come when we understand the whole total process of our being from day to day, in every relationship. And then only is there a possibility of preventing technical knowledge being used for the destruction of man.

Question: Educationists all over the world are troubled by the question of moral education. How can education evoke the deeper core of human decency and goodness in oneself and in others?

KRISHNAMURTI: The good is not the "respectable." The respectable man can never know what is good. Most of us are respectable, and therefore we do not know what it is to be good. Moral education can only come, not with the cultivation of respectability, but with the awakening of love. But we do not know what love is. Is love something to be cultivated? Can you learn it in colleges, in schools, from teachers, from technicians, from the following of your gurus? Is devotion love? And if it is, can the man who is respectable, who is devoted, know love? Do you know what I mean by respectability? Respectability is when the mind is cultivating, when the mind is becoming virtuous. The respectable man is the man who is struggling consciously not to be envious, the man who is following tradition, he who says, "What will people say?" Respectability will obviously never know what truth is, what good is, because the respectable man is only concerned with himself.

It is love which brings morality. Without love there is no morality. You may be a great man, a moral man; you may be very good; you may not be envious; you may have no ambition, but if you have no love, you are not moral, you are not good, fundamentally, deeply, profoundly. You may have all the outer trimmings of goodness, but if you have no love in the heart, there can be no moral, ethical being. Is love something to be taught in a school? Please follow all this. What is it that prevents us from loving? If you can be taught in the school and in the house to love, how simple it would be, would it not? Many books are written on it. You learn them and you repeat them, and you know all the symptoms of love without having love.

Can love be taught? Please, sirs, this is really an important question; please do follow it. If love cannot be taught, what are the things that are preventing love? The things of the mind, the thoughts, the jealousy, the anguish, the ideas, the pursuits, their suppressions, the motives of the mind—these may be the things that prevent love. And as we have cultivated the mind for several centuries, it may be that the mind is preventing us from loving. So perhaps the things that you are teaching your children and the things that you are learning through universities and colleges may be the things which are at the root of the destruction of love because you are only developing one side—the intellectual side, the so-called technical side—and that is becoming more and more important in an industrial world; other things become less and less valuable; they fade away. If love can be taught in school through books, shown on the screen in cinemas, then it would be possible to cultivate morality. If morality is a thing of tradition, then it is quite simple; then you condition the student to be moral, to be a communist, to be a socialist, to think along a particular line and say that that line is the good line, the true line; any deviation from it is immoral, ending up in concentration camps.

Is morality something to be taught—which means, can the mind be conditioned to be moral? Or is morality something that springs spontaneously, joyously, creatively? This is only possible when there is love. That love cannot exist when you cultivate your mind, which is the very center of the 'me', the 'I', the thing that is uppermost in most of us day in and day out—the 'me' that is so important, the 'I' that is everlastingly trying to fulfill, trying to be something. And as long as that 'I' exists, do what you will, all your morality has no meaning; it is merely conformity to a pattern based on security, for your being something some day, so that you can live without any fear. Such a state is not a moral state; it is merely an imitation. The more a society is imitative, following tradition, the more deteriorating it is. It is important to see this, to find out for oneself how the self, the 'me' is perpetuating itself, how the 'me' is everlastingly thinking about virtue and trying to become virtuous and establishing laws of morality for itself and for others. So the good man who is following the pattern of good is the respectable man, and the respectable man is not the man who knows what love is. Only the man who knows what love is, is the moral man.

January 31, 1953

Fourth Talk in Poona

As this is the last talk here and as it is not possible to enter into more detailed thinking-out of certain ideas, may I suggest that you do not reject or accept what I have been saying, that you do not say, "This is not for me, or this is only for the few"; do not compare what I have said to what you already know.

Our problems are very complex because we have, I feel, fundamentally lost—or perhaps we never had—freedom, self-reliance, and vigor to search out happiness and to find out the truth of any problem. We are not happy beings, just normally, healthily happy; we have too many burdens, too many worries; our security, physical as well as psychological, is being threatened all the time; there is no faith in anything any longer, no hope; the faith that we had has evaporated. The leaders have led us to more confusion, to more misery, to more strife; and out of this confusion we have chosen our gurus, our political leaders; naturally, when we choose a leader or a guru out of confusion, out of misery, out of strife, that which we choose will invariably be confused, will also be striving, struggling. So, when we follow somebody, we invariably follow those who represent our state, not something entirely different; those who represent us may perhaps be a little more glorified, a little more polished, but they are never the contrary of what we are.

I think it is very important, especially when we are facing a crisis, to be very clear in ourselves because no one is going to represent us any more. I think there is nothing extraordinary in that if we realize that there are no more leaders, no more gurus, because we have lost complete faith in them; we cannot turn to any political panacea for a solution, so we are invariably forced to think out the problem by ourselves and for ourselves, to see for ourselves the truth of the problem we are faced with now, to think out for ourselves, if we can, individually and perhaps later collectively, every problem that confronts us.

Truth or happiness or what you will cannot come through choice; it is not a matter of choice. But our minds are only capable of choosing, differentiating, and therefore not having insight into the problem. Our minds are petty, small, narrow, shallow. It does not matter if the mind is a most learned, most experienced mind; such a mind is still shallow, still petty. So if you think over the problem of what I am saying, what I am suggesting, do not reject it, don't say, "It is not for me, it is too much for me," but investigate it, think it out for yourself.

As long as we are choosing between what is good and what is bad, between the noble and the ignoble, between this guru and that guru, between that political leader and this political leader, as long as there is choice, there can be no truth. Choice is only the capacity of the mind to differentiate, and the process of differentiation springs from a confused mind, and however much you may choose—analytically, subjectively, or by investigation of all the circumstances—still that choice will invariably produce conflict. What is necessary now is not choice between this and that but to understand each problem in itself, completely, without comparing, without judging, by going into it from every aspect, deeply, by putting aside one's own inclinations and prejudices and by really investigating. Our minds have been made petty through choice, through the capacity to differentiate. Please think it over, don't reject it.

Our minds at present are so cunning, so confused, so distorted, that we are incapable of seeing directly, immediately in an experience the thing that is true. We want confirmation, and a man who is really seeking confirmation can never find or experience that which is truth. But it is very difficult for us whose minds are shallow, who are thinking in terms of tomorrow or of immediate results, to bring about a fundamental revolution in our thinking. This fundamental revolution is essential if we have to create a different world which is not based on communistic or capitalistic or religious ideas.

There must be a transformation in our thinking, and that can only come about if we really investigate into the question of choice—which does not mean that we should become obstinate. The mind that is analytical, that has the capacity to see what is worthwhile and what is not worthwhile, that is choosing, will invariably build a society based on results, on past memories, on immediate necessity. Therefore, such a mind will be utterly incapable of creating a world in which there is this sense of an integrated outlook on the total process of life.

So, if I may suggest, if you are really serious and earnest, please follow what I am saying. Our problems are so complex that there can be only a simple and direct approach to them. You cannot approach them through any book nor through a philosophy, nor through a system, nor through any leader. You can approach them only through the understanding of yourselves, by seeing yourselves in your daily relationships exactly as you are and not what you should be. This 'should be' is always the choice, is always away from *what is*. 'What I am' actually is important, not what 'I should be'. 'What I should be' is theoretical and ideological and has no value; it is only an escape from 'what I am'. Our society, our religious and moral structure is based on 'what should be', which is an escape from 'what I am'. What is important is to find out 'what I am' actually from moment to moment, in which there is no choice whatsoever. As long as the mind is incapable of choosing 'what should be', then it will deal with *what is*. The *what is* is important not only in the world of action but psychologically, inwardly. There can only be direct action if I understand *what is,* not 'what I want to be'.

As long as we introduce choice in our action, the choice is based on our conditioned thought, and therefore there is no release from fear; therefore, there is always struggle, there is always pain; and if we can understand *what is*—which is constantly changing, which is never static—that very understanding is dynamic, and therefore it is creative and, in that, there is release. We must really observe our relationships from day to day, from moment to moment, the exact state of what we are, and not try to transform it into something noble. You cannot transform stupidity into intelligence; all that you can do is to understand stupidity, and the very understanding of that stupidity is intelligence. Please see the importance of this and we will create a new world. As long as you are striving to be something other than what you are, there will be destruction, there will be misery, there will be confusion. It is only when I understand the thing which I am from moment to moment that the understanding leads me to the various unconscious depths of my being; therefore, through that there will be release from fear, and the release from fear is the state of happiness.

Question: You seem to imply that all action, thought, and ideals are forms of self-fulfillment. You confuse us further by asserting that "to be is to be related" and that "not to be related is death." In one breath you uphold renunciation; in another you are refuting that view. What do you mean by self-fulfillment? Can one live at all without fulfilling oneself in one form or another?

KRISHNAMURTI: Is not everyone trying to fulfill in something? The mountaineer climbing the great heights, to him that is the action of fulfillment; through marriage and children, through your son, you try to fulfill; and the politician with a huge crowd in front of him, getting the thrill of the crowd, is fulfilling himself through the crowd. If you reject these outward expressions of action and activities which are self-fulfilling, then you turn to inward, psychological, spiritual actions; you want to fulfill—in an idea, in God, in virtue. So each one of us is trying to fulfill in different ways—that is, to be something through identification. You want to fulfill through identification with a political party; you deny yourself and say the party is all-important. The party represents what you believe is true, so the party is a means through which you fulfill. The mountaineer fulfills in the delight of climbing great heights, and the ambitious man fulfills himself in attaining his ambition. So this is what you are doing, are you not?

The desire to fulfill, the desire to become, the desire to achieve, to gain, that is our relationship, is it not? I want something from you, and therefore I treat you very nicely and very politely. I give you garlands, but I treat contemptuously those from whom I receive nothing. And this is the constant process of our being. Sirs, is there such a thing actually as "self-fulfillment"? Do you follow? 'To be' is to be related, that is an obvious fact. I cannot live without being related to something, and that something is that through which I try to fulfill—my wife, my child, my house, my property, my painting, my poem, or the talk which I am giving now. If I am doing that, obviously it is a form of self-expansion; I am important, not you, not what I am talking about. So the means of self-fulfillment becomes much more important to me and to you than the truth of finding out whether there is ever such a thing as fulfillment.

All action, as it is now, is based on self-fulfillment; that is what we know. We may try to cover it up, camouflage it, we may use any words, any nice-sounding words, phrases, but essentially every action is the outcome of the desire to fulfill through that action. When I say India, I identify myself with India, and India then becomes the means for my fulfillment. These are the obvious facts. Let us go a little bit further into that. Is there such a thing as fulfilling? From childhood to maturity and until death, we are always seeking fulfillment in different forms, are we not, and there is always frustration. The moment you are fulfilled, there is some other higher fulfillment, and you are everlastingly struggling. So behind our fulfillment, behind our urge for self-fulfillment, there is the fear of frustration. Watch your own minds and hearts, and you will see whether what I am saying is true or not. You do not have to accept what I am saying.

Where there is desire, the unconscious or conscious desire to fulfill, there must be the fear of frustration. So our actions invariably lead us to frustration. Being frustrated, we seek further fulfillment to escape from that frustration. So we are caught in this everlasting prison of fulfillment and frustration. And is it not important to free the mind from this desire to fulfill itself in action, in idea, in something? When I am seeking to fulfill myself through my wife and children, is it love? When I am trying to fulfill myself in speaking to large or small audiences, am I really concerned with the truth, with the fundamental desire to free men, or am I fulfilling myself through you?

Sirs, this is not a discussion meeting. So, is it not important to find out if there is not a different way of thinking out this problem, a different approach which is not based on self-fulfillment, an action which is not seeking a result? Don't say, "Yes, that is what the Bhagavad-Gita says, what the Upanishads say," and so brush it aside. When you say that, you are actually not listening to another person. And what is important is to listen. Really, if you know how to listen, the miracle takes place. If you can listen to the pure sound, to the silence between two notes, then perhaps you will find out the truth of something. But as long as you are comparing, rejecting, accepting with the constant activity of explanation and rejection, you are not actually listening.

I am suggesting that perhaps there can be a different way of acting in which there is no longer self-fulfillment, which is not preserved for the few. If I can understand, if I can watch myself in my daily activity, how I am fulfilling myself all the time and therefore living with frustration and fear, when I actually realize that—not merely accept it—then I see that there is no fulfillment of myself in anything. When you actually see, from moment to moment in your daily activity, how every action is the prompting of self-fulfillment and that self-fulfillment invariably brings frustration, if you realize the whole thing, if you are awake to that without argumentation, without disputation, without trying to compare—you know, all that juggling that the mind does—then from that, there must be a new action, an action not of self-fulfillment but of something else.

Obviously, when each one of us is trying to fulfill, there is chaos in society, and in order to overcome that chaos, our minds turn to a particular pattern or condition. If you can realize all that, if you are really listening to what I am saying, you will see the truth of this—that there is no self-fulfillment. Do what you will, climb to whatever heights—there is no such thing as self-fulfillment. If one really, actually sees that, inwardly feels it out, then there is a possibility of action which is not the outcome, the result of compulsion, of fear, of frustration.

Question: You seem to stress the importance of the individual exclusively. Is not collective action necessary to be effective? Why do you denounce all organizations—social, political, or religious?

KRISHNAMURTI: "You seem to stress the importance of the individual exclusively. Is not collective action necessary to be effective? Why do you denounce all organizations—social, political or religious?" Sirs, this is the question.

Now, let us go into the question of what we mean by collective action. Can there ever be such a thing as collective action? I know that is the popular phrase—mass action, collective action, doing things with a spirit of cooperation. But, what does collective action mean? Can we all paint a picture together? Please follow this. Can we all write a poem together? Can we plough a field together or work in a factory? Surely, we do not mean collective action there! We mean collective thinking, not action; we mean action born of collective thinking. So, we are concerned with collective thought, not collective action. Now, action may come out of collective thinking—that is, if you can all agree together as to what is good for India or for a country, if the authorities can so condition your thinking, then there will be collective action—action presenting a collective form, carried out by you as an individual; and if you do not carry it out, there are always ways of making you do it—such as compulsion, liquidation, punishment, reward, and so on.

Essentially the nature of collective action is collective thinking. Now what do we mean by collective thinking? Can you and I and millions together think out a problem—economic, social, political, religious, or what you will? Can we independently think out the problem, or are we persuaded by punishments, rewards, traditions, conditioning influences? Can there be collective thinking? Please find out, observe yourselves, think. Are you not the result of collective thought? When you call yourself a Hindu, Brahmin, Christian, is it not a result of collective thinking? You are conditioned by collective thought to be a Hindu, to be a Buddhist, a Christian, or a Roman Catholic, or a Communist; and every group, every society and every religion conditions, impinges its ideas on the mind. Is it possible to think collectively when we are together, conditioned in a certain way? We are collective; we cannot think independently. There is no thought which is independent because thought is the outcome of a conditioned mind, thought is the symbol of the reaction to memory, so all thinking—conscious or unconscious—must be collective. You cannot think independently because your mind is already conditioned as a Communist, as a Catholic, and so on. Sirs, there is no freedom of thought. Collective action is collective thinking.

When we say we try to make man think differently, not in the old pattern, but in the new way of thinking, it is still a continuance of the old, modified. That is all we are concerned with, and that is what we mean by collective thinking. When we have that kind of collective thinking, we must have propaganda to urge us to think in a certain way, we must have newspapers. Then we become slaves to authority, to the compulsions of subtle minds putting various forms of impressions on us constantly. So collective thinking may produce individual action, but it will be in a field of conditioned thought, and therefore there is no freedom. Freedom is only possible when we realize this and admit that we are conditioned completely. Then there is a possibility of breaking through and finding out a state of mind in which there is no conditioning, and when you and I perceive the truth of that, in that there can be action which is truly collective and which is not the conditioned collective thought.

When you and I say that all our thinking is conditioned—whether as a Catholic, a Communist, or a Hindu, a Buddhist, or a Muslim—when we realize that, when you do not want me to become a Communist or I do not want you to become a Catholic—because that is the modified continuance of the old, in which is implied fear, threat, compulsion, liquidation, concentration camps and all the various forms of propaganda to make you do things—when you and I realize that all our thinking is conditioned and therefore there can be no fundamental revolution, no fundamental transformation in society, then perhaps we shall, you and I, come to the realization of that truth which is not the outcome of a conditioned thought. When you and I realize that, then there can be truly collective action.

Is that not our vocation, yours and mine, to find that truth which is beyond the conditioned mind so that you and I can work together, create a new world which is ours, yours and mine, our world—not communist, not capitalist, not socialist, nor Hindu. But perhaps you will say that this is an impossible state, and very few of us can realize this, and so, brush it aside. Sirs, it is our world. We can transform the world, we can bring it about for ourselves and our fellow beings, but we must give care and thought to all this. True collective action, not the collective action of a conditioned mind, can only be possible, can only come about when you as an individual can understand the total process. That is why organizations—political, religious, or social—will not lead man to happiness.

Man may have all the clothes he wants, all the food he wants, all the shelter he wants, but there is something much more significant in life than the mere acquisition of things. This does not mean that you should become a saint, a sannyasi, and withdraw into a cave, which is the ultimate escape. But when we do realize the implications of the mind that is unconditioned and when therefore all actions can take place from that, that is the true revolution.

Question: What do you mean by the 'whole'? Is it only a new term to define the absolute God? And can we at all shift our outlook from the part to the 'whole', except through image, idea, or aspiration?

KRISHNAMURTI: I am not substituting the word *whole* for God or for truth. It is what you do; I am not doing that. What I am trying to point out is that through the part, we cannot understand the 'whole'. Wait a minute, sir; we will go into what the 'whole' is.

Through studying part of a picture, of a particular painting, taking a part, one corner of it, you don't see the whole picture. Perhaps if we see all the picture and understand what the painter intends to convey, then we can study the part, the corner; but if we begin to study the corner, the angle, instead of the whole of the picture, then we will never have the comprehension of the whole. It is a very simple fact; that is, if we emphasize only the economic side of our total living and give all our thought, all our considerations, all our experiences to the economic solution of man, we will miss the whole struggle of man, the whole existence of man, his different states—the psychological, physical, inward, outward. And will this study of the part lead you to the comprehension of the whole totality of man? As most of us—the specialists, the experienced ones, the learned ones, the great ones—are all concerned with the part and legislating for the part, perhaps we miss something—the whole of man, the whole of the being of man—which if we understand, we may find a different solution, a different answer, a quicker way of approach to our economic problem. That something is, after all, the totality of my being or your being; it is made up of all these parts, is it not? I am the body, the clothes I put on, the hunger, the thirst, outwardly; and inwardly, I am all the desires, all the ambitions, psychological struggles, frustrations, urges, the compulsion to fulfill, to seek something beyond the mind; I am the total process of all that, as you are.

Is it not important to help each other to understand the total process of you and me, and not just legislate for one part of me, for one layer of me? Sir, I need food, clothes, and shelter; so do you, and we also need something much more fundamental. We want to fulfill, we want to be painters, we want to be writers, we want to be saints, we want to be helpers, we want to be evil beings; there is the feeling of hatred, ambition, envy; how can you leave all that aside and just concern yourself with a particular part—it may be a glorified part—and talk about that particular part and bring about a revolution? Is not my existence a total process, is it not the whole process of my being at different levels, the conscious as well as the unconscious? Have you not to take all that into consideration, have you not to have the vision of the whole of me—not of some extraordinary God? The 'me' is related to the 'whole' that is the 'me' of everyone, I do not exist independently of it, I cannot. The total process of the 'whole', of me and of you, has to be understood. If I can understand as you can, the total process of the whole being, and regard and concern myself with the 'whole' and not with the part, then we shall find a different answer to all our problems. But the enrichment and the glorification of the part is not going to solve the problem of the 'whole'.

It is so much easier to occupy ourselves with the part. We are concerned with the part—which indicates our shallowness, the pettiness of our minds. It is only when we can understand the total process of our being from day to day, in all our relationships, then there is a possibility of discovering something which is beyond the mind. But we cannot find that which is beyond the mind through the emphasis of the part. And without discovering what is beyond the mind, we shall have no happiness, we shall have no peace for mankind; our lives will be a constant struggle and misery. These are obvious facts; you don't have to study them in innumerable psychological books; you don't have to pass an examination; you don't have to know a technique to discover what is in your mind and heart from time to time, from moment to moment, everyday. All that it needs is watchfulness, and not the following of a guru or leader. It needs no discipline, but the mere observing of simple things—anger, jealously, the desire to fulfill, the desire to acquire, the desire to be powerful. You observe these things in your relationships, in your everyday life, and you will see how the totality of your being works, whether you are the center, whether without the alteration at the center, fundamentally, radically, you can bring about a revolution at the periphery. As long as we are polishing the outer—not that the outer should not be bright—such an approach will not solve our problems. But if we can understand the total process of our being and then perhaps be able to go beyond and, from there, approach all our problems, then we shall find the true answer. The answer will not then be productive of further problems, further misery, further sorrow.

Question: I am troubled by my dreams night after night. Can one not free oneself from this exhausting process?

KRISHNAMURTI: Let us find out together what is the right answer to this problem—together, you and I. Don't listen to me merely as if I am the talker and you the listener, but together we shall find the truth of this because it is your problem.

What do you mean by waking and dreaming? When are you awake? At least, when do we think we are awake? And when do we think we are dreaming? Please, this is not a psychological question. Just follow it step by step, simply. Do not translate it and say, "Yes, Shankara, Buddha, said so," and then wander away. I am talking very simply; what is the actual fact? When do we think we are awake? When our conscious mind is functioning, is it not? That is, there is the mind that is operating every day, and when that is functioning, we are awake. You are awake when you have a job, when you are studying, when you are getting into the tramcar or into the bus, when you are following, when you are scolding someone, when you are ambitious or sexual or what you will. That is, during the day we think we are awake, and when we sleep we think we are in a state when the mind has gone to sleep—rather, has been put to sleep.

Now, is the mind ever asleep? Is it ever at rest? The mind is both the conscious as well as the unconscious. The conscious shows very little; that which we call the conscious is very superficial, but there is a dreaded part, undiscovered, hidden, below this conscious part, which is the unconscious, and our mind is both the conscious as well as the unconscious. The conscious mind is urged, propelled, driven, or held back by the unconscious. You may think you are outwardly a very peaceful person, that outwardly you are not ambitious, but below, hidden deep down, there is the bellowing going on in your heart—your urges, compulsions, desires, motives. The unconscious is the reservoir of all the past of humanity—not the past of your being only, but of your father, of your forefathers, of your nation, of human beings—the racial traditions, the caste prejudices; all that is held in the unconscious.

The conscious mind is occupied during the day with trivial things, and the occupation with those trivial things we call the waking state. When we go to sleep, the mind goes on being active; it is still thinking out the problems of the day in relation to, and colored by, the unconscious; and when the unconscious wants to put some idea, some impression on the conscious mind which it is not capable of doing during the day, then you have dreams. That is, your conscious mind is occupied throughout the day; it cannot receive new impressions, new promptings, new hints, because it is too occupied; and then you go to sleep, and the unconscious projects into that semi-active conscious mind, its impressions. When you wake up, you say you have had a dream. Then begins the translation of that dream by the conscious mind, and you say you have had a marvelous experience.

So, as long as you are not consciously aware at the time—throughout the waking time, throughout the waking period—of the promptings of the unconscious, as long as you are not open to every impression or every hint from the unconscious, you must continue to dream; there must be a conflict between the conscious and the unconscious. Sirs, these are all very simple facts. If you observe your own being, your own thoughts, your daily activities, if you are aware of them, you will see that this is the actual process going on. There is nothing mysterious about it.

The whole process—the unconscious, the conscious, the promptings, the hints, the impressions, and the translating of all those impulses by the conscious—all that is your being; that is what you are. If you are not open, if the mind is not open to the total process but is only occupied with the part, naturally there must be dreams—dreams being the impressions and the projections of the unconscious. So there is this constant struggle going on between the conscious and the unconscious because the conscious can never compete completely with the unconscious, because the conscious is trying to translate every impression according to certain demands, activities, and results.

Sirs, it is only when we begin to understand this total process of our being, the actual state in which we are, that then there is a possibility of an integrated human being. Surely that is the beginning of meditation, is it not? Meditation is not merely concentration on some idea, on some picture, or the desire to be something—that is just immature, childish; it is not meditation. Meditation is this understanding of the total process, the observation, the awareness of the responses of the conditioned thought to every challenge so that the mind remains aware of its content, its activity, its pursuits, its hidden motives, so that through that constant awareness without choice, there is freedom, there is an integration—this whole process is meditation. A mind that is capable of observing without choice, seeing things as they are without trying to interpret them, without translating them, without twisting them, without distorting them—such a mind, through awareness, shall know what peace is, such a mind is capable then of being truly silent. Then only, in that silence, that *which is* comes into being. But the mind that is seeking a result can never find truth.

February 1, 1953

Bombay, India, 1953

First Talk in Bombay

As we are going to have a series of ten talks, I think it is very important to establish the relationship between the speaker and yourselves; otherwise, sirs, we shall have misconceptions, and inevitably misunderstandings will follow from those misconceptions. You see, I am speaking not to convince any one of you of any particular theory, or of a particular mode of conduct, or to drive in certain ideas, because the intention is not in any way propagandistic. Propaganda implies the conditioning of certain minds to certain attitudes. That is not my intention at all. If you have ideas of which you want to be convinced, if you want to have certain ideas to cherish, to follow, if you want a definite course of thought leading to certain results, or if you wish to bring about a certain revolution in ideas, I am afraid you will be very much mistaken. Because, I feel that what is fundamentally important is the revolution in the unconscious—not the conscious revolution, and of this, I shall explain presently when we go on with the talk.

But before we do that, as I said, you and I must know each other not only at the verbal level but more deeply if we can. Because, if we can know your intention as well as mine, then there is a possibility of our meeting together to talk over our problems. But if you have certain set-up ideas, and I contrary ideas, then obviously there is no meeting point between us. So, I think it is very important that we should, from the very beginning, establish the right relationship between us. I am not your guru, or a leader, so you cannot look up to me. I do not think that our problem, the present crisis in which we are, can dissolve in any way by following any leader, political or religious, or any guru. As I said, it requires a fundamental revolution in the unconscious, not merely a change of ideas on the superficial level.

So, is it not very important to find out what I am going to say or what I have said? Because, I am not going to convince you of anything. This is not propagandistic. I mean what I say; I am not here to convince you of any particular idea. Conviction implies the process of rejection and acceptance, confirmation or denial, and that is not my intention at all. What we are trying to do is to find out the true answer, the right answer to all our problems. You can only find the right answer when you are not projecting any particular idea, when you are not merely accepting a certain thesis and rejecting your own particular form of thinking. We are concerned with the whole problem of thinking, and not what to think. That is, without thinking rightly, obviously, all our actions will lead us to further confusion. So what we are concerned with is not the rejection or the acceptance of ideas, but how to think rightly together—that is, our relationship together—to find out how to think about the problems that confront us rightly. I am using the word *rightly* not in contradiction; there is only one way of thinking, not the right or the wrong. We shall find out if it is at all possible to pursue a thought and discover the truth of that thought, of that particular problem.

Is it not important to differentiate between hearing and listening? Most of us casually hear, as we hear the noise that is going on; and gradually, we get accustomed to hearing particular noises, and then we pass them by. We read papers and we hear the familiar voices about us. But there is a difference, is there not, between hearing and listening? In listening, there is neither acceptance nor rejection; you really listen to find out. You listen to another person to find out what he wants to convey not merely at the verbal level but at deeper levels of understanding. But listening is denied if we merely object or interpose our particular ideas, instead of really listening to find out actually what the other man is saying. After all, we know our minds so that we do not have to listen to that, but perhaps if we can listen without any interpretation, without translation, if we can really listen, then perhaps there may be a possibility of that radical revolution at the unconscious level, which is the only revolution that is worthwhile.

We have got innumerable problems, and the more we consciously think about them and try to resolve them, the greater the complications, the more the problems. Because we are dealing with problems which are not the products of the superficial mind but which are the result of deep unconscious struggles, conflicts, ambitions, strifes, without a fundamental and radical change at that deep level, the mere tinkering reformation on the superficial level—economic, social, political, or otherwise—will have very little significance. You can see that revolutions have not fundamentally altered the process of our living. The change at the conscious level is merely a modified continuity because there the mind is superficially calculating, judging, weighing, but the calculating, weighing, and judging process is a continuity of that which is conditioned, so through that, you have not resolved the problem at all; you have only modified it, only altered its course, but the course is still confused.

As long as we tackle our problems on the superficial level with the conscious mind, opposing idea by idea, argument by argument, cunning by cunning, logic by logic—which are all reactions of the superficial mind—obviously, the results which the mind has thought out will be the product of conditioned thought. Therefore, in that process there is no fundamental, deep, psychological revolution. I think what is important now is not the revolution on the superficial level but the revolution at the deep, unconscious level because we live there much more and have our being there more than on the superficial level.

So, is it not important to listen so that the unconscious is absorbing, if I can so put it—so that the revolution is not a conscious revolution? I think it is very important to listen so that the change is unconscious, so that our whole outlook on life is not a conscious, deliberate alteration but that revolution which comes without the deliberate process of thought.

After all, we have so many problems at different levels, economic, social, religious—the problem of love, death, the problem of relationship, starvation, what is God, if there is continuity, what is mortality, what is that state of 'timelessness', what is creativity, so on, and so on. We have innumerable problems, and we have always approached these problems with the intention of solving them by the conscious mind, by the everyday mind, by the mind that has thoughts, by the mind that is the result of time, that is the result of tradition, that is the result of so-called education—which is the process of conditioning, to a particular thought or pattern or particular action, such as communist, socialist, capitalist, or Catholic. And with that conditioning, we approach the innumerable problems; and obviously, a conditioned mind can never solve these problems.

We need to have quite a different approach, quite a different revolution—psychologically, inwardly, fundamentally. I think that is only possible when you know how to listen to everything, not to me only, but to the conversation that is taking place about you—the talk that you have with your wife, with your husband, with your children, with your boss, on the tramcar, on the bus, when you are listening to the beggar or to a song, when you listen to the birds or to the surge of the sea. If you know how to listen without interpretation, without translation, then there is a possibility of that unconscious revolution taking place. I think that is the revolution which is most essential at the present time—not the chain of leaders, not which political system you should follow, because they have all failed completely, because the systems they have advocated or created are the result of the conditioned mind, and their result will still be conditioned, and so you will be everlastingly caught in the net of problems; that way does not lead to human happiness, human creativity, and the discovery of what is true.

The discovery of what is true does not come about through a conscious effort. If we really understand this—it is my intention during these talks to approach this problem from every point of view—we come to that state when the conscious mind realizes it is incapable of dealing with these problems. Then, perhaps, there is a possibility of uncovering a different source of action, a different source by which or through the discovery of which we shall find a new way of thinking, feeling, living, being.

Our problems are not individual—because there is no such entity as an "individual." The individual, you, may have a different name, a different form, you may live in a separate house, but the content of your mind is the content of my mind also. What you think, I think; you are ambitious, so am I; what you are, I am, and your neighbor is. It is a collective problem, not an individual problem. You, as an individual conditioned to a certain set of ideas, cannot dissolve this problem of existence; you can only resolve it when you and I can think out the problem together, and not separately. The collective action can only come, take place, when there is thinking which is not collective. But as we know now, collective action implies collective thinking; collective thinking is conditioned thinking, and that is what we are concerned with, through various forms of propaganda, education, compulsion, concentration camps, and so on, and so on. You are made to think collectively, traditionally, whether that tradition is new or old; you are made to conform, to think along a collective line, thereby hoping you will produce collective action, but collective action is not possible as collective thinking is only conditioned thinking.

We will discuss that as we go along. But surely there is a way of acting which is not yours or mine, which is not the communist, socialist, or Catholic or the Christian or the Hindu or the Buddhist; that is the way of acting which springs from the discovery of what is truth. The discovery of what is truth is not dependent on you and me, on your conditioned mind or on my conditioned mind. That discovery of what is truth can only come about when you and I recognize our conditioned mind, our conditioned state.

If you and I can discover what is truth, from there, there is collective action. But collective thinking does not lead to collective action; it only leads to further misery, which is actually shown at the present time. But, if we can—you and I together because it is not I who am leading you, and you who are following me—we shall uncover the process of our thinking. I cannot uncover it for you and you merely accept or deny; you have to uncover it as we go on together; you have to observe your own state of mind not only at the conscious level but also unconsciously at every moment of the day, in your relationships, not only while you are hearing me here but when you have gone away from here.

The feeling that discovery of truth is not individual, that truth is neither collective nor individual but it is truth, can only come about when you understand the whole process of thinking. Thinking is collective; you cannot think independently; there is no individual thinking; what you think is the collective thinking because you are conditioned as a Hindu, Christian, or a Muslim, because you are holding yourself in the frame of tradition which is collective thinking. You may be conditioned in the framework of the supposed individual, but the framework is collective; or you may be conditioned as a communist, but the conditioning is still collective. The collective can never find what is true nor can the individual because there is no individual thinking, because all is collective thinking.

Please listen to this; don't reject it; find out the truth of what I am saying.

After all, the words that I am using, the thoughts that I am expressing, the ways of our thinking, all this is the result of collective thought and action; though I may call myself a separate individual, give myself a name, live in a hovel or in a rich house, the whole process of me is the collective. Can the collective ever find what is true? The collective is the conditioned mind; it is a mind that is bound to tradition, to authority, to every form of fear, conscious or unconscious; it is a mind that is constantly seeking security. Can such a mind, which is the collective mind, find what is truth? Truth is that which is uncontaminated, which cannot be conceived, which cannot be premeditated, dictated, or read about in books, which cannot be given to you by another. The only solution to our problems is the discovery of what is truth. That is the only revolution which will radically affect our existence, our daily everyday life, our daily life of relationship.

As the discovery of what is truth is of vital significance and importance, should we not, coming to these talks for the next five weeks or so, earnestly inquire if the mind is capable of peeling itself from all its conditioning and perhaps thereby discovering what is truth? This discovery of what is truth does not come about through any conscious effort. I think it is very important to understand that you cannot come to truth. Truth can come about only unknowingly when you are not expecting. Every form of expectation, every form of hope, is a form of projection—the projection of the 'me', the 'me' being the collective. And so our problem is the understanding of conflict, of struggle, the everyday life, our relationships, our ambitions, our passions and pursuits, our imitativeness and the appalling degradation that is going on within us, the corruption, the darkness, the death that is constantly with us—being aware of all that, to discover something which is beyond the mind. And that state can only come into being when we understand the process of our mind, not when we try to imagine what it is or speculate about it. It is only when we understand the process of our thinking, how our minds are conditioned completely, then only is there a possibility of discovering what is truth, which alone will liberate us from our problems.

After every brief talk I shall be answering questions, and I am afraid you will be disappointed if you are waiting for an answer. The mind that is expecting an answer is a schoolboy mind because you are only concerned with the results, like a schoolboy who looks at the end of the book to find the answer without really studying the problem or going into the problem deeply. When you put questions, you want answers; most of you are not interested in questions, you just want an answer—an answer being an explanation or combination of explanations. So, you who are seeking the answer are not really concerned with the problem.

Sirs, please don't take photographs. Sirs, may I say something? This is a serious meeting; I regard it as a religious meeting—in the deeper sense of the word, not in the religious sense, which is stupid. There must be a certain sense of dignity, and that is not possible when you are asking for autographs, taking photographs, yawning. It requires seriousness. When you are serious, you are quiet; you do not fidget about; you are concentrating, listening. So, please do not take photographs or take notes because then you are not paying attention, you are not listening. As this is a serious meeting and as you have come with serious intention, let us spend an hour with the purpose of understanding and finding out because our problems are tremendous, because we are destroying each other.

As I was saying, a mind that is only concerned with an answer, which is a result, which is really the combination of explanations, is satisfied with words; such a mind can never understand what the problem is. As I am concerned with only the problem and not with the answer, you will be disappointed if you are waiting for an answer. You will say, "I cannot put my teeth into it." But if we can see, the answer is in the problem; the answer to the problem is in understanding the truth of the problem. But the discovery of the truth is a very arduous process. It requires mature thinking—not glib answers or conclusions or judgments, either of the left or of the right or what you have learned in your books or from your experiences. It requires real consideration. As we are only concerned to uncover, to discover the ways of our thinking and thereby to find out how to bring about that fundamental revolution, perhaps we can go together into these problems in the maze of questions.

Question: There is a famine in this country; men starve, and you sit here talking of things which do not fill empty stomachs. Are you not helping us to lose all sense of responsibility to our starving neighbors?

KRISHNAMURTI: If I offered an escape through some means, dialectical or religious, or some kind of phony arguments, that would be an irresponsible action, would it not? But if together we can find out how to solve this problem, not only in this country, but throughout the world, then perhaps we shall not be sitting, talking in vain. Can these stomachs which are empty now be filled by any system, by any economic system, by any revolution at the economic or political level? If you had a new kind of revolution—it does not matter what you call it—which will alter the top layer of bureaucrats, will that solve our problem? We think it will. We hope that if there is a revolution of values, of economic systems, we shall be able to feed the world. Is that possible? Is revolution economic, or is revolution a total process, not just a partial process? After all, we have had revolutions based on economic systems, and they have not fed men. They have always promised that they will feed men, but in that promise there are always concentration camps, tyranny, totalitarianism, wars, destruction, more misery. We are quite familiar with this; the newspaper every morning carries it.

Is our problem the problem of the part—which is, economic revolution—or the problem of the total—which is, revolution in our thinking? When we are talking about starvation, we are concerned about giving food to starving people—which is only the part, though an essential part, and which is only one segment of our existence. The more we concentrate on the one part, one corner of our whole life, we will never solve the problem. We can solve the problem only when we comprehend the whole picture; then we can completely understand; then we can apply our understanding to the part. But from the part we cannot go to the whole. All our revolutions are based on the change of the part, not of the whole.

I am talking of the whole, total process of our being, not of the part. Real revolution is, and must be always, in the total being, in the total thinking, and not in the part thinking. We don't live by bread alone. We need bread, we need food, we need clothes, we need shelter; but if we emphasize them, if we are concerned with alterations or with revolution in the economic field only, then we shall invariably end in greater confusion and misery. But if we can understand the total process of our being and bring about a revolution in the psyche—in the inward nature of our being—then we can apply that revolution, that understanding, to the part. Surely, that is our problem. Please don't misunderstand. There must be no neglect of food, clothing, shelter; on the contrary, they must be provided. But there must be the right approach to it, and the right approach can only come about not on the superficial level but only when there is a fundamental revolution in our being, in our thinking, in the psychological state of our existence. We have tried economic revolutions and they have not fed man; on the contrary, there is more misery, more destruction, more wars. It is only possible to end starvation, famine, when we understand the whole and thereby bring about a revolution fundamentally, deeply.

Question: We have heard you for many years. Still we are mean, ugly, and full of hatred. Often we feel abandoned by you. We know you have not accepted us as disciples, but need you shirk your responsibility completely towards us? Should you not see us through?

KRISHNAMURTI: Sirs, this is a roundabout way of asking, "Why don't you become our guru?" (Laughter) Now, sirs, the problem is not abandoning or seeing you through because we are supposed to be grown-up people. At least physically we are grown-up; mentally, we are the age of fourteen and fifteen, and we want somebody glorified—a savior, a guru, a Master—to lead us out of our misery, out of our confusion; to explain to us the chaotic state; to explain, not to bring about a revolution in our thinking, but to explain it away, and with that we are concerned.

When you put this question, you want to find a way out of this confusion; you want to be free from fear, from hatred, from all the pettiness of life, and you look to somebody to help you. Or, other gurus have perhaps not succeeded in putting you to sleep by giving you a dose of opium, an explanation, so you turn to this person and say, "Please help us through." Is that our problem—the substitution of a new guru for an old one, of a new Master for an old one, of a new leader for the old? Please listen to this carefully. Can anybody lead you to truth, to the discovery of truth? Is discovery at all possible when you are led to it? If you are led to truth, have you discovered it, have you experienced it?

Can anybody—it does not matter who it is—lead you to truth? When you say you must follow somebody, does it not imply that truth is stationary, that truth is there for you to be led to, for you to look at and take?

Is truth something to be discovered or something that you are led to? If it is something that you are led to, then the problem is very simple; then you will find the most satisfying guru or leader, and he will lead you to it. But surely the truth of that something which you are seeking is beyond the state of explanation; it is not static; it must be experienced; it must be discovered, and you cannot experience it through guidance. How can I experience spontaneously something original if I am told, "This is original, experience it"? Hatred, meanness, ambition, pettiness are your problems, and not the discovery of what is truth. You cannot find what is truth with a petty mind. A mind that is shallow, gossiping, stupid, ambitious—such a mind can never find what is truth. A petty mind will create only a petty thing; it will be petty, empty; it will create a shallow God. So our problem now is not to find, not to discover what God is, but to see first how petty we are.

Sir, look. If I know that I am petty, that I am miserable, that I am unhappy, then I can deal with it. But if I am petty and say, "I must not be petty, I must be big," then I am running away—which is pettiness. Please understand this.

What is important is to understand and discover *what is,* not to transform *what is* into something else. After all, a stupid mind, even if it is trying to become very cunning, clever, intelligent, is still stupid because its very essence is stupidity. We do not listen. We want somebody to lead our pettiness to something bigger, and we never accept, we never see *what is,* actually. The discovery of *what is,* the actuality, is important; it is the only thing that matters. At any level—economic, social, religious, political, psychological—what is important is to discover exactly *what is,* not 'what should be'.

Please listen. In this question there are several things implied. The questioner wants someone to help him to free himself from the complications of his life, so he is seeking a leader. The leader whom he seeks is the outcome of his confusion, of his misery, and therefore the leader is himself confused. Sir, don't you know what is happening in the world? You are confused with all this turmoil, and a political leader comes along; you vote for him out of your confusion, and so you have created a politician who is also confused, and he is leading you. Similarly, the guru or the teacher or the leader whom you choose; you choose him out of your confusion, out of your desire for gratification, to get security, so you project what you want, and that guru is your creation. Because he is going to satisfy you, you accept what he gives—which indicates that you are never confronted with *what is* in yourself, with actually what you are. It is only when your mind is not running away, avoiding, pursuing the ideal—that is, when the mind says, "This should not be, but that should be," and so on—that you can discover how to deal with *what is.* Then you will solve the problem. You can only solve the problem when you discover what is actually the 'me'. If you know that you are petty, that your mind is shallow, that you have hatred for people, when you are aware of that fact, then you can deal with that fact. We can discuss how to deal with that fact. But if you say, "I must not hate, I must love," then you are entering into an ideological world—which is the most stupid way of escape from *what is.*

So, in this question, we are not concerned with the understanding of the truth of our problems. It is only the truth that will free us. Understanding comes only when we are not following anybody, where there is no authority of any kind—either the authority of tradition, the authority of books, the authority of the guru, or the authority of our own experience. Our own experience is the result of our conditioning, and such an experience cannot help us to discover what is truth.

So those who are really earnest, who really want to find out the truth of these problems, must obviously set aside all authority. That is very difficult because most of us are so frightened. We want somebody to lean on, somebody to encourage us, the big brother—the big brother in Russia or in England or in America or behind the Himalayas or round the corner. We all want someone to help us. As long as we lean on somebody, we shall never understand the process of our own thinking, so we shall deny the discovery of truth for ourselves.

Please listen to this; don't reject it because you have not solved your problem, because you are just as unhappy as you were before. When you are following your guru or your political leaders, you are confused. There is only one way to resolve this problem, and that is through the understanding of yourself in your relationships, from moment to moment, from day to day—the antagonisms, the hates, the passions, the transitory love, and so on. You are caught in it, and you can only resolve it when you accept it, see it as it is. It is only when you resolve it, there is a possibility of freeing the mind from its own conditioning and thereby letting truth be.

Question: Do you have a technique which I can learn from you, so that I, too, can carry your message to those who are full of sorrow?

KRISHNAMURTI: Sir, what do you mean by carrying a message? Do you mean repeating the words—propaganda? The very nature of propaganda is to condition the mind. Every form of propaganda—the Communist propaganda, the religious propaganda, and so on—is to condition the mind, is it not? If you learn a technique as you call it, a way, and you learn it by heart and repeat it, you will be a good propagandist; if you are keen, clever, if you are capable of using words, you will condition those that hear you in a new way instead of the old way, but it is still conditioning; it is still limited. And that is our problem, is it not?

Our problems arise because we are conditioned. Our education conditions us. Is it possible for the mind ever to be free from conditioning? You can only discover that state. You cannot say whether it is possible or not possible. When you ask, "Have you a technique?" what do you mean? Perhaps you mean a method, a system, which you learn like a schoolboy and repeat it. Sir, surely the problem is something much more fundamental, radically different, is it not? There is no technique to learn. You do not have to carry my message, what you carry is your message, not mine, sirs.

This existence, this misery, this confusion is your problem. If you understand it, if you can understand the experience of a conditioned mind and go beyond, then you will be the person who is teaching; then there will be no teacher and no disciple. But then, you have to understand yourself, not learn my technique or carry my message. Sir, what is important is to understand that this is our world, that together we can build this world happily, that we—you and I—are related together, that what you do and what I do inwardly matters, that how we think is important, and that thought, which is always conditioned, will not solve our problem. What will solve our problem is to understand the ways of our thinking. The moment we understand how we think, there will be a radical change inwardly; we will no longer be Hindus, Christians, Communists, socialists, or capitalists; we shall be human beings, human beings with passion, with love, with consideration. That cannot come about by merely learning a technique or carrying somebody's message.

You cannot have love through technique. You can have sensation through a technique, but that is not love. Love is something that cannot be told, that cannot be carried across through newspapers or through techniques or through propaganda. It must be felt, it must be understood. But if you repeat love, love, love, it has no meaning. You will know of that love when the mind is quiet, when the mind is free from its conditioning, from its anxieties, from its fears. And it is that love which is the true revolution that will alter the whole process of our being.

February 8, 1953

Second Talk in Bombay

As we were saying last Sunday, the conscious effort made to bring about alteration in one's attitude to values or ideals does not fundamentally or radically bring about a change. I may have to go deeply into that problem because I feel it is very important that we understand this question of how to bring about a fundamental change, what is the process, and how it can come about.

Most of us consciously endeavor, in one way or another, to conform to a certain pattern of action—political, religious, or so-called spiritual. Consciously we make an effort, with deliberate intention, to bring about a certain change, either within oneself or within society, economically or culturally. We make every kind of effort consciously, at the upper level of our mind, to bring about what we call a change. Is such a change a radical revolution? Or does it merely bring about a temporary effect at the superficial level—which is not fundamental transformation. The more we see, the more we observe in the world and in ourselves this superficial change; we see that it only produces more problems, not only within ourselves, but in our relationships, in society.

I think it is fairly obvious, if you think it out a little more deeply, that the more we make an effort consciously to change, to bring about a transformation within ourselves, the more problems we have. That is, I want to change: I am angry or I am greedy or what you will. I make a conscious effort to change, and in the process of that change, there are various forms of resistances, of suppressions, and sublimations; there is constant effort made, and thereby there are more problems involved in the very desire to bring about a change in myself.

I do not know if you have noticed that the more we make an effort, the more the complications, the more the problems. So perhaps there is a different form of approach to this question. However much the conditioned mind may make an effort to change itself, does it not produce further conditions, responses, and activities which further increase our problems? So, if we realize that, there must be a different approach to this problem of change, a radical transformation within ourselves. I suggested last Sunday that this transformation, this revolution, can only be at the unconscious level, not at the conscious level at all because all effort is a process of imitation, and therefore there is no fundamental change.

There is only fundamental change, radical transformation, when the conscious mind has ceased to make all effort, which means, really, that there is understanding at the unconscious level. That is why I said that it is very important how we listen to everything about us—not only to what I am saying, but to every incident, to every thought, to the sounds about you, to the voice of the bird, to the noise of the sea—so that as you listen, you begin to understand without any conscious effort. The moment you make a conscious effort, the process of imitation is set going—the imitation being conformity to the pattern which is already being established through the experience, through the ideal, through the desire to achieve a result. If we really comprehend this, I think there will be a fundamental revolution in ourselves. If we comprehend that all psychological effort, in any form, leads to imitation, to conformity, we see that when we desire to be efficient, directive, purposeful in our effort, there must be a process of imitation, conformity, and so, there is no change at all; there is only a change of the pattern of action from one pattern to another, from one reaction to another, and therefore we only increase our problems.

Is it possible to bring about a revolution outwardly as well as inwardly, without effort? Please, this is not a cynical question to be brushed off easily. We see that every effort we have made has not produced the thing we have searched out and longed for, worked for—politically, religiously, or economically. Therefore, that approach must be utterly wrong. If that is not the right approach, there must be a different approach to all our problems.

Can the mind, which is the result of time, of imitation, of the desire to seek security and conformity, can such a conditioned mind ever—however much it may make an effort—bring about a change? Can such a mind bring about a revolution within itself? That is, to put the question differently, will conscious effort, the action of will, bring about a change? We are used to the action of will—"I must or I must not"; "I shall be or I shall not be"; "there must be good, there must be bad"; "there must be a different state of society, a different pattern of action"; "I am violent and I must be nonviolent," and so on and on. This is the conscious effort made by will. In that very process of "must be" and "must not be," there are innumerable problems of control and of suppression, various forms of psychological desires that arise from suppression and from control, various efforts made, and the struggles, failures, frustrations in the process of achieving that which you think is truth. If you have at all thought about it, if you are aware of it, this is our problem, not only individually, but collectively, socially, in the world. How is a serious person, whose intention is to bring about a change fundamentally within himself, to bring about the change? Through conscious effort or by listening to the truth of the falseness of effort?

Seeing the truth of the whole implication of effort, can you just listen without translation, without interpretation, to what is being said? All effort is a process of imitation; imitation is always conditioning, and the conditioned mind can never find the truth of any problem. Can I, can you, listen to that without any interpretation, without any judgment? Can I look, see, hear the truth of it? That can only be done not at the conscious level but at the unconscious level when the mind is not struggling to understand, when the mind is not making an effort to imitate. That can only happen when the conscious mind, the mind which is so active all day and all night, ceaselessly building, destroying, altering, shaping, when that mind is quiet for a few seconds and hears what is truth. I think that is our problem, and not what to do—how to feed the poor or how to bring about an economic revolution or what kind of gods and rituals we should have.

Fundamentally our problem is to bring about a revolution in our ways of thinking psychologically, fundamentally. Such a change cannot be brought about by any conscious effort because, as I said, the conscious mind is built around tradition, by experiences which are the outcome of conditioned action. So, a mind that is thinking out, planning out, and acts according to that plan—through compulsion, through conformity, through imitation—

such a mind cannot find an answer to all our problems. We have been brought up from our childhood to cultivate our memories. Memory is essential at a certain level of our existence, but memory does not give the true answer to any problem; it can only translate the problem according to its condition, its experience. After all, if you, as a Hindu, experience something, you will translate it according to your conditioned mind, or if you are a communist, you will meet the experience or translate the experience in terms of dialectical materialism or what you will. So you are never meeting the experience without a conditional mind, and the conditioned mind, creating a pattern, an action, only further creates more problems, more sufferings, more misery. That is what we have to realize. I think it is very important to see that effort in any form, inwardly, is a process of imitation; effort is imitation, conformity, and through conformity there can be no radical transformation.

Now, is it possible for me to hear a statement of that kind and to see the truth of that? I say life is a process of imitation. The very language which I am using is the result of imitation, the cultivation of memory, knowledge. The acquisition of information is a process of imitation. The very desire to be good is the result of fear which urges me to conform. I see that memory, experience, knowledge are essential at certain levels of our existence because if I did not know how to use language, I would not be able to communicate. But when I make effort to bring about a change psychologically, inwardly, to be different, the very process of becoming different creates other problems. So I am caught in a net of innumerable problems, and there is no release. But there is a release at the unconscious level if I can hear, without translation or without interpretation, the truth of anything that is being said. You can experiment with this yourself, and you will find the truth of this.

Sirs, this is not a discussion meeting. This meeting is not open to any kind of discussion.

Here is a very difficult problem; the mind has cultivated memory for centuries upon centuries, and that is the only instrument we have, and we have used that instrument to solve our problems; we worship intellect—which does not mean that we must become sentimental or devotional or sloppy. It is very difficult to see the limitations of the mind. It is very difficult to see that our problems cannot have an answer through the mind, through the application of the process of thought, because thought is always conditioned. There is no freedom of thought because thought which is memory, which is the result of various past experiences, is conditioned, is limited; and such a thought, when used to solve our problems, can only increase the problems further, add more problems. Can I realize the truth of that thought and allow a revolution to take place at the unconscious level? Because, in the unconscious level, there is no limitation, there is no conformity because the mind there is not interfering to search for a result; there, the mind is not trying to suppress or to be anything; it is only there, the mind can understand what is truth. Truth is not the process of analysis nor the mere observation of knowledge. What is truth can only be understood at the unconscious level when the mind is very quiet, noninterfering, nontranslating. If we once realize this fundamentally, we will see there is a radical change in our ways of thought. But, as I said, the mind is trained to interfere, to constantly seek a result in action. It is only at the unconscious level there can be love. And it is love that can alone bring about revolution.

Question: Who is the truly religious man? By what will his action be known?

KRISHNAMURTI: What is religion? Before we define what a religious man is, what is religion? Is religion the performance of certain rituals, the acceptance of certain dogmas, the conditioning from childhood by certain beliefs to be a Hindu, a Christian, a Buddhist, or a Muslim? Does the conditioning of the mind by a belief constitute religion? Because I call myself a Hindu or what you will, does that make me religious? Or, is religion the state of mind in which there is an experiencing which is not of memory, which is a state in which all conditioning by time has ceased? Is religion the belief in God? Is the man who does not believe in God, is he nonreligious? And is the man who does good works, who is socially active—feeding the poor, everlastingly active in the performance of his duty, concerned with reform, with the pattern of the betterment of man—is he a religious person? The man who is pursuing virtue, the virtue of nonviolence, the virtue of nongreed, is he a religious man? Or is he merely conforming to a particular pattern, projected for his own self-satisfaction? So, must we not first find out what it is that we mean by religion?

Surely the realization of truth does not depend on any belief; on the contrary, belief acts as a barrier to the realization of truth. A man who believes, who is caught in dogma, can never know what is the real. He can never experience that state of ecstasy, of love. Dogma, belief, and experience stand in the way, for experience is merely the continuance of memory. A man who is well-seasoned in memory, in experience, in knowledge, can never find out what God is, nor can the man who professes continually his belief in God find reality. Reality comes into being only when the mind is free, when the mind is still, not compelled, not coerced, not disciplined. When the mind is still, then at the unconscious level there is revolution.

Can you judge a man's action by his good work? By that, will you know whether he is religious or not? How will you judge him? Please, this is not a sophisticated, clever argumentation. By what standards, by what conditioning, will you judge him? If he does good work for his neighbor, if he feeds the poor, puts on ashes, puts on a saffron robe, shaves his head, if he renounces, would you call him religious? Renunciation is intoxication, and a man who is intoxicated through his own actions will never find what truth is. It is only when there is the complete cessation of the 'me', of the 'I', of the ego, which cannot come about through any effort, any will, through any conscious act, it is only when there is love that there is a possibility of such a mind being religious.

But to say what is love, to question whether love shall be this or that, to cultivate love, is not love. All this requires a great deal of understanding, great penetration. The penetration of the conscious mind is only to create further entanglement. But when I am aware of this whole process of the 'me', of the 'I' trying to become something—religiously, politically, socially—I see that as long as that 'me' is becoming virtuous or nonviolent, it is only conforming to the pattern of respectability, and that 'me' which renounces in order to achieve God is only a man intoxicated by his own imagination, and such a man can never find what is love, what is truth.

We know this in our hearts; we have felt deep down in the unconscious that there must be the realization of this, but the world is too much with us. The pressures, the traditions, the examples are too much, and we are carried away by the things that are trivial because from childhood, we are brought up to follow the example, the hero, the great man, so we ourselves become trivial; we ourselves become petty, and we shall never find what truth is. That which is truth, which is the only religion, can only be found—or rather, it can only come into being—when the mind is utterly still, not wanting, not projecting, not desiring to do or not to do; this does not mean withdrawal from the world; there is no withdrawal; there is no isolation. To be related is life, and in that relationship we shall find out what truth is, what love is.

Question: I am a writer. I heard you some years ago, and since then I no longer feel the urge to write. Is the dearth of outward expression the inevitable result of self-knowledge?

KRISHNAMURTI: Why do you write? Do you write in order to fulfill? Do you write in order to become famous? Do you write in order to earn a livelihood? Or do you write for no purpose—because, inwardly you are so alive, so rich, that it is a natural expression, not a vocation, not a means of self-fulfillment. If it is a means of self-fulfillment, then the more you know yourself, the more you study yourself, the more there is self-knowledge, the less outcome there is in words. As long as you are fulfilling through a state—through politics, through religion, through activity, through doing good, through writing a poem or painting a picture—as long as you are fulfilling yourself through a particular action, the more you know yourself, then the less there is of that activity.

Where there is action through which you gain satisfaction, through which you rejoice, through which you become something professionally—a politician, a great man, a well-known man—as long as you are using the outward activities as a means for your aggrandizement, then the more there is self-knowledge, there is the diminution of that activity. This is very important to understand because most of us are fulfilling through something, through the wife or the husband, through the children, through virtue. If by addressing a large audience, by writing a poem, you are becoming something, as long as the 'me' is becoming something, the more you have self-knowledge, the less is the 'becoming'. There is no fulfillment of the 'me' through any action.

But you see, from childhood we are brought up to fulfill. We have innumerable heroes, a great many saints, so many authorities to follow, and gurus who will give us what we want, so we are everlastingly caught in the net of our own self-fulfillment. Where there is self-fulfillment, there is frustration, and with frustration there is fear, and so we are caught in the net again. But there is a release of creativity which is not the outcome of self-fulfillment. If we really understood this, there would be a tremendous change in our activity. Through our activities, at present, we are not releasing that creative energy; through our social reforms, through our writing, through our building bridges, or through painting pictures, we are not creating. After all, are you not fulfilling when you call yourself a Hindu or a Christian or communist? When you are active as a communist or a socialist or a religious person, does not that activity give you—you, the 'me'—the urge to become, to act, to be, to continue in that activity? Do you not create problems? Are you not ruthless; do you not divide, destroy, liquidate, have concentration camps, and so on? It may be religion to you and release to you, but in that process of releasing, you are creating misery not only for yourself but for others. Surely, that is not creativity, that is not the real release of the mind from the desire to fulfill.

I say there is a different release, a creativity which is not hedged by conditioned action; that creativity can only come when I understand the process of effort, when there is no imitation. All effort is imitation, and imitation exists when I am trying to become something. It is only when there is the cessation of the 'me', when I am absolutely nothing—which is not a virtue, which is not to be striven after—that a state comes when I understand the whole process of self-knowledge. It is only then that there is a fundamental, timeless release in which there is creativity.

Question: Man is driven to action according to his inherent nature; it is as if he is forced to sin, though reluctantly; what is this that drives him to wrong action?

KRISHNAMURTI: What is sin? What is the thing that we call wrong action or good action? Please, sirs, do listen to this. By listening, find out a release from all these words so that in that release, in that creativity, there is no sin, there is no wrong action; there is only a state of being, a state of love, which is never wrong. Since we do not have that, we have hedged our minds and our activity by what is good and what is bad; we are caught in this duality, and having been caught, we are trying to escape and create another antithesis of duality. To most of us, morality is tradition. We are slaves to circumstances, to society, to tradition, to what our neighbor, the boss, the government, the party says. Any form of deviation from the party lines is a sin, whether the party be religious or political. Any deviation, any wandering away from the traditional, from the respectable, is considered evil. And we have been nurtured, brought up from our childhood in that state, and so the desire to go against that which is traditional we call sin. There is also the urge to conform, and the conformity is considered good, to be respectable.

So, our problem is not what is good, what is bad, what is sin, and what is truth but to be free from fear. The man who is free from fear shall know love, and the man who loves knows no sin, is not compelled by any action or by anything except love. You cannot have love if there is fear, and fear will exist as long as the mind is seeking security—security in the state, security in religion, in belief, in your wife, in your name, in your child, in your property, in your bank account. As long as there is security, there must be fear, and a man who is secure—psychologically secure, certain, imbedded in knowledge—such a man in his heart is afraid. Such a man shall always know what sin is, what good is, and he is caught up in the conflict of duality. But the man without fear has a mind that is not seeking security; in such a mind there is love.

It is only when a man loves, he is free from sin, free from all urges which create anti-social activities, for love is the only true revolution. But that is very difficult to come by. When you use the word love, it will have very little meaning if there is fear which expresses itself through conformity, through acceptance of authority. The mind that is traditionally bound by knowledge, that is always seeking a result, such a mind can never be free from fear. That which is darkness, which is fear, can never find light.

Question: I have been very close to death. The danger has passed for the time being, but I know its inevitability. Teach me how to face death.

KRISHNAMURTI: Sir, it is not a question of being taught. I cannot teach you; do not be disciples of anyone; do not follow anyone, however comforting, however satisfying he may be. Now, this is a very complex question.

What do we mean by death? Dying, ceasing to be. When are you not dying? When do you know you are not dead? Are you ever aware that you are not dying, that you are living? Please follow this. Are you ever aware that you are living? When do you know, when are you conscious that you are living? Are you ever conscious of it? You are only conscious of living when there is friction, are you not? Are you conscious, are you aware when you are joyous, when you are happy, when you love? Can you ever say at any moment that you are happy? And the moment you are aware that you are happy, has not that happiness ceased? It has already become a memory. Please follow all this, sirs. It is not just an argument, just clever words.

There is a state which is beyond death, and I am trying to convey that, to show that—not to tell you how to get there, but so that you find out for yourself, so that you experience. You cannot accumulate experiences which will guarantee you that state because the moment you have accumulated experiences, then you are dying; then there is death.

When are you conscious of life, of living? Only when there is disease, only when you know you are unhealthy. When you are healthy, you are utterly unconscious of your health; it is only when you are in friction, in sorrow, in conflict, in this constant becoming, then you know; then you are aware that you are in a state of friction, in the state of living. When you are well, when everything is smoothly flowing, running without any friction, without any impediment, without any hindrance, then there is no consciousness of living.

So our life is a process of friction. We only live knowing strife, sorrow, pain, misery, and that is our life; we know when we are jealous; we know when we are greedy, when we are running after things—that is our life, and we call that living. The fear of losing a job, the fear of not being, the fear of not accomplishing the thing which we started out to do, the fear of not enjoying tomorrow or not seeing the one whom we love, all that we call love; that is all we know. We do not know anything else. When we do know of something which we call joy, it is already a thing of the past. We live in memory, the thing that is past, and so the young and the old die. So with us, death is always there. We are always dying, we are always afraid of death. Death is with us; that is all we know. Because, everything that we do, every action, everything our hand is put to is deteriorating. There is a shadow of destruction always accompanying us. The thing that we love, we destroy. The thing we admired has gone. The thing which we have cherished is corrupt. Everything we have touched deteriorates. This is not just a fancy, this is an actuality. So we know death only—the decaying, the deterioration—and that is our life. It is only when we realize it, when we actually see it as it is and not try to run away from it, when we are with it and see what it is that there is a possibility of going beyond this mind, beyond memory because what is continuous must invariably hold within it the seed of deterioration, of destruction.

Please listen to this. We are concerned only with continuity. We want to continue in name, in property; we want to fulfill through the country, the state, through our son; we want things to go on. A thing that has continuity is destructive; in it, there is the seed of deterioration. There is renewal, there is creativity only in things that come to an end. I could have renewal if I could experience without continuity, if there is an experiencing without memory—which is very, very arduous because anything that we experience, the sunset or the single star in the heaven, is immediately stored away as memory because the mind wants to accumulate, to store up, to hold together, and the mind is afraid of losing that.

What is it that we are? We are a mass of confusion, of burning desires, of conflicts, of everlasting travail. Since we are dying all the time, because with us death is always there, we are only concerned with continuity. And if you really hear this without interpreting, without comparing it with the Bhagavad-Gita or the Upanishads, if you listen to what I am saying, if you directly experience this thing even for a second—direct experiencing is that state in which the mind is not caught in time, in which there is no experience as memory, in which time is not, in which the mind is just quiet—then you will see there is no death because every moment is an ending. This is not a poetical phrase. This is an actuality which you can experience, and the experiencing of it does not come about through any pattern of action, through any pursuit of virtue. It must come to you. Truth can only come to you; you cannot invite it. It can only come when you are open, when you do not want anything. It is only when your cup is empty, completely empty, when you know you are dead that there is that state when the cup is full, when it can never be empty. Then there is only love, which can never come to an end.

February 11, 1953

Third Talk in Bombay

I think it is one of our greatest difficulties to be serious because we are surrounded with so many frivolities and distractions, with so many teachers and systems and philosophers that it is very difficult for us to choose what is right. It is especially difficult if we are very learned, if we are already committed to a particular pattern of action. The more we are committed to a certain pattern or type of thought, ideal, or action—though we may appear to be very earnest, very serious—we are really not alert or intelligent because the very acceptance of any particular system—religious, political, scientific, or social—is obviously a conditioning and a deteriorating factor in our existence. It seems to me that it is very difficult for most of us to be serious without being trammeled in a particular system of thought or without being caught up in a groove of action because the moment we are serious, we want to be something; we want to act; we want to throw ourselves into a particular action, reform, revolution, and we think that which is not immediately translated into action is not serious.

I think it is very important to consider this: not that there should not be action, not that there should not be a certain revolution, a certain change—economic, social, and so on—but before we plunge into any activity, should we not be very clear what we mean by seriousness and what we mean by being intelligent? Are all serious people intelligent, and are all intelligent people serious? Is the so-called intelligent, well-read man who is up-to-date in scientific knowledge or philosophical systems of thought—is he serious? Is it not important for each one of us to find out what it means to be serious? Because without seriousness, without real earnestness, life has very little significance.

In the case of most of you who are attending these talks regularly, if you are merely caught up in the travail of curiosities, if you want to find a solution for a particular problem, an answer, should you not consider in what way it is important to be serious? You will hear these talks and you will go away. What effect has this on your lives, what does this do in your lives? Is it merely a repetition of certain phrases, words? Is it the learning of a new technique, new words, a sharpening of the mind? Or is it that by really listening, not merely hearing—there is a distinction between hearing and listening—one may find out what this seriousness is? It is not the seriousness of the man who pursues a particular virtue. The pursuit of a virtue only leads to respectability, and therefore it is a thing to be avoided, for the respectable man will never find joy, will never be creatively happy.

So is it not important to find out for ourselves to what extent, to what depth, we are serious? Because, we have to be serious. Does not seriousness go with intelligence? A man who is really intelligent must be a serious man. Let us find out what this intelligence implies.

Now, if I may suggest, let us repeat what I said the other day, without too much boredom; if you can listen rightly, without interpreting or comparing what you have already read about or heard, listen as though you were enjoying yourself and try to find out, to inquire, not to block, not to hinder, but to really find out—which is entirely different from hearing lectures. We are used to going to talks.We hear lots of speeches made up of words, very brilliant or crudely put together. But the effect of true listening is much more revolutionary than that particular action. If I know how to listen to you, to music, to the sound of a wave, if I know how to listen to it, if I let it penetrate into me without any barrier, then that very listening brings about an extraordinary activity which is not a conscious endeavor on my part.

So, perhaps we can try this way of listening—which is not "being mesmerized" to any particular attitude or action. I am not suggesting any kind of activity or any kind of attitude. I am only trying to find out, you and I together, what is this intelligence which is so essential, which will bring about a seriousness, a dedication, an involuntary dedication to life, and not to a particular action because life is not a particular activity; it is a total process. Is it not possible to dedicate oneself unconsciously, involuntarily, freely to the totality of existence? To do that, one must have extraordinary intelligence, native insight; one must be uncorrupted. And is that intelligence possible? Because the more we read, the more there is comparison, and the more we are caught in all this confusion of knowledge.

Is it not possible to find out what is true intelligence so that with the operation of that intelligence, we shall find out true action? True action is action which is not imposed by anyone—by Marx, by the socialist, or by the capitalist, or by some other clever human entity—which is not dominated by one's ambition, knowledge, erudition. Since we probably have never had that intelligence, we have been dominated by others, and the very process of being dominated destroys the cultivation or the discovery of true intelligence.

Intelligence, it seems to me, is devoid of all authority. There cannot be intelligence where there is authority—the authority of the party, the authority of tradition, the authority of books, or the authority of one's own experiences. Because, where there is authority, domination, there must be choice. And where there is choice, there is no intelligence.

Please listen to this; just let what I am saying penetrate; listen to it and you will find the truth of it as we go along. I depend on my experience, thinking that it will bring about intelligence. But, is my experience capable of such intelligence? Is experience ever capable of producing intelligence? What is my experience? It is a series of reactions to innumerable challenges of life. You may flatter me and I react to it, or I react to beauty. This constant relationship between challenge and response is experience, is it not? And that experience is based on a conditioned background. So, the conditioning, the conditioned background, responds to other challenges, and from the challenge I begin to choose; I begin to react according to my background, according to my choice. So my experience gradually becomes authority—the authority from which I am, from which I choose, from which I think. So choice is authority, authority of knowledge which is experience—whether mine or yours or of all the well-learned people.

Is there intelligence where there is the capacity to choose? Choice is the result of experience, mine or another's, and experience is the recording on the conditioned background. All our life is based on choice. I choose this material or that material. I choose this flower or that scent; I choose this philosophy; I choose that guru, that political system, leader, and so on. All my life is based on a series of interpretations and choices, and the higher I choose, the more I think I am capable of distinguishing, the more I think I am intelligent. Is that so? Obviously, choice is necessary at certain levels of existence, in certain fields of thought, of life, of action, but psychologically, inwardly, does not choice based on authority cripple intelligence? Because, after all, when I choose psychologically—I am not talking about the physical fact of choice—but when I choose psychologically, is not that choice the result of my conditioning, my experience? And so the more I choose according to my experience, the more my mind is conditioned, and so the more I choose according to a particular system of thought, according to tradition, according to my conditioning.

Does not the very process of choice based on authority destroy intelligence? And is not intelligence essential, especially in a world where there are a series of crises, where there is domination and the imposition of authority? Is it not essential to free ourselves from all authority—which means, from all choice—and to discover what is truth? Because, what is truth is not the result of choice, is not the outcome of authority. If I choose, then it is not truth. I choose according to my background, according to my experience, or according to the authority which gives me security, the authority through which I shall fulfill, through which I shall carry out certain series of actions which will guarantee what I want. So, choice as we know it, as we exercise it every day, will that lead us to intelligence? And if it does not, is it not important to find out what it is that prevents this functioning of intelligence, which is the freedom from authority of every kind?

Is it possible to live in a world whose structure is not based on authority, on the social, economic, religious, cultural imposition and domination of authority? Is it possible to live without authority, without some form of compulsion, some form of resistance, to hold us in a certain groove of action? Is it not important for us to find out if it is possible to be earnest with this intelligence in which there is no choice? Because, then there is action without reward, without an end—it is a constant revolution, and such action is necessary, especially in us, because we are confused. All the teachers, all the gurus, all the books, everything has failed; all the heroes are merely on the walls—not in our hearts and minds—since they have all failed. Is it not important for us to be free from every kind of authority and to inquire what is truth, without authority, without choice? Because the moment we do not choose, the moment we do not interfere with that activity in which there is no choice, such an action will obviously produce a revolution, not superficially only, but also fundamentally, deeply, inwardly.

It is that creative action which is essential—creativity without choice, in which there is no authority of any kind. Because, then the mind is free from fear; it is only the mind that is afraid that chooses, and the mind that is afraid is not intelligence. And is not all choice based on fear, and can the mind be utterly free from fear? The mind can only be free from fear when the mind is not seeking an end, when the mind is not pursuing a result, when it is not conditioned by any belief, by any authority. Then only is there a possibility of bringing about a revolution, a regeneration, a transformation of the human mind and heart.

Question: My body and my mind seem to be made up of deep-rooted urges and conscious and unconscious fears; I watch the mind, but often it is as if these basic fears overpower me. What am I to do?

KRISHNAMURTI: Sir, let us find out what we mean by fear. What is fear? Fear exists only in relation to something. It is not something by itself. It is only in relation to something—to what you might say of me, to what the public may think of me, to the loss of a job, in having security in my old age, or the fear of the mother's or father's death, or God knows what. It is the fear of something.

Now how am I to be free from fear? Will discipline of any kind dispel fear? Discipline is resistance, the cultivation of resistance to learn. Will that free the mind from fear? Or will it only hold it away from it—like building a wall, but on the other side there is always fear? Fear obviously cannot be got rid of by resistance, by the cultivation of courage because the very nature of courage is the opposite of fear, and when the mind is caught up in fear and courage, there is no solution but the cultivation of resistance, so there is no overcoming of fear through cultivation of courage.

How am I to get rid of fear? Please follow this, sirs. This is our problem, yours and mine, of every human being who wishes to be free from fear because if I can be free from fear, then the 'me', the self which is creating so much mischief, so much misery in the world can disappear. Is not the self, in its very nature, the cause of fear? Because I want to be secure, if I am not economically secure, I want to be secure politically, socially, in name, I want to be secure in the hereafter, I want to have God's assurance, to pat me on the back and say, "You will have a better chance next life"; I want somebody to tell me, to encourage me, to give me shelter, refuge. So, as long as I am seeking security in any form, there must be fear, from which all the basic urges spring. So, if I can understand what fear is, perhaps then there may be a release from that constant choice.

How am I to understand what fear is? How am I—without disciplining, without resisting, without running away from it, without creating other illusions, other problems, other systems of gurus, of philosophers—to really face it, to understand it, to be free of it and go beyond it? I can only understand fear when I am not running away from it, when I am not resisting it. So we have to find out what this entity is that is resisting. Who is the 'I' that is resisting fear? Do you understand, sirs? That is, I am afraid; I am afraid of what the public might say about me because I want to be a very respectable person; I want to succeed in the world; I want to have a name, position, authority. So one side of me is pursuing that, and inwardly, I know that anything I do will lead to frustration, that what I want to do will block me. So, there are two processes working in me—one, the entity that wants to achieve, to become respectable, to become successful; and the other, the entity that is always afraid that I might not achieve.

So, there are two processes in myself operating, two desires, two pursuits—one that says, "I want to be happy," and the other that knows that there may not be happiness in the world. I want to be rich, and at the same time I see millions of poor people, and yet, my ambition is to be rich. So long as the desire for security confronts me, drives me, there is no release; at the same time there is in me compassion, love, sensitivity.

There is a battle going on endlessly and that battle projects, becomes antisocial, and so on and so on. So what am I to do? How am I to be free from this battle, from this inward conflict?

If I can observe one process alone and not cultivate the dual process, then there is a possibility of dealing with it. That is, if I can observe fear in itself and not cultivate virtue, not cultivate courage, then I can deal with fear. That is, if I know *what is* and not 'what should be', then I can deal with *what is.* With most of us we do not know *what is,* for most of us are concerned with 'what should be'. This 'should be' creates the duality. *What is* never creates duality. 'What should be' brings about the conflict, the duality.

So, can I observe *what is* without the conflict of the opposite, can I look at *what is* without any resistance? Because, the very resistance creates the opposite, does it not? That is, when I am afraid, can I look at it without creating resistance? Because, the moment I create resistance against it, I have already brought into being another conflict. Can I look at *what is* without any resistance? If I can do that, then I can begin to deal with fear.

Now, what is *fear?* Is fear a word, an idea, a thought, or an actuality? Does fear come into being because of the word fear, or is that fear independent of the word? Please, sir, think it out with me. Don't get tired. Don't let your minds go off. Because, if you are really concerned with the problem of fear, which you are, which every human being is—fear of death, fear of your grandfather or grandmother dying—since you are burdened with that extraordinary darkness, should you not go into the problem and not just push it aside? If we go into this problem carefully, we see that as long as we are creating a resistance against fear in any form, running away from it, building barriers against it like cultivating courage and so on, that very resistance brings about conflict which is the conflict of the opposites. And through the conflict of the opposites, we will never come to an understanding.

The idea that conflict between thesis and antithesis will bring about a synthesis is not true. What brings about understanding is comprehending the fact of *what is* and not by creating the opposite. So, can I face fear, look at fear without resisting, without running away from it? Now what is this entity that is looking at fear? When I say I am afraid, what is the 'I' and what is the "fear?" Are they two different states, are they two different processes? Am I different from the fear which the 'I' feels? If I am different from the fear, then I can operate on fear; then I can change it; then I can resist it, push it away. But if I am not different from fear, then is there not a different action altogether?

Is this a little bit abstract and too difficult for you, sirs? Please, let us go into it. Listen to it, just listen; don't bother to argue because by listening, not throwing up arguments, by just listening, you can comprehend what I am talking about.

As long as I am resisting fear, there is no freedom from fear but only further conflict, further misery. When I do not resist, there is only fear. Then is fear different from the observer, the 'me' that says, "I am afraid"? What is this 'me' that says, "I am afraid"? Is not the 'me' composed of that feeling which I call fear? Is not the 'me' the feeling of fear? If there was no feeling of fear, there would be no 'me'. So the 'me' and the fear are one. There is no 'me' apart from fear, so fear is 'me'. So there is only fear.

Now there is the inquiry, Is fear merely the word? Does the word fear, the idea, the symbol, the state—is that created by the mind independent of the fact? Please listen. Fear is 'me'; there is no independent 'I' apart from me. The man, the 'I' says, "I am greedy"; the authority is the 'I'. The quality is not different from the 'I'. So long as the 'I' says, "I must be free from greed," it is making an effort, it is struggling. But that very 'I' is still greedy because it wants to be nongreedy. Similarly, when the 'I' says, "I must be free from fear," it is cultivating a resistance, and so there is conflict, and it is never free from fear. So there is only freedom from fear when I recognize the fact, when there is an understanding of the fact that the fear is the 'I', and the 'I' cannot do anything about fear. Please see the 'I' that says, "I am afraid, I must do something about fear." As long as it is acting upon fear, it only creates resistance and therefore increases further conflict. But, when I recognize that the fear is 'me', then there is no action of the 'I'; it is only then that there is freedom from fear.

You see, we are so accustomed to do something about fear, about an urge, about a sexual urge, that we always act upon it as though that urge is independent of 'me'. So, as long as we are treating the desire as independent of 'me', there must be conflict. There is no desire without 'me'. I am the desire; the two things are not separate. Please see this. It is really a tremendous experience when there is this feeling that fear is 'me', that greed is 'me', that it is not apart from 'me'.

There is no thought without the thinker. As long as there is the thought, there is the thinker. The thinker is not separate from thought, but thought creates the thinker, puts him apart because thought is everlastingly seeking permanency and so creates the 'I' as a permanent entity, the 'I' that controls thought. But without thought there is no 'I'; when you don't think, when you don't recognize, when you don't distinguish, is there the 'I'? Is there the 'me'? The very process of thinking creates the 'me'; then the 'me' operates on thought. So the struggle goes on indefinitely.

If there is the intention to be free from fear completely, then there must be the recognition of the truth that fear is 'me', that there is no fear apart from 'me'. That is the fact. When you are faced with a fact then there is action—an action which is not brought about by the conscious mind, an action which is the truth, not of choice, not of resistance. Then only is there a possibility of freeing the mind from every kind of fear.

Question: My life is one constant adjustment with my husband, with my relations. I thought I was happy, but I have heard you, and the bleakness of my life has been laid bare. What is the use of my listening to you if what you talk about does not bring light to my ordinary everyday life?

KRISHNAMURTI: Is it not important to be stripped off of all illusions? Is it not important to find out what actually one is, to find out the events in the world? You cannot do it through a socialist, communist, capitalist, or religious point of view; you must see them as they are. Then you can deal with them. But if you live in an illusory world and through that illusion look at various problems, then there is no resolution of those problems.

The question appears to be this, Should one be stripped of these illusions to see exactly what one is? Is it not necessary to be aware, to be conscious of this bleakness? After all, we are human beings without joy, without happiness, in sorrow, exploiting others; that is our actual state—using others for our fulfillment, either the state or the party or the idea. We are empty human beings. Inwardly, we are very lonely, afraid, dependent on so many people, on so many ideas, without love; that is what actually we are. Can't we look at it and must we not know of it? Can we avoid it? We try to avoid it by going to cinemas, reading books, doing various activities; but the fact still remains that behind these activities, we are dull human beings, unhappy, living in miserable conditions. Is it not important to face that fact, to know exactly what we are? When we know what we are actually, then what happens? Then we try to alter that, to consciously bring about a change. Do you understand, sirs, what I am saying?

We are living in a world of escapes, in a world of mass illusion; we run away from things as they are actually, and when somebody, anybody, brings them to us and makes us look at the actuality of them, we don't like it. And then we try to do something about *what is,* the actuality; this is again creating resistance, again running away from it. So that is our difficulty. If I know I am lonely, if I an antisocial, if I am greedy, if I am afraid, I want somebody to tell me what to do. If I am aware of my greed, if I am conscious of it, then my immediate reaction is to act upon it, to do something about it. So I set the chain going again—which is, to do something about it, to create resistance against it. If I can look at it, be with it, live with it, if I can get acquainted with all the intricacies of it, then there is a possibility of going beyond it. But as long as I am desirous of operating on what I am, I can never deal with it. I am lonely, I am afraid, I am unhappy; if I can look at this without any kind of compulsion, without any kind of interpretation, then an unconscious revolution takes place.

We want to act consciously, and our conscious action is very limited because our minds are conditioned all the time. It does not matter whose thought it is, all thinking is conditioned; all thinking is reaction, and thought is not productive; it does not bring about freedom. What brings about freedom is when the conscious mind is quiet, when the whole being is quiet with the fact—with the fact of loneliness, with the fact of fear, with the fact that "I hate," with the fact that "I am ambitious." When the mind is silent with the fact, then there is an unconscious revolution. The revolution is in releasing creativity. It is that revolution that is so essential in bringing a creative society into being. But, you see, we never come to that point; we are always wanting to do something about the fact—the fact that I am unhappy, the fact that I am depressed, ambitious. The moment I recognize the fact, my mind is operating upon it to alter it, to see whether it can control it, to shape it. That is the mind.

The conscious mind does not face the fact and remain with the fact without any desire to alter, to bring about a change in it. Real acceptance means seeing the thing as it is. Then, I assure you, there is the revolution of the unconscious, the revolution without motives. That is the only true revolution because in that revolution, there is the release of creativity, that creativity which is love.

Question: I hear you and sometimes I feel I understand. Another uses your words and there is no understanding. What is it that is understood?

KRISHNAMURTI: What do you mean by *understanding?* When do you understand? When I say, "I understand you," what do I mean by that? Do I hear merely the words or is it a deeper process at work? Is understanding on the verbal level? That is, I hear you, I translate what you say and I say, "Yes, I have understood." Is that what we mean by understanding? Or, is understanding something entirely different? Understanding is not merely the verbal hearing but the comprehension of the truth of what you are saying or of the falseness of what you are saying.

What is it that understands? Is it a state, is it a reaction? Please listen to this. It is very important to find it out because we may find the key to the whole process of comprehension, of understanding. Do we listen when we are interpreting? Do I understand what you are saying when I am translating what you are saying? When you say, for instance, "be good," what effect has that on me? Do you say it with full intention, with the feeling of being good without any sense of reservation, without any sense of inhibition? And am I capable of listening to it without translating, without saying, "How am I to be good in my circumstances?" Am I capable of listening without translating what you are saying to suit my circumstances? Can I listen to you without any barrier? Is it not only then that understanding comes?

Is not understanding something which is not brought about by any effort? If you are making an effort to understand me, all your knowledge is gone in making the effort; you are not listening to me. If you are not making an effort, if you are merely listening without any compulsion, without any translation, without any interpretation, without comparing—which means, you are allowing the words, the thought, the feeling, the thing that is said, the whole of the thing implied to penetrate—then, is there not a direct communion of something which I see and you also see? Then that understanding—not yours or mine, it is understanding—is the flash of something true. So understanding is not personal. It is not yours or mine. It is a state of being when the mind is capable of receiving what is truth. And the mind is incapable of receiving what is truth if it is bound by authority, by tradition; then the mind is comparing what is said with the Bhagavad-Gita, with the Bible, with this, with that. So understanding surely is a state in which the mind is not comparing, in which there is no authority; it is choiceless awareness, so the mind directly sees without any interpretation, without any mediator. So, if you and I both can see, if you and I are in that state, obviously there is immediate perception of what is true.

But with most of us, our knowledge, our experiences, authority, compulsions, various activities of daily life prevent us from experiencing directly something which is true. However much you may hear me, your minds are so crippled by authority, by knowledge, by experience that you are incapable of seeing things directly. So, understanding comes only when the mind is really quiet, not compelled, not coerced, when the mind in its quietness and stillness is capable of reception. If understanding is not accumulation, you cannot gather understanding; you cannot keep it in store. Understanding comes in flashes or in a series of flashes or in a long flash, which indicates the mind must be extraordinarily quiet, listening, without making any choice. But a conditioned mind, a mind disciplined, held up, hedged by compulsions—such a mind cannot understand, cannot directly experience what is truth. And it is that experiencing of what is truth, from moment to moment, which brings about creative release.

Question: You talk of the revolution in the unconscious, but as the unconscious is a dimension unknown to thought, how can I be aware that there has been any deep revolution? Are you not using these words to hypnotize us into imagining a state?

KRISHNAMURTI: Is not the unconscious also the conscious? That is, consciousness, as we know it, is strife. I am only aware when there is friction, when there is a challenge, when I am in misery, when I make conscious effort to do or not to do. But behind that conscious effort, are there not many motives hidden, many compulsions, urges, traditions which I have inherited after centuries? I am both the conscious as well as the unconscious. Both are the process of thought, are they not? Suppose I perform rituals, puja; it is an action which is the outcome of the great tradition in which I have been brought up; that tradition is based on fear, on the desire to find peace, hope, reward, and so on; that is the unconscious motive which makes me do a certain action. Is not the whole process of consciousness the result of thought? You may not think of the idea; the unconscious may not have thought it out, but is not the whole of that the process of thinking? I may not have thought out puja, but someone else has thought it out and I have been conditioned in that—that is the unconscious, deep down in me. I have been brought up as a capitalist, as a communist, or as a socialist, and from that I act and from that I respond. The unconscious motives, the urges, the conditions are the result of thinking by me or by another, by society, by circumstances.

Can thought bring about a revolution? Please follow this. Thought being conditioned, thought being always conditioned, can it bring about a revolution—which is so essential—a radical revolution, not an economical or partial revolution? Can a deep, fundamental revolution be brought about by thought? Thought, both conscious and unconscious, is a total process. My unconscious may be covered up and I may not have dealt with it. But that unconscious is still there, and it is the result of thought—my forefathers' thoughts, the thought of the books, the knowledge, the experience—all that is the 'me', the conscious as well as the unconscious; it is the product of thought. So I recognize that this whole process is thought, and I see that thought conditions; how then can thought bring about a radical revolution? But there is a revolution which is beyond thought, and it is there, beyond the conscious, beyond thought, that there must be a revolution.

Is love something to be cultivated? Do I know when I love? Is love a conscious process? If I know I love you, is that not sensation and therefore not love? If I am conscious that I am humble, if I am aware that I am kind, is that humility, is that kindness? So, is not love, is not humility something which is a state of which I am unconscious in the sense of thought—thinking?

The revolution which I am speaking of is only possible when thinking, as a reaction, as the conditioned state, comes to an end. It is only then that there is a revolution. Sirs, don't push it aside as some crazy idea, but find out, investigate, feel it out. You will see that every form of thinking is conditioned—the communist, the socialist, the Catholic, or the thinking of a religious person. It is conditioned; and as long as we are acting in a conditioned field, you will have further problems of conditioned actions; and in that, there is no release, there is no creativity. There is creativity, there is release only when the mind is completely silent. That silence is not a thing to be cultivated consciously. I cannot cultivate it because the conscious effort to bring it about is the outcome of a conditioned thought, a desire, an end; therefore, there is no revolution; there is always an ending, a result, and a mind that is seeking a result is not revolutionary.

So, only a mind that is still is capable of receiving what is true—not something extraordinary, but what is true every moment, the truth of what one sees, the word, the thought, the feeling. It is only when the mind is really quiet, without any compulsion, without any urges, that the revolution takes place. That revolution is a revolution of thought which truth brings about not through any form of cultivation but when you listen to what is being said. But you cannot listen if you are arguing with me—which does not mean I am hypnotizing you. After all, you are being hypnotized every day by newspapers, by the politicians, by do-gooders, by your religion, by the Bhagavad-Gita, by the Bible, by people dominating or pushing, by directive or purposive action. Is not all this a process of hypnosis? The whole process of propaganda is a way of hypnosis, and you are caught in it.

I am talking of something entirely different. The two are not compatible, they are of two different worlds. All that I am saying is: If we can listen, then the truth will release creative activity in human beings, and without that creativity, we become utterly chaotic, destructive; however noble our intentions are, all our actions lead to misery, mischief. That creative activity is love. Without love there is no revolution, and love is not a conscious action. Love is something beyond thought. It can only be understood, felt, known, experienced when the mind is utterly still, and only then is there a possibility of bringing about a fundamental revolution in the world.

February 15, 1953

Fourth Talk in Bombay

It seems to me that one of our greatest difficulties is communication. I want to tell you something, and naturally I have to use words. The words are so loaded with different varieties of meaning that it is very difficult for most of us to communicate directly and simply what we want to say to each other. And especially it is difficult when we are dealing with something which is a little more subtle, which is not too definite, and which therefore requires not only mere verbal communication but also communication that is beyond mere words. The mind rebels against something which it cannot get hold of, put its teeth into.

The difficulty with most of us is that we want a definite course of action. We want to find out what to do, how to behave, especially when we are confused, when the very object of our choice is the outcome of our own confusion. When we choose, out of our confusion, the leader or the idea or the system, it can only lead to further confusion, further misery, further sufferings. Because, if I, out of my confusion, choose an action, that action is bound to lead to further confusion. That is an obvious fact which unfortunately most of us do not consider. Since most of us are anxious to find a way, a course of action, it seems to me important to find out not what to do but how to think.

Most of us are accustomed to find out what to do. We have examples, we have heroes, precepts, ideals that we can follow. But what is important is the manner of our thinking because if there can be a revolution there, then perhaps it is possible to bring about a revolution in our action. So, is it not important to find out how to think, not what to do? Because the moment we are conditioned by an activity, by a system of thought, our actions become more and more complex, more and more confusing, more and more irksome, conditioned, disciplined, shaped; and therefore out of that, more confusion arises. So it seems to me what is important is to find out how to think; and perhaps then there is a possibility of changing that thought, bringing about a revolution in our thinking, and thereby creating a new way of life, a new way of action. There is a state of being which is revolution, and there is a state of becoming which is confusion. Most of us are accustomed to 'becoming'—becoming something more, altering a course of action and adjusting it to a particular pattern of thought, following a leader, developing a virtue, changing from greed to nongreed, cultivating or practicing certain ways of thinking—and all that implies, does it not, a 'becoming' in which there is no change at all, no revolution at all. 'Becoming' is only a form of continuity; in that, there is no revolution, there is no transformation ever possible. A transformation and revolution is only possible in a state of being. Now, the 'becoming' can never understand the 'being'. When the 'becoming' watches the 'being', the 'being' is not.

Please follow this literally. I think it is very important to understand this because our minds are so accustomed to 'becoming', to accumulating, to gathering experiences from which to proceed further; our thinking is based on knowledge, experience, examples, memory, which are all in the pattern of continuity; there is a modified change in that continuity, but there is no revolution, there is no transformation.

The 'becoming' always tries to transcend, go beyond itself. I am the result of time, of memory, of experience, of constant choice, of differentiation; I am the continuity in the past of time; my mind, following, rejecting, accepting, resisting, is all in the pattern, in the field of 'becoming', is it not? I am something today and I will be something tomorrow. The projection, tomorrow, is the continuity of today. This is what my mind is accustomed to, which is the result of accumulation, of memory, is it not? This is not complicated. You observe your own thinking; you observe the various ways of your action, your desires, and you will find this is so. We are always trying to become something—the clerk becoming the manager, the manager the executive, the politician becoming the greatest leader, and so on, and so on. There is a becoming something continuously, and in that, we hope to bring about a revolution, a transformation. But it is not possible because that which continues can never bring about a transformation within itself.

Now with that mentality, with that mind, with the process of that thought, we observe the 'being'—the true God, or what you will, of which we do not know. The 'becoming' always speculates about the 'being'; the 'becoming' always watches the 'being', trying to grasp it, to take hold of it, to adjust itself to it. So when you, the 'becoming', the 'me' tries to capture that 'being', that 'being' is not. Because my mind is accustomed to think in terms of time, because my mind is the product of time, I cannot think in any other terms than 'becoming' or not 'becoming'. So in the very process of becoming there is conflict, and through the conflict we hope to achieve a result; that is our life. We want to achieve a result, an end, and we proceed through various means to achieve—always with an effort, with struggle, complications, choice, desiring to be this, shaping and accepting that, so on, and so on. That is our life, is it not? So, the 'becoming' is ever trying to follow a course of action—worship of the hero, the cultivation of virtue, and so on. It is everlastingly trying to capture the state which is the 'being', in which alone there is revolution. It is important, it seems to me, that we should understand that in 'becoming', there can be no change, no radical transformation. Then what is one to do? Do you follow?

I want to tell you something and I have to use words. And you are going to translate those words according to your conditioning, and so communication ceases between you and me. I want to tell you a very simple thing which is: There is no happiness, no transformation, no revolution in 'becoming', and it is only in 'being' that there is a possibility of fundamental, radical transformations. But the 'becoming' can never understand the 'being'. The more you observe, the more the becomer observes the 'being', then the 'being' becomes static, it never moves. So what the mind chooses is caught always in this 'becoming', in the wanting to do something. Do you see the problem?

How can I who have been conditioned—my whole education, my upbringing, my religion, my every endeavor is to become—how can I stop becoming? I do not know if you have ever thought over this problem, but as I am talking, how do you regard this problem? How do you feel about it? All our textbooks, all our religions, all gurus, all the process of thought is to become something—you must be communal, then national, then the world; first you are a child, then maturity and death; you must go through the evolutionary process until you reach the ultimate reality. Our mind is conditioned to the way of thinking that gradually the world can be changed, that a revolutionary state cannot be brought about immediately, that it must come through a gradual process of time, that we must all be dedicated, that we must all be educated in a certain way, that we must think in a certain way of action, and so on. With that process of thinking we are familiar. I say that through that way there is no revolution, there is no change, there is no possibility of any kind of transformation. Yet, transformation is essential in order to produce a different world.

You see the starving beggars on the road, the baby outside. The baby needs care, it needs food, it needs love, it needs freedom of the right type, it needs education to be without fear. Now, is it possible for the world to change immediately, not in a few centuries? Is that not your problem also? There is that child starving, and we have invented a socialistic, a communistic theory which will ultimately feed that baby; in the meantime, that baby dies. And in the course of building a system, there are a great many complications, destructions, misery, liquidation, concentration camps—which are all the process of becoming, are they not?

So, there must be a different approach to this problem. Can my mind, which is so conditioned in the 'becoming', ever stop and be capable of receiving that 'being' which cannot be observed, which cannot be understood by the becomer? How can I, who am the product of time, memory, who am always becoming something, accepting or denying something positively or negatively, how can I bring about in myself a fundamental revolution of values, of thought, of desires, of everything, radically, so that there can be happiness not only in me but in my relationship with the world, with my fellow beings? Is that also not your problem? And if it is your problem as well as mine, how do we act? Do we act in terms of 'becoming' or in terms of 'being'? There is no 'being' if there is 'becoming'.

As I have said previously, please listen. It is very important to listen to something which is true because that very listening to what is true has an extraordinary effect on the mind. If I know how to listen, if I can see beauty without interpretation, that beauty has an extraordinary effect on me. If I am sensitive enough to see the beauty as well as to see the ugliness of life, to see without interpreting, just to see it, it has an extraordinary effect. Similarly, if I know how to listen to something that is true, to something that is right, without translating, without comparing it to what has already been said by some teacher, by the Bhagavad-Gita, or some book, if I can listen without any translation, then that very listening, the receptivity to what is truth, has an extraordinary effect. An unconscious revolution is taking place, if I can listen.

Please listen to this—there can be revolution only when there is 'being' from which action which is true can take place. But as long as the mind is caught in the everlasting process of becoming, there can be no revolution, there can be no change, there can be no love; there can be only misery, more hate, more wars. So, what is the mind to do? It cannot go over to the other state. The mind, which is in itself the 'becoming' process, cannot go over to the other state and bring it to itself; it cannot become the 'being'. It cannot search the 'being'. The moment it is conscious, it is aware of the 'being', the 'being' is dead; the 'being' is no longer a vital thing, it does not dance, it does not live, it has no purposive action. So, what is the mind to do, which realizes that it cannot bring about a revolution within itself? Please listen, don't answer my question. Just listen.

Action is necessary; wars must be stopped; there must be no starvation. We recognize that a revolution is essential—a revolution which is fundamental, wide, not narrow, not partial, not limited. A total revolution is necessary. On investigation, we see that the mind cannot bring about such a revolution. The communist, the socialist, or the so-called religious person cannot bring about a revolution that is total; they can do partial reformation, partial change, but it will all be modified continuity. A total revolution is necessary in order to bring about a different world, a world which is not yours or mine but ours together, and that revolution can only come about when there is 'being' and not 'becoming'. So whatever effort you make in the revolution of being is a denial of that revolution. That is, if I make an effort to understand that state of being in which there is a radical revolution, that 'being' becomes a dead state. So when my mind understands this whole thing, my mind becomes very quiet; then it does not make an effort to be or not to be. Please follow this. The mind becomes quiet, and then you understand the whole process of becoming.

The mind cannot invite the 'being'. The 'being' can only come into existence when the mind is completely quiet, without any pursuit, without seeking any result, without becoming virtuous. Because, the self is the 'becoming', the 'me' is the becomer; and as long as the 'me' exists, there cannot be 'being'. The 'me' can take on different garments of different colors and think it is changing, is bringing about a revolution; but at the center, the 'me' is still there, and the 'me' cannot come to an end by discipline, by control, by sacrifice, by following examples. The 'me' exists because of the very effort it makes to be or not to be. So listen.

As long as the mind makes an effort, that very effort gives strength to the 'me'—the 'me' identifying with the state, with the party, with virtue, with certain systems of thought, with religion, or what you will. Therefore, through that process there is no revolution, there is no transformation; there is only more misery, more confusion, more war, more hatred. When I realize that, when the mind realizes that, then there is tranquillity; then there is that silence which is so essential for the 'being', and it is only then that there is a possibility of radical revolution.

Question: I feel like committing suicide; life to me has no purpose, no meaning whatsoever. Wherever I look, there is only despair, misery, and hatred. Why should I continue to live in this monstrous world?

KRISHNAMURTI: Why do we commit suicide? Are there not different ways of committing suicide? Do you not commit suicide when you identify yourself with the country? Do you not commit suicide when you become a party member, join any sect? Do you not commit suicide when you believe in something? That is, you give yourself over to something greater; the something greater is your projection of what you think you ought to be; the identification of yourself with something greater—the greater being your desire for something nobler—is a form of committing suicide. Do listen to it; don't throw it out, sirs.

Many of you have identified yourself with this country; you have been to prisons, you have struggled. Have you not committed suicide for something which is very small? Another commits suicide because he has no belief; he is a cynic; all his intellectual life has led him to nothing but despair and misery, and so he commits suicide. The man who believes and the man who does not believe have both committed suicide in their own ways because both want to escape from themselves. They want to escape through the country, through the idea of nationalism, through the idea of God; and when God and nationalism fail, or the country or the ideal for which the country stood for fails, then they are in darkness. And when I or you depend on a friend, on the person whom we love, when that dependence is taken away, we are again on the edge, ready to throw ourselves into darkness. So all of us—through identification with something greater, through belief, through various forms of escapes—try to run away from ourselves; and when we are thrown back upon ourselves, we are lost, we are lonely, we are in despair; so we are ready to commit suicide. That is our state, is it not? One whom you love turns away; you are jealous; it reveals the emptiness of your heart and mind, and that frightens you, and therefore you are ready to run away to another form of escape, and so on and on.

So, as long as we do not understand ourselves, we are always on the edge of darkness. We say the world is a terrible place, a miserable place. But the world is what we have created; the world is your relationship to another. If, in that relationship, there is dependence, then there is fear, there is frustration, there is disillusionment, and from that, there is the desire for suicide. And if you have a very strong belief, it holds you, and that very belief consciously conditions your mind so that you have no regard for inner search; that very belief acts as an escape from yourself. The more you are religious, the less you are inclined to commit suicide.

The more you question, the more you investigate, there is the constant fear of coming to that very close knowledge which is the emptiness of one's own loneliness. So must you not face that emptiness without depending upon anything? Must you not come to that state when you are completely lonely, and understand that state? Must you not be alone in order to find that which is alone, that which is not contaminated, which has not been thought about? But you cannot come to that aloneness if you are afraid of your loneliness. Most of us are afraid to face ourselves, and therefore we have many avenues of escapes, and when these avenues of escapes fail, we are thrown back upon ourselves, and it is that moment which we have to regard, to look into ourselves; we have to understand this emptiness, not run away from this emptiness through rituals, through any form of distraction, knowledge, or belief.

You can only look at this emptiness when the mind is completely absorbed in it, when you know of it without any sense of translating it or without desiring it to change—which is a very arduous process. Since most of us are lazy, we escape into some form of belief or commit suicide. So it is only when a person understands what loneliness is and goes through it that that person is purified to be alone, and only that aloneness can meet that which is the 'being', in which there is not the 'me' with all its efforts, contradictions, and confusions.

Question: I have known moments of quietness, a sense of complete equilibrium, but the moment is fleeting; how can this balance be sustained?

KRISHNAMURTI: Why do you want to sustain this balance? Is it not the same desire to continue, the same desire to hold on to something which you have? Happiness is an experience, a sense of quietness, a stillness. You have had that experience, and so you want to hold on. The very desire to hold on is to give it continuity, is it not? And that which has continuity can never experience the new. That is our trouble, is it not?

We are so traditionally bound, our mind is so conditioned by tradition, by yesterday's beauty, by yesterday's sorrow, by yesterday's experience. The mind is saturated by the many yesterdays and no new experience can possibly penetrate; and when by some chance it does, we want to hold on to it; and so the quiet moment becomes a habitual moment, the moment of tradition; and so it is no longer a still mind. It is a mind that is weighed down by acquisition. And the mind that is burdened by the weight of the past is incapable of being still; it only lives on memory, like an old man. A mind that is old, that is burdened by the past, cannot possibly understand a still mind. Please listen to this, and you will find out how to put aside the past and to have a fresh mind.

Our difficulty is not the adoption of new methods, new systems of what to do, but how to be creative. We are not creative in our lives, in our ways of thinking, in our activities. We are just machines of routine, and our education is a cultivation of that routine which is memory, and since we are not creative, any new creative breath becomes the old, gets caught in a tradition, and is lost. So if you can really listen and understand that, you will see that any accumulation of virtue or of money or of possessions burdens the mind, and therefore the mind is incapable of knowing the new, being new, and that what is essential in the world at the present time is the new mind, a creative mind—not an inventive mind. A creative mind is not possible when the mind is becoming, is possessing, is caught in the process of memory.

So, a mind that accumulates happy experiences is not a creative mind. A mind that is burdened by the past, and therefore by fear, is incapable of bringing about the revolution of being. If you can listen to this and let the truth of this operate unconsciously, without any purposive action by the conscious mind, then you will see that the mind becomes free from the past not in some distant future but immediately. That means, you must have the capacity to listen, to listen very attentively, without interpretation. Then only is there a possibility of the mind being creative.

Question: I understand, sir, your emphasis on the need of revolution in the human psyche, and your determined refusal to bless mere ideas; but, sir, our way of life influences our psyche. Why do you not preach voluntary redistribution of land and property, and thus help to create a right atmosphere for the understanding of your teaching by common men and women? Why do you not lay down the minimum condition that a truth-seeker must fulfill?

KRISHNAMURTI: Sir, what is important in this question? The minimum standard for the truth seeker? You have them in your books, have you not? Have you not been told from the very beginning that there must be generosity, that you must do good to others, that you must give what little you have to another, that you must love, that you must not be greedy? Those are all ideals which are good, are they not? Because you have no generosity of the heart, to you the generosity of the heart is an idea. And it is the fact that is more important than the minimum of what you should be.

Will the redistribution of land create a right atmosphere? Will everybody having enough land, enough food, enough clothing, enough shelter create a right atmosphere for the truth seeker, for the human being? Sir, what is the essence of this question? Our minds are petty, small, and we think we can enlarge that mind by regulation, by creating a right atmosphere, by redistribution of land, by economic revolution. The problem is not the distribution of land or what kind of economic system we should have; the problem is the pettiness of our minds. We do not see that.

What constitutes the petty mind? The question that has been put to me is not important, but the questioner is important because it indicates the mind that puts these questions. The question itself can be understood. We can resolve the problem of distribution of land, giving food, clothing, shelter; all these things can be arranged, organized. But, it is the mind that is behind the organization, and that is the thing that must be understood. It is there that there must be a revolution, and a petty mind cannot bring about a revolution. The mind, even when it thinks of God, is still petty because the mind in itself is petty. When the mind creates a revolution, it must be a petty revolution because the mind, do what you will, is still petty because thought is conditioned. Do what you will, thought is always conditioned—conditioned according to Marx, according to Christianity, Buddhism, or Hinduism, and so on. As long as the mind is conditioned, it is a petty mind, and such a mind cannot create a revolution. It can bring about reforms here and there, but that reformation brings more misery; that very reformation which the petty mind creates ends in tyranny, in concentration camps.

So our problem is not redistribution of land or a better economic system but how to break this mind that is so small so that the mind cannot think at all. Sir, it is very important to understand this question because we all want to do something in this world. There is so much misery, starvation, lack of love, unkindness, brutality; we all know the absolute absence of love in our daily life. We want to do something, but our minds have never produced a revolution; they have produced reformations, but those reformations have produced greater wars, greater miseries. Please see this, hear it, let it penetrate; you will understand it. So thought can never produce a happy world. Thought can produce more confusion, more misery, because our thought is always conditioned. There is no free thought because thought is based on memory. Memory is experience; experience is conditioned reaction; from childhood you are brought up as a Hindu, as a communist, a socialist, or what you will; you are conditioned, shaped, hedged about to be in a frame. The revolutionary man says that that frame is no good, and he will put you in a new frame, and if you do not fit into his frame, he will liquidate you, so that is the constant process of modifying, changing thought; that is not revolution; that is not transformation; that is mere modification, the changing superficially. So, as long as we are concerned with thought, with ideas, with experience, our world will be in a state of confusion and misery.

So our problem is not how to redistribute land or to sacrifice or to give up something but how to think, how to bring about the silence of the mind so that a new state can come into being. This revolution is possible only when thought has come to an end. And thinking can only come to an end when I understand the whole process of thought, how thought arises. Thought arises through memory; thought is words. All our action is based on experience, on knowledge which is always conditioned, and if I make an effort to put an end to thought, it is still conditioned. So the mind, realizing this, becomes very quiet. That is true meditation. When the mind—without discipline, without compulsion, without resistance—comprehends this whole process of thought and so becomes quiet, then only is there a possibility of a deep fundamental revolution from which action can take place, which will not be a conditioned action. Therefore, there will be a possibility of producing a different world in which this conflict between human beings—you have everything and I have nothing—has come to an end, and in that world, though you may have something more than me, I do not care because I have something else.

It is only when the mind is no longer seeking to aggrandize itself, seeking a result, seeking to bring about an action through ideas that there is a possibility of a revolution which is not of the mind, which is not the product of thought. That revolution is the revolution of being, of truth, of love. This is not sentimental, a superstition, a religious bogy. This is not a myth but a reality that can be discovered by each one. That reality can only be found when you are really earnest, when you know how to listen to something which is true and let that truth operate, let that cleanse the mind of all thoughts.

February 18, 1953

Fifth Talk in Bombay

For most of us, prejudice or bias is a very strong influence in our lives. Most of us are not aware of our prejudices and of the way they condition our life, and we derive a great deal of strength from prejudices, so it is almost impossible for anything new to penetrate through the thick wall of prejudices and conditioned influences. And the more we make an effort to break through consciously, not only do we further strengthen the prejudices that we have, but also cultivate new ones. I do not know if you have observed that any form of conscious effort to get rid of some particular quality or bias or prejudice brings about another form of prejudice, another conditioning, another wall which creates a resistance and from which we derive strength to act, to live, to continue.

It would be unfortunate if we, in listening this evening to the talk here, try to break through any particular wall of prejudices in order to capture a certain meaning or significance of what I am saying. I think therefore it is very important to listen rightly. I do not think I can repeat it too often that there is an art of listening, which is not the cultivation of a new thought or a new resistance. On the contrary, the very process of listening is really a very unconscious awareness. In that unconscious awareness, in that listening, a new perception, a new understanding can come into being, and any effort made destroys and nullifies understanding. You understand only when the mind is fairly quiet, when you are willing to find out the truth of the matter, but the truth of a matter is not revealed when you make an effort and therefore create resistance. So, if I may suggest, let us try to listen not to mere words or to the definition of a particular word but to the whole content of any particular statement. The more one listens in that way without any effort—without any directive purpose to use what has been said, to do something in life with it, to use it to act, to use it as an instrument to clear our conflicts and miseries—the more we are capable of listening with a passive awareness, with an easy awareness in which there is no choice, with an alertness in which the meaning, the significance comes without any effort on our part.

I want to discuss, if I can this evening, the thing that we call influence—the motive power, the faith, the strength which keeps us going, the machinery of dull routine, the so-called purpose—which having established itself, gives us a certain driving power, and that very force of an idea, of a purpose, of an aim, of wanting to achieve a result, which gives us a great deal of strength to continue. For most of us there is ambition, the desire to achieve a result—whether particular or national or of a party or of a group of people—and when we identify ourselves with a particular idea, we derive a great deal of strength from it, and that keeps us going, that gives us an energy, a drive; and the more we use that energy, the greater is the capacity to achieve a result. But in the wake of that capacity there is always pain, there is always suffering, there is always frustration, and so gradually we lose confidence.

I do not know if you have noticed in yourselves that if you strive after an idea, if you strive after a result, you may achieve it, but in the very process of that achievement there is always a frustration in which there is fear, there is a lack of confidence; being aware of this lack of confidence, you identify yourself with something which sustains you, from which there is strength, and that strength keeps you going. If I have no particular ideal, I have faith in God, and that faith keeps me going; all the troubles I translate with that faith, or that faith sustains me through trouble. But most of us have really no faith at all; we have a verbal assertion of faith, and so we are always looking for something, some idea, some person, some guru, some political party, some system; we identify ourselves with a country, with an idea, from which we derive strength and so keep going, and those of us who have capacity use that capacity as a means to sustain our effort.

As long as there is an outward or inward faith, there is always fear. Most of us try to awaken self-confidence through some kind of experience, the experience of God or the experience of knowledge or the experience of a conditioned state. I believe in a particular religion, in a particular ideal, in God; from that belief, I derive strength that sustains me, and then in the very process of the energy of sustaining, there is the cultivation of the 'me', of the 'I', the self, the ego. If we have no confidence in ourselves, we try to learn the technique of certain practices, and so establish routine, a habit of thought which gives us vitality, the energy with which to confront our daily conflicts and struggles. The more intelligent, the more alert we are, the less faith we have in anything.

So, is there not a way of life in which self-confidence is nonexistent? Let us go into it a little bit. I depend on my parents when I am young, and as I grow older, I depend on society, on a job, on capacity, and when these fail me, I depend upon faith; there is always a dependence, a faith in something; that dependence sustains me, gives me vitality, energy, and as with all dependencies, there is always fear, and so I set conflict going. Or, having no faith, I cultivate consistency, to be constant in my life according to my idea, and that very consistency endangers my self-confidence; the more I am consistent, the less I am strong, vital, clear-cut. Self-consistency—to be consistent to a certain form, to a certain action—is what most of us are striving for, which is the cultivation of self-confidence.

So wherever we try, there is always this desire to depend on something to give us strength—on a person, on a particular idea, on a political party, on a system, or on an experience. So there is always a dependence on something to sustain us, and as we depend more and more, there is the cultivation of fear. Dependence arises because in ourselves we are insufficient, in ourselves we are lonely, in ourselves we are empty. I depend, and therefore I cultivate faith; therefore, we must have more knowledge, and as we become more and more civilized, more and more learned—materialistic or spiritual—we must have faith or we turn cynical.

Now, is there not a drive for action—to do something, to live—without being dependent on anything inwardly? For most of us, self-confidence is necessary, and for most of us, confidence is merely the continuation of an experience or the continuation of knowledge. Does self-confidence ever free the mind from its own conditioning influence? Does this confidence derived through effort bring about freedom, or does it merely condition the mind? And is it not possible to free the mind, to remove all dependencies? That is, am I capable of being aware of my loneliness, of my complete emptiness, being aware of it without running away from it, and not being consistent through any particular form of knowledge or experience? That is our problem, is it not? Most of us are running away from ourselves as we are; we cultivate various forms of virtues to help us to run away. We cultivate various forms of confidence, knowledge, experience; we depend on faith, but underneath it all, there is a sense of immense loneliness, and it is only when we are capable of looking at it, living with it, understanding it fully, that there is a possibility of acting without bringing about a series of efforts which condition the mind to a particular action. Please listen to this and you will see it.

All our life we try to be consistent to a particular thought or to a pattern of thought, and the very desire to be consistent creates energy, drive, gives us strength, and so narrows down the mind. The mind that is consistent is a very small mind, a petty mind. A small mind has enormous capacity for energy; it derives a great deal of strength from its pettiness, and so our life becomes very small, very limited, very narrow. Can we realize this process of dependence from which we derive strength, in which there is conflict, in which there is fear, envy, jealousy, competition, that constantly narrows down all our efforts so that there is always fear?

Is it not possible to look, to be aware of our loneliness, of our emptiness, and understand it without trying to escape from it? The very understanding of it is not to condemn it but to be passively aware of it, to listen to the whole content of that loneliness. It means really to go beyond the self, beyond the 'me', and from there act, because our present action is within the confines of the 'me'. It may be enlarged, extended, but it is always the 'me' identifying with a person or an ideal; and that identification gives us a great deal of strength to act, to do, to be, and that identification strengthens the 'me', the 'I', the self in which there is everlasting conflict, everlasting misery; and so all our actions lead to frustration. Recognizing that, we turn to faith, we turn to God as a source of strength; and that, too, is the enlargement of the 'me', the strengthening of the 'me', because the 'me' is running away from itself, from that loneliness in itself. When we are capable of facing that loneliness without condemnation or judgment, looking at it, understanding it, hearing the whole content of the 'me', of that loneliness, then only is there a possibility of having strength which is not of the 'me'. Then only is there a possibility of bringing about a different world or a different culture.

Question: You have talked so much of beauty. Now tell us of ugliness.

KRISHNAMURTI: We avoid ugliness, we turn our back upon it. We put away the thing that we call evil, and cultivate the thing that we call good. We resist the thing called sin and cultivate virtue. We avoid those things which are ugly—the ugly street, the ugly faces, the ugly habits—and always pursue the thing we call beauty, the good, the noble. Now in this process what happens? When we turn our back on the ugly and turn our faces to beauty, what happens? We become insensitive, do we not?

When you put away the ugly, resist it, turn your back upon it, and turn your face to what is considered beautiful, what are you doing? You are only observing one side of life, not the whole process of life, and the whole process of life, the total process of life, includes the ugly and the beautiful. Is there such a thing as ugliness? And must not the mind be totally sensitive to both beauty and ugliness? Must it not be aware of hatred as well as of love, not as opposed to each other, not as a dual process? Please follow this. For us, hate and love are two opposites; we want to avoid hate, and we want to cultivate love. In the very avoidance of hate, we are cultivating resistance; we create ugliness; we are becoming insensitive; we are insensitive to the whole section which we call ugly, and we try to be sensitive to the whole part which we call beauty.

So there is a dual process going on—the avoidance of that which we call ugly, and the capturing of that which we call beauty—and in that conflict the mind becomes dull, the mind becomes insensitive, unaware. It is like walking down the street and only looking at the beautiful sky or only looking at the trees, the stars. Life is not only the sky, the stars, and the trees, but also the dirt, the squalor, the ugliness, the misery, the children that are starving, the tears and the laughter. The whole process is life. But the mind does not want to be sensitive to understand the whole process; it wants to pursue a particular pattern of thought. And the pursuit of a particular thought is considered noble, good, virtuous; that only leads to respectability, and the respectable mind will never find God. (Laughter) No, sirs, don't laugh! That is what we want. We want to be respectable because we all want to be consistent, and that very consistency gives us self-confidence, and where there is the strengthening of the self, there is respectability, whether through virtue or through denial of virtue.

So life is not merely the pursuit of the beautiful but also the comprehension of that which we call sin, ugly. It requires a great deal of sensitivity and alertness, a passive awareness of both, and then we will find that there is no ugly, no beautiful, but only the state of the mind. But you cannot come to that state of mind by the cultivation of any particular virtue or by pursuing a particular thought which you consider beautiful. That state of mind comes only when we understand the total process of our whole being—anger, envy, jealousy, love, hate, the ugly things of our existence, the tears and the laughter, the whole thing. The man who avoids the squalor and hangs a picture in his room and worships that picture, psychologically or physically, is never satisfied.

Surely what is important is not the cultivation of the beautiful or the avoidance of the ugly but to understand the total process of our existence, everything that we are. And there can be no understanding of everything we are if we are merely concerned with judgment because most of us derive strength from judging others, or judging our own character, our own state. We have values, and according to those values we judge people, experiences, ideas; that very judgment gives us strength, and in that strength, in that judgment we live, and from that, we derive confidence for further action. Such an action, such an activity, such judgment obviously cripples our capacity to understand the whole process of existence. That is why it is very difficult for most of us to live completely open inwardly, psychologically, without any background—to live from moment to moment without the psychological accumulation of judgment, of any pursuit, of virtue, of the denial of sin—because we are not quite aware of the total entity, consciously or unconsciously; we are not aware of the 'whole'.

You are both hate and love, but by merely cultivating love and making a conscious effort to pursue it, love is no longer love. The man who is conscious of love does not know love; likewise, the man who is conscious of his humility surely ceases to be humble; there is only concern with the cultivation of the partial. So what is important in understanding this question is not what is ugly and what is beautiful but to be totally sensitive to the whole process of life, which is you, to the total process of relationship. After all, society is relationship, and if I understand that relationship—conflict, pleasures, pain, sorrow, ugliness, bitterness, the whole of that, then I am a mature human being. But to understand the whole, the total process of life, the conscious as well as the unconscious, requires a great deal of listening to the whole content of myself—which means, there must not be condemnation, judgment.

You see how difficult it is to live without condemnation, to live without comparison, because our mind is always comparing, everlastingly judging, and with that comparison, with that judgment, there is vitality, there is strength, and we are satisfied with that vitality and strength—which is very destructive. If I want to understand, there must be no comparison, there must be no judgment, I must listen, I must go into it. And that requires enormous patience, affection, care—which implies an openness of mind, not a blankness, but a passivity of mind. But the mind will resist all this. The mind exists only in comparing, judging. That is the function of the mind. And when you deprive it of judgment, of comparison, there is no longer the mind, there is no longer the anchorage of it in which the mind can live, so we are afraid of that, and so we cultivate various forms of beauty and avoid various forms of ugliness, and so we are caught everlastingly in the conflict of duality. But if we can understand it as a total process, a unitary process, then there is no conflict of duality; then there is a possibility of the mind going beyond itself, a possibility of quietness, stillness, so that you can receive that which is true.

Question: How can I be free from envy?

KRISHNAMURTI: What is envy? Is not envy the desire for the 'more'? The more knowledge, the more power, the more love, the more adulation, the more understanding—having more and more of things, of ideas, of knowledge. The 'more' implies comparison, does it not? Please listen.

You will see that one can be free from envy completely, not at some future date, but immediately, if one knows how to listen to the truth of the statement, "The mind is the seat of envy." The mind is everlastingly asking for more and more, and our whole civilization is based upon the acquiring of the 'more', the demand for more properties, more money, more, more, and more; therefore, there is always comparison, therefore, everlastingly struggle. Knowing envy, we say we must cultivate nonenvy, which is another form of the 'more', negatively. So is it possible for the mind not to think in terms of the 'more' at all, not to compare, not to judge what it is? This is not stagnation; on the contrary, when the mind is not seeking the 'more', when it is not comparing, you are no longer concerned with time.

Time implies the 'more'—"I will be something tomorrow," "I will be happy in the future," "I will be a rich man," "I will fulfill," "I will be loved," "I shall love," and so on. The comparative mind, the mind that is asking for the 'more', is the mind of time, of tomorrow, is it not? So, when such a mind says, "I must not be envious," it is again another form of time, is it not? Another form of comparison is, "I have been this, I shall be less than that." So, can the mind which is seeking the 'more', stop completely from the demand of the 'more', which is envy? Do you understand the problem, sirs?

The problem is not how to be free from envy—which is a very small affair—but how not to think in terms of the 'more', how not to think comparatively, how not to think in terms of time, how not to think, "I will be"? Can the mind ever not think in terms of the 'more'? Do not say it is not possible. You do not know. All that you do know is the 'more'—more knowledge, more influence, more clothes, more property, more love. If you cannot get the 'more', then you want the less and less and less.

Now, is it possible for the mind not to think at all in those terms? First put the question. Do not help me to be free of envy. Can the mind cease to think in terms of the 'more'? Put that question and listen—not only now, but when you go home, when you are taking the tramcar, sitting in the bus, when you are walking alone, when you see a sari. When you see a man going in a big car, the big politician, the big businessman, put that question and find out and listen to it. Then you will find the truth of the matter; then you will find that the truth frees the mind from the 'more'. The mind then is not the conscious mind making an effort to denude itself of the 'more'. When the mind makes a conscious effort of not asking for more, it is another form of negation of the same thing, of the 'more', so in that, there is no answer. But if you put that question, you can only listen to it when you are not judging, when you don't want a result, when you don't want to use it to produce a certain action. It is only when you are listening that it is possible for truth to come into being, which will free the mind from the 'more'.

Question: You have talked of a state of nonrecognition. How does that state come into being?

KRISHNAMURTI: First of all, let us find out how this state of recognition comes into being. Without memory, there is no mind. Without naming, there is no mind. If I do not recognize, I have no experience, do I? There is no experience without recognition, is there? If I do not recognize you, I do not have an experience of meeting you, have I? So all experience is a process of recognition, is it not? The mind is the process of recognition. Naming, verbalizing, memory is all recognizing. So, my mind, which is the mechanism of recognition, can never see the new. It can only recognize what has been. All experiences are conditioned. They are never liberating because every experience is recognized by me as good, beautiful, ugly, worthwhile, or nonworthwhile. The very process of recognition, that very process of experience through recognition, strengthens the conditioning of the mind. So there is no freedom through experience because, after all, experience is the process of recognizing. I recognize because of a similarity in the past, so that the past is the process of recognition. We say that experience is the liberating force. We say that the more we experience, that the more we recognize an experience, understand it, store it away, the more there is wisdom. Is that so? Every experience only conditions my thinking, does it not? And thinking is the process of recognizing, verbalizing, naming, terming. So my mind is conditioning itself, limiting itself, confining itself through the experience which is already recognized, which has come from the background, from the mind itself. So my mind, which is the mechanism of recognition, can never know what truth is, what reality is.

Reality is the original, the new, the completely unrecognizable. If I can recognize it, it is my projection, something I have already known; therefore, it is not truth. Please follow this. Please listen to this rather than following it. All the gods, all the experiences, all the images and symbols which man pursues in his desire for happiness are projections of his recognition, of his experiences. There is no freedom through knowledge, accumulation of recognition, which is the process of experience.

We know, we are aware that the moment we recognize an experience, it is not new. Can the mind ever be in the state of nonrecognition? Do not say, "No." Please do not shake your heads but listen and find out. If the mind can never be in a state of nonrecognition, then there is no possibility of anything new, there is no possibility of truth or God. The truth which is recognizable, the God which is recognizable, is not truth, is not God but only a projection of my past. You have to see the truth of the fact that so long as the mind is recognizing, there is nothing new, there is no creativity at any time, there is nothing beyond the state of recognition. Now, is there a state which is not of recognition? If I say, "Yes," it would be no answer because it is my statement which has no value, but you have to find out the truth of it. And to find the truth of it is to put the question, to go into it, to let the mind, the unconscious, the deeper things, give hints of the thing which is not recognizable. Have you not experienced this at any time? The mind is quiet, still—it may be for a fleeting second—when it is in a state when something new is happening inwardly to it, but that state of nonrecognition is immediately captured by recognition, by past memories, by past desires. That state is the new, but the mind captures it, recognizes it, and wants more of it. That is all its concern, the 'more'.

Is there not a state when the mind is not recognizing, when it is absolutely still, when it is no longer asking even for an experience, when the whole desire for the 'more', when the whole demand for acquiring, has completely ceased? It is only in that state that there is a possibility of the state of nonrecognition. When the mind is so still, so quiet, without any process of recognition, it is only then that truth can come into being. But the moment you recognize it as truth, it is no longer truth; it is already caught in the net of time. Because truth is something which comes into being from moment to moment, it is not to be accumulated, to be stored away, to be used. If it is stored away, if it is to be used, to be captured, then it is no longer truth; then it is only a memory, a thing that has come and gone. Truth is not to be accumulated. The mind can never understand truth because the mind is a process of recognition. The mind can never experience truth. Truth is a living thing, and a living thing cannot be understood by the mind because the mind is the result of the past; it is a dead thing.

And as truth, that reality is something not of time; the mind cannot comprehend the timeless. The mind can create all kinds of illusions, project various forms of desires, symbols, but that is not reality. That reality comes only when the mind is in a state of nonrecognition, and that state is not to be cultivated. You cannot cultivate a state which you do not know. If you knew it, it is not truth. It is only memory, which is conditioning you to a particular action. So the mind inquiring what is truth, what is reality, can never find it. It can invent, it can theorize, but it can never know what reality is.

That reality can only come when the mind recognizes its own process, how it is conditioned, and when there is then a freedom from its own recognizing process. Then only is there a possibility of the mind being so still that it is capable of receiving that which is truth. Truth is timeless. It is of no time. Therefore it cannot be captured, put away for use, or remembered, renamed. Therefore, truth is creative. It is everlastingly new; the mind can never understand it.

February 22, 1953

Sixth Talk in Bombay

I think it is important to understand the problem of discontent. Perhaps we may find the right answer to our enormous problems if we can search out the deeper significance of discontent. Most of us are dissatisfied with ourselves, with our environment, with our ideas, with our relationships. We want to bring about a change. There is discontent from the villager up to the most learned man, if he is not caught in his knowledge, if he is not a slave to his learning. There is a spreading discontent which makes us do all kinds of actions, and we want to find a way to contentment. If you are dissatisfied, you want to find a way to happiness. If you are battling within yourselves, you want to find a way to peace. Being dissatisfied, discontented, you want to find an answer that will be satisfactory. So the mind is ever groping, ever probing to find out the truth—the true answer to its discontent. Some find an answer in their satisfaction, in an aim, in a purpose of life which they have established for themselves, and finding a means to their desire, they think they have found contentment.

Is contentment to be found? Is peace a thing to be found by the process of the intellect? Is happiness a thing gotten by the understanding or by the creation of the opposite of what it is? This misery and this discontent—is it essential in our life? The fact is we are discontented with *what is,* discontented with things which we have, with what we are, and the discontent arises because of comparison. I am discontented because I see you are learned, rich, happy, powerful. Is that the cause of discontent? Or does discontent come into being when I am seeking a way away from *what is?* If I can understand the way of discontent, perhaps there will be happiness, there will be contentment. There is no way to happiness, to contentment. That contentment and that happiness are not the process of stagnation because if I am discontented and if I want to be contented, then that way leads to contentment which is stagnation, and that is what most of us want. But is there a way?

Can we find out, can we probe into the question of discontentment without trying to create its opposite, without trying to seek its opposite? Because after all, when we are young, we are discontented with society as it is. We want to reform, we want to bring about a change. So we join a society, a party, a political group, or a religious association. And soon our discontentment is canalized, held, and destroyed. Because, then we are only concerned with carrying out a way, a system which will produce a result, and thereby put aside our discontent. Is that not one of our greatest problems? How easily we are satisfied!

Is not discontent essential in our life, to any question, to any inquiry, to probing, to finding out what is the real, what is truth, what is essential in life? I may have this flaming discontent in college, and then I get a good job and this discontent vanishes. I am satisfied, I struggle to maintain my family, I have to earn a livelihood, and so my discontent is calmed, destroyed, and I become a mediocre entity satisfied with things of life, and I am not discontented. But the flame has to be maintained from the beginning to the end so that there is true inquiry, true probing into the problem of what is discontent. Because the mind seeks very easily a drug to make it content with virtues, with qualities, with ideas, with actions, it establishes a routine and gets caught up in it. We are quite familiar with that, but our problem is not how to calm discontent but how to keep it smoldering, alive, vital. All our religious books, all our gurus, all political systems pacify the mind, quieten the mind, influence the mind to subside, to put aside discontent and wallow in some form of contentment. And is it not essential to be discontented in order to find what is true?

Why is it that we are discontented, and does discontent produce revolution, change, transformation? And does transformation, revolution, come about only when we understand the nature of discontent? And with what is there discontent? What is it that we are discontented with? When you can really probe into that question, then you may find an answer. What is it that we are discontented with? Surely with *what is*. The *what is* may be the social order, the *what is* may be the relationship, the *what is* may be what we are, the thing we are essentially—which is, the ugly, the wandering thoughts, the ambitions, the frustrations, the innumerable fears; that is what we are. In going away from that, we think we shall find an answer to our discontent. So we are always seeking a way, a means to change the *what is*—that is what our mind is concerned with. If I am discontented and if I want to find a way, the means to contentment, my mind is occupied with the means, the way, and the practicing of the way in order to arrive at contentment. So I am no longer concerned with discontent, with the embers, the flame that is burning, which we call discontent. We do not find out what is behind that discontent. We are only concerned with going away from that flame, from that burning anxiety.

Surely we are discontented with *what is*. And it is enormously difficult to probe into the actual *what is*, not 'what should be', but into what I am from moment to moment. This is not the inquiry, the probing, into the higher self which is a fabrication of the mind but into *what is*. This is enormously difficult because our mind is never satisfied, never content in the examination of *what is*. It always wants to transform *what is* into something else—which is the process of condemnation, justification, or comparison. If you observe your own mind, you will see that when it comes face to face with *what is*, then it condemns, then it compares it with 'what should be', or it justifies it and so on, and thereby pushes away *what is*, setting aside the thing which is causing the disturbance, the pain, the anxiety.

Is not discontent essential, not to be smothered away, but to be encouraged, inquired into, probed into, so that with the understanding of *what is* there comes contentment? That contentment is not the contentment which is produced by a system of thought, but it is that contentment which comes with the understanding of *what is*. That contentment is not the product of the mind—the mind which is disturbed, agitated, incomplete—when it is seeking peace, when it is seeking a way away from *what is*. And so the mind through justification, comparison, judgment, tries to alter *what is*, and thereby hopes to arrive at a state when it will not be disturbed, when it will be peaceful, when there will be quietness. And when the mind is disturbed by social conditions—by poverty, starvation, degradation, by the appalling misery—seeing all that, it wants to alter it; it gets entangled in the way of altering, in the system of altering. But if the mind is capable of looking at *what is* without comparison, without judgment, without the desire to alter it into something else, then you will see that there comes a kind of contentment which is not of the mind.

The contentment, which is the product of the mind, is an escape. It is sterile. It is dead. But there is contentment which is not of the mind, which comes into being when there is the understanding of *what is*, in which there is profound revolution which affects society and individual relationship. So, discontent is not to be calmed, to be set aside, to be drugged by some system of thought. It is an essential thing. It must be kept alive, burning, in order to find out.

We are in conflict with each other, and our world is being destroyed. There is crisis after crisis, war after war; there is starvation, misery; there are the enormously rich, clothed in their respectability, and there are the poor. To solve these problems, what is necessary is not a new system of thought, not a new economic revolution, but to understand *what is*—the discontent, the constant probing of *what is*—which will bring about a revolution which is more far-reaching than the revolution of ideas. And it is this revolution that is so necessary to bring about a different culture, a different religion, a different relationship between man and man.

Question: Who are you? Whom am I listening to? You say, "Do not rely on any guru"; you say, "Listen to me"; listening to you is to listen to the greatest guru of all. I am puzzled. What am I to do?

KRISHNAMURTI: Does it really matter very much who the speaker is? Surely it does not matter much by whom the microphone is made, but it matters very much what the microphone conveys to your ears. The voice is of no importance. Whose it is, whether it is educated, whether it is the voice of the cultured, it does not at all matter, but what is important is what it says, conveys. And what it says and the understanding of it depends upon you, not on the guru, not on the voice, but on how you understand it, how you translate it, how you put it into action. So again the voice is not important; what is important is listening.

How do you listen? Do you listen with your projections, through your projections, through your ambitions, desires, fears, anxieties, through hearing only what you want to hear, only what will be satisfactory, what will gratify, what will give comfort, what will for the moment alleviate your suffering? If you listen through the screen of your desires, then you obviously listen to your own voice; you are listening to your own desires. And is there any other form of listening? Is it not important to find out how to listen not only to what is being said but to everything—to the noise in the streets, to the chatter of birds, to the noise of the tramcar, to the restless sea, to the voice of your husband, to your wife, to your friends, to the cry of a baby? Listening has importance only when one is not projecting one's own desires through which one listens. Can one put aside all these screens through which we listen, and really listen?

What does this listening mean? That is all we are concerned with—not who the speaker is, it is utterly irrelevant, not whether he is good or bad, not whether he is the guru, small or big. But in listening to the speaker, you are going to find out how you are listening, how you are watching yourself. Do not merely listen to me but watch the process of your own mind—how you project, how you ward off, how you feel shy of certain statements, how you will resist, and how you will put aside a new idea, a new way of looking; all that reveals the process of your own mind, does it not? And when you discard, put aside all these projections of the mind, is there any other way of listening? Can one put them aside and really listen?

Then, is there a guru at all? Then, is a guru necessary at any time? We all think a guru is necessary from the beginning to the threshold. If the guru is not necessary after the threshold, then he is not necessary from the beginning because the end lies in the beginning, and the man who is seeking the threshold of reality must seek at the beginning, not at the end. And because we are sluggish, impatient, doubtful, discontented, we want to find somebody to lead us away from our discontent. The understanding of this is essential, not the entity who leads away, not the system, not the thought that will take us away from what we actually are.

So, is it not important to know how you are listening? And when you listen without these projections, what happens? Please follow this. What happens when you are not projecting your desires through which you hear, through which you translate to suit your particular temperament, your particular idiosyncrasies? When you are not projecting your desires, how do you listen? Is your mind capable of listening? Will it allow you to listen? And then when you are so capable of listening, and when you are listening, what happens? What happens to the mind that is so listening? This is important, but not whether there is a guru or not, not whether you are hearing the voice of the guru who is promulgating the truth to which you are listening, and which makes the guru essential for you. What are you listening to when you are not listening through the screen, through the layers of your own projections? Do you understand?

We are always listening to something—to a noise, to the voice of somebody, to the restless sea. But if you are not listening through your projections, then are you listening to anything? Please watch your own mind, not what I am saying. If you watch what I am saying, you are dependent on me, and if you depend on me, then you have fear; then you are fettered to me, and that is a bondage; that is a travail from which you have to go beyond. So from the very beginning, do not be dependent on anyone. Do not follow anyone because it matters what you are from the beginning, not what you are at the end.

So when the mind is no longer following, no longer listening to the voice of its own projections, its desires, ambitions, satisfactions, then what is the mind listening to? Is there a listening to anything? Is it not a complete openness, a complete state in which there is no reaction, no listening to anything, in which there is no concentration, no absorption with an idea, in any idea? Is it not a state of complete passive activity when the mind is very quiet, not listening to anything in particular, but listening, not projecting, but thoroughly still? Then, in that state, is there a guru? And in that state, is a guru necessary? Is that state not possible from the very beginning? That is, if I want to understand something fundamental, must I not be in that state always? Most of you are projecting your own desires, so most of you do not listen. You are always listening to something. You are not merely listening. You are always listening to your own voice, and that voice always assumes the voice of despair, of hope, of pleasure, of security. But if you are not listening to something, if you merely listen, then is there not an utter stillness of the mind which is not the result of any discipline to be achieved at some far end but which is to be understood right at the very beginning, from now on for the rest of your lives?

Can you completely and totally discard this whole idea of the guru, the awakener, the giver of comfort, the man who will lead you to truth? I say you can completely wipe it away when you see that listening to something is listening to your own projections, to your own desires, that it is translating them to suit yourselves; when you understand that, then there is no listening to anything; then there is only listening; that listening is eternal because it is not of time, because it is not of the mind.

Question: What is happiness? Is it not the search for happiness that makes the mind crave for new experiences? Is there a state of happiness that is beyond the mind?

KRISHNAMURTI: Why do we inquire, "what is happiness"? Is that the right approach? Is that the right probing? We are not happy. If we were happy, our world would be entirely different; our civilization, our culture would be wholly, radically different. We are unhappy human beings, petty, miserable, struggling, vain, surrounding ourselves with useless, futile things, satisfied with petty ambitions, with money, and position. We are unhappy beings though we may have knowledge, though we may have money, rich houses, plenty of children, cars, experience. We are unhappy, suffering, human beings, and because we are suffering, we want happiness, and so we are led away by those who promise this happiness, social, economic, or spiritual. So we want to escape from *what is*—the suffering, the pain, the loneliness, the despair. We want to run away from it, and the very running away gives us experience, and that experience we call happiness. Is there any other kind of happiness?

What is the good of my asking if there is happiness when I am suffering? Can I understand suffering? That is my problem, not how to be happy. I am happy when I am not suffering, but the moment I am conscious of it, it is not happiness. Is it not so? Because the moment I know I am virtuous, I cease to be virtuous. The moment I know I am humble, courageous, generous, the moment I am aware of it, then I am not that. So happiness, like virtue, is not a thing to be sought after, not a thing to be invited. Virtue, when cultivated, becomes immoral because it strengthens the 'me', the 'I', leading to respectability which is the self. So, I must understand what is suffering. Can I understand what is suffering when a part of my mind is running away seeking happiness, seeking a way out of this misery? So must I not, if I am to understand suffering, be completely one with it, not reject it, not justify it, not condemn it, not compare it, but completely be with it and understand it?

Can I listen to the voice of suffering without projections? I cannot listen when I am seeking happiness. So my probing, my inquiry, is no longer what is happiness, nor if there is happiness beyond my mind, nor whether it is permanent or impermanent, nor whether it is an experience and therefore to be stored. The moment I do any of these things, it is already gone; therefore, it is no longer happiness. But the truth of what is happiness will come if I know how to listen. I must know how to listen to suffering; if I can listen to suffering, I can listen to happiness because that is what I am.

I suffer; I am fearful of death; I desire to be secure after death; I desire to be permanent, to have position, wealth, comfort; I am filled with the ache of loneliness. So can I listen to all that? Then, my problem is no longer a way to happiness but to find out how to listen to the voice of suffering, just to listen, without trying to interpret it. And that is a very arduous process because the mind continuously objects to living with suffering—to look at it, not to interpret it, not to justify it, not to translate it, not to condemn it, but to look at it, to know its content, to be acquainted with it, to love it. The mind is capable of listening to that voice which is beyond suffering only when the mind is not running away from it into some futile imagination or illusion or some desire for satisfaction.

So what is important is not if there is happiness but from the very beginning to inquire what is suffering, and to stay with that until the right answer comes. The right answer cannot come if you are seeking. The moment you search for the right answer, the mind is projected because it wants the answer; therefore, it is not concerned with the listening to suffering. It is not concerned with listening, but it is concerned with the answer which will reject this suffering. The moment you wish to reject something, then you will find an answer which will be satisfactory, and so it will be that satisfaction which the mind seeks, and not the understanding of suffering. After all, that is what we all want. We want satisfaction, either in a position, in relationship, or in ideas. And the more we are satisfied, the more the suffering. Because, the mind that is satisfied is never let alone; it is always being challenged on every side of life. So a mind realizing that it is seeking satisfaction—the very desire to find an answer for suffering is to be satisfied—totally puts aside all this. Therefore it is only listening, seeing the whole process of how the mind runs away, how it never can stay with suffering—such as facing fear. Fear comes only when you are running away from it. Fear exists in the process of flight, not when you are confronted with the thing. It is only when you are running away from the thing, in the very running away, fear is created—not when you are watching the thing, the *what is.*

So, similarly, can I look at suffering without running away—which creates sorrow, which creates fear, which prevents me from looking at it? If I can look at it, then there is a possibility of listening to suffering without interpretation, without judgment, without translating, or asking for a result. Then only is there a possibility of listening, of trying to find something beyond the mind.

We cannot find what is beyond the mind if we do not know, if we are incapable of facing *what is.* And it requires enormous attention, great passive awareness to observe without justification, without judgment, just to observe, just to listen. In that, there is transformation. In that, there is happiness which is not measured by time, by the mind.

Question: You talk so much of intelligence. What is it to be intelligent?

KRISHNAMURTI: Again, can a stupid mind see what is intelligent? Can a petty mind, a shallow mind find out what is greatness? Please, sirs, listen to this. A petty mind inquires after God. It is like the rich man who builds temples after exploiting people; after putting away money, he inquires, "What is God?" Shall such a man find what is God? His mind is corrupt, his mind is cruel, ungenerous, unkind, petty, small, and clothed by his own beliefs; shall such a man find what is truth, what is reality, what is God? He may surround himself with images, symbols, prayers, words, books, but shall such a mind find what is God? His mind is petty, and his God is also petty. So a stupid mind, inquiring what is intelligence, can never understand what is intelligence, but if it is aware that it is stupid, then it is already intelligent. Do please listen to this; it is not a matter of emotional, nervous laughter.

As most of us are petty, small, narrow, we create the world in our image, not in God's image. So what is important is not what is intelligence but to be aware of our own narrowness, of our stupidity, of our pettiness without trying to alter it, without saying, "I must make it intelligent, I must make it clever." When the petty mind, which is aware that it is petty, tries to alter its pettiness, then its activity will still be petty. If I realize that I am stupid, if I am aware that I am stupid, and if I set about to alter that stupidity, that very action is born of stupidity, is it not? But can I be aware that I am stupid and listen to it, follow it, understand it, and not challenge it? The stupid mind is still a stupid mind; it cannot alter its course, which is choice; all that it can do is to see that whatever it chooses is still petty. Please observe your own mind. Don't listen to me only, but watch your own minds and see the truth of what I am saying.

Because choice is a factor of deterioration, choice is petty under all circumstances; there is no great choice and no little choice. All our cultural, religious processes are from discrimination to discrimination, climbing higher and higher through choice. But the choice is made by the petty mind because where there is choice, there is pettiness of the mind. A mind which is the result of hate, which is the result of prejudice, which is the result of conditioning, whatever such a mind chooses is still conditioned; whatever its experiences, they are still conditioned. Therefore, a mind that is petty, in choosing, is not liberated from its pettiness. Therefore when a mind chooses something great, the great is still the petty. When the petty mind chooses the guru, a particular guru to follow, it is the petty mind that chooses; therefore, the guru is petty. And so all gurus are petty because you have chosen them.

So intelligence is surely something that is not cultivatable through the process of choice, through the process of experience, through knowledge. A petty mind remains a petty mind, though it has innumerable experiences, because at the center it is still petty. You may read all the Vedas, all the Upanishads, the Gita, all the sacred books of the East and the West; the mind is still petty, so your knowledge is still petty. Is not the mind always petty? Can it be anything other than petty and small? So is it not important to find out not what is intelligence but in what way the mind is choosing, acting, discriminating? Is it not important to find out for yourselves—not to listen to me, not to read a book on what is intelligence—to observe the state of your own mind? Only in the uncovering of *what is,* intelligence comes into being. In the understanding of *what is,* there is that intelligence which is creative.

Question: Every religion advocates prayer. Will you please explain the power of prayer and how prayer differs from meditation?

KRISHNAMURTI: You pray, do you not? And when do you pray? Is it when you are happy? Or is it that you pray in the moment of strain and suffering? You pray every morning when you are doing puja. That is a routine; that is traditional and dull and without much significance. When you are suffering, you pray, do you not? You supplicate, petition, to find an answer for your suffering. And there is a prayer in which there is no routine, which is not the outcome of supplication, but which is complete listening.

The routine prayer of repetition of words obviously produces a certain result; the more you repeat, the more quiet you are. But that quietness of repetition is stagnation because the mind is put to sleep by repeating a phrase, and you think you have done marvelously if you can quieten the mind by repetition, but that quietness is not creative, is it? It is dull; it is like the petty human being who is concerned with household things and prays, repeats words because, in repetition, it is peaceful in its smallness.

Then there is prayer, supplication, petitioning, when there is suffering. Please follow all this, listen to all this. When I suffer, I want an answer. When my son dies, I want to find comfort; I want somebody to tell me that he is all right. When I am dying in my old age, I want an assurance from some guru or from the book or from some friend that everything is all right, that I am secure. So I beg, I petition, I inquire, I ask. When I petition, when I ask, when I beg, I receive what I want because what I want is security, comfort. Because I am confronted with the abyss of darkness, with loneliness, with utter extinction, and not knowing what it is, I ask somebody to give me the answer which I want—which is, to guarantee that on the other side there is light, there is companionship, there is the Father. So when I suffer, I pray, and my prayer is answered according to my desire. This is not a cynical reply, but it is the actual fact.

I am suffering, and somebody comes and tells me that I am suffering because of all the misery that I have inflicted on thousands of people, the way I have behaved. I do not want to face it; I want to be pacified, I want comfort, and I seek the person who satisfied me. Or in that suffering, when I pray, I think about something—about light, about the bird, the sea, about a picture—and my suffering goes; I temporarily put it aside. Have you not noticed that if you can turn your mind from your physical suffering, there is less suffering? Similarly, in praying, if you can turn your mind away from the present conflict, from the present misery, there is peace. But that is an escape. In that, there is deterioration. But it gives you a certain tranquillity, a peace; your mind is at rest, and this peace acts as a drug. You might as well take whiskey as pray because all that you are concerned with is not to suffer, not to inquire, not to find out, not to go beyond; all that you are concerned with is some comfort. So prayer answers what you want, and the more you want, the more strongly you desire, the greater is your satisfaction.

But can one use that word prayer, which has been so misused, for something quite different? If I can understand what is meditation, then I shall perhaps understand what is prayer—the right prayer, not the stupid prayer of the petty mind.

What is *meditation?* To find out what is meditation, you must know what the meditator is—not some higher entity but the meditator, the one who meditates, the one who sits down, closes his eyes and begins to meditate. Without knowing that entity, the process is all a waste, and you cannot know meditation because you cannot separate meditation from the meditator. There is no meditation without the meditator, and without the meditator understanding himself, there is no peace. So to find out what is meditation, one must understand what is the meditator, and in the understanding of the meditator, there is self-knowledge, there is wisdom. Don't listen just to words, but understand yourself.

Self-knowledge is the beginning of wisdom, and a small mind meditating will, even at the end of ten years, still be a small mind, and that is the tragedy of people who meditate. They have enclosed themselves so deeply in their conditioning that nothing can penetrate, and they remain petty, anxious, everlastingly seeking. The meditator must set about to understand himself from moment to moment, from day to day—what it is he is, what it is he is not, at the time when he is getting into the tramcar, when he is talking to his wife, when he is scolding his servant, when he is snobbish—he must study himself at all those moments.

Then, in that self-knowledge, he will find out the operations of the meditator, how the meditator comes into being; then he will find that there is no meditator apart from meditation, that there is only meditation—not the meditator meditating. Then only, when there is only meditation, there is peace because the mind then is no longer meditating upon something, because the mind is no longer seeking through meditation to find something. There is only meditation as there is only listening. There is not the meditator meditating upon something. Then the observer is the observed. Then fear is not. Then only is there peace, and that peace cannot be sought by the mind because the mind is everlastingly petty, small. The mind can never be great. What is great cannot be invited by the mind. The mind can only invite its own pettiness. It cannot invite the great. It cannot invite the truth, the real. And so, the mind can only be quiet, receptive, alone, listening.

February 25, 1953

Seventh Talk in Bombay

One of our problems, it seems to me, is this question of mediocrity. I am not using this word in any derogatory sense, but the obvious fact is that the vast majority of us are mediocre. Will any technique, religious or mechanical, release us from that mediocrity? Or must there not be a revolt against the whole idea of technique? Because it seems to me that the more and more one observes, there are less people who are creative. I am not using that word *creative* in the sense of the man who paints, who writes poems, or who produces inventions, a genius. We shall find out as we go along what it is to be creative.

But should we not inquire—before we find out what it is to be creative—why is it that most of us are so easily influenced? Why do so many of us allow interference in our lives? Why do we want to interfere, and why are we so efficient in judging others? And perhaps we shall find out when we inquire into this that in the things that we have so carefully cultivated—judgment, the capacity to develop a technique, mechanical or so-called spiritual—there may be the very root of mediocrity, and that as long as there is no revolt against technique, there will be imitation, authority, the development of capacity, the following of certain ideas, a mind that is constantly consistent—which all indicate the structure of a mind that is mediocre.

Please listen; don't take notes. This is not a class. I am not a professor speaking to you so that you can take notes which you can think over afterwards. Let us think out together as we go along. I am only saying what is very obvious or fairly obvious, and if you do not listen, you may not experience immediately that state of creativeness which perhaps we can discover together by understanding—that is, by hearing directly what it is that makes for mediocrity.

Creativeness is a state of aloneness. When the mind is not completely alone, there is no creativeness. It is only when the mind is capable of shedding all influences, all interferences, of being completely alone— without dependence, without a companion, without any molding influence and judgment—that in that state of aloneness, there is creativeness. But that state of aloneness is not understood by the mediocre mind, by the mind that is cultivating a practice, the know-how, the way to something.

In the world, more and more technique is being developed—the technique of how to influence people through propaganda, through compulsion, through imitation, through examples, through idolatry, through the worship of the hero. There are innumerable books written on how to do a thing, how to think efficiently, how to build a house, how to put machinery together; so gradually we are losing initiative, the initiative to think out something original for ourselves. In our education, in our relationship with government, through various means, we are being influenced to conform, to imitate. And when we allow one influence to persuade us to a particular attitude or action, naturally we create resistance to other influences. In that very process of creating a resistance to another influence, are we not succumbing to it negatively?

Are we not the result of innumerable influences? Is not our mind, our structure, our being, a network of influences—economic, climatic, social, cultural, religious? It is a mind that is put together, and with such a mind we want to find out what we want to create. But such a mind can only imitate; it can only put other things together; that is why the world is developing more and more technologically. A man who is technologically trained can never be a creative human being. He may produce a marvelous house, put an aeroplane together, but he is not a creative entity. Because his mind is put together, his mind is not a whole mind; it is not an integrated mind.

How can there be an integrated mind when we are segments of various forms of influences? Our mind is the result of these influences; our mind is conditioned by all these influences as a Hindu, as a Muslim, as a Christian. And being conditioned, being subjected to various kinds of influences, we say, "I will choose a particular influence, a guru, the good, the noble; and I will cultivate through various practices, various methods, that nobility." But our mind is still a mind influenced, controlled, shaped, pursuing a deliberate end, and such a mind can never be in revolt, can it? Because the moment such a mind is in revolt, it is in a state of chaos. So a mediocre mind can never be in revolt; it can only move from one conditioned state to another, from one influence to another.

Should not the mind always be in revolt so as to understand the influences that are always impinging, interfering, controlling, shaping? Is it not one of the factors of the mediocre mind that it is always fearful and, being in a state of confusion, it wants order, it wants consistency, it wants a form, a shape by which it can be guided, controlled, and yet these forms, these various influences create contradictions in the individual, create confusion in the individual. You are conditioned as a Hindu or a Muslim, and there is another who is conditioned in being noble, or who is conditioned by certain ideas, economic or religious. Any choice between influences is surely still a state of mediocrity. A mind that chooses between two influences and lives according to that particular influence is still a mediocre mind, is it not? Because, it is never in a state of revolt, and revolt is essential to find out anything.

When the mind is never alone, can it be creative? When you examine your mind, you will find how fearful it is of going wrong, of making a mistake. The mind is constantly seeking security, certainty, safety in a particular consistent pattern of thought, and can such a mind which is never alone be creative? By alone, I do not mean that loneliness in which there is despair; I mean that aloneness in which there is no dependence of any kind on anything—on tradition, on a custom, on a companion. And must not the mind be in such a state in which there is no fear of any kind? Because, the moment I depend, there is the birth of fear, and all initiative, all originality—not eccentricity, but the capacity to think out—is lost. Must not the mind have the capacity to fathom—not to imitate, not to be shaped—and to be without fear? Should not such a mind be alone and therefore creative? That creativeness is not yours or mine, it is anonymous.

Please listen to all this because most of us are mediocre. Is there a possibility of complete and immediate transformation into this creativeness? Because, that is what is needed at the present time in the world—not reformers, not ideologists, not great philosophers, but you and I who, realizing our mediocrity, immediately bring about that state of aloneness in which there is no dependence, no fear—which is completely alone, uninfluenced, which cannot be interfered with, which is not imitative, not following. Can you and I produce together immediately such a state of mind? Because, without such a mind, do what you will, your reforms will produce more misery and more chaos.

Is it possible for a mind that has been mediocre, that has been interfered with, put together, shaped, controlled, that is dependent, immediately to realize that aloneness? Do not say, "It may be possible, but I cannot do it; someone else can do it," but just listen, not to the words, but the meaning of the words. Can a mind that has been interfered with, that is the result of interference, that is the result of time, of influence, can such a mind put away everything and be alone? For, in that aloneness there is creativity. It does not matter what words you use. That creativity is not of time, it is not yours or mine, it is completely anonymous. And as long as you are cultivating a technique, there is no anonymity because most of our minds are occupied with how to do this, how to stop being influenced, how to break away from our conditioning. When one says, "I will practice this and I will get it," "I will discipline myself, and then I shall not be influenced," or "I shall build a wall around myself against all influences," it indicates that the mind is inquiring the way, the technique. Is such a mind capable of ever being free, ever being in revolt? And is not such a mind mediocre? Therefore such a mind can never be alone.

If you have to create a new world, a new civilization, a new art, everything new, not contaminated by tradition, by fear, by ambitions, if you have to create something anonymous which is yours and mine, a new society, together, in which there is not you and me but an "ourness," must there not be a mind which is completely anonymous, therefore alone? This implies, does it not, that there must be a revolt against conformity, a revolt against respectability, because the respectable man is the mediocre man because he wants something, he is dependent on influence for his happiness, on what his neighbor thinks, on what his guru thinks, on what the Bhagavad-Gita or the Upanishads or the Bible or the Christ says. His mind is never alone. He never walks alone, but he always walks with a companion, the companion of his ideas.

Is it not important to find out, to see, the whole significance of interference, of influence, the establishment of the 'me', which is the contradiction of the anonymous? Seeing the whole of that, does not the question inevitably arise: Is it possible immediately to bring about that state of mind which is not influenced, which cannot be influenced by its own experience or by the experience of others, a mind which is incorruptible, which is alone? Then only is there a possibility of bringing about a different world, a different culture, a different society in which happiness is possible.

Question: I have been a cripple since I was 40 days old. You talk of securities, but I have none—no home, no friends, no job. How am I to face my life?

KRISHNAMURTI: How do we face life, whether we are healthy or unhealthy? Actually how do we face it?

If you are secure financially, if you have a gift, if you have capacities, if you have a backing or influence, you can face it fairly well, can't you? But the vast majority of people have no security, no influence with the big ones; they are crippled, mentally, physically, and how are they to face life? Surely as best as they can. That is what is actually taking place.

But those who are capable of thinking anew of this whole problem, who are not crippled, who want to find out a different way of existence—that is, you and I, we who are not mentally crippled—can those find a different process of action, a different way of thinking? Surely you and I are responsible to create a new world because you have leisure, you have the capacity to think, you are fairly secure, economically. It is your responsibility, is it not, to help those who are not capable of thinking, who are crippled physically, mentally, intellectually, who have to face life with dread, with fear? It is our responsibility, is it not? And if you do not do it, who is going to do it?

Is there any other way for this questioner to find a job? Most of us are not able to give him a job. If we do, we are always critical, bossy; we are incapable of giving a little of the little we have; we have lost our generosity; we have none, if we ever had it. So we keep the weak always weak, and we always look up to the strong and so keep ourselves weak.

So, that is our life—confusion, mediocrity, pain, insufficiency inwardly, and outwardly, the burning with innumerable desires which we suppress—and we cannot really create a different world unless there is a complete revolt from all this—a revolt not to join some society, not a revolt from this group, to join a communist group or a socialist group. I am talking of total revolt because then only is there that strength which comes when the mind is alone, when it is no longer capable of being influenced—which does not mean obstinacy, which does not mean the strength derived through experience, through knowledge; that is not being alone; there is dependency when there is knowledge and experience. This aloneness is totally devoid of all the crutches of the mind. It is in revolt not only towards something but in revolt as a total process. Then only can there be a different world, then only can the questioner find a right answer to his problem.

Question: Will you please explain the interval of which you speak between a thought and a thought? Most of our thinking is trivial and of no significance. Is it necessary to pursue such trifling thoughts?

KRISHNAMURTI: Sir, have you noticed in your thinking that there is a gap between two thoughts? However trivial, however stupid the thoughts be, there is an interval, is there not? It is not one continuous thinking. If you observe, if you are aware, you will see that there is a gap, an interval. Merely to pursue, analyze, be aware of any particular thought is utterly useless if we have not understood or observed the interval between two thoughts. Because, after all, when I think out a particular thought, however small, the mind that thinks it out is still a trivial mind, a small mind, a mediocre mind, a mind which is judging, comparing, condemning; and such a mind, when pursuing a thought, cannot understand. And to say, "I must not judge, I must not compare," still binds thought all the more; it limits thinking because the moment I say I must not judge, I have already limited thought, I have already put a resistance against judgment and so conditioned the mind more. But if I observe that there is an interval between thoughts, if my mind is concerned with that interval, watching, being aware of it, then I will see that the trivial thoughts will fade away without judging, without comparing, without disciplining, without compelling. Because in that interval there is no thought functioning. There is an interval, it may be a second, but the moment you want that second to become ten seconds, you have set mediocrity into action.

Please follow this; you will see it clearly if you are rightly listening. That is, if you observe an interval between two thoughts, and being aware of that interval, the mind wants to continue in that interval, to lengthen that interval, and when you so desire, have you not set into motion a particular influence which you want, and thereby crippled the mind to a particular influence, to a particular experience, and thereby reduced the mind to mediocrity, to a state of pettiness, smallness, narrowness? When the mind desires to experience a particular experience and to maintain that experience, does it not indicate consistency? And is not a mind that is consistent a mediocre mind, a mind that is frightened? Therefore, however much such a mind may pursue or analyze a particular thought, the analyzer is still the entity which is caught in mediocrity.

So being aware of that interval is sufficient if there is no pursuing, no trying to establish that, no lengthening that interval—which means, really, infinite self-knowledge, does it not? Because you cannot maintain that interval, in that interval a new and different feeling can come into being, but the moment you pursue that interval and try to lengthen that interval, the mind is interfering with it, and a mind that interferes, influences, conditions. So the more you are aware of the process of thought and of the interval, the greater is the self-knowledge—self-knowledge not from a book, not according to any pattern of thought, but the understanding of yourself as you are from moment to moment, from day to day, from month to month. This is an extraordinarily arduous process. Without that knowledge, the conditioned influence cannot be understood, and so the mind submits to every form of influence and interference, and therefore the mind is in a perpetual state of imitation, dependency, and fear.

Please listen to this. If you really understand this, you have not to do a thing consciously. You do not have to do a thing because all conscious interference is conditioning. That is why it is important to listen so that there is unconscious, deep revolution, not the revolution brought about by the mind, by the upper level of the mind, because the upper levels of the mind are the result of influence, of interference, of conditioning. Such interference by the mind cannot produce something new, something totally different. So, is it not important to know oneself without judgment, to know oneself as one is, not according to judgment?

We only know ourselves when we compare. At least we think we do. But comparison prevents the understanding of the thing as it is. I am ugly, I am greedy, I am envious. The moment I compare myself with somebody who is envious, have I not used my energy, dissipated my energy, distorted it? And must I not be completely concerned with *what is?* Because, when I compare, I want to change *what is* into something that it is not. And is not the desire to change *what is* into something which is not an utter waste of energy and time, and is it not an escape? Can I, without comparison, see *what is?* Is it possible to look at what I am without comparative knowledge? Please follow this. When I say I am greedy, is that not itself comparative? I only know greed because I am comparing the feeling—the feeling of the 'more', the wanting more power, more position, more security, more experience, more knowledge. The 'more' is the comparative. Can I look at my thought without comparison when my mind is comparative? So the moment I find my mind is capable of thinking, looking, observing without comparison, will greed exist? Please follow all this.

Because my mind is comparative, when the mind says, "I must not be greedy," which is the condemning, that very condemnation creates a comparative state. It strengthens the comparative state. Is it possible for me to look at greed which is the product of the 'more', which is the result of the 'more', which is the desire for the 'more', without comparison? And is that not the only way to free the mind from all greed?

So, self-knowledge is the beginning of wisdom. And this wisdom cannot be bought. No guru, no book, no experience will give it because experience is of time; experience is accumulative; it implies the 'more', the cultivation of technique through experience. It is the revolt against experience, against technique, against the 'more' that will bring about the liberation of the mind so that it is completely alone.

Question: What is forgiveness? Are forgiveness and compassion identical? To forgive another may be possible, but is it not necessary to forgive oneself?

KRISHNAMURTI: What is forgiveness? And when do you forgive? And is forgiveness ever necessary? I have hurt you; you store that hurt. Either time heals it, or you deliberately set about cultivating forgiveness. First you store the hurt; you accumulate it; you guard it, and later on, you forgive. But if there was no storing, there would be no necessity for forgiveness.

Is not forgiveness different from compassion? Can a man who is hurt and is forgiving—can he ever know compassion? Surely love is a state in which there is no hurt. Hurt exists only, does it not, when the 'me' is dominant in that love, when I am expecting something in that love. When I want to be loved, in that love I am still the dominant factor. When the 'me' or the 'I' is wanting—"I want to be loved," "I want to be looked after," "I miss the person"—I am still the center, and that center gets hurt or pleased; and when it gets hurt, it stores it up; and later on, it forgives, according to pressure, interference, influences, fears. Is compassion a state in which the 'me'—the center, the ego, the self—is ever conscious of itself being compassionate? In compassion is consciousness of the 'me' necessary?

When you know that you are compassionate, when you are conscious that you are compassionate, is that compassion? When you know you are forgiving, is that forgiveness? And the moment I am conscious of virtue, is that virtue? So, does not the conscious act of forgiveness, of being hurt, the conscious act, does it not strengthen the entity, the 'me', that is always gathering, always accumulating, comparing, judging, weighing? And can such an entity ever be free, ever know what it is to love, what it is to be compassionate? Please find out for yourself, don't listen to my words.

What is it to be compassionate? Please find out for yourself, feel it out, whether a mind that is hurt, that can be hurt, can ever forgive. Can a mind that is capable of being hurt ever forgive? And can such a mind which is capable of being hurt, which is cultivating virtue, which is conscious of generosity, can such a mind be compassionate? Compassion, as love, is something which is not of the mind. The mind is not conscious of itself as being compassionate, as loving. But the moment you forgive consciously, the mind is strengthening its own center in its own hurt. So the mind which consciously forgives can never forgive; it does not know forgiveness; it forgives in order not to be further hurt.

So it is very important to find out why the mind actually remembers, stores away. Because, the mind is everlastingly seeking to aggrandize itself, to become big, to be something. When the mind is willing not to be anything, to be nothing, completely nothing, then in that state there is compassion. In that state there is neither forgiveness nor the state of hurt, but to understand that, one has to understand the conscious development of the 'me'—the 'me' that is growing, becoming big, virtuous, respectable, the 'me' that is ultimately going to find God. That is, one has to understand the emphasis on the self, the cultivation of the self, the ego, whether one places that ego on the higher level or on the lower level.

So, as long as there is the conscious cultivation of any particular influence, any particular virtue, there can be no love, there can be no compassion because love and compassion are not the result of conscious effort.

Question: How can I be free from the past?

KRISHNAMURTI: Perhaps if I can understand what my mind is occupied with, then I shall perhaps see how to free the mind from the past.

What is your mind occupied with? Is it not occupied with something of the past, with what you should have done, what you should have thought, with what your experiences are, how sorrowful you are, how you want to be happy, how you have been hurt, how you would like to fulfill? Your mind, your consciousness, is the past, is it not? The 'what you should be' is the outcome of what you have not done. The future is the projection of the past, is it not? So our minds are occupied with the past. Our mind is the past, and you ask, "How am I to be free from the past?" But I who ask that question am still the past; the 'I' is not different from the mind which is the past. That is, my mind which says, "I want to be free from the past." That 'I' is part of the mind—is it not? It is part of thought, is it not? And that thought is the result of the past.

When the mind says, "I must be free from the past," is it not separating itself from the past? And is not the desire to free itself from the past a total process, a unitary process, not the 'I' separate from the past? Is there not only one state, the past, which projects into the future? So when the mind, the consciousness, is occupied with the past, how can such a mind ever free itself? Please follow this: How can my mind, which is the result of the past, which is the result of time, how can such a mind be free from the past? When you examine what the mind is, you see that the mind is memory, the mind is experience, the mind is the growing in time—which is the past.

So the mind is time, is the past, and when the mind asks, "Can I free myself from the past?"—is that valid? And when you see this whole, total process, what happens to the question which you have put, "Can I be free?" If I say you can be free, it has no validity, it is not your experience, it is not a fact. All that you will then do is to make an attempt to be free, to free the mind from all the occupations of the past. But if you understand the whole structure of the past, then you will never put that question. And by not putting the question, you will find the right answer because the mind, which is the sum total of experience, of influences, and which is put together, can never see the eternal, can never see that which is not made up, because the mind can never experience or understand or comprehend what is the eternal. The eternal is something entirely apart from the mind because it is not of time. The mind is of time. If the mind realizes that it is time, that it is the product of time, the product of memory, the product of experiences, of influences, of interferences—when the mind completely realizes that, then there is a revolution in itself, a revolution which is not created by the mind.

As long as the mind is seeking the eternal through experience, it will never find it. That is why you put the question, "Can the mind be free from the past?" It can be when it understands the total process of itself, when it is aware that it has put that question and thereby is aware of its structure. You will find that any movement from that structure is still the outcome of the past. When the mind realizes this, there is no movement at all; therefore, there is complete stillness of the mind. Any movement from the past is of time, and such a mind cannot understand, cannot be in a state to receive the eternal.

Question: God is not something so easily denied. You are attacking the very concept of God. What then have you to offer to this world? Without belief in God, life is sterile, vicious and can only lead to darkness.

KRISHNAMURTI: Whether you believe or do not believe, whether I brush aside or destroy the concept of God, reality exists. That reality cannot be found through any belief, for belief is the outcome of the desire to be secure. The mind that is fearful, anxious, wanting something to depend on, seeing the transiency of the world, creates an idea, but the idea of God is not God. God is not something projected by the mind, so the mind cannot possibly at any time comprehend God.

Your belief in God surely has separated man, has put man against man because, to you, God is not important but belief is. And do you not make the world darker by your belief? Look at the innumerable beliefs that you have! In the name of God you kill, do you not? The man who throws an atomic bomb, he believes in God, destroying thousands in a few seconds. And the man who does not believe in God, the communist, he also destroys in order to produce a better world. So you are not very much different, are you? Those who believe and those who do not believe both bring destruction and misery to man. The Christian believes and the Hindu believes; they are poles apart, fighting, wrangling, ambitious, destroying, liquidating, believing and yet they all profess to believe in God. And is God to be denied? And is God the projection of our minds?

Surely reality, or whatever name you call it, is something beyond the mind. But you cannot find that reality if the mind does not understand itself. If the mind is not still, quiet, it cannot know what that reality, that extraordinary thing is.

But belief is not what makes the mind quiet. On the contrary, belief cripples the mind, belief conditions the mind, belief shatters the mind. The mind that is fearful, seeking security, something to hold on to—such a mind has no value. Then belief acts as a personal security. Belief becomes, then, not anonymous but something upon which you can depend. Belief divides people, it destroys people. And can such a mind ever find reality? Seeing all this, must not the mind be alert, free itself from all beliefs—which means, be free of fear? Then only the mind becomes very quiet, still, without any projection, without any desire, without any book, without any hope. A mind in despair can never find reality. When the mind is in despair, it seeks hope, and hope then becomes the reality projected by a despairing mind.

So, seeing all this, the mind is very quiet. It is only then that reality comes. You cannot invite it. You cannot bribe it. There is no sacrifice that you can make in order to get it. There is no virtue that will reward you with that reality. It is only when the mind is completely still—not expecting, not hoping—that reality can come to that mind which is still.

March 1, 1953

Eighth Talk in Bombay

I think it may be said that most of our lives are very confused, and being confused and in constant struggle, we try to find a way out of the confusion. So we turn to anyone who can give us help. When we are economically strained, we turn to the economist or the politician, and when there is confusion psychologically, inwardly, we turn to religion. We turn to another to find a way, a method, out of our confusion, out of our misery. And I would like, if I can this evening, to find out if there is a method, a way to overcome our sufferings through any accumulation of knowledge or experience; or, if there is quite a different process, quite a different attitude, quite a different way that is far more important than the search for a system, a technique, or the cultivation of a particular habit.

So if I may, I would like to quietly and hesitatingly explore this question, and in this exploration, you are going to take part also, because it is also your problem. The problem is a way out, a system to help me fundamentally to resolve the cause, the substance, or the very nature of the mind that creates the problem. Is that possible through any form of accumulation, both of knowledge and of experience? Knowledge is the outward accumulation, which is the gathering of technical knowledge, and the inward accumulation of psychological experience, the "knowing," the capacity to know. Will these actually help to bring about complete freedom—not a momentary alleviation, but a total freedom—from this constant battle within myself? Because, it is this battle, this conflict, this incessant uncertainty that creates outward activities which produce mischief, which produce chaos, which bring about the expression of personal ambition—the desire to be somebody, the aggressive attitude towards life.

I think it is very important to understand whether by the cultivation of any particular attitude or by the development of any particular knowledge or technique, suffering can come to an end. Or can suffering come to an end only with a mind that is not seeking, that does not know, that is not gathering? Most of us have certain attitudes towards life, certain values with which we approach our activities, which create the pattern which we have established culturally, outwardly or inwardly, and we say, "I know, I know what to do." Do we know what we know? And should we not very earnestly endeavor to probe into the question of what we call "knowledge," whether we can know anything at all, and whether it is fallacious thinking to say, "I know"? Is it not very important to find out, when a mind says, "I know," what it does know? And will that knowledge at any time dissipate the conflicting process of the mind which creates such innumerable conflicts within one, so many frustrations, fears?

The problem is: Can knowledge dissipate suffering? We know that technological knowledge at one level can dissipate suffering when the body is ill physically, psychologically. At one level knowledge is essential, is necessary. Knowledge is also necessary when we are concerned with the evil of poverty. We have the technological knowledge to put an end to poverty, to have plenty, to have sufficient clothing and shelter. Scientific knowledge is essential to make life more easy, purely on the physical level. But the knowledge that we accumulate, the knowledge that the mind gathers in order to be free, in order not to have suffering—the practices, the techniques, the meditations, the various adjustments the mind makes in order not to have conflict—will they bring about the cessation of conflict? You read various books and try to find a method, a way of life, a purpose of life, or you go out to find it from another, and according to that purpose, you act; you try to live, but the suffering goes on, the conflict goes on.

The constant adjustment of *what is* to 'what should be' is the deteriorating factor of struggle. So our life inwardly is full of tears, turmoil, and suffering, and there must be a way of meeting life not with the accumulated knowledge of experience but a different way in which this battle is not going on. We know how we meet life, how we meet the challenge always with knowledge, with experience, with the past. That is, I say, "I know." "I have accumulated experience," "Life has taught me," so I always begin with knowledge, with a certain residue of experiences, and with that, I meet my suffering. The suffering is the conflict between *what is* and 'what should be'. We know the inward nature of suffering—the death of someone, the suffering of poverty, the psychological inward frustration, the insufficiency, the struggle to fulfill, and the everlasting pain of fear—and we meet suffering always with knowledge, do we not? So I say, "I know what to do," "I believe in reincarnation, in karma, in some experience, in some dogma," and with this, I meet the everyday occurrences of life.

Now I want to question that knowledge, that thing with which we say we meet life. There is never a sense of complete humility in a mind that says, "I know." But there is a complete humility which says, "I do not know." And is that not an essential state, an absolute necessity when you meet life, when you meet a problem, when you meet suffering, when you meet death? That sense of humility is not induced, is not cultivated, is not brought about, is not put together. It is the feeling that you do not know.

What do you know? What do you know of death? You see bodies being burned, relations dying, but what do you know except the things that you have learned, the beliefs? You do not know what is the unknown. Can the mind, which is the result of time, which is the result of accumulation, which is the result of the total past, can such a mind know the unknown, namely, "What is after death"? Hundreds of books have been written about what is after death, but the mind does not know.

So is it not essential in order to discover anything true, to have that complete sense of humility of not knowing? Then only is there a possibility of knowing. It is only when I do not know what God is, there is God.

But I think I know. I have already tasted the idea of what God is—not God, but the idea of God. I have sought him out, I have suffered; therefore, I go to the guru, to the book, to the temple. My mind has already got a glimpse of what is reality; I know, I have a little experience, I have read, I have tasted. So there is, in essence, vanity, a strange sense of vanity which is based on knowing. But what I know is only a memory, an experience—which is a conditioned response, an everyday movement of life. So I start with vanity: "I know God speaks to me," "I have knowledge," "I have visions," and I call that wisdom—which is absurd. I organize schools of thought, I gather, and there is never a moment when I can honestly say with complete humility, with complete integration that, "I do not know." Because, I think I know. But what I know is the past accumulation of experience, of memory, and that does not solve my problem of suffering, nor the problem of how to act in life with all its confusion, its contradictions, its pulls, its influences, and urges.

Can your mind, which is already contaminated by vanity, by knowledge, by experience, can such a mind be completely free? Can it have that feeling of complete humility? Not to know is humility, is it not? Please follow, please listen. When you realize that you do not know, then you are beginning to find out. But the state of not-knowingness cannot be cultivated. The state of not-knowing comes only with complete humility. Then, when such a mind has a problem, it is not-knowing, and the problem gives the answer—which means, the mind that is giving answers must completely, totally, inwardly, deeply, profoundly be without vanity, in a state of complete not-knowing. But the mind objects strongly to that state. Watch your own minds, sirs. You will see how extraordinarily difficult it is for it to face itself and to say, "I do not know." The mind objects to that statement because it wants something to lean on. It wants to say, "I know the way of life," "I know what love is," "I have suffered," "I know what it means"—which is really a mind clothed in its own knowledge. Therefore, it is never innocent. It is the innocent mind, the mind that says, "I do not know," which has no vanity, no trimmings; it is such a mind that can find the real, which is the true answer. It is only a mind that says, "I do not know," which receives that which is truth.

When the mind inquires the way to freedom, the way to truth, the way of any psychological technique, all that it is concerned with is the accumulation of knowledge by which it hopes to dispel this constant struggle within itself. But that knowledge does not dissolve it. You know that, don't you? From your books, from the experiences of your everyday life, you know sufficiently, but has that prevented you from suffering?

Is it not possible for a mind to be completely in a state of not-knowing, so that it is capable of sensitivity, so that it can receive? Is not the highest form of thinking the completely negative state of the mind in which there is no accumulation, in which, therefore, there is complete poverty of mind—poverty in the most dignified, profound sense? It is new soil, it is a mind in which there is no knowledge; therefore, it is the unknown. It is only then the unknown can come to the unknown. The known can never know the unknown. Sirs, this is not just a statement, but if you listen to it, if you listen to the real meaning of it, you will know the truth of it. But the man of vanity, the man of knowledge, the scholar, the man who is pursuing a result, can never know the unknown; therefore, he cannot be a creative being. And at the present time it is the creative being—the man who is creative—that is essential in our daily life, not a man who has a new technique, a new panacea. And there can be no creativeness if there is already a residue of knowledge. The mind must be empty to be creative. It means, the mind must be totally and completely humble. Then only is there a possibility of that creativity coming into being.

Question: In a world that needs collective action, why do you emphasize the freedom of the individual?

KRISHNAMURTI: Is not freedom essential for cooperation? Must you not be free in order to cooperate with me, or I with you? And does freedom come into being when you and I have a common purpose? When you and I intellectually, verbally, theoretically establish a common purpose, a common aim, and you and I work together, are we really working together? Does the common end bind us? You think I have a common aim, but when I have a common aim, am I free? I have established an aim, a purpose, because of my knowledge, because of my experience, of my erudition, and I say that is the purpose of man. When I have established it, has that aim not caught me? Am I not a slave to it? Therefore, is there creativeness? To be creative, we have to be free of common purpose.

Is collective action possible, and what do we mean by collective action? There can be no collective action because we are individuals. You and I cannot paint a picture together. There is no collective action; there is only collective thinking, is there not? It is collective thinking that brings us together to act together. So what is important is not collective action but collective thinking.

Now, can there be collective thinking? And what do we mean by collective thinking? When do we all think alike? When we all are communists, when we are all socialists, Catholics, then all of us are being conditioned to a certain pattern of thought, all of us are acting together. And what happens when there is collective thinking? What happens? Does it not involve concentration camps, liquidation, control of thought so that you must not think differently from the party, from the whole which the few have established? So collective thinking leads to more misery; collective thinking leads to destruction of people, to cruelty, to barbarity. What is necessary is not collective thinking but to think rightly—not according to the right, not according to the communist, socialist, but to know how to think, not what to think.

We think that by conditioning the mind to what to think, there would be collective action. But that only destroys human beings, does it not? When we know what to think, has not all creative investigation, the sense of complete freedom come to an end? So our problem is not collective action or collective thinking, but to find out how to think. And this cannot be learned from a book. The way to think, which is thinking, can only be found in relationship, in self-knowledge. And there cannot be self-knowledge if you have no freedom, if you are afraid you are going to lose a job, if you are afraid of what your wife, your husband, your neighbor says.

So in the process of self-knowledge there comes freedom. It is this freedom that will bring about collective action, not the conditioned mind that is made to act. Therefore, there is no collective action in any form of compulsion, coercion, reward, or punishment. It is only when you and I are capable of finding what is truth through self-knowledge, that there can be freedom; then there is a possibility of real collective action.

There is no collective action when there is common purpose. We all want a happy India, a cultured India, a cultured world; we all say that is our aim; we know that, we repeat it, but are we not throwing it away all the time? We all say there must be brotherhood, there must be peace and love of God; that is our common aim, and are we not destroying each other, though we profess we have a common purpose? And when the leftist says there must be collective action through collective thinking, is he not destroying, bringing about misery, war, destruction? So a common purpose, a common idea, the love of God, the love of peace, does not bring us together.

What brings us together is love, which comes into being with self-knowledge and freedom. The 'myself' is not a separate unit; I am in relationship with the world; I am the total process. So in understanding the total process, which is the 'me' and which is the 'you', there is freedom. This self-knowledge is not the knowledge of 'me' as a separate entity. The 'me' is a total 'me' of every one of us because I am not isolated; there is no such thing; no being can exist in isolation. The 'myself' is the total process of humanity; the 'myself' is 'you' in relation with one another. It is only when I understand that 'myself', there is self-knowledge; then in that self-knowledge there is freedom. Then the world becomes our world—not your world or a Hindu world or a Catholic world or a communist world. It is our world, yours and mine, in which to live happily, creatively. That is not possible if we are conditioned by an idea, if we have a common end for all of us. It is only in freedom which comes with the understanding of the 'me', which is the total process of man, that there is a possibility of collective thought and action.

That is why it is important in a world that is torn apart by religions, by beliefs, by political parties, that this should be very clearly understood by each one of us. Because, there is no salvation in collective action; that way lies more misery, more destruction, and more wars; it ends in tyranny. But most of us want some kind of security. The moment the mind seeks security, it is lost. It is only the insecure that are free, but not the respectable, not the man who is secure. Please listen to this. In any enriching of the mind, in any belief, in any system, there is never freedom. And because the mind is secure in some form or pattern of action, because of its bondage, it creates action which produces more misery. It is only the free mind—that is, when you understand the process of the self, the 'me' with all its contents, the mind is free—that can create a new world. Then that is our world; it is a thing we can build together, not create to the pattern of some tyranny, of some god. Then you and I can work; then it is our world to be built, to be nurtured, to be brought into being.

Question: When I see and hear you, I feel myself before an immeasurable sea of stillness. My immediate response to you is reverence and devotion; surely, that does not mean that I establish you as my authority. Is it not so?

KRISHNAMURTI: Sir, what do we mean by reverence and devotion? Reverence and devotion surely are not to something. When I am devoted to something, when I reverence somebody, then I create an authority because that reverence and devotion unconsciously, deep down, gives me comfort, a certain sense of gratification; therefore, I depend upon it. As long as I am devoted to somebody, as long as there is reverence towards something, I am a slave, there is no freedom.

Is reverence, devotion, not capable of existence by itself? That is, you revere a tree, a bird, the child in the street, the beggar, or your servant; the reverence is not to something; it is not to somebody, but it is in yourself, the feeling of respecting. The respect of somebody—is that not based on fear? Is not the feeling of respecting more important and essential than respect to some deity, to some person? If that feeling exists, then there is equality. The equality which the politicians, the lawyers, the communists are trying to establish is not equality because inequality will always exist when you have a higher capacity, better brains, more gifts than I. But when I have that respect, not to somebody, but the respect in itself, then that inherent respect is love, not love of something. When I am conscious that I am revering something outside of me, a person or an image, then there is no love; then there is the division between you, whom I revere, and me, who am lowly.

So devotion and reverence surely are inherent when I begin to understand the whole process of life. Life is not merely the 'me' in action but the life of the animal, the life of nature, the child begging in the street. How often do we look at a tree? Do you ever look at a tree or a flower? And when you do, is there a sense of reverence—not to the flower that is going to fade away but to the beauty of the flower, to that strange thing that is life? This means really, the complete sense of being humble without any sense of begging. Then your mind in itself is still; then you do not have to see somebody who is still. And in that stillness there is no you and I, there is only stillness. And it is in that stillness you will find that there is respect not in something but in itself. Life is then extraordinarily vital, there is no authority, the mind is completely still.

Question: When I am aware of my thoughts and feelings, they disappear. Later, they catch me unawares and overwhelm me. Can I ever be free from all the thoughts that plague me? Must I always live between depression and elation?

KRISHNAMURTI: Sir, what is the way of thought? What is thinking? I am asking you a question; I am sure you have an answer. Your mind immediately jumps and answers. It does not say, "I do not know; I am going to find out." Watch your own mind and you will find an answer to this.

What is thinking, not right thinking and wrong thinking, but this whole process of thinking? When do you think? Only when you are challenged. When you are asked a question, you begin to respond according to the background, according to your memory, according to your experience. So thinking is the process of response to a challenge, such as, "I am unhappy, I want to find a way out," so I begin to inquire. "I want to find a way out"—that is my problem, that is my question. If I do not find the answer outside, then I begin to inquire within myself. I depend on my experience, on my knowledge, and my knowledge, my experience, always responds—which is, to find a way out. So I start the process of thinking.

Thinking is the response of the past, the response to the past. I do not know the way to your house, and you tell me because you know it. I ask you what God is, and you immediately respond, because you have read, your mind is conditioned, and that condition responds. Or if you do not believe in God, you will respond also according to your conditioning. So thinking is a process of verbalization to the reaction of the past.

Now the question is: Can I be aware of the past and thereby put an end to thinking? The moment I think fully, focus fully, there is no thinking. Observation of an idea, of an action—the concentration on something—still implies thinking because you are concentrating, in which there is exclusion. The mind is focused, concentrated on an idea, writing a letter, in thinking out a problem; in that concentration, there is exclusion. In that, there is a process of thinking, conscious or unconscious.

But when there is total awareness—awareness not of an idea, not the concentration on an idea, but the awareness of the whole problem of thinking—there is no concentration; there is awareness without exclusion. When I begin to inquire how to be rid of a particular thought, what is implied in it?

Please follow this and you will see what I mean by awareness. There is a particular thought that is disturbing you, and you want to get rid of it. And so you proceed to find a way of resisting that particular thought. But you want to keep the pleasant thoughts, the pleasant memories, the pleasant ideas. You want to get rid of those thoughts that are painful and hold on to things which are pleasurable, which are satisfying you, which give you vitality, energy, and drive. So when you want to get rid of one thought, you are at the same time holding on to the things that give you pleasure, memories which are delightful, which give you energy, and then what happens? You are concerned not with the total process of thinking but only how to hold on to the pleasant and how to get rid of the unpleasant. But here we are concerned with the whole, with the total process of thinking—not with how to get rid of a certain thought. If I can understand the whole past, and not just how to get rid of a particular past, then there is the freedom of the past, not of a particular past.

But most of us want to hold on to the pleasant and put away the unpleasant. That is a fact. But when we are inquiring into the whole question of the past from which there is thinking, then we cannot look at it from the point of view of the good thought and the bad thought, what is the good past and what is the unpleasant past. Then we are only concerned with the past, not with the good and the bad.

Now can the mind be free from the past, free from thought—not from the good or bad thought? How do I find out? Can the mind be free from a thought, thought being the past? How do I find out? I can only find out by seeing what the mind is occupied with. If my mind is occupied with the good or occupied with the bad, then it is only concerned with the past, it is occupied with the past. It is not free of the past. So, what is important is to find out how the mind is occupied. If it is occupied at all, it is always occupied with the past because all our consciousness is the past. The past is not only on the surface but on the highest level, and the stress on the unconscious is also the past. So can the mind be free from all its occupations? Watch your own minds, sirs, and you will see.

Can the mind be free from occupation? This means—can the mind be completely without being occupied and let memory, the thoughts good and bad, go by without choosing? The moment the mind is occupied with one thought, good or bad, then it is concerned with the past. It is just like the mind sitting firmly on the wall watching things go by, never occupied with anything as memory, thought, whether it is good, pleasant, or unpleasant—which means, the total freedom of the past, not just the particular past. If you really listen—not just merely verbally, but really profoundly—then you will see that there is stability which is not of the mind, which is the freedom from the past.

Yet, the past can never be put aside. There is a watching of the past as it goes by, but not occupation with the past. So the mind is free to observe and not to choose. Where there is choice in this movement of the river of memory, there is occupation; and the moment the mind is occupied, it is caught in the past; and when the mind is occupied with the past, it is incapable of seeing something real, true, new, original, uncontaminated.

A mind that is occupied with the past—the past is the whole consciousness that says, "this is good," "that is right," "this is bad," "this is mine," "this is not mine"—can never know the real. But the mind unoccupied can receive that which is not known, which is the unknown. This is not an extraordinary state of some yogi, some saint. Just observe your own mind—how direct and simple it is. See how your mind is occupied. And the answer, with what the mind is occupied, will give you the understanding of the past and therefore the freedom from the past.

You cannot brush the past aside. It is there. What matters is the occupation of the mind—the mind that is concerned with the past as good or evil, that says, "I must have this" or "I must not have this," that has good memory to hold on to and bad memory to let go. The mind that is watching the thing go by, without choice, is the free mind that is free from the past. The past is still floating by; you cannot set it aside; you cannot forget the way to your home. But the occupation of the mind with the past—in that, there is no freedom. The occupation creates the past, and the mind is perpetually, everlastingly, occupied with good words, with virtue, with sacrifice, with the search for God, with happiness; such a mind is never free. The past is there; it is a shadow constantly threatening, constantly encouraging and depressing. So, what is important is to find out how the mind is occupied—with what thought, with what memory, with what intention, with what purpose.

Question: Talk to us of meditation.

KRISHNAMURTI: Are you not meditating now? Meditation is when the mind, not knowing, not desiring, not pursuing, is really inquiring; when the mind is really probing, not towards any particular idea, not to any particular image, to any particular compulsion; when the mind is merely seeking—not an answer, not an idea, not to find something. When do you seek? Not when you know the answer, not when you are wanting something, not when you are seeking gratification, not when you want comfort. Then, it is no longer seeking. It is only when the mind, understanding the whole significance of comfort and of wanting security, puts aside all authority, only when the mind is free, that it is capable of seeking. And is not that the whole process of meditation? Therefore, is not the seeking itself devotion, is not the seeking itself reverence?

So, meditation is the stillness of the mind when it is no longer wanting, vibrating, searching out in order to be satisfied. It is not meditation when it is repeating words, cultivating virtue. A mind which is cultivating virtue, repeating words, chanting—such a mind is not capable of meditation; it is self-hypnosis, and in self-hypnosis you can create marvelous illusions. But a mind that is capable of real freedom—freedom from the past—is a mind that is not occupied; therefore, it is extraordinarily still. Such a mind has no projections; such a mind is in the state of meditation. In that meditation there is no meditator—I am not meditating, I am not experiencing stillness—there is only stillness. The moment I experience stillness, that moment it becomes memory; therefore, it is not stillness; it is gone. When a mind is occupied with something that is gone, it is caught in the past.

So in meditation there is no meditator; therefore, there is no concentrator who makes an effort to meditate, who sits cross-legged and shuts his eyes to meditate. When the meditator makes an effort to meditate, what he then meditates on is his own projection, his own things clothed in his own ideas. Such a mind cannot meditate; it does not know what meditation means.

But the man who understands the occupation of his mind, the man who has no choice in his occupation, such a man will know what is stillness—the stillness that comes from the very beginning, the freedom. Freedom is not at the end; it is at the very beginning. You cannot train a mind to be free. It has to be free from the very beginning. And in that freedom the mind is still because it has no choice; it is not concentrating, it is not absorbed in anything. And in that stillness, that which is unknown is concentrating.

March 4, 1953

Ninth Talk in Bombay

Perhaps if we can go into the question of initiative then there may be a possibility of understanding self-fulfillment. For most of us fulfillment in some form or other becomes urgent, becomes necessary. In the process of fulfilling, so many problems, so many contradictions, so many conflicts arise, and there is everlasting misery in fulfillment. And yet, we do not know how to escape from it, how to act without fulfilling, for in the very fulfillment of action there is sorrow.

Action is not merely doing something, but is it not also thinking? Most of us are concerned with doing something, and if that action is satisfactory, if it sufficiently guarantees the fulfillment of one's desires, cravings, longings, then we are easily pacified. But if we do not discover the incentive that lies behind the urge to fulfill, surely we shall always be haunted by fear, with frustration, so is it not necessary to find out what this incentive is that is driving us? It may be clothed in different paints, with different intentions, with different meanings, but perhaps if we can hesitatingly, tentatively explore this question of incentive, then we shall begin to understand an action or a thought which is not always born from this consciousness of fulfillment.

Most of our incentives spring from ambitions, from pride, from the desire to be secure or to be well-thought-of. Now, you may say or I may say that my action is the outcome of the desire to do good, or to find the right values, or to have an ideology, a system that is incorruptible, or to do something that is essentially worthwhile, and so on. But behind all these words, all these pleasant sounding phrases, is not the motive—the urge in some form or another—ambition? I seek the Master, the guru; I want to achieve; I want to arrive; I want to have comfort, to know a certainty of mind in which there is no conflict. My incentive is to achieve a result and to be assured of that result in the same way as the man who accumulates money and who also seeks security, so in both these forces, there is the drive which we call ambition, upon which all our activities, our outlook, our energies are spent. Is it possible to act without these ambitions, without these desires to fulfill? That is, I want to fulfill—I want to fulfill through my nation, through my children, through property, through name—I want to be "somebody." And the pride of being somebody is extraordinary because it gives extraordinary energy without doing anything; merely the sense of being proud in itself is sufficient to keep me going, to keep me resisting, controlling, shaping.

You watch your own minds in operation. You will see the activities, and you will see that behind them, however much you may cover them up with pleasant words, the drive is for fulfillment, for being somebody, to achieve a result. In this drive of ambition, there is competition, ruthlessness, and our whole structure of society is based on that. The ambitious man is looked upon as being worthwhile, as being somebody who is good for society, who will through his ambition create a right environment, and so on, and so on. We condemn ambition when it is worldly; we do not condemn it when we call it spiritual. A man who has given up the world, renounced it, and is seeking, he is not condemned. Is he not also driven by ambition to be something?

Everyone of us is seeking fulfillment—fulfillment through ideas, fulfillment through capacity, fulfillment through release in painting, through writing a poem, in loving, in being generous, in trying to be well-thought-of. So, are not all our activities the outcome of this urge to fulfill? And behind that urge is ambition. When I hear that, when I know that, and when I realize that where there is fulfillment, there must be sorrow, what am I to do? Do you follow what I mean?

I realize my life is based on ambition. Though I try to cover it up, though I suffer, though I sacrifice myself for an idea, all my activities are an outlet for self-fulfillment. You see me burned out, and you set yourself to do something worthwhile; that "worthwhileness" is still the urge for fulfillment. This is our life; this is our constant urge, our constant pursuit, conscious as well as unconscious. When I realize this, when I know the content of all this struggle, what am I to do?

This urge to fulfill is one of our most fundamental problems, is it not? This urge to fulfill is in little things and in big things—to be somebody in my house, to dominate over my wife, my children, and to submit myself in the office in order to rise, in order some day to be somebody. So, that is the process of my life; that is the process of all our lives. Then how is such a mind to put aside the desire for fulfillment? How am I to free myself from ambition?

I see that ambition is a form of self-fulfillment, and where there is fulfillment there is always the sense of being down and out, of being broken, frustrated; there is fear, a sense of utter loneliness, of despair, and everlasting hope. That is our life, is it not? That is our state from day to day. Behind everything there lurks this desire to fulfill, this urge to be ambitious, this ambition for power, position, prestige, to be well-thought-of. Knowing the whole content of that, what is the mind to do?

Is there any activity, any form of movement of the mind which is not based on this? Do you understand? If I brush aside, control, shape ambition, it is still ambition because I say, "It does not pay me to do this, but if I do that, that will pay me." If I say I must not fulfill, then there is the conflict of not fulfilling, the resistance against the desire, and the very resistance against the desire to fulfill becomes another form of fulfillment.

Why is the mind seeking fulfillment? Why is the mind, the 'me', which is the thought, why is it proud, ambitious? Why does it want to be well-thought-of? Can I understand that? Can the mind realize what it is that is pushing outwardly all the time? And when the outward movement of consciousness is cut, then it turns inward, and there again it is thwarted.

So our consciousness is this constant breathing in and out—to be important and not to be, to receive and to reject—this is our daily life of consciousness. And behind it, the mind is seeking a way out. If I can understand that, if the conscious can dwell on it, can know its full significance, then perhaps it is possible to have action which is not of ambition, which is not of pride, which is not of fulfillment, which is not of the mind.

To seek God, to try to find God, is another form of pride, and is it possible for me and you to find out what it is that is making us continuously go out and come in, go out and come in? Are we not aware of a state of emptiness in us, a state of despair, of loneliness, the complete sense of not being able to depend on anything, not having anybody to look up to? Don't we know a moment of extraordinary loneliness, of extraordinary sorrow, without reason, a sense of despair at the height of success, at the height of pride, at the height of thought, at the height of love; don't we know this loneliness? And is this loneliness not pushing us always to be somebody, to be well-thought-of?

Can I live with that loneliness, not run away from it, not try to fulfill through some action? Can I live with it and not try to transform it, not try to shape and control it? If the mind can, then perhaps it will go beyond that loneliness, beyond that despair, which does not mean into hope, into a state of devotion, but on the contrary. If I can understand and live in that loneliness—not run away from it, but live in that strange loneliness which comes when I am bored, when I am afraid, when I am apprehensive, not for any cause or with cause—when I know this sense of loneliness, is it possible for the mind to live with it, without trying to push it away?

Please listen to this; do not just listen to the mere words. As I talk, if you have observed your own minds, you will have come to that state of loneliness. It is with you now. This is not hypnosis because I suggest it, but actually, if you have followed the workings of your own mind, you will have come to that state of loneliness—to be stripped of everything, every pretense, every pride, every virtue, every action. Can the mind live with that? Can the mind stay with it without any form of condemnation? Can it look at it without interfering—not as the observer looking at it? Is not, then, the mind itself that state? Do you follow?

If I look at loneliness, then the mind operates on the loneliness, tries to shape it or control it or run away from it. The mind itself, not as the observer, is alone, lonely, empty. It cannot tolerate for a single minute a state in which it is completely empty, a state in which it does not know, a state in which there is no action of "knowing," so a mind, seeing that, is fearful of it; it runs away into some activity of fulfillment.

Now, if the mind can stay in that very extraordinary sense of being cut off from everything, from all ideas, from all crutches, from all dependencies, then is it not possible for such a mind to go beyond, not theoretically, but actually? It is only when it can fully experience that state of loneliness, that state of emptiness, that state of nondependency, then only is it possible to bring about an action which is without ambition. Then only is it possible to have a world in which there is no competition, no ruthless pursuit of self-enclosing activity. Then that action is not the action through the narrow funnel of the 'me'. That action is not self-enclosing. You will find that such an action is creative because it is without motive, without ambition; it is not seeking a result. But to find that, must the mind go through all this? Can it not suddenly jump?

The mind can jump if I know how to listen. If I am listening rightly now, without any barrier, without any interpretation, with an open door to discover, there is freedom, and through freedom alone I can discover.

That freedom is the freedom from fear, the freedom from being well-thought-of, the freedom from pride, the freedom from the desire to fulfill. And that freedom cannot come about except through the realization of the complete negation of all thought, when the mind is totally empty, lonely, when the mind is in a state in which there is neither despair nor fulfillment. Then only is there a possibility of a world in which ruthlessness, brutality, competition can come to an end.

Question: You have been talking of freedom. Does not freedom demand duties? What is my duty to society, to myself?

KRISHNAMURTI: Are freedom and duty comparable? Can the dutiful son be free? Can I be dutiful to society and yet be free? Can I be dutiful and yet be revolutionary in the right sense, not in the economic sense? Can I, if I follow a system, political or religious, ever be free? Or do I merely imitate, copy? Is not this whole system imitation? Being a dutiful son, doing what my father wants me to do, doing the right thing according to society—do these not themselves connote a feeling of imitation? My father wants me to be a lawyer; is it my duty to become a lawyer? My father says I must join some religious organization; is it my duty to do so?

Does duty go with love? It is only when there is no love, when there is no freedom, that the word *duty* becomes extraordinarily important. And duty then takes the place of tradition. In that state we live, that is our state, is it not?—I must be dutiful.

What is my duty to society? What is my duty to myself? Sirs, society demands a great many things of you: you must obey, you must follow, you must do certain ceremonies, perform certain rituals, believe. It conditions you to certain forms of thought, to certain beliefs. If you are finding what is real—not what is dutiful to society, not trying to conform to a particular pattern—if you are trying to find out what is truth, must you not be free?

Being free does not mean that you must throw something aside, that you must be antagonistic to everything; that is not freedom. Freedom implies constant awareness of thought; it implies that which is unfolding, the implications of duty, and out of which—but not by merely throwing aside a particular freedom—freedom comes. You cannot understand all traditions, you cannot grasp the full significance of them if you condemn or justify or identify yourself with a particular thought or an idea.

When I begin to inquire what is my duty to myself or to society, how shall I find out? What is the criterion? What is the standard? Or, shall we find out why we depend on these words? How quickly the mind that is searching, seeking, inquiring, is gripped by the word duty! The aging father says to his son, "It is your duty to support me," and the son feels it his duty to support him. And though he may want to do something else—to paint pictures which will not give him the means of livelihood to support his father and himself—he says his duty is to earn and to put aside what he really wants to do, and for the rest of his life he is caught, for the rest of his life he is bitter; he has bitterness in his heart, and he gives money to his father and mother. That is our life; we live in bitterness, and we die with bitterness.

Because we really have no love and because we have no freedom, we use words to control our thoughts, to shape our hearts and feelings, and we are satisfied. Surely love may be the only way of revolution, and it is the only way. But most of us object to revolutions, not only superficially, the economic revolutions, but the more essential, the deeper, the more significant revolution of thought, the revolution of creation. Since we object to that, we are always reforming on top, patching up here and there with words, with threats, with ambitions.

You will say at the end of this question that I have not answered your questions, "What is my duty to society, to my father, and to myself?" I say that is a wrong question. It is a question put by a mind that is not free, a mind that is not in revolt, a mind that is docile, submissive, a mind that has no love. Can such a mind which is docile, submissive, without love, with that shadow of bitterness, ever be dutiful to society or to itself? Can such a mind create a new world, a new structure?

Do not shake your heads. Do you know what you want? You do not want a revolt; you do not want a revolution of the mind; you want to bring up your children in the same manner in which you have been brought up. You want to condition them the same way, to think on the same lines, to do puja, to believe what you believe. So, you never encourage them to find out. So, as you are destroying yourselves in your conditioning, you want to destroy others. So the problem is not what is my duty to society but how to find or how to awaken this love and this freedom. When once there is that love, you may not be dutiful at all.

Love is the most revolutionary thing, but the mind cannot conceive that love; you cannot cultivate it; it must be there; it is not a thing to be grown in your backyard; it is a thing that comes into being with constant inquiry, constant discontent, and revolt, when you never follow authority, when you are without fear—which means, when you have the capacity to make mistakes and from the mistake to find out the answer. A mind that is without fear is really not petty, and it is capable of real depth; then such a mind shall find out what love is, what freedom is.

Question: Please explain to us what you mean by time and what you mean by the timeless. Can there ever be freedom from time?

KRISHNAMURTI: Explanations are comparatively easy. Words put together are explanations, and most of us are satisfied with explanations, with conclusions. But to really experience requires an extraordinarily arduous mind, not a mind that says, "Words are enough for me."

Surely the mind is the process of time; thought which is the verbalization of a reaction is the result of time; words are of time, as explanation is of time. A mind which is content with words, explanation, with time, tries to go beyond time through explanation, through words, through symbols, through the symbol of eternity. Though the mind tries to use the symbol to go beyond, obviously, it is still within the field of time—time being memory, what I remember of yesterday, and the projection of yesterday to today and to tomorrow. The yesterday, today, and tomorrow is the process of time, is the process of thought.

Then there is time that is implied from childhood, to manhood, to death—time as progress. I will be something tomorrow or in the next life; now, I am a clerk; in three years time I am going to be the boss. There is time as implied in the cultivation of virtue: I am afraid, I am violent; I will cultivate nonviolence—which is sweet deception. The mind that is violent can never be nonviolent, however much it may practice nonviolence. The very practice of nonviolence is violence. Sirs, listen. Do not smile.

The very practice of virtue strengthens the violence which is the 'me'. That is time. The mind, caught in this time, says, "Please explain to me what is the timeless; please help me to experience something which is not of myself." The mind is, in its very essence, the past; the past is time; the past is the future; the past is what is present. Such a mind is inquiring, trying to find out what is the timeless. It can only find what it projects; it cannot find the timeless because the instrument itself is of time.

The mind can speculate, it can argue, it can project what should be the timeless and so on, but it can never experience the timeless, and if it experiences the state of timelessness for a few seconds, then it expresses it and puts it away into memory. For instance, "I have experienced the beauty of the sunset yesterday; now I must have it again today." So everything the mind does is the process of capturing that extraordinary movement of life and putting it into the past.

Please listen. The problem now is not to find out what is the timeless, not how I can find the timeless, not how the mind can find the timeless but to find out the state in which the mind can experience the timeless, which is a state of experiencing, not experience. The moment I am conscious that I have experienced, it is already in the past; the particular experience is of the past.

Please listen; you will find out what I am talking about; it is not mysterious. You do not have to go into the deep intoxication of renunciations and pujas and controls; what you have to do is to understand the structure of the mind, the anatomy of thought. When you understand it, when the mind sees how it is caught in time, then the mind becomes fully focused; it is all full attention, the attention that is not exclusive. In that attention, there is the coming and going of the conscious; there is the reacting to that noise of the train, and the reaction is memory. At the same time, the mind is not concentrated but is fully focused—focused not through any volition, not through any action of will, but the mind is fully called to pay attention to itself; on the periphery, on the outskirts, there are always the impression and responses going on.

But when the mind sees what the function of thought is, the whole process of time, then it is completely focused, completely attentive, not to something, but listening; when the mind is completely still, then there is the timeless. But a man who makes the mind still is caught in the net of time. So it requires enormous vigilance, and that state is experiencing; there is no experiencer experiencing, there is only experiencing. At that moment, there is no experiencer, there is only experiencing; a moment later it becomes the experiencer, and so we are caught in time.

Can the mind be in a state of experiencing, not in a state of experience which is what we know, which is the accumulative past, which is of time? Please put the question and listen to the question; you will find the answer for yourself. I am not hypnotizing you by words.

Can the mind be in a state of experiencing? That is the state of experiencing what is timeless, and in that experiencing, there is no accumulation, no knowledge, no entity that says, "I am experiencing." The moment there is the experiencer, he is introducing time.

So, can the mind be in a state of experiencing God? That is meditation—the meditation which is not of pursuit, not of a particular idea, the meditation which is not the mere concentration which is exclusion. In that meditation, there is experiencing without the experiencer. And I assure you it is very arduous. It is not just sitting down and closing the eyes and getting some kind of fancy visions and ecstasy.

If I know how to listen rightly, if I know how to listen to thought, then thought will inevitably bring about this state—the state in which there is no experiencer, therefore, no accumulator, the person that gathers, holds. Therefore, experiencing is a state of constant unknowingness; therefore, it is timeless, it is not a thing of the mind.

Question: Modern scientists have placed vast powers of destruction in the hands of political rulers of America and Russia. There seems to be no place for simple kindliness between man and man. What is the meaning of human existence in this age of cruelty?

KRISHNAMURTI: The questioner says: There is no human kindliness, the simple kindliness between man and man. Have you and I that simple kindliness? Because we have not got it, we have created America and Russia. Please don't separate yourself from America and Russia. We have the potential capacities of being Americans and Russians. We are Russians and Americans at heart. We pose in the name of liberty, and given that liberty, we become tyrants. Are you not tyrants in your homes, over your children, in your offices, over your wives and the wives over you? (Laughter) Yes, sirs, how easily we laugh at these things!

Though we may live thousands of miles away from Russia and America, we have created this world, you and I; our problem is the world problem because the 'you' is the world. You, Mr. Smith, and you, Mr. Rao, you are the world living in Russia and America; their misery is our misery. Though we might like to separate ourselves, though we may like to condemn them and say that they are politically this and they are politically that, that they are trying to use this and that—you know the things that newspapers cultivate as propaganda—you and I are the Russians and the Americans. We all want power, position, prestige. We are all cruel, we all feel proud, we are all full of pride. Then how can we be kind, unsuspecting, innocent? We cannot. And it is no good condemning Russia and America, and to fight them is to become like them.

So, there must be a revolution in the ways of our thinking. When there is no identification with India, with any political or religious system, when we are common humanity—not labeled as Hindus, Russians, Germans, English, Americans, Christians, and so on—then only there is a possibility for peace to be; until then, there is no possibility. Stalin will come and go, and others will come. There will be war until there is a real revolution in our heart.

That revolution is not possible through any economic revolution, through any superficial change because such a change is merely a modified continuity, whereas a revolution is not. The revolution that is necessary cannot come about by any compulsion. It must come spontaneously out of ourselves. Because we do not want it, we resort to war, we resort to various forms of reforms which need further reforms, and so, we are everlastingly caught.

Question: What is God? What is love? What is death?

KRISHNAMURTI: Is it not possible to experiment to find out what is God, what is love, and what is death? As we are sitting here, can we not find out? Do not just listen to my explanation. I am not going to explain because explanations do not satisfy the hungry man; the description of food will not satisfy me if I am hungry.

Since I am hungry to find out what is God, what is love, and what is death, can I find it out? I can only find out if the mind can completely free itself from the known. If the mind can put aside everything it has learned—the Bhagavad-Gita, all its experiences, everything that the Upanishads have said—if all its conditions can completely be wiped out, then only is it possible to know, to experience that state of living.

Can one know what death is? Death is the unknown. But a mind that clings to the known, which is the continuity of what I am from day to day, cannot know the unknown. The unknown is death, is it not? Death has no 'knowing'. Though I may have read many descriptions of it, I have to leave all symbols. All words must be put aside, must they not? And can I put them aside—not with any effort, but just as I am listening?

Can I completely enter into the state of 'unknowing'? Then though I am living, there is the 'unknowing' which is death. That means, there must be no fear, no fear of dying—the dying being the ending of continuity. That which continues, deteriorates; it is only the ending that is creative.

So, can I know death while I live? Death is not the word, not the corpse, not the thing that you see being carried down the road to be burned, but the thing which is not the word, which is a state of 'unknowing'. Surely I can feel it out.

And is God a thing to be found by the mind? God is not of time. I may imagine, I may think this is God, that is not God, but I do not know what God is. The word is not God. So, as I do not know, can the mind be in a state in which there is no ending—when the mind is completely empty, completely still, without any formulations, without any hope to find, innocent, in which there is no demand, no asking? The moment you ask, you are given, and what you are given is given with a curse. The mind can never ask because it can only hear the answer according to the words, according to the past. So can the mind, listening, be still, without asking, without expecting?

And is not love also something which is not brought into being by the mind? The moment the mind is conscious that it loves, surely it is no longer love, is it? And can I not feel even for a second, in the stillness of the mind, this thing that we call God—the word—and to go beyond the word and to see and to experience that state in which there is no knowing, which is death? And that word love, which is not of the mind, which is not of time, can the mind in its complete stillness feel it, but not be able to recognize, because the moment you recognize, it is of time? So, there must be the state of nonrecognition, an experience in which there is no experiencer; it is only then in that real stillness of the mind the unknowable comes into being.

March 8, 1953

Tenth Talk in Bombay

I think it might be worthwhile if we went into the question of how quickly the mind deteriorates and what are the primary factors that make the mind dull, insensitive, quick to respond. I think it would be significant if we could go into this question of why the mind deteriorates because perhaps in understanding that, we may be able to find out what is really a simple life.

We notice as we grow older that the mind, the instrument of understanding, the instrument with which we probe into any problem, to inquire, to question, to discover—that mind, if misused, deteriorates, disintegrates, and it seems to me that one of the major factors of this deterioration of the mind is the process of choice.

All our life is based on choice. We choose at different levels of our existence. We choose between white and blue, between one flower and another flower, between certain psychological impulses of like and dislike, between certain ideas, beliefs—accepting some and discarding others. So our mental structure is based on this process of choice, this continuous effort at choosing, distinguishing, discarding, accepting, rejecting. And, in that process, there is constant struggle, constant effort. There is never a direct comprehension, but always the tedious process of accumulation, of the capacity to distinguish, which is really based on memory, on the accumulation of knowledge, and therefore, there is this constant effort made through choice.

Now, is not choice ambition? Our life is ambition. We want to be somebody, we want to be well-thought-of, want to achieve a result. If I am not wise, I want to become wise. If I am violent, I want to become nonviolent. The 'becoming' is the process of ambition. Whether I want to become the biggest politician or the most perfect saint, the ambition, the drive, the impulse of becoming is the process of choice, is the process of ambition, which is essentially based on choice.

So, our life is a series of struggles, a movement from one ideological concept, formula, desire, to another, and in this process of becoming, in this process of struggle the mind deteriorates. The very nature of this deterioration is choice, and we think choice is necessary, choice from which springs ambition.

Now can we find a way of life which is not based on ambition, which is not of choice, which is a flowering in which the result is not sought? All that we know of life is a series of struggles ending in results, and those results are being discarded for greater results. That is all we know.

In the case of the man who sits alone in a cave, in the very process of making himself perfect, there is choice, and that choice is ambition. The man who is violent tries to become nonviolent; that very becoming is ambition. We are not trying to find out whether ambition is right or wrong, whether it is essential to life, but whether it is conducive to a life of simplicity. I do not mean the simplicity of a few clothes; that is not a simple life. The putting on of a loincloth does not indicate a man that is simple; on the contrary, it may be that by the renunciation of the outer things, the mind becomes more ambitious, for it tries to hold on to its own ideal which it has projected and which it has created.

So if we observe our own ways of thinking, should we not inquire into this question of ambition? We see that ambition breeds competition—whether in children, in school, or among the big politicians, all the way up—the trying to beat a record. This ambition produces certain industrial benefits, but in its wake, obviously there is the darkening of the mind, the technological conditioning, so that the mind loses it pliability, its simplicity and therefore is incapable of directly experiencing. Should we not inquire, not as a group, but as individuals—you and I—should we not find out what this ambition means, whether we are at all aware of this ambition in our life?

When we offer ourselves to serve the country to do noble work, is there not in it the fundamental element of ambition, which is the way of choice? And is not therefore choice a corruptive influence in our life because it prevents the flowering? The man who flowers is the man who is, who is not becoming.

Is there not a difference between the flowering mind and the becoming mind? The becoming mind is a mind that is always growing, becoming, enlarging, gathering experience as knowledge. We know that process full well in our daily life, with all its results, with all its conflicts, its miseries and strife, but we do not know the life of flowering. And is there not a difference between the two which we have to discover—not by trying to demarcate, to separate, but to discover—in the process of our living? When we discover this, we may perhaps be able to set aside this ambition, the way of choice, and discover a flowering, which is the way of life, which may be true action.

So if we merely say that we must not be ambitious without the discovery of the flowering way of life, the mere killing of ambition destroys the mind also because it is an action of the will, which is the action of choice. So is it not essential for each one of us to find out in our lives the truth of ambition? We are all encouraged to be ambitious; our society is based on it—the strength of the drive towards a result. And in that ambition there are inequalities which legislation tries to level out, to alter. Perhaps that way, that approach to life is essentially wrong, and there might be another approach which is the flowering of life, which could express itself without accumulation. After all, we know when we are conscious of striving after something, of becoming something; that is ambition, the seeking of a result.

But there is an energy, a force in which there is a compulsion without the process of accumulation, without the background of the 'me', of the self, of the ego; that is the way of creativity. Without understanding that, without actually experiencing that, our life becomes very dull; our life becomes a series of endless conflicts in which there is no creativity, no happiness. And perhaps if we can understand not by discarding ambition but by understanding the ways of ambition—by being open, by comprehending, by listening to the truth of ambition—perhaps we may come upon that creativity in which there is a continuous expression which is not the expression of self-fulfillment but is the expression of energy without the limitation of the 'me'.

Question: In the worst of misery, most of us live on hope. Life without hope seems dreadful and inevitable, and yet very often this hope is nothing but illusion. Can you tell us why hope is so indispensable to life?

KRISHNAMURTI: Is it not the very nature of the mind to create illusion? Is not the very process of thinking the result of memory, of verbalized thought which creates an idea, a symbol, an image to which the mind clings?

I am in despair; I am in sorrow; I have no way of resolving it; I do not understand how to resolve it. If I understand it, then there is no need for hope. It is only as long as I do not understand how to bring about the dissolution of a particular problem that I depend on a myth, on an idea of hope. If you observe your own mind, you will see that when you are in discomfort, in conflict, in misery, your mind seeks a way away from it. The process of going away from the problem is the creation of hope.

The mind going away from the problem creates fear; the very movement of going away, the flight from the problem, is fear. I am in despair because I have done something which is not right, or some misery comes upon me, or I have done a terrible wrong, or my son is dead, or I have very little to eat. My mind, not being able to resolve the problem, creates a certainty, something to which it can cling, an image which it carves by the hand or by the mind. Or the mind clings to a guru, to a book, to an idea which sustains me in my difficulties, in my miseries, in my despair, and so I say I shall have a better time next life, and so on and on and on.

As long as I am not capable of resolving my problem, my sorrow, I depend on hope; it is indispensable. Then I fight for that hope. I do not want anyone to disturb that hope, that belief. I make that belief into an organized belief, and I cling to that because out of that, I derive happiness, because I have not been able to solve the problem which is confronting me, hope becomes the necessity.

Now, can I solve the problem? If I can understand the problem, then hope is not necessary; then depending on an idea or an image or a person is not necessary because dependence implies hope, implies comfort. So, the problem is whether hope is indispensable, whether I can resolve my problem, whether there is a way to find out how not to be in sorrow—that is my problem, not how to dispense with hope.

Now, what is the factor essential to the understanding of a problem? Obviously, if I wish to understand the problem, there must be no formula, there must be no conclusion, there must be no judgment. But if we observe our minds, we will see that we are full of conclusions; we are steeped in formulas with which we hope to resolve the problem. And so we judge, we condemn. And so, as long as we have a formula, a conclusion, a judgment, a condemnatory attitude, we shall not understand the problem.

So the problem is not important, but how we approach the problem. So the mind that is wishing to comprehend a problem must not be concerned with the problem but with the workings of its own machinery of judgment. Do you follow?

I started out with the establishment of a hope, saying that it is essential because without hope I am lost. So my mind is occupied with hope, I occupy it with hope. But that is not my problem; my problem is the problem of sorrow, of pain, of mistakes. Is even that my problem, or is my problem how to approach the problem itself? So what is important is how the mind regards the problem.

I have altogether moved away from hope because hope is illusory, it is unreal, it is not factual. I cannot deal with something which is not factual, which has been created by the mind; it is not something real; it is illusory, so I cannot grapple with it. What is real is my sorrow, my despair, the things that I have done, the crowded memories, the aches, and the sorrows of my life. How I approach the aches and sorrows and miseries in my life is important, not hope, because if I know how I approach them, then I shall be able to deal with them.

So what is important is not hope but how I regard my problem. I see that I always regard my problem in the light of judgment—either condemning, accepting, or trying to transform it—or looking at it through glasses, through the screen of formulas of what somebody has said in the Bhagavad-Gita, what the Buddha or the Christ has said. So my mind, being crippled by these formulas, judgments, quotations, can never understand the problem, can never look at it. So can the mind free itself from these accumulated judgments?

Please follow this carefully—not my words, but how you approach your problem. What we are always doing is pursuing the hope and everlastingly being frustrated. If I fail with one hope, I substitute another, and so I go on and on. And as I do not know how to approach, how to understand the problem itself, I resort to various escapes. But if I knew how to approach the problem, then there is no necessity for hope. So what is important is to find out how the mind regards the problem.

Your mind looks at a problem. It looks at it obviously with a condemnatory attitude. It condemns it in distinguishing it, in reacting to it, or it wants to change it into something which it is not. If you are violent, you want to change into nonviolence. Nonviolence is unreal, it is not factual; what is real is violence. Now to see how you approach the problem, with what attitude—whether you condemn it, whether you have the memories of what the so-called teachers have said about it—that is what is important.

Can the mind eradicate these conditions, free itself from these conditions and look at the problem? Can it be unconcerned with how to free itself from these conditions? If it is concerned with it, then you create another problem out of it. But if you can see how these conditions prevent you from looking at the problem, then these conditions have no value because the problem is important, pain is important, sorrow is important. You cannot call sorrow an idea and brush it aside. It is there.

So, as long as the mind is incapable of looking at the problem, as long as it is not capable of resolving the problem, there must be various escapes from the problem, and the escapes are hopes; they are the defense mechanism.

The mind will always create problems. But what is essential is that when we make mistakes, when we are in pain, to meet these mistakes, these pains, without judgment, to look at them without condemnation, to live with them and to let them go by. And that can only happen when the mind is in the state of noncondemnation, without any formula; which means, when the mind is essentially quiet, when the mind is fundamentally still; then only is there the comprehension of the problem.

Question: Will you please tell us what you mean by the words our vocation? I gather you mean something different from the ordinary connotation of these words.

KRISHNAMURTI: Each one of us pursues some kind of vocation—the lawyer, the soldier, the policeman, the businessman, and so on. Obviously, there are certain vocations which are detrimental to society—the lawyer, the soldier, the policeman, and the industrialist who is not making other men equally rich.

When we want, when we choose a particular vocation, when we train our children to follow a particular vocation, are we not creating a conflict within society? You choose one vocation and I choose another, and does that not bring about conflict between us? Is that not what is happening in the world because we have never found out what is our true vocation? We are only being conditioned by society, by a particular culture, to accept certain forms of vocations which breed competition and hatred between man and man. We know that, we see it.

Now is there any other way of living in which you and I can function in our true vocations? Now is there not one vocation for man? Please listen, sirs. Are there different vocations for man? We see that there are: you are a clerk, I polish shoes, you are an engineer, and I am a politician. We see innumerable varieties of vocations, and we see they are all in conflict with each other. So man through his vocation is in conflict, in hatred, with man. We know that. With that we are familiar every day.

Now let us find out if there is not one vocation for man. If we can all find it, then the expression of different capacities will not bring about conflict between man and man. I say there is only one vocation for man. There is only one vocation, not many. The one vocation for man is to find out what is real. Sirs, don't settle back, this is not a mystical answer.

If I and you are finding out what is truth, which is our true vocation, then in the search of that, we will not be in competition. I shall not be competing with you, I shall not fight you, though you may express that truth in a different way; you may be the prime minister; I shall not be ambitious and want to occupy your place because I am seeking equally with you what is truth. Therefore, as long as we do not find out that true vocation of man, we must be in competition with each other, we must hate each other, and whatever legislation you may pass, on that level you can only produce further chaos.

So, is it not possible from childhood, through right education, through the right educator, to help the boy, the student, to be free to find out what is the truth about everything—not just truth in the abstract, but to find out the truth of all relationships—the boy's relationship to machinery, his relationship to nature, his relationship to money, to society, to government, and so on? That requires, does it not, a different kind of teacher who is concerned with helping or giving the boy, the student, freedom so that he begins to investigate the cultivation of intelligence, which can never be conditioned by a society which is always deteriorating.

So, is there not one vocation for man? Man cannot exist in isolation; he exists only in relationship, and when in that relationship there is no discovery of truth, the discovery of the truth of relationship, then there is conflict.

There is only one vocation for you and me. And in the search of that, we shall find the expression wherein we shall not come into conflict, we shall not destroy each other. But it must begin surely through right education, through the right educator. The educator also needs education. Fundamentally, the teacher is not merely the giver of information but brings about in the student the freedom, the revolt to discover what is truth.

Question: When you answer our questions, what functions—memory or knowledge?

KRISHNAMURTI: It is really quite an interesting question, is it not? Let us find out.

Knowledge and memory are the same, are they not? Without knowledge, without the accumulation of knowledge which is memory, can you reply? The reply is the verbalization of a reaction, is it not? There is this question asked: What is functioning, memory or knowledge? I am only saying memory and knowledge are the same thing essentially, because if you have knowledge but have no memory of it, it will have no value.

You are asking what functions when I answer a question. Is knowledge functioning? Is memory functioning? Now what is it that is functioning with most of us? Please follow this. What is functioning with most of us when you ask a question? Obviously knowledge. When I ask you the way to your house, knowledge is functioning, memory is functioning. And with most of us that is all that functions because we have accumulated knowledge from the Bhagavad-Gita or from the Upanishads or from Marx or from what Stalin has said or what your pet guru says or your own experience, your own accumulated reactions, and from that background, you reply. That is all we know. That is the actual fact. In your business that is what is functioning. When you build a bridge, that is what is functioning.

When you write a poem, there are two functions going on—the verbalization, the memory, and the creative impulse; the creative impulse is not memory but when expressed, it becomes memory.

So without memory, verbalization, the verbalizing process, there is no possibility of communication. If I do not use certain words, English words, I could not talk to you. The very talking, the verbalization, is the functioning of memory. Now the question is: What is functioning when the speaker is answering, memory or something else? Memory obviously, because I am using words. But is that all?

Am I replying from the accumulated memories of innumerable speeches I have made during the last twenty years, which I keep on repeating like a gramophone record machine? That is what most of us are. We have certain actions, certain patterns of thought, and we keep on repeating them. But the repetition of words is entirely different from that because that is the way of communication. In the repetition of experience, the experiences are gathered and stored away, and like a machine, I repeat from that experience, from that storehouse. Here again, there is repetition, which is again the memory functioning.

So you are asking if it is possible, while I am speaking, that I am really experiencing, not answering from experience? Surely there is a difference between the repetition of experience and the freedom of experiencing which is being expressed through memory, which is the verbalization. Please listen. This is not difficult to understand.

I want to find out what ambition means, all that it implies. Do I really, now as I am speaking, investigate afresh the whole process of ambition? Or, do I repeat the investigation which I have made yesterday about ambition, which is merely repetition? Is it not possible to investigate, to experience anew all the time, and not merely rely on a record, on memory, on the experience of yesterday? Is it not possible to flower, to be, all the time, now as I am speaking, without the repetitious experience of yesterday, though I use words to communicate?

Your question is: What is functioning when I am speaking? If I am repeating merely what I have said ten days ago, then it is of very little value. But if I am experiencing as I am talking, not an imaginative feeling, but actually, then what is functioning? The flowering is functioning, not through self-expression, not the 'me' functioning, which is memory.

So it is very important, not for me alone, but for all of us, to find out if we can keep our minds from being this storehouse of the past, and whether the mind can be stable on the waters of life and let the memories float by without clinging to any particular memory, and when necessary to use that memory as we do use it when we communicate. Which means, the mind constantly letting the past float by, never identifying itself with it, never being occupied with it; so that the mind is firm, not in experience, not in memory, not in knowledge, but firm, stable in the process, in the way of experiencing continuously.

So, that is the factor which brings about no deterioration, so that the mind constantly renews. A mind that accumulates is already in decay. But the mind that allows memories to go by and is firm in the way of experiencing—such a mind is always fresh, it is always seeing things anew. That capacity can only come when the mind is very quiet. That quietness, that stillness, is not induced, cannot come about through any discipline, through any action of will, but when the mind understands the whole process of accumulation of knowledge, memory, experience. Then it establishes itself on the waters of life, which are always moving, living, vibrant.

Question: With what should the mind be occupied? I want to meditate. Would you please tell me on what I should meditate?

KRISHNAMURTI: Now, let us find out what is *meditation*. You and I are going to find out. I am not going to tell you what is meditation. We are both going to discover it afresh.

The mind that has learned to meditate, which is to concentrate, the mind that has learned the technique of shutting out everything and narrowing down to a particular point—such a mind is incapable of meditation. That is what most of us want. We want to learn to concentrate, to be occupied with one thought to the exclusion of every other thought, and we call that meditation. But it is not meditation. Meditation is something entirely different, which we are going to find out.

So our first problem is why does the mind demand that it should be occupied? Do you understand? My mind says, "I must be occupied with something, with worry, with memory, with a passion, or with how not to be passionate, or how to get rid of something, or to find a technique which will help me to build a bridge." So the mind, if you observe, demands constant occupation, does it not? That is why you say, "My mind must be occupied with the word *om,*" or you repeat *Ram Ram,* or you are occupied with drinking. The word *om,* the word *Ram Ram,* or the word *drink* are all the same because the mind wants to be occupied, because it says if it is not occupied it will do some mischief, if it is not occupied it will drift away. If the mind is not occupied, then what is the purpose of life? So you invent a purpose of life—noble, ignoble, or transcendental—and cling to that, and with that, you are occupied. It is the same whether the mind is occupied with God or whether it is occupied with business because the mind says consciously or unconsciously it must be occupied.

So, the next thing is to find out why the mind demands occupation. Please follow this. We are meditating now. This is meditation. Meditation is not a state at the end. Freedom is not to be got at the end; freedom is at the beginning. If you have no freedom in the beginning, you have no freedom at the end. If you have no love now, you will have no love in ten years. So what we are doing now is to find out what is meditation. And the very inquiry of what is meditation is to meditate.

The mind says, "I must be occupied with God, with virtue, with my worries, or with my business concern," so it is incessantly active in its occupation. So the mind can only exist as long as it is active, as long as it is conscious of itself in action, not otherwise. The mind knows itself as being when it is occupied, when it is acting, when it has results. It knows itself as existing when it is in motion. The motion is occupation towards a result, towards an idea, or denial of that idea negatively.

So, I am conscious of myself only when there is motion, in and out. So consciousness is this motion of action, outward and inward, this breathing out of responses, of reactions, of memories, and then collecting them back again. So my mind, 'I am', is only when I am thinking, when I am in conflict with a thing, when there is suffering, when there is occupation, when there is strain, when there is choice.

So the mind knows itself as in motion when it is ambitious and drags itself there, and seeing that ambition is dull, it says, "I will occupy myself with God." The occupation of the mind with God is the same as the occupation of the mind with money. We think that the man whose mind is occupied with God is more sacred than the man who is thinking of money, but they are factually both the same; both want results, both need to be occupied. So, can the mind be without occupation? That is the problem.

Sirs, can the mind be blank without comparing because the 'more' is the way of the mind knowing that it exists? The mind that knows it exists is never satisfied with *what is;* it is always acquiring, comparing, condemning, demanding more and more. In the demand, in the movement of the 'more', it knows itself as existing, which is what we call self-consciousness, the conscious on the surface and the unconscious. This is our life; this is the way of our everyday existence.

I want to know what meditation is, so I say I want to be occupied with meditation. I want to find out what meditation is, so my mind is again occupied with meditation. So, can the occupied mind—please follow this, listen to this—can the occupied mind ever be capable of meditation? Meditation surely is the understanding of the ways of the mind. If I do not know how my mind operates, functions, works, how can I meditate? How can I really find out what is truth? So, the mind must find out how it is occupied; then it begins to see with what it is occupied, and then finds that all occupations are the same because the mind then is filling itself with words, with ideas, with constant movement, so that there is never a quietness.

When the mind occupies itself with the discovery of what love is, it is another form of occupation, is it not? It is like the man who is occupied with passion.

When you say you must find out the truth, will you find truth? Or, does truth come into being only when the mind is not occupied, when the mind is empty to receive, not to gather, not to accumulate. Because, you can only receive once. But if what you have received you make into memory with which you are occupied, then you will never receive again. Because the receiving is from moment to moment. Therefore it is of timelessness.

So the mind, which is of time, cannot receive the timeless. So the mind must be completely still, empty, without any movement in any direction. And that can only take place with a mind that is not occupied—not occupied with the 'more', with a problem, with worry, with escapes; not conditioned in any belief, in any image, in any experience. It is only when the mind is totally free, then only is there a possibility of immense profound stillness, and in that stillness that which is eternal comes into being. That is meditation.

March 11, 1953

London, England, 1953

First Talk in London

It seems to me that one of our greatest problems in this rather confused world is "what to do?" There is starvation in Asia, and there is the threatening of war. There is extraordinary progress in science, and though we may want to keep up with this so-called progress morally, we are behind. And the difficulty in this confusion is to find out—intellectually even—how to behave, how to act, and what to think. Because, though we look to leaders, intellectual philosophers, or scientists, it seems to me that the difficulty is that we no longer have confidence in philosophers, in the teachers, in the scientists. The more we observe, the greater we see the confusion to be. Though we may have a welfare state, inwardly, psychologically we are extraordinarily poor. We may have all the outward things—shelter, food, clothing—that go to create comfort, but inwardly we are poor, insufficient, utterly miserable, confused, not knowing what to do, where to find either happiness, salvation, or that sense of reality which is not dependent on any particular religion, on any philosophy.

Seeing all this, surely we must begin to find out what we mean by a moral life. Is morality consistent with progress? And, can morality be consciously, deliberately planned out and cultivated so as to meet this extraordinary progress that man is making in other directions? Is inward progress ever possible? And can man be happy without this deliberate, conscious effort at morality? Is morality cultivable? And when morality is developed, does it lead to happiness, to creativity, to freedom? Or, is morality something which is not to be cultivated but a revolution, an unconscious revolution?

We may cultivate virtue, compassion, love, but will intellectual cultivation—the deliberate process of becoming something, becoming noble, and so on—will such a deliberate act bring about that unconscious freedom from the restraints that modern society and our own limitations place upon each one of us? Surely, is it not important to find out whether this constant struggle towards greater and greater intellectual development will solve any of our problems, or whether there is a totally different approach? Because, if I consciously follow a particular course of action, plan out my life, intellectually think it out, analyze it and set a course, naturally I will achieve certain results. But will that bring about a sense of freedom, that creativity which is the reality of actual experience? Or, does that creativity, that freedom, come about entirely differently, through a different process?

Perhaps we can go into this and find out whether through a deliberate process, through a cultivation of the mind, through various disciplines and compulsions, the mind can go beyond itself. Because, intellectually we are very far advanced; intellectually we know a great many things, but inwardly we are insufficient; there is no richness. We depend on others for our psychological well-being; there is fear, there is frustration, there is anxiety, a sense of being bound. And, is it possible to break through this intellectuality by the cultivation of any particular virtue or virtues? Will intellect free us from our own bondage, will intellect free us from fear, will intellect cultivate that feeling of compassion? And yet, that is what we are trying to do, are we not?

Though we may have a welfare state where everything is planned for us, we are aware that there is an insufficiency of affection, love; and there is fear. And we intellectually set about cultivating various forms of resistance to fear—denying anxiety or analyzing it, going into it very, very carefully all through the intellect, through the mind. And can the mind resolve the problems which it has created? We cultivate virtue, morality, to keep up with the progress we are making, but will that cultivation of morality by the intellect bring about the well-being of man?

So, that is one of our major problems, is it not? Scientifically we are making extraordinary advances in the world, and so we say to ourselves, "Morally also we must progress." But the more we cultivate virtue, the stronger the resistance, which we call the 'me', the 'I', the ego. Is that not so? When I am consciously, deliberately, cultivating humility or fearlessness, am I being humble, free from fear? When I am deliberately trying to be nonviolent, am I so? Or, is virtue something that cannot be cultivated at all? The person who is conscious of his morality surely is not moral, is he? And yet, there must be morality; there must be an unconscious moral well-being which is not the result of the intellectual cultivation of any particular virtue.

I do not know if I am making myself clear. Because, it seems to me that this is one of our greatest problems. Because, to meet this progress, obviously there must be a freedom from the ego-consciousness; otherwise, we are going to make more misery for ourselves, more sorrow. And, is the freedom from this ego-consciousness the result of the cultivation of any particular virtue? Because, all religions deliberately set about to cultivate particular qualities in the follower. This conscious cultivation is surely the development of the intellect and not of virtue. The more I am conscious that I am virtuous, the less I am virtuous. And yet, every activity of a religious person, every activity of a person who is trying to meet this world problem, the world crisis, is the deliberate cultivation, conscious effort, towards some particular form of virtue, of morality, of well-being. It is a conscious, deliberate effort. And I wonder if such an effort does bring about morality, the well-being of man so as to meet the progress that the world is making?

Is not true revolution not of the mind but at quite a different level? Because, planned revolution—economic, social, or of any other kind—is still on the intellectual level, and the intellect cannot possibly bring about a revolution. Intellect can only bring about a continued change, but that change is not a revolution. An economic change, thought out, planned out by the mind, is not a revolution for the total well-being of man; it is only a revolution at a particular, narrow level. And if we are concerned with the total revolution of man—not the development of one particular quality at one particular level—must we not be concerned, not only with the revolution at the superficial, conscious level, but at the deeper levels of our being also?

And is the mind, the conscious mind, capable of digging into or analyzing the unconscious and thereby bringing about a revolution? Because, it is obvious that we need a fundamental, radical transformation in ourselves which cannot be brought about by the mind. The mind cannot produce that revolution. That revolution can only come about when there is a direct experience of reality, or God, or what you will. But the intellect cannot experience that; it cannot, through any of its efforts, realize that truth. Any cultivation of morality, any belief, any doctrine, is still on the intellectual level, on the superficial level. And yet with that mind, that intellect, we are trying to grasp, trying to experience, something which is beyond the mind.

Is God, truth, or what you will, to be discovered by the mind, by the intellect? Or, is it to be experienced when the totality of the mind—not only the conscious, but also the unconscious—when the whole mind is utterly still, not struggling to achieve a result, not struggling to find something, not trying to go beyond itself? It seems to me this is very important to understand. All our effort so far is at the level of the intellect because that is all we have; that is what we have cultivated for generations. And with that mind we are trying to find a reality, a truth, a God, which will give us happiness, give us virtue, bring about the inward well-being of each one of us. Is that really to be found through the mind? Yet without that reality, do what we will, whatever progress we make will always bring about more confusion, more sorrow, more wars, more divisions; and without finding that reality, progress has no meaning.

So how is one to find that new state? How is one to awaken to that reality, to that creativeness which is not merely a verbal expression or a myth or a fantasy? It is to be found. But it cannot be found by the mind. The mind is only the result of time, memory, reactions—a storehouse of knowledge of the past. The mind is the past. In its very nature it is put together through time, through the ages. And we are trying to find something which is beyond time, which cannot be named, which cannot be put into words, which no description can ever cover. Without the discovery of that, life has very little significance; life becomes one series of struggles—sorrow, pain, suffering, constant anxiety. So, how is one to find that?

Is it not to be found—or rather, does it not come into being—when the whole of my being is very still? Because in that state I am not asking for anything; I am neither virtuous nor not-virtuous; I am not thinking of myself as progressing, advancing, growing, attaining a result; there is no longer the drive of ambition, of wanting to put the world in order. The world can be put in order only when I have found that reality. That reality will bring about order without my making an effort to do something. So, is it not important for me to understand myself, the ways of my own mind? For that understanding brings about that state of stillness in which there is an unconscious revolution—the revolution in which the 'me' is no longer important. And so when I see all this, the mind becomes very quiet, no longer seeking, no longer demanding, no longer struggling to be something; and in that quietness, in that stillness, reality comes into being. It is not a fancy; it is not some oriental mysticism. Without that reality, do what you will, there will be more wars, more destruction; man will be ever against man.

That reality cannot come into being, I feel, without self-knowledge—self-knowledge which is discovered from moment to moment in the mirror of relationship so that all illusion is stripped away, so that the mind does not build fantasies, escapes. When the mind is no longer caught in beliefs, it begins to understand *what is*—*what is* in relationship. So, through the constant awareness in action of the self, of the 'me', one discovers the ways of one's mind. It is a book that cannot be read all at once. The man who says, "I must read it at once and understand it totally," will never understand the mind. It is to be read constantly, and what one reads is not to be accumulated as knowledge. Because, knowledge prevents reality; knowledge is accumulated memory; knowledge is of time, is of so-called progress. But reality is not of time; it cannot be stored up and used; it comes only when the mind is utterly quiet. And that quietness comes into being not through any discipline but through the understanding of the ways of the ego, the 'me', the mind, through awareness of all relationships.

So, no discipline, no cultivation of virtue, will bring reality into being. The cultivation of virtue merely becomes an impediment to reality, without which the various problems that life creates will ever continue. It is only when I begin to understand myself that the mind becomes quiet; only in that quietness, in that stillness of the mind, that creative reality comes into being.

Some questions have been sent in, and I will try to answer them. But before I do so, I think one or two things must be made clear. If you are looking for an answer, I am afraid you will be disappointed. Because, the problem is more important than the answer; how one approaches the problem is more significant than seeking a solution. If one knows how to approach a problem, then the answer is in the problem, not away from it. But we are so eager to find an answer, a remedy, to be told what to do, that we never study the problem itself.

And I think, also, that it is very important to know how to listen. Because, we rarely listen; we are so full of our own ideas, our own objections, our own prejudices, or we have read a great deal; we know so much. Our own experience, our knowledge, and other people's knowledge prevent us from listening not only to the speaker but to everything in life. The more we listen, the greater the understanding. But it is very difficult to listen. To listen, one must be extraordinarily quiet—not concentrated because concentration is merely an exclusive process. But when one listens to find out, one discovers because then one is open; there is no barrier; one's own projections have stopped, and psychologically one is not demanding.

So, it is very important, is it not, to know how to listen not only to me, that is not so important, but to everything—to your neighbor, to your wife, to your children, to the politicians—so that in the very process of listening, there is that confidence which is not of the 'me'. Because, most of us lack confidence, and so we seek to cultivate it, which merely becomes the egocentric certainty of the 'me', the confidence that is self-enclosing. But if I know how to listen not only to everything about me but also to all my inner compulsions, urges, demands, to listen without interpreting, without translating, then I begin to understand the fact of *what is.*

And so with that, perhaps I can answer some of these questions.

Question: What need has one who belongs to the welfare state to come to meetings like this?

KRISHNAMURTI: Sir, you may have all the physical necessities supplied to you by the state. And then what? Is it not important to find out why man is pursuing physical utopia? We want salvation on the physical level. We want a well-ordered society. We want the perfect man, the perfect state. And we are getting lost in planning the perfect state. We think we make progress along that line, forgetting the total process of man. Man is not just this outward physical entity. There are all the psychological processes, the extraordinary resistances, fears, anxieties, frustrations. Dealing only with one part of man without understanding the whole, total process surely does not bring about the well-being, the happiness of man. Is it not important also to find out the other parts, the hidden, the different levels, and not merely concentrate on physical well-being?

This does not mean that we must neglect physical well-being, go off into some monastery, into isolation. But, should we not deal with the total process of man? If you are emphasizing only the progress towards a perfect utopia, leaving out the enormous depths, the difficulties, the resistances, fears of man, surely you have not solved the problem! I do not think you will have utopia without understanding the total man. Surely religion—not belief, not organized ritual, and so on, but true religion—is the discovery of man's total process, and so, to go beyond the mind. Because the mind will not solve our problems, we need a different quality. And that quality can only come about with inward revolution.

Perhaps you have come to this meeting to find out for yourself if it is possible, as an individual, to go beyond the limitations of the mind, beyond its conditioning influences—to find out for yourself. Because, I feel without experiencing that reality, mere economic planning, trying to bring about a perfect state will lead us nowhere. I think we are beginning at the wrong end. If we begin at the right end—that is, the discovery of reality—then the other is possible; then the other, the perfect state, the perfect society, has significance. But to begin with the perfect society and deny the other will only lead us to further confusion, to concentration camps, to the liquidation of those people with whom we do not agree, and so we will be everlastingly against each other.

Through understanding this process of conditioning, through understanding how the mind is conditioned—whatever its activities, whatever its projections, the mind will always be conditioned—through realizing that, perhaps it is possible to go beyond. And perhaps that is the reason some of you are here.

Question: I watch my thoughts and feelings, but it does not seem to lead me any further because I continually slip back into the old routine of casual escape and thought, so what am I to do?

KRISHNAMURTI: A small mind, a petty mind, watching its own thought and feeling, still remains within its own limitations, does it not? If my mind is petty, shallow, small, I can watch my thought everlastingly, and naturally it will lead me nowhere. Because, my small mind wants certain results, and so, it is observing, watching for the results. My mind being petty, small, whatever I think is also small; my gods, my beliefs, my activities, my objections, controls, disciplines, are still petty, small, bound by my own limitations. That is the real problem—not how to watch the mind, but is it possible for the mind which is small, narrow, petty, to go beyond itself?

Merely watching your thoughts and feelings will not help a petty mind, will it? After all, I watch my thoughts in order to bring about a change; I watch my feelings in order to transform them. But the entity that is watching, the entity that is trying to change the thought and the feeling, is itself the result of feelings and of thoughts. The entity is not different from the thought and the feeling. Without that feeling and that thought there is no entity. I am made up of my thoughts, feelings, experiences, conditioning, and so on; I am all that. And one part of me says, "I will watch the various thoughts, various feelings, and try to change them, try to bring about a transformation." But the 'I' that is trying to do something about these thoughts is still within the field of thought. So the mind, separating itself as the superior and trying to control, to change thought or feeling, is still part of the feeling, is still part of that thought.

Do please think it out with me. I am not different from my thoughts and feelings, am I? I am made up of thoughts and feelings—the fears, the anxieties, the frustrations, the longings, the innumerable desires—I am all that, all of that. And one part of me, watching and trying to control thought and feeling, will obviously not produce any result. I can change them, but the entity that changes is still petty, small. So what am I to do? Because, I see the necessity of bringing about a fundamental change in my thinking—I want to put aside ambition, various forms of fear, and so on; I see the fundamental necessity of it. Then, what am I to do? The 'I' which is made up of this ambition, made up of fear, frustration, that 'I' which is itself part of frustration, when it tries to go beyond or to fulfill, will only create further frustration.

If I see the truth that whatever I do with regard to frustration—trying to become happy, trying to fulfill, or trying to put aside any desire for fulfillment—will only lead me to further frustration, if I see the truth of that, is there any necessity to struggle against frustration? Then I do not have to watch my thought and feeling. I only watch my thought and feeling in order to change them, in order to control them, in order to discipline them to fit into a particular pattern of thought or action. But the 'I' is not different from those thoughts and feelings. The 'I' cannot change those thoughts. It can modify them, change the pattern, but it cannot bring about a revolution in thinking. Revolution can only come about when the 'I' is not conscious of making an effort to change.

Please see this. When you desire to change a particular thought or feeling, you make a deliberate, conscious effort to change, but that consciousness is itself the result of struggle, of pain, of frustration, of wanting a certain result. So it is a planned action of the mind, of the 'me', of the 'I', of a particular thought process. That is not a revolution. That is only a modified continuity of a particular thought. And so one sees, does one not, the importance of a fundamental revolution, a revolution in the unconscious, which must come about without one's making a conscious effort. Such a change, such a revolution, is only possible when I understand the total process of my thinking. Therefore, I deliberately do not do a thing. I realize that any conscious action on my part will only hinder that unconscious revolution.

Fundamental revolution in oneself comes about without any act of will. As long as I will to act in a particular direction, I am only cultivating, strengthening the 'me' which is always anxious to achieve a result, to bring about a change. Please, think about this, and you will see that so long as you desire to bring about a particular change in habit, in thought, to alter a particular relationship, to free yourself from fear, so long as you deliberately set about consciously to change fear, you will never succeed. But, if you can be aware of the total process of fear and leave it alone, then you will find that there is an unconscious transformation, a fundamental change in which there is no longer any fear.

But the difficulty with most of us is that we want to act, we want to alter, whereas the mind cannot bring about a radical change. The mind can modify, but it cannot bring about fundamental freedom from fear because the mind itself is made up of fear. So, if you can understand this total process, if as you listen to this, you understand it, then you will see that in spite of your conscious efforts there is a transformation going on which will free the conscious mind from fear.

The conscious mind cannot free itself from anything. It can modify, it can alter, but in the background of it there is still fear. To be radically free from fear is to be aware of fear and to leave it alone without any judgment, without trying to do anything about it. Just to know that there is fear and to be quiet brings about a fundamental revolution in which fear has no longer any place.

March 30, 1953

Second Talk in London

Is not the conditioned mind—the mind that is held, limited, confined to various forms of beliefs, to many experiences, to a particular mode of conduct, to certain prejudices, attitudes—one of the major causes of confusion? Such a mind obviously does create confusion because each of us is conditioned—you as a Christian, another as a Hindu, a Buddhist, or a communist, a socialist, and so on. So, whether this conditioning is externally imposed through education or inwardly imposed through our own fears, our own experiences, through knowledge, through certain capacities, the conditioned mind obviously is incapable of being free. And it seems to me that it is only in freedom that one can discover what is true, and that as long as the mind is conditioned, it is incapable of that discovery. Only in the discovery of what is true can there be a harmony, a real love between man and man.

Is it possible to be free from this conditioning? And what is the factor that goes to make up the conditioning? If we can understand what it is, without making an effort to uncondition the mind, perhaps then we shall find out what it is to be free from the various limitations which the mind has imposed upon itself.

After all, each society, each group of people, the various religions, they all impose certain conditions on us. From childhood, we are all conditioned—climatically, geographically, religiously, socially, economically. These influences are constantly impinging on our minds. And we do not seem to be able to free ourselves from these conditionings imposed from our childhood or the experiences that we have acquired—experience being the conjunction of the past with the present in the moment of reaction.

Is it ever possible to be free of this conditioning? After all, so long as I am a Hindu or a Buddhist or a Christian, I think of reality or God in the framework in which I have been brought up; I believe that there is only one church through which salvation can be found, or only one economic system through which society can be saved, or I have innumerable beliefs imposed or cultivated through anxiety, through fear. Surely such a mind is incapable of finding any reality! It can only find what it has been conditioned to find. If you are conditioned one way and I another way, there must be confusion, contention in our action, in our attitude, in our relationship. We have each been brought up in a certain framework, and each separate group of people thinks they alone have found certainty, reality, that theirs is the best way. But life is in constant movement; it is not capable of being held in a particular system of thought, and so there is always conflict between the conditioned mind and the vital, living movement of life.

Realizing this, we say, "Is it not possible to uncondition ourselves?" All that we can do, surely, is to put the mind into a better pattern, a better framework, make it more sociable, more moral. Can a mind which is so conditioned find reality? And, what is the factor that makes the mind conditioned, held in limitation? Perhaps if we understand that, we may be able to step out of conditioning almost immediately. The gradual unconditioning of the mind is really not possible because in the very process of gradual unconditioning, you are conditioning it in another direction.

So, what is the factor that conditions the mind? Is it not the power of the mind to acquire and to hold on to what it has acquired? The mind is constantly seeking knowledge, security, experience. It has become a storehouse. And through that screen we translate everything. So long as the mind has the power, the urge to acquire, it must obviously be conditioning itself all the time; it is never in a state of freedom; it is limited by its own acquisitions, by its own knowledge, by its own capacity.

So, can the mind be free from this power to acquire and to retain what it has acquired, whether it is knowledge, capacity, or experience? Can it not let experience, knowledge, pass by and yet remain without being conditioned? Can I not realize how I am conditioned as a Hindu, a Christian, or what you will, and understand how that conditioning comes into being socially, morally, in my relationships? Can I not see how the mind in that conditioning feels secure, feels that it has acquired certain knowledge, certain experience, that it is certain in itself? Cannot knowledge be used for action, without the action or the knowledge limiting the mind, conditioning the mind?

These things have to be felt out, thought out. It is not a question of being convinced or being persuaded to a certain attitude. What we have to find out is whether, being conditioned, it is possible to free oneself from that conditioning, inwardly, totally. Because, then there may be a possibility of the mind being so deeply free as to discover what is real, to discover what is God. And it seems to me that if the mind is not capable of freeing itself from this constant acquisition—acquisition in becoming something, in being certain, in safeguarding itself—if the mind continues to hold on to this power to store up what it has learned, to gather experience and retain it, obviously the mind will ever be conditioned. We are experiencing all the time, but cannot the mind experience and let it go by without holding, never identified with it, never calling it "mine?"

Surely, if we can feel that out—not intellectually, abstractly as an idea, but actually see, feel out, directly experience this mind that is acquiring, storing, and then acting—then, surely, we shall comprehend that state in which the mind experiences and lets the experience go by, without itself being caught in the experience. Then, it seems to me, there is a real freedom, not the so-called freedom within the framework of a conditioned state.

As a Christian or as a Hindu, one says one is free, but that is not freedom. To be free within a conditioned state is still to be conditioned, and in that state it is obviously not possible to discover what is real, what is the 'highest'. Any projection of the conditioned mind is still the result of its own experience, the outcome of its past conditioning. So, is it possible for me—knowing that I am conditioned, and the factors that condition me, the causes—is it possible to be so aware of it that without any effort, without any action of will, I can let the experience, the knowledge go by without the mind being caught in it? After all, the mind is memory, is it not? It is the past, it is of time. And most of us are occupied with memories. We cannot deliberately put memory aside, but we can let the memories go by without corrupting the mind, without being occupied with any particular memory, pleasant or unpleasant. It is this occupation that conditions the mind, this concern with the particular memory from childhood or from yesterday which I have acquired and to which I cling.

Is it possible to go into this whole process of acquiring and be free from it? We seem to think that freedom is not possible as long as we are bound economically. Perhaps we shall always be bound economically. I do not think freedom lies in that direction. But perhaps freedom is to be found not in the seeking of physical comforts but in the freedom from acquisition, the freedom from being conditioned, so that the mind is always in a state of quiescence, quietude, not being disturbed by any experience, by any shadow. Surely such a state is necessary if one would know what is real, what is true creativeness.

Question: I am always hungry. Where can I find the food that will fill me forever?

KRISHNAMURTI: We want to find contentment, do we not? We want to fulfill ourselves in some action, in some person, in an idea. And we try one thing after another—join one society, one group after another, attach ourselves to certain ideas, beliefs, and then push them aside when they do not satisfy, when they no longer give us what we want. So we keep on moving, everlastingly hungry. The hunger becomes painful only when it has nothing to feed upon. But the moment it has found something it can feed upon, there is no pain. Pain exists only when I cannot find food when I'm hungry. But if I find food when I'm hungry, there is no pain.

So, being hungry, inwardly insufficient, frustrated, I want to find something that will give me everlasting fulfillment, everlasting happiness. So I seek, I try one thing after another. That is our state, is it not? Being discontented, being hungry, being frustrated, we want to find an outlet somewhere where one can find contentment, where there is no such thing as frustration. So, I try to quieten my discontent by theories, by explanations, or by identifying myself with the state, throwing myself into some social activity, or joining a society, a religious group. But always there is hunger, there is anxiety, there is fear, there is discontent.

Now, why shouldn't I be discontented? What is wrong with the discontent? It is only painful, surely, when I want to alter it. Discontent in itself is not painful. It is only when I wish I could find contentment, it is only in relationship to contentment that the main pain of discontent arises. So, being discontented, I am seeking contentment. And when I cannot find it, then there is pain. So I go from door to door, from Master to Master, from saint to saint, from one teacher to another because my intention is to find contentment, to find satisfaction, perpetual peace. In myself I am in turmoil, confused, frustrated, and as I cannot find the means of alteration of the state in which I am, from that arises pain.

So, can I understand what is discontent and not ask how to transform it, how to become contented? It is very simple, is it not, how to be contented? I can take a drug, condition myself to certain beliefs, become active socially, politically, or follow some authority, and so on; thereby, it is fairly easy to find contentment, but there is always pain, fear, behind that contentment. But if I can understand discontentment—that flame, that thing that is constantly active, inquiring, searching, that thing that is not satisfied—then that very understanding may be the essential thing, not contentment at all. If I am not capable of constant inquiry, constant watchfulness of the things that are happening, taking shape in me—the thoughts, the feelings, the experiences—if I am not capable of that questioning, inquiring, then only is it that discontent becomes a pain. And from that pain I want to escape. And so I want to find food that is everlastingly satisfying.

Is it not necessary to be discontented and not to find an easy channel through which the discontent can be pacified? Discontent, this feeling of searching to find out what is true, to be inwardly in revolution, is essential, is it not? Then that flame will give a new life, a new relationship to everything that the mind invents, so that the mind's power to create illusion is burned out. That power to create illusion is not burned out by experience because experience creates illusion. It is only the understanding of the accumulative process of experience that gives freedom.

So, is it not important not to seek satisfaction, contentment, the everlasting food, the manna from heaven, not to ask for it? Because, the moment you ask you are given, and what you are given turns to ashes. Is it not important to have this capacity of discontent—perhaps that may not be the right word—to have that feeling of not being easily satisfied, of not seeking satisfaction at all, not being in pursuit of any form of gratification; and so, to be in this permanent state of revolution, not doubting—doubting has no place in it—but inquiring, fathoming, searching out? Such a mind cannot be conditioned because it has never a resting place, never calls anything 'mine'.

Surely we must have such a mind. But the moment you say, "How can I have such a mind?" the method becomes the factor of your conditioning. If we can see the truth of that, feel it out inwardly—not merely intellectually or verbally—then an unconscious revolution is taking place; then the mind no longer is satisfied; it can never be satisfied; it is not thinking in terms of satisfaction then at all. And therefore the mind is not caught in frustration, despair, and hope; it is not held in that terminology or in that field.

So is it possible for the mind, for you and me—who are just ordinary people, not geniuses, but ordinary, mediocre, struggling people—is it possible for us to free ourselves from this craving for satisfaction? Because, the moment we are satisfied, we cease to be creative. Creation is not the mere writing of a poem or the painting of a picture; I'm not talking of that. I am not talking of the projections that the mind creates and calls reality but of that reality which comes when the mind is capable of receiving it, which alone is creativeness. So, should not the mind be constantly in revolution, never acquiring, never having a place where it feels safe, being ever in that state where no experience can enrich it? Because, the moment you are enriched, revolution has ceased to be, and therefore creativeness is not.

So, is it not possible for the mind, which is seeking food for its satisfaction, to be timelessly in a state of nonacquisition so that it is no longer struggling and is therefore extraordinarily still? Because, in that stillness, perhaps that which is the creative, the timeless, can come into being.

Question: Sleep is necessary for the right function of the physical body. Apart from that, what is the function of sleep?

KRISHNAMURTI: Without making sleep and what happens during sleep into all kinds of mystical nonsense—you know all the things that we invent—can we not find out what actually takes place, the truth of the matter, not the invention of the mind, not what the mind would like to be happening? Because, something does happen during sleep. Problems are solved; new discoveries are made. I may have been thinking over a problem for days, and suddenly in sleep the answer may be revealed. Sleep is necessary. And perhaps we can, by understanding it, going into it, discover what actually happens—not theoretically, not what we would like to happen, not all the explanations which various societies invent as to what happens during sleep. But cannot we, putting aside all those, really deeply inquire into it and find out the truth of the matter?

Obviously sleep is essential not only for physical well-being but also for psychological well-being. Because, during that period, obviously, the so-called conscious, active mind, the daily mind—the mind that goes to the office, the mind that is tied to the kitchen, the mind that nags, the mind that quarrels, the mind that is perpetually occupied with some silly thing, with what your neighbor says, with the coronation, and so on—that mind is quiet; actually, it is quiet when you sleep. But that is only one part of the mind, the very, very superficial part. The rest of the mind is going on acting. It is never asleep, surely. You can see that when any deep problem, when any deep trouble, anxiety, when a fundamental question in the waking consciousness has been touched upon and no answer found, the deeper mind which does not sleep is still inquiring, searching out. And because it is searching out without the interference of the superficial mind—the mind that is occupied with the trivial things of daily life—the deeper mind is more free to inquire. That is why suddenly we may wake up in the morning and say, "By Jove, that is the answer!" or, you have a new idea, a new outlook, a new impression. That new impression comes into being, does it not, when the so-called superficial mind is quiet. I dig into a problem, look at it all round, talk about it, discuss, and when I have given up finding a solution and go to sleep, out comes the right answer. It has happened to all of us. And perhaps it is because the superficial mind is no longer interfering.

And so, sleep becomes very important. But as most of us live and have our being in the superficial mind, we never touch the other. Perhaps, occasionally through dreams, the other gives hints, but these hints are translated by the trivial mind, and in the very process of translating, that which has significance is made trivial.

So, sleeping and waking—keeping fully awake during the day—both have significance, have they not? So, can I not during the day keep awake?—not be a slave to the superficial mind, but keep awake to the whole process of the mind, the various levels of consciousness; not just live on a certain level, the level which I choose, the level on which I have said, "This is the perfect state, and in that state I am going to live." Is it not possible during the day to be aware of the total process of the mind, not just one segment? That process is understood more significantly in sleep, and so again, the waking consciousness becomes much more vital.

So, what is important is not what happens during sleep and the interpretation of dreams with all its complications, but to be awake to the whole process of the mind, of consciousness, during the day so that at night sleep becomes a deeper, a further understanding of what is going on. For in that sleep there are a great many hints, suggestions, that the conscious mind cannot possibly think of.

But as long as there is an interpreter, the translator, the censor, the one that judges or condemns, the total process of consciousness is not understood. There can be no entity that is looking at the consciousness and translating the hints. The total process cannot be understood by the part, by the entity that is observing, that is translating. That is why a silent mind is necessary, a mind that no longer condemns, judges. Then the whole process of consciousness reveals itself through every action, through every word. Therefore the waking consciousness and the sleeping are both important because then the greater depths of consciousness are revealed.

Question: My son is dead. How am I to meet that sorrow?

KRISHNAMURTI: Actually, how do we meet sorrow? Do we ever meet it? We do not know what sorrow is; we are forever running away from it. That is all we know. If I know how to meet it, how to meet the fact, then the fact will do something to me. I cannot do anything about the fact, but I want to do something about it. So my very desire to translate, to interpret the fact, helps me to run away from it.

Look, and see what actually happens. My son is dead, and I am in sorrow. So my mind in pain, in anxiety, in fear, wants some consolation. The natural response, not the cultivated response, is, "I want comfort for that pain, for that fear, for that loneliness." So I turn to something—to a belief, to a seance, to mediums, to reincarnation, or rationalization of the fact of death—hoping to find some assurance. So, the mind is everlastingly active about the fact. The fact is—my son is dead. And I cannot face it. So the mind begins to invent, symbolize, find assurance, hope, in something. So the mind is never meeting sorrow.

When you say, "How am I to meet sorrow?" what you are concerned with is not meeting sorrow but how to deal with sorrow—what you should do about sorrow, with what attitude, value, you should look upon it. So, you are really concerned not with meeting sorrow but how to have the self-protective attitude with which to meet it. After all, when I have a belief in reincarnation, that I'm going to meet my son next life, I do not meet sorrow. Or, if I resort to a seance, of course I do not meet my sorrow. Or, if I try to forget it by becoming active socially, in dozens of ways, I still avoid sorrow. And that is what we are actually doing.

If I want to meet sorrow, my mind must not escape from the fact—which does not mean that I accept the fact. The fact is a fact; I don't have to accept it; it is so. If I cultivate the attitude of acceptance, then I again prevent myself from meeting the fact. So, the mind is everlastingly finding ways, devices, not to meet the fact. And yet sorrow can only be understood when I meet it. And it is only possible to meet it when the mind is really still, not interpreting, not accepting, not trying to find the reasons, the explanations, not indulging in theories, speculations.

When the mind is completely still, not because it wants to understand the fact, but because it knows its own process, then only can I meet the extraordinary experience of death—that unknowingness, that sense of not knowing what death is, despite the innumerable books that have been written about it. Only when the mind is quiet, completely still, can I understand the fact which is: there is sorrow and there is no explanation. Surely, in such a state of mind, when it is completely silent before the fact of death, something extraordinary happens. This is not a promise. So do not cultivate quietness of the mind. But when the mind is not seeking any solution, has no beliefs, has no hope, is completely silent, then only can it meet sorrow. And in that state, sorrow ceases to be.

March 31, 1953

Third Talk in London

If we can find out what are the factors of deterioration, then perhaps we shall be able to set aside mediocrity and come to a realization or to a feeling of what it is to be creative. Is not one of our problems, perhaps the major one, that we are constantly living in the shadow of death, in the shadow of deterioration, decay? The circumstances, the various compulsions of life about us make us mediocre, closed in, ineffective, and there is soon deterioration, not only physical, but the much more important psychological deterioration. Perhaps if we can find out what it is that we are seeking, what it is that we are searching after, that we want, then we may be able to solve this problem of mediocrity and decay.

Why is it that most of us are so utterly, inwardly empty, miserable, always seeking, running after things, trying to find out, longing for something which we never seem able to get? Is that not one of our problems? If we can really try to find out what it is that we are seeking, perhaps we shall be able to answer or to go beyond this psychological decay, the mediocrity of the mind.

We can see, most of us, that at one level we are seeking comfort, physical well-being—to be comfortable, to have money, to have love, to have things, to enjoy things, to travel, to be able to do certain things. All these we want at the superficial level. And if we go a little bit deeper, at another level we want happiness, we want freedom, we want to have the capacity to do things grandly, greatly, magnificently. And if we go still deeper, we want to find out what there is beyond death, and what is love, to work for an ideal, for a perfect state. And if we go deeper still, there is the desire to find out what is reality, what is God, what is this thing that is so creative, that is always new. And we are caught between these many layers, are we not? We would like to have all of them. We want to live in perfect relationship; we want to work collectively, to have the right vocation, and so on. We are constantly seeking something, even though we may not be fully aware of it. Perhaps we have never inquired into the matter. We just drift along, pushed by circumstances until death comes, and there is the end of things, or perhaps the beginning of a new torture.

So, we have never really sat down and looked into ourselves to find out what it is that we are searching after. I think if we can find that out, not merely at the superficial level, but fundamentally, deeply, what it is we want, then I think we shall be able to solve this question of mediocrity and decay. Because, most of us are mediocre. We have nothing alive, nothing new, nothing creative in us. Anything that we create is so empty, so tawdry, with such little significance. So, should we not find out what it is that we want?

If we really examine it, go into it, we find we want something permanent, don't we?—permanent love, a state of permanent peace, a joy that can never vanish, that can never fade, the realization of some beauty, a perfection. We want, do we not, a state in which there is joy and permanency. That is what most of us are searching for, to find a permanent state—something that cannot be destroyed by the mind, by any circumstances, by any physical disease, something that is beyond the mind, a joy that does not depend on the body, a creativeness that is independent of the withering effect of the mind. Surely that is what most of us want, do we not? Perhaps not when we are young, but as we grow old, more thoughtful, more mature, we want something permanent. That is what most of us are seeking, are we not? Put it in any other words you like, but that is the direction of our striving.

Now, is there anything permanent? Though I want it, though in my longing, in my search, in my struggle I am constantly seeking that state which can never be destroyed, a state which is beyond the mind, is there really anything permanent which the mind can have? Most of us want a permanent relationship of love, a permanent experience which is timeless, a thing that can never be destroyed. That is what most of us want, if we go beyond the superficial, immediate demands. But is not this demand for the permanency of experience, of knowledge, for the continuity of a certain state, is that not one of the main factors of deterioration? Because, is there anything permanent? Yet the mind is forever pursuing and seeking out a state which will be forever the same. If I have an experience which gives me joy, I want that state to continue forever; I do not want to be disturbed from it. So the mind clings to that experience.

So, if I want to find out, must I not inquire if there is anything permanent at all?

Surely, to find out if there is something which is beyond the mind, must I not put aside in myself any demand for the continued state? Because, after all, to find creativity—not the mere writing of a poem or the painting of a picture, but creativity which is of no time, which is not the invention of the mind, not a mere capacity or gift, but that creativity which is ever renewing itself—must not the mind be capable of being enthusiastic and persistent in its inquiry? Most of us as we grow older lose our enthusiasm—which is not the superficial enthusiasm of certain actions, which is not the enthusiasm that one has when one is searching with an end in view, when one is going to be rewarded, but which is that enthusiasm which is not dependent on the body, that enthusiasm which is constantly probing, inquiring, searching out, never satisfied.

Now, to be free to inquire, must there not be virtue? Because, the virtue that gives freedom is not the virtue that is pursued, caught, and cultivated, for that only creates respectability, which is the sign of mediocrity. But without the cultivation of virtue, to be virtuous is essential, is it not, if one would find out what is true without any illusion. So I want to find out if there is something beyond the mind, something which is permanent. And to find out, there must be freedom to inquire, that extraordinary vitality of the mind which is not dependent on the physical state. To inquire, there must be freedom, and virtue gives freedom, but not the virtue that one cultivates, which is merely a bondage.

So, to inquire, to find out, must there not be that innocence which is not contaminated by experience? Because if experience is used as a guide to inquiry, then experience conditions thought, does it not? Whatever experience I have conditions all further experience. All knowledge conditions further knowledge, does it not, because my experience interprets every reaction. All experiences are translated by past experience. So, experience is never liberating; it is always conditioning. So, can the mind be innocent, free of knowledge, free of memory, free of experience? Because, after all, that is innocence, is it not? The mind that is burdened with knowledge, with experience, with memory, such a mind is not an innocent mind.

So, in order to find out if there is a permanent state, must there not be that virtue, that enthusiasm, that innocence? Then only, it seems to me, can we go beyond the demands of the mind. Because the mind, when it inquires, can never find that which is true. The mind can only project from its past experiences, and what it finds will be the effects of its own conditioning, its own knowledge, its own experience.

So, can one find out what is creativity or God or whatever name you like to give to it? Because that is the one factor that makes all things new. Though I may be living with death, when there is that creativity, death has quite a different significance. That creativity frees the mind from all mediocrity, from all deterioration. And if that is the thing which I am seeking, I have to be very clear, have I not, so as not to create any illusion, so as to free the mind to really discover—which means, surely, that the mind must be utterly still to find out. Because, creativity cannot be invited; it has to come to you, to the mind. God cannot be invited; it has to come. And it cannot come when the mind is not free. And freedom is not the outcome of a discipline.

So, our problem is really very complex. Unconsciously we are pursuing, we are demanding, we are longing for some permanent quality, permanent state. And this desire for permanency, for security, brings about mediocrity, deterioration. Because that is what we want, do we not, psychological security. And by devious means and ways, we try to capture it. But if once we really understand that there is no such thing as psychological security, then there is no decay, is there, because then there is no resting place. There is decay only when there is something permanent, something continuous. But when there is a constant ending, constant dying, then there is a constant renewal which is not continuous.

Please, this is not something mystical. If you really listen to what I am saying, then you will experience something directly, which frees the mind from all this horror of trying to be secure in some corner. It is only when the mind is really free that it is able to receive that which is creative.

Question: What, precisely, do you want to do, and are you really doing it? Do you just want to talk?

KRISHNAMURTI: I am not turning the tables on you. But precisely why are you here? Why do you listen? Why do you attend these meetings? I may perhaps answer why I talk, but it is much more important for you to find out, is it not, why you are here. Because, if you are here merely to listen to another talk, to another lecture, to capture some mysterious something or other, surely that would be utterly a waste of time, would it not? But if you are here to find out, to actually discover for yourself, to actually experience, then it is very important to find out the relationship between you and me. If our relationship is of one who instructs you, and you who listen and follow, then you will never discover; you are merely followers. Then there is no creativity; in yourself there is no renewal. And if you are merely listening to find out a state, a feeling, which you can take home and keep, then obviously our relationship is not mutual.

But if in listening you are discovering yourself, how your mind thinks, operates, functions—which is the whole problem of existence—then as you discover it, understand it, your being here has value, has it not? If in listening there is an awakening, a revolution in the right sense of the word, if there is a deep, inward, psychological revolution which brings about a wider, more significant understanding, then your being here has significance, has value.

And what is it that I am trying to do? Talking is only a means of communication, is it not? I want to tell you something, perhaps the way to find out what is reality—not the way as a system, but how to set about it. And if you can find this for yourself, there will not be one speaker, there will be all of us talking, all of us expressing that reality in our lives wherever we are. That is what is important, is it not? Because, one solitary voice has very little significance in a world of confusion, in a world of so much noise. But if each one of us is discovering reality, then there will be the more of us. Then perhaps we may be able to bring about a totally different world. That is why I am talking, and I hope that is why you are listening, so that each one of us is alive to himself, so that each one of us is creative, free to discover what truth is, what reality, what God is, not ultimately, but from moment to moment, without any sense of accumulation.

Truth cannot be accumulated. What is accumulated is always being destroyed; it withers away. Truth can never wither because it can only be found from moment to moment in every thought, in every relationship, in every word, in every gesture, in a smile, in tears. And if you and I can find that and live it—the very living is the finding of it—then we shall not become propagandists; we shall be creative human beings—not perfect human beings, but creative human beings, which is vastly different. And that, I think, is why I am talking, and perhaps that is why you are here listening.

Question: How can I free myself from my conditioning?

KRISHNAMURTI: As this is rather an important and complex question, let us patiently go into it. Because, perhaps by very careful delving into the problem, we shall be able to free the mind from its conditioning immediately.

Most of us are conditioned, are we not? We may be unaware of it, but we are conditioned as Christians, as the English, as the French, as the Germans, as the Communists, as the Hindus, and so on; we are all conditioned. That is, I have certain beliefs, certain experiences, knowledge which is imposed upon me from childhood through education, through various forms of compulsion, and also my own experiences have conditioned me. Religiously, you and I are conditioned, and also politically, economically, in various ways, consciously or unconsciously, we are conditioned. Perhaps we are not aware of it. And when we do become aware of it, then what happens?

I am aware that I have been conditioned as a Hindu, with certain beliefs. And being dissatisfied with those beliefs, I turn to other forms of belief: I become a Christian or a Buddhist or a Communist. So, my movement is always from what I am to something which I think is better. That is what is happening constantly, is it not? I am moving from what I am, hoping to break what I am, the conditioned state in which I live, by moving away from it to something better, to another conditioning. That is always so, is it not?

Please, this is not a question of argument, to be discussed and torn to pieces, but this is actually what is happening in our daily life. We are moving from one conditioned state to another conditioned state which we think is better, wider, more significant, of greater value, more helpful, and so on. And when the questioner says, "Can I be free from conditioning?" does he mean entirely, totally free, or is he inquiring for a better conditioning? Do I, as a Hindu, want to break down my conditioning totally, or do I want to go to a better conditioning?

Please ask yourself this question. Because, on that depends the answer, the right answer, the truth of the matter. If I am aware of the conditioning, do I want to break down totally my conditioning, or do I merely want to go to another, better, superior conditioning? If I merely want to go towards a better conditioning, then the problem is entirely different. There may be a better conditioning, or there may not be. It may be merely another illusion in which the mind is caught. But if I want to find out, break down the total conditioning, then my problem is entirely different. Because then, I am not concerned with moving towards something else. Then I am concerned with being aware of the total process of conditioning.

Now, if I am so aware, what is the thing that is conditioning me? What is it that conditions the mind? I am a Hindu. What is a Hindu? Certain traditions, beliefs, customs, and so on, which are all ideas, thoughts, are they not? You as a Christian are conditioned by certain other ideas, by certain other beliefs. So, one is conditioned by the idea. As long as there is the idea, there must be conditioning. As long as I believe as a Hindu, that belief conditions me. As long as you believe in certain forms of salvation, that idea conditions you. So conditioning takes place when there is idea.

And when you say, "I want to be free from conditioning," what is your immediate response? Do you understand? That is, I say, "I must be free from conditioning." The immediate response to that question is, "How am I going to be free?" is it not? The "how" becomes very important; the "how" is the immediate reaction, is it not? If I am aware of my conditioning, and I see the importance of breaking it down, the immediate reaction after that is to ask myself, "How am I going to break it down?"

So, the "how" is again the idea, is it not? I am again caught in the idea of how to break it down. So the "how" becomes the pattern of action, which conditions my mind. So as long as I am looking at my conditioning with the idea of how to break it down, the "how" creates another pattern in which the mind is caught.

So, how do I look at my conditioning? With an idea? Or, am I breaking it down? I do not know if I am making it clear. Because, I think it is really important to find out whether we are dealing with idea or with actuality. Because, after all, when I call myself a Communist, I have certain ideas, and if I want to break down those ideas, I do so by introducing another series of ideas, do I not? So I am always dealing with ideas. And ideas obviously are the conditioning factor.

So, as long as I am dealing with ideas, conditioning will go on. Because, my conditioned state is merely a set of ideas. And I can only break down that conditioning, not through further ideas, but by being free from the idea altogether. I believe, as a Christian, in a Savior; that is an idea. And to be free from that conditioning, I cannot introduce another idea. Yet that is what the mind is always doing. I can only be free when the idea is not. So, the conditioned mind can never be free through ideas because the ideas themselves, thought and belief, condition the mind. It is only when the mind is free from the creation of ideas that there is immediate freedom from conditioning.

Question: In the past I have done harm. How can I now achieve peace of mind?

KRISHNAMURTI: We all make mistakes, do we not? We all hurt people; we make grave mistakes. And it has left a mark, regret, repentance. And, how is one to be free from the mistake that one has made? Will repentance dissolve the mistake? It is done. My repenting over it, will that wipe it away? My calling it a sin, will that wipe it away? Or, confessing it to you, will that wipe it away? What will free my mind, my being, my consciousness, from the error, from a grave mistake that I have made?

Surely this is our problem, is it not? Because, the moment we say, "We must never make a mistake," then we are working for an ideal—the perfect man—which is again an idea which will condition the mind. We do make mistakes; that is a fact. So, how are we to deal with a mistake that we have made, a grave error?

Now, what does the mind do with regard to that error? How does the mind respond? I know I have made a mistake; I have hurt somebody. What am I to do? I can go and apologize, but the fact remains: I have done harm. Now, how does the mind respond to that? What is its next action? It wants to put it right, does it not? It has already put it right in the sense that it goes to the person and apologizes for whatever it has done, and so on; that is the ordinary thing to do. But the mistake, the hurt, is still there. So, is it not important for me to find out how my mind reacts to that mistake which I have made?

Is it not occupied with that mistake, building it up, enlarging it, being concerned with it everlastingly, dreaming about it, condemning itself? That is what most of us do, do we not? So, the very occupation of the mind with a mistake that has already been made becomes another mistake. From that there arises the idea of forgiveness, repentance, and so on—the continual occupation of the mind with an error. It is done; you have tried to correct it, but the occupation of the mind with the mistake is another form of the mind trying to correct it, without any effect.

So, as long as I am concerned with the mistake, with the error, with the hurt, and my mind is occupied with it, it becomes a fixation, does it not; it becomes another barrier. The fact is: I have made a mistake; all that I am now concerned with is to see why the mind not only occupies itself with the mistake, with the error, but why the mind is frightened of ever making a mistake. Because, as long as I live and you live, we are hurting each other in some way or other. Though I don't want to hurt you and you don't want to hurt me, we are hurting each other in most subtle ways. And, what am I to do? Am I to withdraw completely into isolation? The very existence of me, the very breath of me, destroys; I am exploiting somebody and somebody else is exploiting me. So, realizing that, shall I withdraw into isolation and never move?

Whereas, if I know how to meet the errors, the mistakes, that I have made, then there is a freedom, is there not? Then I will know what to do. So I do not say to myself that the perfect entity will never make a mistake. But, after making the mistake, can I not acknowledge it and then let it go by and not be occupied with it? Because, that gives a freedom to the mind, to be conscious that one has made a mistake and to acknowledge it, to do what has to be done about it, and then to let it go by, and not be occupied with it.

That requires a great deal of understanding, a great deal of subtle freedom. To know that one is capable of making a mistake and not have a standard according to which one is living, that way the mind is set free to make, perhaps, more mistakes. But, to know how to deal with the mistake is what is so very important. The important thing is to acknowledge it and leave it alone, not to worry, not to be occupied with it.

Question: Is there any possibility of the individual becoming perfect and so creating a perfect world?

KRISHNAMURTI: Can the individual, you and I, become perfect and so create a perfect world? Again, we are dealing with ideas, are we not? The perfect man is the ideal man, the man which the mind has conceived as being perfect. Mind has conceived and projected that pattern, and I live according to that. The mind projects the idea of the perfect state and tries to bring this perfect state about. That is, we are concerned only with the mind when we say, "Can man be perfect?" And when you say, "We want to create a perfect state," it is still again within the field of the mind.

So, when perfection, reform, is within the field of the mind, then, to produce the perfect state, there is cruelty; then there is liquidation, concentration camps, tyranny; you know the whole business of it. So long as we consider that man can be made perfect, then brutality is endless. The mind then is only dealing with ideas, and idea has no relationship with reality.

But, can the mind discover what is real, not the idea of what is real? Can the mind allow reality to come into being? If it does, then the relationship of man to man, of man to society, is entirely different. After all, if I want to create a perfect state, then I not only compel myself to live according to a certain pattern of thought, but I also compel others to live according to that ideal pattern. The perfect man is never a free man. It is the most materialistic form of achievement; it is not spiritual at all—the idea that man should become perfect.

But, man can find what is true, what is the real, what is God. And then, reality can operate. Then that reality will produce quite a different state from the perfect state which the mind can think of. So, we must first seek reality, not how to make ourselves perfect or to make society perfect.

So, can the mind which is conditioned, which is perpetually seeking perfection as a security, can such a mind free itself from the idea of perfection and seek reality? Because, we do not know what reality is. Mind can only deal with ideas; it cannot deal with a fact. It can translate the fact, it can interpret the fact, but the mind is not the fact. So, as long as I am seeking perfection, I am not seeking God, truth. And if I am seeking a perfect state, then I inevitably create a society in which compulsion, every form of coercion, discipline, tyranny, becomes essential. But if I am seeking reality, seeking the unknown, the unknowable, then there is a possibility of creating a different world.

But to find the unknown, mind must be extraordinarily quiet; it cannot be projecting ideas. Because, the very idea controls the mind, conditions the mind. A conditioned mind is not a perfect mind, is not a free mind. It is only when the mind is free from idea that there is a possibility for it to receive that which is creative.

April 1, 1953

Fourth Talk in London

I think if one can understand the power that creates superstition, then there is a possibility of understanding what is true religion. But without understanding or going deeply into the matter of this problem of illusion, what it is that breeds illusion, without deeply and fully comprehending that, it is almost impossible to find what reality is. Most of us have got so many illusions, so many superstitions. We have not only the economic superstition of the perfect state, the illusion of creating a perfect man, but also the superstition of what reality is or what God is. And is it possible to free the mind from creating, from breeding, throwing up any kind of illusion so that we can find out what truth is without any barrier, without any interpretation, see it simply and directly with a clear mind, a mind that does not have premeditated ideas, theories, speculations?

It seems to me it is very important, if we are at all earnest, to find out how this sense of illusion arises, this feeling that one is caught in a trap of one's own making. So perhaps we can really go into it and dissolve it, not bit by bit, slowly, gradually, but completely because I do not think there is such a thing as the gradual dissolution of any particular idea, superstition, or desire; either one dissolves it completely or not at all.

Is it possible to dissolve the power that creates illusion? Most of our religions throughout the world are ritualistic, dogmatic; they condition our thinking. We have been brought up in a particular pattern of thought or action, and our mind clings to it. And it seems almost impossible, being born in a particular pattern of philosophy, organized thought, to free the mind from its symbols, from the words which we have learned since childhood.

To find out what is reality, surely mind must be extraordinarily free, without any symbol, without any reaction to a particular word, without projecting ideas or experiences that it has had so that the mind is very clear, very simple, and direct, without any illusion or the power to create illusion.

Now, what is it that makes for illusion? Is it not the desire, the wish, to seek comfort, to seek gratification, salvation, this desire for fundamental security, this deep demand for some kind of hope, for some escape from deep frustration? Does not the power to create illusion arise when the mind puts out a hand in supplication, in petition, wanting to know? Because, behind that desire there is the whole unconscious background of our conditioning, of the innumerable impulses, fears, anxieties, the conditionings of a particular race, of a particular philosophy. And with that background we demand a salvation, a comfort, a hope. Because we cannot find in this world happiness, a sense of freedom, a complete fulfillment without any fear or frustration, so we turn to the other world. We know we cannot be perfect in this world; man cannot make himself perfect because he can only make himself perfect through his own mind, and mind can never make itself perfect. Mind can never be free from thought, and thought conditions the mind. So we look to various forms of salvation, trying to find out what is reality, what is God, what is happiness, what is immortality, something beyond and above the transient. So the mind already in its demands, through its desire, is creating further illusion.

Can such a mind, which is wanting, desiring to find, discover what is the real? I think it is very important to go into this matter. Because as long as we are seeking without understanding the background, we shall find what we seek, but it will be an illusion.

So, can I free myself from my background without going through the process of analysis? Because I can see that by analyzing the background, I have not resolved it. I can strip, I can explain, I can see the various implications involved in it, but I am not free of it; the mind is still unconsciously held by it. Because, there is still the analyzer observing, and therefore the analyzer always translating what he observes, according to his conditioning.

So, can I be entirely free from the background, not in some distant future, but now, so as to be able to stop creating any form of desire for truth, for happiness, for some unknown thing? Because, desire is the root cause, is it not, of this creating of illusions to which the mind clings. And can I be free from psychological desire, not through any compulsion, not through any discipline, resistance, but by seeing the significance of this feeling, of this demand for more and more and more? I want more knowledge, more virtues, more freedom, more happiness; I want to understand more. Surely it is the demand for the 'more' that creates the illusion—which does not mean I must be content with what I have. If I am content with what I have, that is also another form of illusion because I can never be content with what I am, with what I have accumulated.

So, can the mind free itself from this demand for the 'more'? This means, really, can the mind recognize *what is* without trying to alter, without trying to transform *what is* into 'something that should be'? Can one psychologically, deeply, inwardly, understand this thing—that the demand for the 'more' creates the illusion? Because, mind then invents the process of time: "Ultimately, through perfection, through perfecting the mind, by cultivating virtue, I will attain that happiness." So the mind is everlastingly struggling, experiencing, gathering, in order to be free, in order to recognize what is true.

So, can I completely strip myself of this desire for more, completely put it away from myself? I think one can if one understands the whole implication, if one really listens to the inward nature of it, the unconscious urges of the moment. I think then there is a possibility of breaking down the power that creates illusion. After all, that is what we all want. We want more and more comfort, more and more happiness, more and more assurance, certainty. And being caught in that, the mind creates the pattern of action which will give the 'more'.

Surely we have had enough explanations, descriptions. And if we are at all serious, if we really, earnestly are intending to find out what is true, surely we have put aside all explanations, words, and we are concerned directly with trying to find out. But our mind is incapable of finding out so long as we want more.

So it seems to me that the important thing is for the mind to be in a state when it can allow itself not to ask, not to demand—which does not mean acquiescence, acceptance, but that the mind is really silent. The mind being thought—thought as the verbalization of certain experiences, thought as memory, thought that is seeking, investigating—cannot such thinking come to an end, so that the mind is no longer projecting, is really still? For then only is it possible for the mind to be free from all illusion. Then only shall we find out what is reality—not the description of reality, not the explanations, not the speculations, not the reality of someone else who has experienced it; those things are utterly valueless; they have no meaning. But when the mind is really in that state when thought as we know it has come to an end—thought which is always strengthening the background of the conditioned mind—then we shall find out what that nameless thing is.

But it is very difficult for the mind to be quiet, for it not to project, seek, try to find out. That stillness can only come not through any form of well-thought-out pattern of action but when we understand this whole problem of the power of the mind to create anything it desires—the Master, the savior, the various forms of innumerable superstitions in which we are caught. So, can the mind, my mind and your mind, not through any sense of compulsion, come to that extraordinary stillness, that peace of mind which is not of its own creation? It is only possible when I understand the necessity of it, when having wandered through all this labyrinth of illusions, I have finished with it. Then only is there a possibility of reality coming into being.

Question: Looking at my fellow creatures in bus or tube, I find everyone, myself included, mediocre and commonplace. How can I tolerate this ugliness of everyday life?

KRISHNAMURTI: We ourselves are mediocre; we ourselves are ugly. We do not have to look at our neighbors; we do not have to look at the woman or the man sitting across the other seat in the tube or the bus. We have lost all vitality, all zest, all true appreciation of beauty. Our life is a routine, a boredom, a thing really that has no great significance. So being ourselves ugly, mediocre, what is our reaction? When I recognize that I am ugly, mediocre, that my whole life has very little significance, being merely the routine that I have to carry on with, on recognizing that, what is my immediate reaction? I condemn it, do I not? I condemn mediocrity; I want to be more beautiful, I want to have a different quality, I want to have joy, a sense of freedom. So I cling to beauty, do I not? I want to have beauty. So I cultivate beauty and condemn the mediocre, the ugly. That is our normal reaction, is it not?

And when I condemn, have I understood, have I changed in any way, has there been some new thing taking place? All that I am concerned with is the cultivation of beauty. I want that; I want to be sensitive to beauty, and I want to put away the ugly. But the putting away of the ugly and holding on to beauty makes me insensitive, does it not? Please see this. When I deny the ugly, condemn it, try to put it away from me, am I not becoming less sensitive to beauty? It is like cutting away my own arm which is ugly and trying to cultivate beauty in other directions.

Is it not important to be totally sensitive, not merely sensitive to one thing? And does sensitivity arise through condemnation of that which I think is ugly? If I condemn envy, saying it is ugly, am I sensitive to that state in which there is envy? Have I not to be totally sensitive both to envy and to that state which is not envious? So, the important thing is sensitivity, is it not?—not how to be more beautiful or more virtuous, not how to avoid the ugly, the everyday hideousness of life, but to be sensitive to both. I cannot be sensitive if I condemn and hold on to one particular thought, idea, or picture which I think is beautiful. If I see all that, then I do not condemn, I do not say, "It is ugly, mediocre." Then I see that the very word has a neurological significance; it acts upon me, as the word *beauty* acts upon me.

So it is important, is it not, to be sensitive both to the ugly and to the beautiful. Then there is a possibility of observation, of looking across at the ugly without condemning it. And out of that sensitivity, something new may arise, a quality of love. But love is not something to be cultivated; it comes only if we can understand this whole background of our condemnation. Every society, every religion, every culture, condemns; we are brought up to condemn, to judge, to weigh, to say, "This is right, this is wrong"—not that there is not right and wrong. Our instinctual response is to condemn, which is a form of resistance, and through resistance there can be no sensitivity either to beauty or to ugliness.

But if we do not condemn, perhaps there may be a new breath, a new vitality, a feeling of love which will transform, which will give a different outlook to our ugly daily life.

Question: I feel very lonely and long for some intimate human relationship. Since I can find no such companion, what am I to do?

KRISHNAMURTI: One of our difficulties is, surely, that we want to be happy through something, through a person, through a symbol, through an idea, through virtue, through action, through companionship. We think happiness or reality or what you like to call it can be found through something. Therefore we feel that through action, through companionship, through certain ideas, we will find happiness.

So, being lonely, I want to find someone or some idea through which I can be happy. But loneliness always remains; it is ever there, under cover. But as it frightens me, and as I do not know what the inward nature of this loneliness is, therefore I want to find something to which to cling. So I think that through something, through a person, I will be happy. So, our mind is always concerned with finding something. Through furniture, through a house, through books, through people, through ideas, through rituals, through symbols, we hope to get something, to find happiness. And so the things, the people, the ideas become extraordinarily important because through them we hope we shall find. So we begin to be dependent on them.

But with it all there is still this thing not understood, not resolved; the anxiety, the fear, is still there. And even when I see that it is still there, then I want to use it, to go through, to find what is beyond. So my mind uses everything as a means to go beyond and so makes everything trivial. If I use you for my fulfillment, for my happiness, you become very unimportant because it is my happiness I am concerned with. So, when the mind is concerned with the idea that it can have happiness through somebody, through a thing or through an idea, do I not make all these means transitory? Because, my concern is then something else, to go further, to catch something beyond.

So, is it not very important that I should understand this loneliness, this ache, this pain of extraordinary emptiness? Because if I understand that, perhaps I shall not use anything to find happiness; I shall not use God as a means to acquire peace or a ritual in order to have more sensations, exaltations, inspirations. The thing which is eating my heart out is this sense of fear, my loneliness, my emptiness. Can I understand that? Can I resolve that? Most of us are lonely, are we not? Do what we will, radio, books, politics, religion, none of these can really cover that loneliness. I may be socially active; I may identify myself with certain organized philosophies, but whatever I do, it is still there, deep down in my unconscious or in the deeper depths of my being.

So, how am I to deal with it? How am I to bring it out and completely resolve it? Again, my whole tendency is to condemn, is it not? The thing which I do not know, I am afraid of, and the fear is the outcome of condemnation. After all, I do not know the quality of loneliness, what it actually is. But my mind has judged it by saying it is fearful. It has opinions about the fact; it has ideas about loneliness. And it is these ideas, opinions, that create the fear and prevent me from really looking at that loneliness.

I hope I am making myself clear. I am lonely, and I am afraid of it. What causes the fear? Is it not because I do not know the implications involved in loneliness? If I knew the content of loneliness, then I would not be afraid of it. But because I have an idea of what it might be, I run away from it. The very running away creates the fear, not the looking at it. To look at it, to be with it, I cannot condemn. And when I am capable of facing it, then I am capable of loving it, of looking into it.

Then, is that loneliness of which I am afraid merely a word? Is it not actually a state which is essential, the door maybe through which I shall find out? Because, that door may lead me further so that the mind comprehends that state in which it must be alone, uncontaminated. Because all other processes away from that loneliness are deviations, escapes, distractions. If the mind can live with it without condemning it, then perhaps through that the mind will find that state which is alone, a mind that is not lonely but completely alone, not dependent, not through seeking something to find.

It is not necessary to be alone to know that aloneness which is not induced by circumstances, that aloneness which is not isolation, that aloneness which is creativeness, when the mind is no longer seeking either happiness, virtue, or creating resistance. It is the mind which is alone that can find—not the mind which has been contaminated, made corrupt, by its own experiences. So perhaps loneliness, of which we are all aware, if we know how to look at it, may open the door to reality.

Question: I am dependent, primarily psychologically, on others. I want to be free from this dependence. Please show me the way to be free.

KRISHNAMURTI: Psychologically, inwardly, we are dependent, are we not, on rituals, on ideas, people, things, property. We are dependent, and we want to be free from that dependence because it gives us pain. As long as that dependence is satisfactory, as long as I find happiness in it, I do not want to be free. But when the dependence hurts me, when it gives pain, when the thing on which I have depended runs away from me, dies, withers away, looks at somebody else, then I want to be free.

But do I want to be free totally from all psychological dependence or only from those dependencies which give me pain? Obviously, from those dependencies and memories which give me pain. I do not want to be free totally from all dependencies; I only want to be free from the particular dependence. So, I seek ways and means to free myself, and I ask others, someone else, to help me to free myself from a particular dependence which causes pain. I do not want to be free from the total process of dependence.

And, can another help me to be free from dependence, the partial dependence or the total dependence? Can I show you the way—the way being the explanation, the word, the technique? By showing you the way, the technique, giving you an explanation, will you be free? You have still the problem, have you not; you have still the pain of it. No amount of my showing you how to deal with it, your discussing it with me, will free you from that dependence. So, what is one to do?

Please see the importance of this. You are asking for a method which will free you from a particular dependence or from total dependence. The method is an explanation, is it not, which you are going to practice and live in order to free yourself. So, the method becomes another dependence. In trying to free yourself from a particular dependence, you have introduced another form of dependence.

But if you are concerned with the total freedom from all psychological dependence, if you are really concerned with that, then you will not ask for a method, the way. Then you ask quite a different question, do you not? You ask if you can have the capacity to deal with it, the possibility of dealing with that dependence. So the question is not how to free myself from a dependence but, "Can I have the capacity to deal with the whole problem?" If I have the capacity, then I do not depend on anybody. It is only when I say I have not the capacity that I ask, "Please help me, show me a way." But if I have the capacity to deal with a problem of dependence, then I do not ask anyone to help me to dissolve it.

I hope I am making myself clear. Because I think it is very important not to ask, "How?" but, "Can I have the capacity to deal with the problem?" Because, if I know how to deal with it, then I am free of the problem. So, I am no longer asking for a method, the way. But, can I have the capacity to deal with the problem of dependence?

Now, psychologically, when you put that question to yourself, what happens? When you consciously put the question, "Can I have the capacity to free myself from that dependence?" what has psychologically happened? Are you not already free from that dependence? Psychologically you have depended, and now you say, "Have I the capacity to free myself?" Obviously, the moment you put that question earnestly to yourself, there is already freedom from that dependence.

Please, I hope you are following not merely verbally but actually experiencing what we are discussing. Because, that is the art of listening, is it not? Not to merely listen to my words, but to listen to what is actually taking place in your own mind.

When I know that I can have that capacity, then the problem ceases to be. But because I have not the capacity, I want to be shown. So I create the Master, the guru, the savior, someone who is going to save me, who is going to help me. So I become dependent on them. Whereas if I can have that capacity of resolving, understanding the question, then it is very simple, then I am no longer dependent.

This does not mean I am full of self-confidence. The confidence which comes into being through the self, the 'me', does not lead anywhere because that confidence is self-enclosing. But the very question, "Can I have the capacity to discover reality?" gives one an extraordinary insight and strength. The question is not that I have capacity—I have not the capacity—but "Can I have it?" Then I shall know how to open the door which the mind is everlastingly closing by its own doubts, by its own anxieties, fears, by its experiences, knowledge.

So when the whole process is seen, the capacity is there. But that capacity is not to be found through any particular pattern of action. I cannot comprehend the whole through the particular. Through a particular analysis of a special problem, I shall not comprehend the whole. So, can I have the capacity to see the whole, not to understand one particular incident, one particular happening, but to see the whole, total process of my life with its sorrows, pains, joys, the everlasting search for comfort? If I can put that question in earnestness, then the capacity is there.

And with that capacity I can deal with all the problems that arise. There will always be problems, always incidents, reactions; that is life. Because I do not know how to deal with them, I go to others to find out, to ask for the way to deal with it. But when I put the question, "Can I have the capacity?" it is already the beginning of that confidence which is not the confidence of the 'me', of the self, not the confidence which comes into being through accumulation but that confidence which is renewing itself constantly, not through any particular experience or any incident, but which comes through understanding, through freedom, so that the mind can find that which is real.

April 7, 1953

Fifth Talk in London

I would like this evening for us to consider a problem that may be rather difficult to go into; I want to talk over with you the problem of consciousness. Because, without understanding the function of the mind, what the mind is, however much one may earnestly seek to transform oneself, to bring about a deep, fundamental revolution in oneself, it seems to me that it will not be possible. It is obviously a very difficult subject. Because, each one of us has very definite opinions, unfortunately, on what the mind is or should be. We have, after reading a great many books, come to definite conclusions about what consciousness is. But perhaps if we can put aside our particular knowledge, the things that we have learned, the things that we have experienced, if that is possible, and examine it anew, then we may find out how to bring about this fundamental transformation and not merely a superficial change.

So, what is the function of the mind? Can the mind bring about an entire change, transform itself? And the 'I', the 'me', the ego, is that different from the mind? At whatever level one may place the 'I', the ego, the 'me', and however much it may struggle to bring about a transformation within itself, is that not still within the field of the mind, of consciousness? And can there be a transformation—not permanent in the sense of continuity, but a complete revolution within itself—without any cause, without any motive, without any desire to seek a result?

I think if one can go rather hesitantly into this question of what is consciousness and what the function of the mind is, then we may be able to discover what is wisdom.

So, what is consciousness? What is the thing that is functioning all the time, that chooses, that struggles, that creates ideals, images, symbols, that allows itself to be conditioned and demands to uncondition itself, that feels pain and avoids any pursuit that might entail fear? What is this thing that is constantly seeking permanency, comfort, security, and what it calls God? What is this total thing—not just the superficial part that shrinks through fear or enlarges through pleasure? What is this 'me'—the 'me' that is constantly endeavoring to become better, the 'me' that allows itself to be disciplined in order to achieve a result, the thing that is driven by ambition, that is always seeking to overcome any barrier, and so always being afraid of frustration—and where is its center?

Is not all this what we call consciousness—not only the consciousness that is functioning daily, but also the consciousness that is hidden, the consciousness of the race, in which all the traditions of the past are embedded? The things that one has learned, the things that one has acquired, the experiences, the prejudices, and so on, and also, the 'me' that tries to go beyond the limitations, the conditionings, is not all that our consciousness?

And is not the unconscious a part of the whole of mankind? Is not my unconscious the totality of the thought of India, as yours is of another race, another clime?

Is not all this, the total process, what we call consciousness? Is not that the mind—the mind being the result of time, of cultivation, the 'me' that is always being put together through contact, sensation, desire, and the accumulation of experience through that desire? And, when we talk of experience, is it not memory, the word, the symbol, the idea? So, as we—plain people, not very highly theological or erudite people—know it, that is our mind, is not? That is our consciousness—desire, experience, memory, and knowledge—and within that sphere we function.

Will the consciousness of the 'me' bring about wisdom? Will knowledge bring about wisdom—not the wisdom of books, not the wisdom that one learns through going to a school of wisdom?

So, what I want to find out is, can the mind which is the product of time—which has been put together through experience, through memory, through symbols; which is constantly aspiring, despairing, hoping, feeling itself frustrated, in bondage, in pain, in misery; which is ever choosing, and in its very choice being caught by the bigger choice, the better choice—can that mind discover what is wisdom, what is truth, what is God? And if the mind experiences reality, is not that mind of the nature of reality at the time when it experiences reality?

You follow what I mean? I see that my mind is the result of time. That is fairly obvious; we need not go into that in too great detail. It has been put together through generations of experience. I am the result of all the thought, the struggles, the pain, the superstitions of the world; my mind is that. And yet, this mind is seeking some reality which obviously must be out of time, which cannot be gathered, accumulated, stored up to be used. And, yet, the mind being the only instrument with which we can feel, experience, surely in the moment of experiencing reality, the mind is of the quality of truth, the quality of timelessness?

So, how does this transformation take place? And can the 'I', the 'me', which is the result of time, bring about the change within itself, a transformation within itself? Because, that is our problem, is it not? I want to change; I want to bring about in myself a transformation. Because, my life is very dull; I am unhappy; I am conditioned; it is a constant struggle with the pleasures and joys and depressions that make up the 'me'. And in that consciousness, at the center, there must be a revolution. I do not want to change just on the outward periphery because that has no meaning. If I am at all serious and in earnest, I want a transformation at the center, a transformation which is not merely of time, of convenience, of varying moods, or even of necessity. And I have no other means than the mind. I cannot put aside my mind because I am the mind. The things which I think, the things which I feel, the aspirations, the longings, the fears, the loves and the hates, the inevitable death and the unknown—all that is me. And at the center of that self-consciousness there must be a revolution.

And how is that possible? Will the unconscious, which is the result also of time, will that bring about any revolution? Will the unconscious aid, help the conscious mind to stop accumulating so that at the center there is complete abnegation? I think this is very important. Even though I may put it clumsily, use words that have a different meaning to each one of us, that is the fundamental question, is it not? Because, every attempt leads to dreariness, leads to routine, to degeneration, to slow withering away. There are moments of supreme happiness, ecstasy, and then, a few days later, everything has faded away.

So, seeing all this extraordinary complexity, is it not necessary to inquire whether it is possible to come to that revolution, to that inner transformation, without the interference of the mind? Can the mind change itself? Can the mind transform itself? I know there are moments when it perceives reality, unbidden, unasked. At that moment the mind is the real. When the 'I' is no longer struggling, consciously or unconsciously, no longer trying to become something, when the 'I' is totally unaware of itself, at that moment that state of worship, that state of reality is there. And so, the mind at that moment is the real, is God.

So, the problem is, can the mind, which is the result of time, the mind which is the self, the 'me'—however much it may like to divide itself into the higher self and the lower self, as the observer and the observed—can that 'me' whose whole consciousness is the result of accumulation of experience, of memory, of knowledge, can that 'me' come to an end, without desiring, without hoping for the 'me' to be dissolved? Because, I have only one instrument, which is the mind, the mind which evaluates, judges, condemns. And can such a mind, which is of time, which is not of truth—the mind knows knowledge, but knowledge is not truth—suddenly cease, so that the other mind, the other state of being, the mind which experiences reality can be, and therefore the mind itself is the real.

By asking, by inquiring seriously, I think, one finds the answer. Can the mind, which is the only instrument we have, can the self cease to be, cease to accumulate? Can the mind which has accumulated knowledge, experience, memory, completely free itself? Can it allow itself to watch the memories, the experiences, knowledge, go by, and itself remain on the bank of the stream, as it were, without attaching itself to any particular memory, to any particular experience, and so, be free and remain anchored in its freedom?

Because we cannot put aside our knowledge or experiences or the memories, they are there. But we can watch them go by without clinging to any one of them, either the pleasurable or the painful. This is not a thing to be practiced. Because, the moment you practice, you are accumulating, and where there is accumulation, there is the strengthening of the 'me'. The 'me' of time, the 'me' that pursues virtue and cultivates virtue, is accumulating. Reality has nothing to do with acquired virtue. But yet, there must be the virtue of the nonaccumulative state. The man who is observing his experiences, his memories, his knowledge, watching them go by, he does not require virtue; he is not gathering. And when the mind is no longer accumulating, when the mind is awakened to the whole process of consciousness with all its memories, the unconscious motives, the impulses of generations, of centuries, and can let it pass by, then is not the mind out of time? Then is not the mind, though aware of the experiences, not holding on to them at all, no longer caught in the net of time?

Because, what makes for time is the occupation with memory, the capacity to distinguish different forms of memory. And is it possible for the mind to remain out of time, out of knowledge, which is memory, which is experience, which is the word, the symbol? Can it be free from that and so be out of time? Then is there not a fundamental revolution or transformation at the center? Because, then the mind is no longer struggling to achieve, to accumulate, to arrive. Then there is no fear. Then the mind in itself is the unknown; the mind in itself is the new, the uncontaminated. Therefore it is the real, the incorruptible, which is not of time.

Question: I find I am deeply afraid to give up certain habits which give me pleasure, and yet I feel I must give them up, as their hold on me is too great. What can I do?

KRISHNAMURTI: Can habits be broken without creating another habit? My problem is, surely, not that I want to give up one particular habit which is painful or cling to a habit which is pleasurable, but, can I be free from all the habit-forming mechanism? Can I be free from the whole pattern of action, not only from the particular, but from the whole pattern-making thought? That is, can I break down, be free from the thought, the pattern, which has been made, created for centuries, without creating another pattern? That is what most of us indulge in; we break one pattern and go and join, create, or take on another pattern. If I am a Hindu, I break it and become a communist, but it is still a pattern of thought, an organized philosophy. Or, if I am a communist, I break that and become a Catholic. So, I go from one pattern to another; that is my life. I am always seeking better patterns of action, better patterns of thought, a better framework of reference. I revolt against one pattern and take on another.

So, the problem is, can I, can the mind, break from all patterns? Can it be in revolt, not merely against any one particular pattern, but be essentially in revolt? When we are in revolt, we are against something, are we not? As a traditional Christian, I may be in revolt against communism, or the communist may be in revolt against capitalism. We are always in revolt against something, are we not? The very revolt against something creates the pattern. When I, as a Hindu, am against Christianity or communism, does it not create yet another pattern of action? So, can I be in revolt, not against something, but be in essence in a state of revolution?

That is the problem, is it not?—how to be in oneself in revolt, and not how to break down one pleasurable habit, one particular pattern of action, or how to find a better framework, another reference of ideas—because, we go through that process everlastingly; there is no end to it. But if I am concerned with breaking down the whole pattern-forming mind, must I not be in revolt, not against something, but be in myself in revolt? The pattern comes to an end, surely, only when I am not in opposition to something.

What is happening when I am in opposition, when I am against something, when one idea is opposed by another idea? If I, as a Hindu, am against Christianity, my idea opposes your idea. And it is this idea that creates the pattern, even though it may be a so-called new idea. So, if I would be free from all patterns, there must be revolt without a motive, a revolt without the new idea. Such a revolt is surely creative; that state is creativeness; it is the pure thing, unadulterated, uncorrupted because there is no hope even; it is not against anything; it is not caught in any particular pattern.

But that transformation is only possible when the mind understands the whole structure of the pattern, the whole process of idea opposing idea, belief opposing belief, one experience contradicting another experience. So long as the mind is caught in its own experience, in its own knowledge, it can never free itself; there must ever be the pattern. The mind can see, surely, how the patterns are made. The formation of idea to which the mind clings, the adherence to a belief, to a habit, to a pleasure, all these create the form, the framework, in which the mind is held. So, can the mind be free from idea?

Thought is the creator of the pattern; thought is always conditioned; there is no freedom in thought because what I think is the result of my background, and all thinking is the reaction to the background. So, the question is not how to be free of a particular pattern or habit of thought but whether the mind can be free from creating ideas, from clinging to belief, from holding on to experience, to knowledge, to memory. Then only is there a possibility of breaking the pattern, of being completely free of all pattern.

Question: Christians, including Roman Catholics, promise heaven. What do you offer?

KRISHNAMURTI: Why are you seeking heaven? Why are you wanting something? Why do you say, "Others give me something; what have you to offer?" If you are promised something because you are stretching out your hand, begging, is what you get the truth?

What is heaven, and what is hell? What is the heaven that religions offer? Security in some form or another, is it not? A hope, a reward, a better life, a greater happiness on the other side, salvation beyond death, and a secure place for each one of us hereafter. That is what we all want. And each religion promises the ultimate reward, so each religion has its own monopoly on heaven. This is what we want, and we create all these heavens and hells for ourselves. It is not merely that religions offer them; they are what we want. We want security; we want a permanent happiness, never to be in a state of unknowingness.

But, the unknown is reality. Heaven is a state of unknowingness, and hell is the state of knowing. And we are caught between the knowing and the unknowing. And as all our life is a state of knowing, we are always afraid of that which is not known. God, the real, the heaven, is the unknown. And we want a place in the unknown. So any religion, any state, any political party that promises us a place of security, we accept, and we become either Catholics, Communists or join some other organized philosophy. So long as we are seeking a permanent place—a happiness that knows no variety, no change, a peace that shall never be disturbed, that is everlasting—we shall find, we shall organize philosophies, religions that will satisfy us.

So, as long as I am seeking permanency, I shall create dogmas, beliefs. And in those dogmas, beliefs, theories, I shall be caught. And that is all we want. Fundamentally, deeply, we never want to be in a state in which there is no 'knowing'. Even though the thing that I have known becomes the routine, the chore, the tiresome, the unknown is something of which I am afraid. And as I feel there is the unknown, I want a place in that. So I am in constant battle between the thing that I know and the thing that I do not know. That is my hell.

So, is it possible for the mind to put aside all its knowledge, all its experiences, memories, and be in that state of unknowing? That is the mystery, is it not, not the mystery of superstition, dogmas, saviors, and Masters, but the mystery of the unknown. Cannot the mind itself become the unknown, be the unknown? That requires, does it not, extraordinary freedom from the known. So the mind, with the burden of the known, tries to capture the unknown. And there is this constant battle between the past and something not knowable by the mind which is caught in the past.

But when the mind is free from the past, the past of experience, of memory, of knowledge, then the mind is the unknown. To such a mind there is no death.

These are merely words unless you experience it. Unless it is a direct revolution which the unknown brings, mere repetition of words will have little meaning. And, is it possible for plain people like us to come to this thing? The simpler and plainer we are, the nearer. The man of erudition, the man of vast experience, the man who is burdened with innumerable memories can never come to it. But unfortunately the plain man, the ordinary man, is grasping to become the 'more', to become wiser, to acquire more knowledge. But if he remains simple, plain, not acquiring, then there is a possibility, is there not, for the mind itself to become the unknown. Therefore the mind itself becomes the heaven, the unfathomable.

Question: The words "the thinker and the thought are one" seem incomprehensible to me and arouse my resistance. Can you tell me why I find the idea so extremely difficult to understand?

KRISHNAMURTI: Probably the idea is difficult because you are meeting idea with idea, because we have been conditioned from childhood to think that there are two different states—the thinker and the thought, the higher self and the lower self, the God and the non-God—the one trying to dominate, control, shape the other. That is what we are always taught, are we not? We are conditioned in that way, prejudiced, biased. We think these two states are separate. And so there is a constant battle between the thinker and the thought.

Please notice your own minds, your own thoughts, and you will see this is an ordinary, everyday fact—there is the thinker controlling, disciplining his thought, shaping it, making it more noble, more virtuous, more respectable, inhibited. That is what we are doing, is it not?

And, if you are at all awake, why do you ask the question whether the thinker is separate? Is there a thinker as an entity, a spiritual essence, or call it what you like, a higher self, apart from thought? Is there a thinker apart from the very quality of thinking? Obviously not. If I do not think, there is no thinker. So, thinking creates the thinker.

Please, you do not have to accept anything I say; just observe your own ways of thought.

And so, we are everlastingly in conflict, the conflict between the thinker and his thought. I want to concentrate, and my thoughts go off; I am jealous, and I must not be jealous; at one end of the scale I am very noble, at the other end I am ugly. So, there is this battle going on. And if one wants to transcend, to go beyond this battle, to be free from this everlasting struggle, must one not find out if the thinker is a reality, if there is a thinker apart from the thoughts? Thoughts are transient, aren't they?—they change. And the mind, seeing this vast transient chain going on, naturally desires to establish a thinker which is not destructible. So, 'I', thought, have given myself a quality of imperishability. So there I have established, by thought, a thinker—the thinker that knows, the thinker that accumulates, the thinker that can choose, the thinker that can overcome all difficulties. But the thinker is part of the thought. There is only thinking.

Can the thinking process free itself from the struggle, from the constant battle of achievement, the constant desire for permanency? After all, thought is the result of the known; thought is the reaction of the known, of memory, of experience, of knowledge. You cannot think without words, without symbols, or without memory. And thought, in its struggle to become something greater, creates the ideal. And then there is the ideal and the actual, the 'what should be' and the *what is*. And so there is a battle ever going on, a constant effort, constant struggle to achieve, to become, to be better.

And yet one really wants to understand and be free from the struggle. Because, struggle, conflict, is uncreative; like all war, it is destructive. And if there is to be creativeness in the highest sense of that word, there cannot be conflict. And if I am serious in my desire to find out how to put an end to conflict, I must be clear about this question of the observer and the observed. As long as there is the observer, the thinker, the experiencer, apart from the experience, the observed, the thought, there must be conflict.

Seeing this whole process, how the mind invents the thinker, the separate entity, the ego, the higher self, the atma, is it not possible for the mind not to divide itself but only be concerned with thinking? Is it not possible for the mind to be free of ideation, of thought—thought being the memory, the background from which there is the reaction through words, through expression, through symbols?

Surely, when the mind is free from struggle, from conflict, when the mind is still, when there is that stillness which is not induced by the background, by thought, then only is there the cessation of all conflict. That stillness is not an idea; it is a fact. It is the unfathomable, the unknown. And then the mind is the real.

April 8, 1953

Sixth Talk in London

Again this evening I would like to talk over with you the question of renewal, of being reborn—not in an afterlife, a next life, but whether it is possible to bring about the complete regeneration of consciousness, a rebirth, not a continuity, but a complete revolution. It seems to me that is one of the most important questions to go into and to consider—if it is possible for the mind which is the only instrument we have of perception, of understanding, of investigation, of discovery, to be made completely new. And if we can discover it, if we do not merely listen to words but actually experience that state of renewal, of complete regeneration, something new—then it may be possible to live the ordinary life of every day routine, of trials, fears, mistakes, and yet bring to these mistakes and fears a quite different significance, a different meaning. So it may be worthwhile this evening to talk over this question—whether there can be a complete transformation of the unconscious. In understanding that, we may be able to find out what is the true function of the mind.

Now as I talk, perhaps it would be worthwhile if you would not merely listen to the words but actually experience the significance of the words by observing your own minds, not only following what I am saying but watching the operation of your own mind as it is functioning when you listen. Because, I think, if we can go into this question, we may find the key to this creativeness, to this complete state in which the unknowing, the unknowable, can come into being.

What we now know of life is a series of struggles, of adjustments, of limitations, of continual compulsions; that is our life. And in that process there is no renewal; there is nothing new taking place. Occasionally there is a hint from the unconscious, but that hint is translated by the conscious mind and made to conform to the pattern of our everyday convenience. What we do know is struggle, a constant effort to achieve a result. And will strife, struggle, the conflict between the thesis and the antithesis, hoping to find a synthesis—will that struggle bring about this quality of something new, original, clear, uncorrupt?

Our life is a routine, a wasting away, a death—the death of continuity, not the death that brings a new state. We know this; this is our life, conscious or unconscious. And is it possible for this mechanical mind, the mind that is the result of time, that is made up of experience, memory, and knowledge—which are all a form of continuity, the mechanism of the known—is it possible for such a mind completely to renew itself and become innocent, uncorrupted? Can the mind, my mind and your mind, which is caught in various habits, passions, demands, urges, which is forever following a series of convenient, pleasant habits, or struggling to break down habits that are not pleasant—can such a mind put aside its activities and be the unknown?

Because, it seems to me, that is one of the major problems of our existence—how to be able to die to everything of the past? Can that take place? Can the mind die to all the past, the memory, the longings, the various conditionings, the fears, the respectabilities? If not, there is no hope, is there? Because then, all that we know is the continuity of the things that have been, which we are continually establishing in the mind, in consciousness. The mind is constantly giving birth through memory, through experience, through knowledge, to a state of continuity. That is all I know. I want to continue, either through property, through family, or through ideas; I want this continuity to go on. And can the mind which is seeking security, seeking permanency either in pleasure or in strife, or trying to go beyond its own fears and so establish a state of permanency, which is the reaction of its own desire for continuity—can such a mind come to an end?

Because, what continues can never renew, can never give birth to something new. And yet, deep down in all of us there is the desire to live, to continue, to be as we are, only modified, better, more noble, having greater significance in life through our actions, our relationships. So, the function of the mind, as we know it, is to give birth to continuity, to bring about a state in which time plays a very extraordinarily important part as a means of becoming. And so we are constantly making an endeavor, struggling, striving to maintain this continuity. And that continuity is the 'me', the 'I', the ego. That is the function of our mind up to now; that is all we know.

Now, can such a mind, which is so embedded in time, put an end to itself and be in that state in which the unknown is? The mind is mechanical because memory is mechanical, experience is mechanical, and knowledge, though it may be stimulating, is still mechanical, and the background of the mind is of time; can such a mind cease to think in terms of time, in terms of becoming, in terms of the 'me'? The 'me' is the idea, the idea being memory, the experience, the struggle, the fears. Can that mind come to an end without desiring to come to an end?

When the mind desires to arrive at an end, it can intellectually come to that state; it can hypnotize itself to that state. The mind is capable of any form of illusion, but in that illusion there is no renewal.

So, the problem is, knowing the function of the mind as it is, can such a mind renew itself? Or, is such a mind incapable of seeing the new or receiving the new, the unknown, and therefore all that it can do is to be completely silent? And it seems to me that is all that it can do. Can the mind, which is so restless, discursive, wandering all over the place, gathering, rejecting—please follow your own mind—can such a mind immediately come to an end and be silent?

Because, in that silence there is the renewal, the renewal that is not comprehensible by the mind of time. But when the mind is silent, freed from time, it is altogether a different mind, in which there is no continuity of experience because there is no entity that is accumulating. In that silence, in that state, there is creativity, the creativity of God or truth. That creativity is not continuous, as we know it. But our mind, the mind that is mechanical, can only think in terms of continuity, and therefore it asks of truth, of God, that it should be continuous, constant, permanent. But the mechanical mind, the ordinary mind, the mind that we use every day cannot experience the other; such a mind can never renew itself; such a mind can never know the unknowable.

But if the mind that is the continuous mind—the mind of time, the mind that functions in memory, in knowledge, in experience—if such a mind can come to that silence, that extraordinary stillness, then in that there is the creativity of truth. That truth is not for all time; it is only from moment to moment, for in it there is no sense of accumulation.

And so creativeness is something which is never, in terms of the ordinary mind, continuous. It is always there, but even to say, "It is always there" is not true. Because the idea that it is always there gives it a permanency. But a mind that can be silent will know that state which is eternally creative. And that is the function of the mind, is it not? The function of the mind is not merely the mechanical side of it, not merely how to put things together, how to struggle, how to break down and again be put together. All that is the everyday mind, the plain mind—where there are hints from the unconscious, but where the whole process of consciousness is in the net of time—the mind that is constantly reacting, which it should; otherwise, we are dead entities. We cannot dispense with such a mind. Such a mind is born of technique, and the more you pursue technique—the "how," the method, the system—the less there is of the other, the creative. Yet we have to have technique; we must know how to do things. But when that mechanical mind—the mind of memory, experience, knowledge—exists by itself and functions by itself, irrespective of the other, it obviously must lead to destruction. For intellectuality, without that creativeness, reality has no meaning; it only leads to war, to further misery, to further suffering. And so, is it possible for that creative state to be, while at the same time the mechanical, technical mind is yet going on? Does the one exclude the other?

There is only exclusion of the real, surely, when the intellect, which is the mechanical, becomes all-important; when ideas, beliefs, dogmas, theories, the inventions of the intellect become all-important. But, when the mind is silent and that creative reality comes into being, then the ordinary mind has quite a different meaning; then the ordinary mind also is in continuous revolt against technique, the "how"; then such a mind will never ask for the "how"; then it is not concerned with virtue because truth is beyond virtue. The silent mind—the mind that is utterly still, knowing, being the unknown, that creativity of the real—does not need virtue. For in that, there is no struggle. It is only the mind that is struggling to become which needs virtue.

So, as long as we give emphasis to the intellect, to the mind of knowledge, of information, of experience, and memory, the other is not. One may occasionally catch glimpses of the other, but that glimpse is immediately translated in terms of time, of demanding further experience and so strengthening memory. But if, seeing all this—this whole process of consciousness—the mind naturally is no longer caught in the net of beliefs, ideas, then there is a stillness, a silence, an unpremeditated silence, not a silence that is put together by will, by resistance. Then in that silence there is that creative reality which cannot be measured, which cannot be made as an end to be got hold of by the mechanical mind. In that state there is happiness of a kind the mechanical mind can never understand.

This is not mysticism, a thing from the East. But on the contrary, this is a human thing, wherever one is and whatever the clime. If one can really observe this whole process of consciousness, the function of the mind as we know it, then, without any struggle, that extraordinary stillness of the mind comes into being. And in that there is creative reality.

Many questions have been sent in. And I hope those who have sent them will forgive if all are not answered; there are too many of them. But each evening we have tried to answer the representative ones. And if your particular question is not answered, perhaps in listening to the other questions which have been answered, you may solve or understand your own problem.

As I said, it is very important to know how to listen, to listen to everything—not only to me, which is not very greatly important. But if one knows how to listen, then there is no authority, then there is no imitation. For in that listening there is great freedom. The moment I am incapable of listening, then I create resistance, and to break down that resistance, I need further authorities, further compulsions. But if one knows how to listen without interpretation, without judgment, without twisting, without always bringing to it one's reactions, the reactions of one's conditioning, if one can put aside all that and listen to everything, listen to one's wife, one's children, one's neighbor, to the ugly newspapers, to all the things that are taking place about us—then everything has an extraordinary significance, everything is a revelation.

We are so caught up in our own judgments, in our own prejudices, in what we want to know, but if one can listen, it reveals a great deal. If we can really quietly listen to everything that is happening in our consciousness, to our own impulses, the various passions, the envies, the fears, then that silence of which I spoke earlier comes into being.

Questions: How is collective action possible when there are so many divergent individual interests?

KRISHNAMURTI: What do we mean by collective action? Let us take that up first, and then see if we have fundamentally divergent interests which come into conflict with the collective action.

What do we mean by collective action? All of us doing something together, creatively doing things together, building a bridge together, painting together, writing a poem together, or cultivating the farm together? Collective action, surely, is only possible when there is collective thinking. We do not mean collective action; we mean collective thinking, which will naturally produce an action in which we all conform.

Now is collective thinking possible? That is what we all want. All the governments, all the religions, organized philosophies, beliefs, all of them want collective thought. We must all be Christians or Communists or Hindus; then the world will be perfect. Now, is collective thinking possible? I know it is made possible now through education, through social order, through economic compulsion, through various forms of disciplines, nationalism, and so on; collective thinking is made possible, in which you are all English or Germans or Russians or what you will. Through propaganda, through education, through religion, there are various elastic frames in which we all think alike. And because we are individuals with our peculiar idiosyncrasies, with our peculiar drives and urges and ambitions, the framework is made more and more solid so that we do not wander away from it; and if we do, we are liquidated, we are excommunicated, we are thrown out of the party—which means losing the job.

So we are all held together, whether we like it or not, by the framework of an ideology. And the more that work becomes solid, firm, the more we are happy, relieved, because responsibility is taken away from us. So every government, every society, wants to make us all think alike. And we also want to think alike because we feel secure in thinking alike, don't we? We feel safe. We are always afraid lest we do not create the right impression, afraid of what people will say about us because we all want to be respectable.

And so, collective thinking becomes possible. And out of it, when there is a crisis, we all come together, as in wars, or when we all are threatened religiously, politically, or in any other way.

Now, is such a conditioning of the individual creative? Though we may yield to this conditioning, we are inwardly never happy; there is always a resistance because, in that yielding to the collective, there is no freedom; the freedom of the individual becomes merely verbal. And the individual, because he is so held by conventions, by tradition, is always expressing himself, wanting to fulfill himself through ambition. So society again curbs him, and there is a conflict between the individual and society, an everlasting war.

And is it not possible to have one vocation for all of us, not divergent aptitudes, divergent interests, but one true interest for all of us, which is the understanding of what is true, what is real? That is the true vocation, surely, of all us—not that you become an engineer or a sailor or a soldier or a lawyer—the true vocation, surely, of each one of us is to find that reality. Because, we are human beings, suffering, inquiring; and if we can have that true vocation by right education from the very beginning, through freedom and so on, if we can find that reality, then we shall in freedom cooperate together, and not have collective thought everlastingly conditioning us and making us act together. If we as human beings can find that reality, then only is true creative action possible.

Question: How can our poor, faulty human love become incorruptible?

KRISHNAMURTI: Can that which is corruptible become noncorruptible? Can that which is ugly become beautiful? Can the stupid become very intelligent? Can I, who become aware that I am stupid, struggle to become intelligent? Is not the very struggle to become intelligent, stupid? Because, fundamentally I am stupid, though I may learn all the clever tricks; still, in essence, I am stupid. Similarly, if my love is corruptible, I want to make it pure, incorruptible. I do not think it is possible. The very becoming is a form of corruption. All that I can do is to be aware of the whole implication of this love with its envies, jealousies, anxieties, fears, its bondage, its dependence. We know that; we know what we mean when we say we love, the enormous background that lies behind that word. And we want the whole of that background to become incorruptible—which means, again, the mind making something out of love, trying to give the timeless a quality of time. Is that possible?

Please, see this. Because the mind knows the pain of love, the anxiety, the uncertainty, the separation, the fear, the death, it says it must change it, it wants to make love into something that cannot be corrupted. Does not the very desire to change it make love into something which is of the mind, which is of sensation? The mind cannot make something which is already corrupt into something noble, and that is what we are always trying to do, are we not? I am envious, and I want to be nonenvious, and so I struggle because the mind feels the suffering of envy and wants to transform it. I am violent, and it is painful, so the mind wants to transform violence into nonviolence—which is still within the field of time. And so there is never a freedom from violence, from envy, from the decay of love. As long as the mind makes of love something which is of time, there must always be corruption.

Then is human love not possible? One will find that out if one really understands the significance of how the mind corrupts love. It is the mind that destroys. Love is not corrupt. But the mind that feels that it is not being loved, that feels isolated, that is conditioned, it is that mind which destroys love. We love with our minds, not with our hearts. One has to find out what this means. One has to inquire, to go into it, not just repeat the words.

But one cannot comprehend it without understanding the whole significance of the function of the mind. One must come to understand the whole consciousness of the 'me' that is so afraid of not being loved, or, having love, is so anxious to hold the love that depends on another for its sustenance; that is all part of that mind. The 'me' that says, "I must love God, truth," and so creates the symbol and goes to church every day, or once a week, or whenever you will, is still part of the mind. Whatever the mind touches with its mechanical memory, experience, and knowledge, it corrupts.

So it is very important, when we are faced with a problem of such a kind, to find out how to deal with it. One can only deal with it and bring about that quality which is incorruptible when the mind, knowing its function, comes to an end. Then only, surely, is love incorruptible.

Question: Are there not as many ways to reality or God as there are individuals? And is not yoga or discipline one of the ways?

KRISHNAMURTI: Is there a path to the unknowable? There is always a path to the known, but not to the unknown. If we really saw that once, felt it in our hearts and minds, really saw the truth of it, then all the heavens that religions promise, and our own desire to find a path through which reality can be found, would be broken down.

If reality is the known—as you know your way home to your house—then it is very simple; you can make a path to it. Then you can have a discipline; then you can bind yourself to it with various forms of yogas, disciplines, beliefs so as not to wander away. But is reality something known? And if it is known, is it the real? Surely, reality is something from moment to moment, which can only be found in the silence of the mind. So there is no path to truth in spite of all the philosophies because reality is the unknowable, unnameable, unthinkable. What you can think about truth is the outcome of your background, of your tradition, of your knowledge. But truth is not of knowledge, is not of memory, is not of experience. If the mind can create a God, as it does, surely it is not God, is it? It is merely a word. The mind can only think in words, in symbols, in images. And what the mind creates is not the real.

The word is all we know. And to have faith in that God which the mind has created, obviously gives us a certain strength. That is all we know. We have read, we have been conditioned—as Christians or Buddhists, as Communists or what you will—and that conditioning is all we know. There is a path always to the known, but not to the unknown. And can any discipline lead us to that—discipline being resistance, suppression, sublimation, substitution? We want to find a substitute for the real. Because we do not know how to allow the real to come into being, we think it will come through control, through virtue. So we cultivate virtue, which is again the mechanical habit of the mind, and thus make of virtue something which gives not freedom but respectability, a safeguarding from fear.

When we use discipline, there is no understanding. Surely a mind that is disciplined, controlled, shaped, can never be a free mind—free to inquire, to find out, to be silent. Because, all that it has learned is to strengthen the process of thought, which is the reaction of memory, reaction according to a conditioned demand, hoping thereby it will achieve some happiness, which it calls truth.

So can we not see all this, how consciousness, the mind, operates; how the 'me' is everlastingly seeking, gathering, accumulating in order to be secure and projecting heaven or God, which is its own creation, which is the urge to be safe, to be singularistic? Such a mind obviously cannot come upon truth. A mind that is suppressed, that has never looked within itself, that is always fearful of what it may find within itself and so always escaping, running away from *what is,* such a mind obviously can never find the unknown.

For the unknown comes into being only when the mind is no longer searching, no longer asking, petitioning. Then the mind, fully comprehending the whole process of itself, naturally comes to that silence in which there is creative reality.

April 9, 1953

Ojai, California, 1953

First Talk in The Oak Grove

I think it is very important to know how to listen, but most of us have innumerable opinions, ideas, experiences, and foregone conclusions through which we filter everything that we hear, and so we never listen to anything anew; we always translate what we hear according to a particular bias. So perhaps it is important to know how to listen without translating, without interpreting, but this is really quite a difficult problem. Most of us do not want to listen to anything completely, fully, because in that process we may discover what we are; therefore, we are always throwing up screens between ourselves and what is being said. So it would obviously be a good thing if we could simply listen, because we have a great many problems—not only personal, but also social, political, economic—to all of which we have to find the right answer, and I do not think we will find the right answer through any opinion, through any book knowledge, or through listening to any talks, including my own. Surely, to find the right answer, we must know how to listen to the issue, to the problem itself, and we are not listening when we merely interpret the problem to suit our particular idiosyncrasies or opinions. There must a right answer to all our problems, but the right answer does not lie through analysis, through judgment, comparison, or through any amount of learning. The right answer comes into being only when the mind listens quietly, almost indifferently, so that it is capable of considering the problem without any special motive or intention, without an end in view—which is a very difficult thing to do, for most of us want a particular result, a satisfactory answer. To find the right answer to our human problems, we must have a great deal of patience, especially those of us who are used to living in a mechanistic world where the answer to so many technical problems is very quickly discovered. If we have a problem, we want an immediate answer, so we turn to a book, to a doctor, to an analyst, a specialist, or we battle within ourselves to find a solution. We are impatient for results and therefore in constant conflict.

So, even though we may have heard before everything that is going to be said during these talks, it may be profitable if we can listen with a great deal of patience. What is important, surely, is that each one of us shall find lasting freedom from all the conflicts, from the innumerable responses which create such chaos in the mind, and through that freedom perhaps we shall discover something which is beyond the mind; but before we can be free, we must obviously understand what is the self, the 'me.'

Can you and I ever be free from our problems, from our suffering, from our innumerable wants? To be free implies a complete aloneness, which is freedom from fear. It is only then that we are individuals, is it not? We are individuals only when there is a complete cessation of fear—the fear of death, the fear of what our neighbors say, the fear arising from our own desires and ambitions, the fear of not fulfilling, of not being. To be alone is entirely different, surely, from being lonely. It is our very loneliness that creates fear, and as a defensive measure we have a great many blockages, a great many ideas, shelters, securities. Most of us are not true individuals, are we? We are the result of the various influences of society, of the impressions we have gathered, of the inner problems that crush our minds and our hearts. We are not individuals in the sense that we are not free from fear, and it seems to me that without being free from fear, we can never find a true answer to any of our human problems.

Now, is it possible for us to be completely free from fear? And of what are we afraid? Of being insecure, of not having everything one wants physically, of not complying with a particular political or religious system, and so on. The desire for security implies fear in our relationship with each other. To be capable of expressing the truth which we see, independently of all the threats around us, requires a great revolution in our thinking, does it not? And is it possible for each one of us to be completely free from the desire to be secure, which engenders fear? If we can understand this matter fundamentally, deeply, I think many of our problems will be solved. Freedom from fear, surely, is the only revolution, for when we are free from fear, we are neither American nor Hindu; we do not belong to any organized religion; there is no longer the sense of ambition, the desire for success, for achievement, and therefore we are not pitting our strength against another.

Freedom from fear is not an idea, nor is it an ideal to be striven after, but when one puts to oneself that question, "Can one be free from fear?" what is the inward response? Fear is a basic impediment, a fundamental blockage in all our relationships, in our search for reality, and can you and I, without a series of efforts, without analysis, be free from that contagion which brings about so many problems? Can one be totally free from fear? It is a difficult question to answer to oneself, is it not? To be free from fear is really to be free from any desire to be secure economically or socially or to find security in one's own experience. Surely, this is a very important question because our whole outlook is biased through fear; our education, our religion, our social structure, our efforts in every field are essentially based on fear. And can one be free from fear through any practice, through any form of discipline, through self-forgetfulness, through self-immolation, through the pursuit of any belief or dogma, or through identification with any country? Obviously, none of these things can give us freedom from fear because the very process of imitation, of conformity, of self-immolation, is rooted in fear; and when one recognizes the futility of these things and sees how the mind in its various activities is constantly projecting defenses, taking shelter in belief, in knowledge—in all of which lurks fear—what is one to do? How then is one to be free from this state we call fear? If we are at all serious, is that not a fundamental question which we have to ask ourselves? From childhood we have been brought up to think in terms of fear; all our defenses, psychological as well as physical, are based on fear, and how can a mind which is so educated, so conditioned, free itself from fear? Can the mind free itself from fear? Can any activity of the mind bring freedom to the mind? Is not the mind, is not thought itself, the very process of fear? And can thought ever negate fear?

Please, this is a problem not easily to be answered; but what one can do is to be aware of fear without fighting it, without analyzing it and thereby throwing up other defenses; and when the mind is really very quiet, passively aware of all the various forms of fear as they arise without acting against them, then in that quietness there is a possibility of the resolution of fear, which is the only real, fundamental revolution; and then there is individuality. As long as there is fear, there is no uniqueness, there is not an individual. At present most of us are merely the result of various influences: social, economic, political, climatic, and so on; we are not true individuals; therefore, we are not creative. Creativeness is not the expression of a talent, a gift; it arises only when there is no fear, that is, when the individual is completely alone.

Surely, this question of how to be free from fear is one of our major problems, is it not? Perhaps it is the only problem because it is fear, lurking in the innermost recesses of our minds and hearts, which cripples our thinking, our being, our living. So it seems to me that what we need now is not more philosophy, better systems, or greater knowledge and information but true individuals who are utterly free from fear, because it is only when there is no fear that there is love.

Now, can you and I set about freeing ourselves from fear? Can we put aside all opinions, all dogmas, all beliefs, which are merely expressions of fear, and come to the source, the fundamental issue, which is fear itself? Surely, as I said, creativeness is not a mere talent, a gift, a capacity—it is far beyond all that; and it can come into being only when the mind is utterly quiet, no longer hedged about by fear, by judgment, by comparison, when it is not burdened with knowledge and information. But with most of us the mind is constantly agitated; it has many problems; it is everlastingly seeking its own security, and how can such a mind be alone, uninfluenced, unafraid? How can it comprehend that creativeness, that reality, whatever it be, or find out whether or not that creative state exists? It is only when the mind is utterly free from fear that there is a possibility of bringing about a fundamental revolution—which has nothing to do with economic or political revolution; and to be free from fear requires not quick judgment but constant watchfulness, a great deal of patient and persistent awareness of the whole process of thought, which can be observed only in relationship, in everyday activity. Self-discovery lies through the understanding of *what is,* and *what is* is the actual process of thought at any given moment. Surely, that is meditation, and it requires a quietness of spirit in which there is no demand. It is only when you and I begin to know ourselves that the mind can be free from fear, and then there is a possibility not only of inward peace but of outward happiness for man.

Question: How can we know what is right and what is wrong without commandments or books?

KRISHNAMURTI: Why do you want to know what is right and what is wrong? Can anyone tell you? Can any book, can any teacher impart to you the knowledge of what is right and what is wrong? If you follow the authority of a book or of a teacher, you are merely imitating a pattern of thought, are you not? And do you discover anything through imitation, through conformity? You follow in order to achieve a certain result, and is that process not based on fear? Is that which is right to be discovered through fear, or only through direct experience? As long as the mind is caught in the dual process of right and wrong, there must obviously be incessant conflict. But is it not possible to discover what is true all the time without being caught in the conflict of right and wrong? That is our problem, is it not? What is right and what is wrong will vary according to the conditioning and experience of each person, and therefore it has very little significance, but to know what is true all the time—surely, that is important.

Please listen to this very carefully. As long as we are caught in the conflict of duality, which is the choice between what is right and what is wrong, we shall never know what is true all the time. What is right and what is wrong may be an opinion—what we have been brought up on from childhood, the imprint of a particular culture, of a particular society—and as long as we are imitating, conforming to a pattern, however noble, there must be this endless choice between right and wrong—the desire always to do the right thing and therefore the fear of making a mistake, which only leads to respectability. But to know what is true all the time, inwardly, deeply—that is not an opinion, a judgment, a dogma. What is true does not depend on any belief. To find out what is true is to understand *what is* from moment to moment, and that requires a great deal of alertness in which there is no judgment or comparison, an openness of mind to observe, to feel out, to be sensitive. What is true does not create conflict, but when the mind chooses between what is true and what is false, that very choice produces conflict. Most of us have been brought up to think rightly and to eschew certain things which are said to be wrong, and therefore our minds are always seeking the one and avoiding the other, and that process of thinking is in itself a conflict, is it not? The "right" may be what the priest says, what your neighbors or your political leaders say, so the pattern of conformity is set going, and the mind that conforms can never be in revolt, and therefore it can never find that which is everlastingly creative.

So is it possible to discover what is true all the time? Surely, there cannot be discovery as long as there is the conflict of choice. To discover, the mind must be basically quiet, free from the fear of making mistakes. But we want success, do we not? From childhood we are brought up to think in terms of success, and every book, every magazine exemplifies it—the poor boy becoming the president, and so on. Seeking security in success, the mind must conform to what is right, and so the battle is set going between what is right and what is wrong, the everlasting conflict of duality. In that conflict one never finds out what is true. What is true is *what is* and the release that comes from the understanding of *what is*. Do please listen rightly to this; think it over, and if you can understand that which is actually taking place from moment to moment, you will see what a release there is from the conflict of right and wrong. That understanding cannot come about if you are judging or condemning *what is* or comparing it with past experience, and when there is no understanding of *what is*, there is no release. To understand *what is*, the mind must be free from all condemnation and judgment, but that requires infinite patience, and it may produce an extraordinary revolution in your life, of which the mind is afraid, so you never look at *what is*; you merely give opinions about it. As long as the mind is caught in the choice between what is right and what is wrong, it remains immature, and that is one of our difficulties, is it not? Our minds are immature; we have been told what is right and what is wrong, and we want to conform. Conformity is the very nature of an immature mind, whereas the understanding of *what is* is the revolutionary factor in creativeness.

Question: Although I am aware that I am flattered by admiration and resentful of criticism, my mind continues to be swayed by these influences; it is drawn or repelled like the compass needle in the presence of a magnet. What is the next step to be really free?

KRISHNAMURTI: The difficulty is that you want to be free; you do not want to understand the problem. You are antagonistic to both flattery and criticism. You resent being criticized, and while you want to be attractive, you want to be admired, yet you despise yourself for being so childish, and you want to be free from both. So you have three problems, have you not? And that is what we always do; having one problem which we do not know how to resolve, we introduce other problems, and so multiply problem after problem.

Now what is the question? Not how to be uninfluenced by admiration and criticism, but why do you want to be admired, why do you mind so much when you are criticized? That is the problem, is it not? Why do you want admiration? Because when you are admired, you feel happy; it gives you encouragement; it makes you work better. You want to be encouraged because in yourself you are uncertain, and so you look to others for support, and you are sensitive to criticism because it uncovers what you are. That is why you are always running away from criticism and longing for admiration, encouragement, flattery, so again you are caught in this battle of wanting and not wanting. Surely, all this indicates an inward poverty of being, does it not? There is no deep sense of confidence. I don't mean the aggressive confidence of experience, which is only a strengthening of the 'me' and therefore without much significance. I am talking of that confidence which arises when you begin to understand yourself, when you begin to see all the implications of admiration, of encouragement, of criticism. The understanding of yourself does not depend upon anyone; it comes if you are aware, alert, meeting *what is* from moment to moment without judgment. Self-knowledge gives a confidence in which the self does not become important. It is not the confidence of the 'me' who has gathered innumerable experiences, or the 'me' who possesses a large bank account, or the 'me' who has a vast store of knowledge. In that there is no confidence; there is always fear. But when the mind begins to be aware of itself and its responses, when it sees all its own activities from moment to moment without any sense of comparison or judgment, then out of that knowledge there is a confidence free of the self. Such a mind does not seek admiration or avoid criticism; it is no longer concerned with either because it is finding release from moment to moment in the understanding of *what is.*

What is is the reaction, the response, the urge, the desire of the mind at any given moment, and if you really observe *what is,* become fully aware of all its implications, you will find that there is an extraordinary freedom which comes into being without the mind seeking it. When the mind seeks freedom, it is freedom from something, which is not freedom at all; it is only a reaction, like the political revolution, which is a reaction against the existing regime. The freedom which comes with the understanding of *what is* is not a reaction against something; it is a creative release, and therefore it is complete in itself. But to understand *what is* requires great insight, quietness of mind. Freedom does not come about through any form of compulsion, through any attraction, through any desire; it comes only when the mind is aware without judgment, without choice, so that at every moment it is seeing itself as it is. The mind that seeks freedom will never find it because to seek freedom is to block, to push aside *what is,* but when the mind begins to understand *what is* without choice, that very understanding brings about a creative release, which is freedom. Freedom is alone; it is true individuality, and in that there is bliss.

June 20, 1953

Second Talk in The Oak Grove

I would like this morning, if I can, to talk over the problem of change. Considering the world situation—the starvation, the wars, the competition, the incessant conflict between man and man, the extraordinary prosperity of some nations and the extreme poverty in the East, where millions of people have one meal or less a day—taking all this into consideration, it is clear that there must be some kind of radical transformation, a revolutionary change. And I think it is fairly obvious, if one has thought about this matter, that any change through conformity, compulsion, or fear is no change at all. Mere peripheral change, adjustment on the outward circle, whether economic, political, social, or even so-called religious, is no revolution. Revolution must naturally be at the center, not on the circumference, on the outside, and how is this revolution at the center to take place? I am using the word *revolution* advisedly, for if there is change at the center, it is a revolution, a complete transformation of thought, and it is only when there is this revolution at the center that there can be significant changes on the outside, on the periphery. But most of us are concerned not with the revolution at the center but with changes on the outside; we want a better economic position, more riches, more comfort, more prosperity, more luxury, a greater variety of entertainments and distractions. With that most of us are concerned. Or we change from one special activity to another, from one religion to another, from one dogma to another, which is merely going from an old cage to a new one. And if we are somewhat inclined to be serious, we talk about the stopping of war—again considering how to bring about a change on the outside. Scientific research, social reform, political adjustment, are all concerned with outward change, as are the various religions and sectarian societies.

Now, how is one to bring about a change at the center? That is the problem for most of us, is it not? If we are at all serious and see the superficiality of merely seeking a better job or an immediate solution for our problems, whether economic, political, or religious, we will naturally want to know if it is possible to bring about a change at the center, which will in turn bring about a transformation in our relationship with our family, with our immediate partners, and so on, which is society.

I do not know if you have thought about this matter, but I consider it a fundamental issue, not easily to be put aside. For years we have tried to reform ourselves outwardly; we have sought to transform our manners, our thoughts, our conduct, our society, and it has not brought about a radical change, a creative release; and it seems to me that without this deep, inward revolution at the center, whatever effort we exert to change things on the outside is utterly useless. It may bring about changes which are satisfactory for the moment, but if the revolution does not take place at the center, mere alteration on the circumference, on the outside, is of very little significance, and it may ultimately lead to greater mischief. So realizing that, let us find out how to bring about this change, this revolution at the center.

What is the center? Surely, it is the mind, and we are going to find out if the mind can change, can bring about a revolution within itself. The mind is obviously made up of the conscious as well as the unconscious levels, and any effort to change itself on the part of the conscious mind is still on the outside. Please see the importance of this.

As I said yesterday, if I may repeat it in a different way without boring you, it is important to know how to listen. When you make a conscious effort to listen, to understand, then understanding is thwarted by that very effort. When your whole attention is given to trying to find out, your mind is in a state of tension, and therefore there is no listening, there is no penetration, there is no spontaneous response to something that is not completely or fully understood. And yet to listen requires a certain attention; you cannot just go to sleep. But to listen is entirely different from hearing. You may hear what I am saying and comprehend the significance of the words, but if the mind does not go beyond the mere verbal communication between you and me, there is no real understanding. What I am trying to convey is not so much the verbal implication but much more the things that lie between words, the space, the interval between thoughts. If the mind can be quiet, attentive to that which lies between the words, if it can be so attuned, then it can listen wholly, totally; and perhaps it is that very listening which brings about a revolution, and not the conscious effort to achieve understanding.

Most of us know only the conscious effort to change, to discipline the mind, and therefore what we call change is a partial process; it is not a total revolution. I am talking of that total, integrated revolution, not a partial, a superficial action; and that total revolution cannot take place through any conscious effort on our part. We know what consciousness is; we are familiar with the conscious mind that thinks and desires, that is moved by impulse, by motive, and brings about conformity. The conscious mind is constantly making an effort in a particular direction, either to conform through fear or through fear to change itself to fit another pattern of action. So any conscious effort to change must be influenced by conformity, by fear, by the desire to succeed, or to better oneself in order to achieve a certain result, either in this world or in the world of sainthood. It is imperative that there should be a deep revolution, but that revolution must obviously be unconscious because if I deliberately bring about a revolution in myself, it will be the result of desire, of memory, of time. I want to be better, I want to achieve a result, I want to find out what God is, what truth is, I want to be happier—so I say there must be a change. Positive or negative effort, the effort to be or not to be, is based on fear, on the urge to gain, to find comfort, peace, security; so any change through conscious effort is not a change at all; it is merely an adjustment to a different pattern. Of that one must see the truth completely. Like all economic revolutions, whether of the right or of the left, it is still not a change at the center. Both bring about tyrannies. So the wise man is not concerned essentially with peripheral changes; he is concerned with that revolution which is inward, which is at the center. And how are you and I to bring about that change?

I do not know if you see the importance of this question. All schools of religion, all religious societies, seek to bring about a change through conscious effort, through discipline, through conformity, through fear, through the desire to achieve a better state, whether socially, religiously, or psychologically—all of which is on the outside. But surely, the man who is consciously becoming virtuous is immoral because he is virtuous for his own security, for his own comfort, for his own happiness. We are not talking of such a change, such a transformation.

So how is one to bring about this revolution at the center? We see that the deliberate, conscious effort of everyday thought cannot do it. And can the unconscious do it? Do you understand what we mean by the unconscious? The unconscious is the residue of the past, is it not? It is the result of the racial instincts, of the cultural imprints, of all that we have been in the past, of the whole human struggle with its hidden urges, compulsions, drives. Can that unconscious help to bring about a change, a revolution at the center? And is there a difference, a gap, a hiatus between the unconscious and the conscious? Surely, the conscious mind, the mind that is awake during the day, functioning in our daily activities, is only the outer edge of the unconscious, is it not? There is not a fundamental difference between the two. As the leaf of a tree is the outcome of the deep roots in the earth, so the conscious mind is the outcome of the deep unconscious. There is not a division between them; the two things are not different, only we are not familiar with the unconscious. We are familiar with the conscious mind: the everyday activity of greed, competition, jealousy, envy, wanting this and not wanting that, the ceaseless struggle—but the same urges are also at the deeper level, are they not? So can one look to the unconscious to bring about a radical transformation?

If you really listen to all that I am saying and follow it easily, you will find the right answer, and the finding of the right answer is the revolution at the center. What is the state of the mind when there is no effort either by the conscious or the unconscious? Is there a center then? With the majority of us there is a center, which is the 'me', the ego, the self, and whether that center be at a higher or a lower level is not of great significance. The center is the 'me', the acquisitive instinct which expresses itself through the ownership of property, through the desire to become better, to acquire virtue through control, through discipline, and all the rest of it. The fears, the anxieties, the affections, the longings, the hopes, the failures, the frustrations—that is the center we know, is it not? And for that center to cease completely is the only revolution, but that revolution cannot come about through any effort on the part of the conscious or the unconscious.

Now, when one realizes all this, what is the state of one's mind? Obviously, the first response is an extraordinary sense of anxiety, of fear, of not knowing what is going to happen. The 'me', the center which is an accumulation of innumerable reactions, of innumerable cultural, political, and religious influences—it is that center which has been functioning; and if that center has to go completely for the mind to be pristine, incorruptible, single, alone, the first reaction is obviously a sense of tremendous negation, of not being; and very few of us can stand that, which is to face what we actually are. So at the center there is fear, and from that center we begin to create defenses; we cling to gifts, capacities, talents, thereby bringing about the constant conflict between what we actually are and what we should like to be. And yet, at intelligent moments, we perceive that this mere traffic with the outward affairs will never bring about a deep, lasting, fundamental revolution. So those of us who are at all serious and religiously inclined must obviously be concerned with this question of revolution at the center.

Since neither the conscious nor the unconscious mind can bring about a radical change at the center, what is the mind to do? Can the mind do anything? As we have seen, the mind is the conscious as well as the unconscious activity of thought, of reaction, of memory. Mind is the result of time, and time does not bring about revolution. On the contrary, it is the cessation of time that produces the fundamental revolution at the center. The center is used to time; the center is time—the whole psychological process of yesterday, today, and tomorrow, "I have been," "I am," "I shall be," the frustration, the fear, and the hope. So the mind cannot produce a revolution; when it does, it creates more brutality, more tyrannies, more horrors, a totalitarian compulsion. And if the mind cannot bring about a radical change, then what is the function of the mind?

I hope you are following all this because I am talking not only for myself but also for you. I feel that if this extraordinary revolution could take place in each one of us, we would bring about a different world; we would be missionaries of a totally different kind, not those who convert, but who liberate.

So what is the function of the mind when it realizes that neither a conscious effort nor an unconscious urge on its part can bring about complete transformation? What is it to do? It can only be still, can it not? Any effort on its part to change itself is the outcome of its conditioning, of its fear, of its desire for success, of its hope that things will be better, and such effort only thwarts the discovery of the right answer. Please see the importance of this. If I realize that the fundamental revolution cannot be brought about through any response of the mind, conscious or unconscious, that all such responses are based on acquisitive fear, on memory, on time, and are therefore on the outside, on the periphery—if I realize that, then the mind has to be completely quiet, has it not? So the mind's function is only to see how these responses arise and not seek to capture a particular state or try to bring about a change at the center through an action of will. All that it can do is to watch its responses. But to watch requires infinite patience, and if you are impatient, then that very watching becomes a drudgery because you want to get on, you want to achieve a result. It is only when the mind is constantly aware of its own responses of fear, of greed, of envy, of hope, that these responses come to an end; but they cannot come to an end if there is any condemnation, comparison, judgment. They come to an end by mere observation, by complete cessation of all choice. Then the mind becomes extraordinarily quiet, utterly still, and in that stillness there is a revolution at the center. Only then is there a possibility of being truly individual because then the mind is alone, uninfluenced. That state is creativeness. There is no longer an experiencer who is experiencing. As long as there is an experiencer, there is the process of time.

So this revolution at the center, which is so obviously essential, is not possible through any form of compulsion or discipline, which is all childish; it can come about only when the mind is utterly quiet, choicelessly aware of its own responses, outward and inward, as a total process. Then you will find that there comes an extraordinary sense of inward bliss—which is not a promise nor a reward for your valiant effort of days or years to come to it. That happiness, that bliss, is not the opposite of sorrow; it has nothing to do with sorrow. But in the understanding of sorrow, and being free from sorrow, that state comes into being.

In considering some of these questions, I hope you and I are really thinking over the problem together. You are not waiting for my answer because I am not giving an answer. It is very simple to give answers, to say yes or no, like a school teacher. What is important is that you and I together uncover the answer in the problem, which is the only right answer; and to do that, you must be alert, and I must be alert. The right answer is not easily found. Most of us are so eager to find the answer and get on with the next problem that we never examine the problem itself. There is only one problem, though it may have different expressions, and to understand that problem through its various expressions requires a great deal of wisdom, penetration, insight, and a patience which is not laziness. To penetrate, to understand, the mind must be free from all authority, from all book knowledge, from what someone else has previously said. Unfortunately, most of us have read so much; we know so well what the Buddha, the Christ, or someone else has said that we are incapable of thinking the problem right through. But if we are to find the right answer together, you also have to think, to inquire, to penetrate into the question.

Question: You say that to be free of the self is an arduous task, and at the same time you assert that any effort to be free is an impediment to that very freedom. Is this not a vicious circle? How can one perform the arduous task without effort?

KRISHNAMURTI: What do we mean by effort? When do you make an effort? And if there is no effort, does it imply laziness, stagnation? So let us begin to find out what we mean by effort, in what direction we are making effort, and why we make effort.

When we talk of making an effort, we always mean exerting ourselves in order to achieve a result, do we not? We want better health, better understanding, a better social, economic, or political position, and so on, which means that we are always making an effort to arrive somewhere. Or we make an effort to remove certain psychological blocks. If we are envious, we say we must not be envious, and therefore we create a resistance against envy. Or we want to be very learned; we want more in order to impress, or to have a better job; therefore, we read, we study. That is all the effort we know, is it not? For most of us, effort is either positive or negative; it is a process of becoming or not becoming, and that very process is the center of the self, is it not? If I am envious and I make an effort not to be envious, surely the entity who makes that effort is still the self, the 'me'. Any effort to dominate the self, positively or negatively, is still part of the self, and therefore it only further strengthens the self; and in that vicious circle one is caught. So the problem is how to break that vicious circle, that continuous chain of effort which only gives greater strength to the 'me'.

Now, please follow this. You can break the vicious circle only if you are aware of it as a total process. When the mind sees that it is envious, it wants to be unenvious because it thinks that not being envious will pay it in some way; it derives a certain satisfaction from the effort not to be envious; it makes a spiritual record. So in not being envious, the mind finds security, shelter, and the maker of the effort is still the 'me', the ego, the self. Please just realize that, only that. Then the problem arises, what am I to do when I am envious? I am used to denying, creating resistance against envy; now I see the futility of that, the absurdity of one part of me denying another part, when I am the whole. So what am I to do? But we never come to that point; we never recognize that we are both the envy and the desire not to be envious. When we are envious, we exert effort to dominate envy, and we think that that effort is beneficial, that it will bring about freedom from the self. It will not. But when I understand, when I am fully aware that envy and the desire not to be envious is a total process, then is there an effort? Then something entirely different takes place, does it not? Is all this too much for this morning?

Audience: No, no.

KRISHNAMURTI: All right. The moment we are conscious that we are envious or angry or jealous, a process of condemnation is set going, and as long as one is condemning, there is no comprehension. The very words *envy, anger, jealousy,* imply judgment, comparison, condemnation, do they not? Through centuries of education, of culture, of religious training, these words have come to connote a sense of denunciation; they stand for something to be put aside, resisted, fought, and our whole reaction is in that direction. So I find that when I name certain feelings, I am already in a position of condemnation, and the very act of condemning, of resisting a feeling, strengthens it. If I don't condemn envy, will I yield to it? Will I become more envious? Surely, envy is always envy, it is not more or less. The demand, the direction may vary, but envy is always the same whether its object be a Ford or a Cadillac, a large house or a small one. So not to name, and therefore not to condemn envy, is not to indulge in it. When one understands that the very word *envy* connotes condemnation, that the feeling of antagonism to envy is embedded in the word itself, then a freedom comes into being. That freedom is not opposed to envy; it is not freedom from envy. Freedom from a particular quality is not freedom at all, and the man who is free from something is like the man who is against the government; as long as he is against something, he is not a free man. Freedom is complete in itself; it is not from any position or against any state or quality.

So all effort to overcome, to be free from something, only strengthens the 'me', the self, the ego; and when one really understands this, when one is aware of the quality and its opposite as a total process and sees how the word itself contains condemnation or encouragement, then one is no longer caught in words, and therefore the mind is free to regard, to observe *what is*. The understanding of *what is* and the freedom that it brings is not the outcome of a persistent practice, of a drudgery to which you devote so many minutes every morning; it comes into being only when one is aware throughout the day of the trees, of the birds, of one's own reactions, of the things that are happening inwardly and outwardly as a total process. When there is condemnation or justification, comparison or identification, there is no comprehension of *what is*, and that is why it is very arduous to be aware. *What is* can be understood only from moment to moment, which means that one must be completely aware that one is judging, that every word has either approval or denial. As long as the mind is the verbal expression of its own conditioning, it can never be free. There is freedom only when the mind is empty of all thought.

June 21, 1953

Third Talk in The Oak Grove

Perhaps this evening we could consider the significance of authority in life and the relationship between authority and fear. During the last two meetings we have been going into the question of individual freedom and whether it is possible to be individual in the sense of being free from fear, and I suggested that there can be individuality only when there is no fear at all. It is one of the most difficult things to be free from fear because fear takes so many forms. When the mind is completely absorbed in a certain idea, that absorption may be an escape, and the man who disciplines his mind according to a pattern of thought may still be caught in fear. When we conform to a particular standard of morality in which there is authority, compulsion, are we free of fear? To follow authority in any form without fully understanding the whole significance of authority is surely to be burdened with fear.

So let us go into this question of authority, but before we do so, I would like to suggest that you listen rightly. To listen rightly is not to conclude. When you jump to any conclusion, you are not open to find out, to discover. You cannot be led to discover; discovery must be spontaneous. If you are listening in order to be led, you will never discover. That is fairly clear, is it not? If you are waiting to be shown, you will never find out anything for yourself; you will find out only what the speaker wants you to find out. Therefore you must listen not merely to what I am saying, to the description I am giving, but rather to what is taking place in your own mind—which is to be aware. Though I may use certain words and phrases as a means of communication, what I am actually describing is what each one of us is thinking, whether consciously or unconsciously. If you are merely listening to me, you are not listening to yourself; you are only following a description. But if through this description you begin to be aware of the activities of the mind with all its tendencies and idiosyncrasies, then there is a possibility of discovering, of becoming fully conscious of what is actually taking place within your own being, and that, it seems to me, is very important.

I am not saying anything that is so very difficult to understand, but if you merely listen to words, you will miss the whole point. I am describing what is actually going on, consciously or unconsciously, within ourselves, and what is going on is a very complex affair which requires a great deal of patient attention, an awareness in which there is no judgment, an observation without choice. If we can listen with that attitude of mind, then I think we shall begin to understand the whole significance of authority. Surely, as long as the mind is caught in authority, it is not an individual at all; and to find out what is real, what is God, what is truth, to discover that which is nameless, must one not be completely individual? To be individual means complete freedom from all fear, from all compulsion, from the desire to find a right way of living. That is what we all want, that is the cry in our hearts—to find a right way of action, a right way of conduct, a right method to live happily, to have peace. And does not that very cry create authority, the authority of a book, of a person, of an idea? We want to be told what to do, how to live, in what manner to overcome the innumerable problems that we have, and with that desire in our minds and in our hearts, we pursue those who can give us what we are seeking, those who we think will lead us to reality, to happiness, to God. So we set up an entity, a teacher, who is the result of our own projection, and we cloak him with what we want. The urge to guide our lives through teachers, through books, through any form of compulsion is essentially the desire to be secure, is it not? That is what we want—to be secure in our relationships, to be secure in this world and also in the next.

Now, desire for security sets going the mechanism of compulsion, of resistance, of conformity to a pattern, to an idea, or to a person who represents the idea, and that is our life, is it not? So must one not be completely free from this desire for security, which creates authority? Authority is a very complex problem. There is authority at different levels: the governmental, the social, the religious, and the individual authority of one's own experience. From childhood we are compelled to conform. Our education, our social and religious training, our whole environment encourages us to conform, to resist, or to follow, which is our daily mechanism of thought, and as long as you and I are in that state, can we be free individuals? If we are not free, obviously we can never discover what is real, and to be free requires a great deal of understanding of this problem of authority. You cannot just throw aside all external authority and follow what you want because the very following of what you want creates authority. You may reject external authority, but there is the inward authority of experience, and that experience is based on your conditioning. It is fairly easy to reject all external authority, but one is still the result of that authority, of tradition, of society, of the culture, the civilization about one. To reject the outer and follow the inner is not to be free of authority. Surely, authority is a unitary process. There is no division between outer and inner authority—there is only authority. And can a mind which is following authority in any form ever discover what is true?

Please listen to this very carefully; don't jump to conclusions. Compulsion, resistance, discipline, the following of authority, is the outcome of fear, and can a mind hedged about by fear ever be free? It is only when the mind is free that there is individuality, but to bring about that freedom of the mind is extremely difficult—difficult in the sense that mere desire, mere effort will not bring it about. Desire and effort are the reactions to our conditioning, and reaction is not freedom. So can the mind be free from all resistance, from all desire to find a way out of our problems?

I do not know if I am making myself clear. This is really quite a difficult subject to deal with because when we approach it, we are immediately confronted with the thought, "If I have no authority, no mode of conduct, how shall I guide myself tomorrow? If I cannot use my past knowledge to discover what is true, then what am I to do?"

Now, is it not possible to live from moment to moment, understanding each incident, each experience, each relationship, as it arises? Cannot the truth of things be seen from moment to moment? Must I have the burden of knowledge, the authority of experience, to discover what is true? To understand, must not the mind be totally free of the past? Must it not stop translating the immediate experience according to its previous knowledge, which becomes the authority? But that is what we are doing, is it not? When we have a problem, how do we deal with it? We translate the problem in terms of the background of our conditioning, our previous experience; we evaluate it according to the standards which we have established, or which society has set up, and in translating the problem, we are never free to comprehend the truth of that problem. Can the truth of any human problem be understood through the authority of experience or of knowledge? Is not intelligence the freedom of understanding from moment to moment?

Life is very complex, and the mind is still more complex, with extraordinary capacities, and to understand any human problem, must not the mind come to it anew, afresh, and not from a center which has gathered, which has accumulated? After all, that is creative understanding, is it not? The center which accumulates is the 'me', the ego, the self, and therefore any action from that center will only increase the problem. Reality, God, or what name you will, must be something totally new, never experienced before, completely original; and can a mind which is the residue of time, of the past, of authority, of compulsion, resistance, fear—can such a mind understand, see the significance of what is true? Yet every church, every religious organization, every sect is always talking of God, and those who believe in God have visions which strengthen their belief. Surely, that which you can recognize has already been known; therefore, it is not true. That which is true has never been known; therefore, the mind must come to it afresh, anew, and one of our major difficulties is how to denude the mind of all compulsions, of all fears, of all resistances, of all authorities, so that it is free to observe, to listen, and to understand. Tomorrow is never the same; the next reaction is never what has been, and it is because we translate every reaction, every tomorrow, every next moment in terms of the old that more and more complications arise.

There is never a moment when we can look at life, at the trees, at the birds, at every incident, originally, freely, fully.

Surely then, the question is not how to be free of problems, or how to find the answers to our problems, or how to be free of authority but rather can we look at all the extraordinarily complex and subtle problems of life with a mind that is pristine, original, uncorrupted? It is possible to do that only when we are free of fear because it is fear that breeds authority, whether it be the authority of a person or the authority of a church, of a belief, a dogma; and though we may be free of dogma and belief, if we are slaves to what our neighbors think or to that which we have known, we are obviously still bound by fear.

So it is fear which breeds authority, and can the mind be free from fear, the fear of being insecure in all our relationships, the fear of not knowing, of not being? In our desire for security, in our fear of the unknown, we create heaven and hell, we create gods, visions—it is out of our own minds that all these things are born. Because intrinsically, deeply, there is a fear of being completely alone, the cunning mind begins to accumulate property, knowledge, experience; and being caught in that process, we project what reality or God should be, which is mere speculation and therefore of no significance; we create innumerable forms of belief behind which the mind takes shelter.

Now, can the mind be free of this whole process and live simply from day to day, understanding life as it arises from moment to moment? After all, that is the timeless, the nameless eternity—when the mind itself is the unknown. At present the mind is the known; it is the result of time, of yesterday, of accumulated knowledge, experiences, and beliefs; and such a mind can never know the unknown. This is not some vague form of mysticism. Surely, if I want to know something that has never been experienced before, that is not of time, that cannot be put in the frame of authority, my mind must be totally free from the past, which means that it must be free from fear. To this the immediate reaction is, "How am I to be free from fear? I know I am afraid, but how am I to be free?" Is that not your instinctive response? Please listen to the question and you will find the answer. Can the mind, which has created fear, free itself from fear? In its desire for security, the mind takes shelter in belief, thereby engendering fear and rendering itself incapable of facing the unknown, and can the entity which is giving birth to fear ever be free from fear? Surely, its very desire to be free from fear is the outcome of fear; therefore, any effort of the mind to be free from fear is still part of fear. All that the mind can do is to be aware of fear and be completely passive with regard to it. In that passive awareness there is no choice, no overcoming; and when the mind is so aware, you will find that there is no fear at all. But the mind cannot be in that state as long as there is any effort to overcome.

Please listen carefully and you will see the truth of this. The mind, which is thought, creates fear, does it not? Most of us are lonely, and we do not know what that loneliness means; we have never gone into it, understood it, because we are always running away from it through some form of distraction. We can understand loneliness only when we can look at it, and we can look at it only when we are not afraid of it. Fear comes in when we are running away from loneliness; the running away, the flight is fear. So the mind is creating fear all the time—fear of what is going to happen tomorrow, of what will happen when we die. Thought, which is the result of the past, is projecting itself into the future and creating fear.

The mind can never be free of fear as long as it is making an effort to get away from fear. All that it can do is to be aware that it is frightened and be completely passive, without any choice. Then you will see that the mind becomes extraordinarily quiet, and in that quietness the problem of fear can be resolved. In that stillness of mind, authority has wholly vanished. What need have you of authority when from moment to moment you are seeing what is true? Truth is not dependent on valuation, on judgment, and if once the mind sees that completely, then the mind itself is both the experiencer and the experienced; therefore, the mind is capable of going beyond itself.

All this requires a great deal of patient attention, an awareness in which there is no desire to become, to avoid, or to gain. It is because we are everlastingly desiring to achieve, to be successful, or to avoid something that we engender fear. Fear multiplies problems; fear cripples the mind and holds it to the past, and so the mind itself is the center of fear. Only when the mind understands the full significance of not desiring to be something, of being, not blank, but completely empty, utterly silent—only then is it possible for the mind to resolve every problem as it arises.

Question: I would like not to be competitive, but how is one to exist without competing in this highly competitive society?

KRISHNAMURTI: You see, we take it for granted that we must live in this competing society, so there is a premise laid down, and from there we start. As long as you say, "I must live in this competing society," you will be competitive. This society is acquisitive; it worships success, and if you also want to be successful, naturally you must be competitive.

But the problem is much deeper and more significant than mere competition. What lies behind the desire to compete? In every school we are taught to compete, are we not? Competition is exemplified by the giving of marks, by comparing the dull boy with the clever boy, by endlessly pointing out that the poor boy may become the president or the head of General Motors—you know the whole business. Why do we lay so much stress on competition? What is the significance behind it? For one thing, competition implies discipline, does it not? You must control, you must conform, you must toe the line, you must be like all the others, only better, so you discipline yourself in order to succeed. Please follow this. Where there is the encouragement of competition, there must also be the process of disciplining the mind to a certain pattern of action, and is that not one of the ways of controlling the boy or the girl? If you want to become something, you must control, discipline, compete. We have been brought up on that, and we pass it on to our children. And yet we talk about giving the child freedom to find out, to discover!

Competition hides the state of one's own being. If you want to understand yourself, will you compete with another, will you compare yourself with anyone? Do you understand yourself through comparison? Do you understand anything through comparison, through judgment? Do you understand a painting by comparing it with another painting or only when your mind is completely aware of the picture without comparison?

You encourage the spirit of competition in your son because you want him to succeed where you have failed; you want to fulfill yourself through your son or through your country. You think that progress, evolution, lies through judgment, through comparison, but when do you compare, when do you compete? Only when you are uncertain of yourself, when you do not understand yourself, when there is fear in your heart. To understand oneself is to understand the whole process of life, and self-knowledge is the beginning of wisdom. But without self-knowledge, there is no understanding; there is only ignorance, and the perpetuation of ignorance is not growth.

So, does it require competition to understand oneself? Must I compete with you in order to understand myself? And why this worship of success? The man who is uncreative, who has nothing in himself—it is he who is always reaching out, hoping to gain, hoping to become something, and as most of us are inwardly poor, inwardly poverty-stricken, we compete in order to become outwardly rich. The outward show of comfort, of position, of authority, of power, dazzles us because that is what we want.

All this is obviously true, but if you are listening to it with the thought that you have to live in this world, you are not listening; you are only comparing. If you do not compete, you may lose your job; if you lose your job, what about your responsibilities, who will feed your children? And so you go round and round. A man who is intent upon finding out what is true, who is in a state of revolt, must obviously go through a great deal of physical discomfort, must he not? He may lose his job. Why not? The mind that clings to security can never find reality. It is only when the mind understands the real that our problems will be resolved, not until then. Do what we will, however cunning our minds may be, however much knowledge we may acquire, whatever process of analysis we may go through, until we find the real, which is at every minute to be discovered, there can be no lasting solution to our human problems.

Competition arises when there is the desire to be successful, to become something, whether in the material world or in the world of knowledge, of psychological intention; and as long as the mind is competing, comparing, judging, it can never know the real. It is only when the mind is completely choiceless—not comparing, judging, or condemning—that there is a possibility of seeing what is true from moment to moment, and in that lies the resolution of all our problems.

June 27, 1953

Fourth Talk in The Oak Grove

I think it is important with what attitude we come to these meetings because to me, they are very serious. You are not here to meet your friends, which you can do afterwards, or to spend an hour in entertainment, in mere verbal discussion, opposing one idea or opinion with another. What we are trying to do is to go into the very complex problem of living, and for that there must be a great deal of earnestness. Bearing that in mind, it is obviously quite out of place to take photographs or to ask for autographs, which are among the many flippant things we do when we are not really in earnest, and I would beg of you to regard our meeting here not as a curious gathering of very odd people but as a coming together of those who are seriously endeavoring to find out the full significance of living. At least, that is my approach, and I am very earnest about it. There is such chaos, such misery and confusion in the world, and however small our gathering may be, if we can go into this problem very intently—not just for an hour or so on Saturday afternoon or Sunday morning, but continuously throughout the week—then perhaps we shall come to a point when we ourselves will be the missionaries, not merely the listeners, when we ourselves will begin to talk of these things out of our own depth of understanding and experience. So my intention in talking here is not to express or to fulfill myself, which would obviously be most childish, but rather to see if we cannot together awaken that intelligence, that integrated outlook on life which will enable each one of us to be the flame that brings about a fundamental, radical revolution in our own thinking and so perhaps in the world about us. If there is a sense of quietness, a sense of dignity, a mutual respect which demands equal attention on the part of all, then perhaps we can go deeply into these problems and not be satisfied with descriptions, with mere scratching on the surface.

This morning I would like, if I can, to talk over the problem of what it is to experience, and if we do not bring about a fundamental revolution at the center, whether there is any possibility of experiencing, except as a mere continuation of past experience. Now, what is this center? Surely, it is the 'me', the self, the ego, the mind—the mind which is so sensitive, so extraordinarily capable, which can understand such a variety of experiences, which can store up innumerable memories, which can invent, which can design a plane capable of flying at forty thousand feet and at six hundred miles an hour. This center, which is a complex machine with unlimited potentialities, is hedged about with the thought of 'me'—my pleasure, my security, my vanities, my possessions, my advancement, my fulfillment. It is a center of affection, of hate, of passing pleasures, of envy, greed, and pain. And can I bring about a revolution at this center so that the self, the 'me' is nonexistent? Because, the 'me' is the source of misery, is it not? Though the 'me' may have passing satisfactions, superficial joys and affections, it is constantly multiplying problems, producing pain. However high I may place the self, at whatever level, it is still within the field of thinking, and thinking, with most of us, is pain, suffering, a constant battle between what I am and what I should be. And yet this machine, this mind which is always thinking about itself and its own security, is also capable of infinite unfoldment.

I do not know if you have ever thought what extraordinary significance, what nuances, what subtle profundities words like *love* and *death* have for the mind. And yet this mind, with all its subtleties and swiftness of movement, is bound by the thought of 'me'—the 'me' that is not loved and must be loved, the 'me' that should love, the 'me' that is going to die. And is it possible for this 'me', the self, to completely come to an end? That is fundamentally our problem, is it not? All religions, not the organized churches, but all real teachers, all civilizations and cultures have always struggled to eliminate the 'me', the sense of separate effort. Various governments have made extraordinary efforts to destroy the 'me' through tyranny, either of the left or of the right, through the totalitarian domination over the thought of 'me', hoping to bring about a culture of cooperative work. Yet this 'me' is constantly asserting itself; it is always translating every experience, every reaction, every movement of thought in terms of its own center. The 'me', the self, the ego, is the source of conflict, of pain, of the everlasting strife to become, to achieve, to gain; and as long as we do not see this fact, however capable, however subtle and learned the mind may be, it will only create more problems, produce more misery. So those of us who are really in earnest must obviously direct our inquiry to finding out if this 'I' can come to an end.

Now, what is this 'I'? It is a process of recognition, is it not? It is a center of experience, of fear, of joy, of passing fulfillment, of memory. If the 'I' is not, there is no experience with which the mind identifies itself as my experience.

I am not telling you anything new. On the contrary, I am just describing what is actually taking place in each of us. My verbal expression must inevitably be very limited, but if, as you listen, you observe this process in yourself, you will begin to see the intricacies, the extraordinary subtleties of your own thinking; you will become aware of your own center, of this aggressive or negative state of the mind which is called the 'me' and which is constantly reaching out to gain through acceptance or denial.

So the 'I' is a center of recognition and experience, and as the mind translates every experience in terms of this center, it is constantly limiting itself. As long as the 'I' is there, the mind cannot go beyond, however capable, however fantastically subtle it may be. When every experience is translated in terms of the self, in terms of like and dislike, how can the mind go beyond? A mind that is caught in the pursuit of gratification and the avoidance of pain, that is always limiting itself by its efforts, by its demands, by its fears—how can such a mind ever experience or comprehend that which is beyond itself? And yet, if we are at all earnest, that is what we are seeking, is it not? Of course, if we are satisfied to be caught in the pleasures and pains of daily life, there is no problem; we will merely go on substituting one pain for another, one pleasure for another, one belief or dogma for another. But if we want to go beyond, to search out, to discover, surely the 'me' which is everlastingly putting a limit on the mind must come to an end.

Now, how is this 'I', the self, the ego, this self-centered and self-enclosing movement of thought, to come to an end? This center is fed by experience, is it not? And what is experience, whether it is conscious or unconscious? Please, this is a very important question, so let us think it out together.

Experience is a continuation of memory, is it not? If I meet you and you are a complete stranger, there is no recognition. But if I know you, there is set going the process of recognition, which is the experiencing of pleasure or pain, of flattery or insult. So the mind is always translating experience in terms of the known. Therefore the unknown, that which cannot be found out, becomes something fearful, something to be afraid of—tomorrow, death, the future. Being afraid, the mind builds theories, hopes, ideas, all of which further strengthen the 'me'. That is the process we know. But if we can find out how not to feed the 'me' at any level, high or low, then perhaps we shall negatively be capable of bringing about the ending of the 'me'. It cannot be done positively but only negatively, by finding out how this 'I' nourishes itself and continues to survive. Surely, the 'I', the mind, can think only in terms of past experience, in terms of the known. Our religions, our culture, our outlook, our ideals are all in terms of the known, and the mind, the 'I', clings to these things and strengthens itself through its knowledge of the known.

So, being aware of this whole process, can the mind free itself from the known and come to a state in which the unknown can be? Surely, that is the only revolution—when the fear of the unknown is not. And that revolution can take place only when the mind sees the futility of the known. But consciously or unconsciously we are always seeking the known; it is our desire for the known that creates gods, heaven, the ideal future, the perfect state. We project what should be and force man to fit into the known, and that is our utopia.

Man can never perfect himself because
his perfection is always the known. Please, it is very important to think this out. We are striving to make ourselves more and more perfect, technologically as well as psychologically. The effort to bring about technological perfection one can understand. But the desire to make oneself inwardly, psychologically more perfect is always to conform to the known, to something which has already been experienced—which implies that the mind can perfect itself only in terms of the past or in terms of reaction to the past. As the communist society is a reaction to the capitalist state to which it is constantly op-

posed, so the mind's effort to perfect itself is a reaction to its conditioning, and reaction is never perfect; it is only an extension of the known.

The 'me' is a total entity. Though we talk of the conscious and the unconscious, actually there is only one state—consciousness. We are aware of that part which we call the conscious, and of the other part we are hardly aware, but the mind is a total process which includes both the inner and the peripheral consciousness, the hidden as well as the open. Now, can one be aware of this total consciousness which is the 'me', with its desires, its anxieties, its fears, its motives, its constant struggle to better itself, its urge to fulfill—can one be completely aware of this process without strengthening the activity of the 'me'? And can this whole process of the 'me' come to an end? Surely, it cannot come to an end by any act of volition, nor by any trick, nor by repeating phrases, chants, mesmerizing oneself with words, nor by losing oneself in some idiotic fantasy such as that of the nation or the fantasy of God.

If you will really go into it, you will see that this is a very important inquiry because the solution to our human problems does not lie at any conscious level. Our consciousness is now limited by the 'me', and any answer that comes out of the 'me' will only produce further mischief, further sorrow. Knowing this, being aware of the total process of the 'me', can there be an ending to the 'me'?

Do you understand how we have tried to end the 'me', the self? We have tried it through discipline, through controls, through defenses, through resistance; we have tried it through compulsion, through conformity to dogma and belief. We have tried it through various forms of self-immolation, forgetting oneself for the bigger thing, for one's property, for one's wife and children, for the state, for the world. We have tried to forget ourselves in war, in service, in loving another, and ultimately in the idea of God. We have tried all these tricks—and they are tricks—and have only brought about more misery, more tyranny, more chaos in the world.

You don't have to read a great deal to understand all this. You are the result of the past, of all human struggle, of all human endeavor, joy, and sorrow. The whole story of humanity is in you, and if you know how to read that, then you don't have to read a single book. To discover that, no philosophy, no system is necessary. So the question I am putting to myself, and which I hope you will also put to yourself is: Can this thing called the 'me', which runs like a thread through every action, through every thought, through every movement of affection, come to an end? Please just put the question to yourself; don't try to find an answer because whatever you find will be a positive answer, which is an invention of the mind, and therefore it will become another means of perpetuating the 'me'. But if you put the question to yourself, being totally aware of this whole process, then you will find not a verbal answer but that spontaneous answer which is a revolution, and which comes into being only when you ask the question without any volition, and that is true listening. If you become choicelessly aware of the 'me' in all its activities, of the whole process of your thinking, the cognitive as well as the hidden, if you see it without judgment or condemnation, you are bound to bring about that revolution at the center. Then the mind becomes extraordinarily subtle, astonishingly active and alert.

At present our minds are crippled by our fears, by our frustrations, by the desire to succeed; but if without judgment, without condemnation or choice, we begin to be aware of this whole process of consciousness that is going on, whether we are awake or asleep, then we will find that in spite of ourselves and our desires, in spite of our conflicts, our wars, and brutalities, there is a revolution at the center; and like a wave that reaches further and further from the center, all our difficulties will be solved. But if merely approached from the outside, our problems can never be solved. It is from the center that all human problems arise, and if there is an ending, a complete cessation at the center, that in itself will bring about a total revolution. But a mind that deliberately tries to bring about a revolution, to deny the center, will only create further misery. Then it becomes an ideal, and an idealist is not a revolutionary; he is merely conforming to a pattern of his own invention.

So, please just listen to all this, absorb it silently, and you will see that creativeness is a thing that comes into being when the mind is quiet, when the 'me' is totally absent. The creativeness which we occasionally know through turmoil is not the same as the creativeness which is free from the center. Creativeness free from the center is not of time because it is not the invention of the mind, and without that creativeness life has very little significance, though we may have all the prosperity, all the latest gadgets in the world. We soon get tired of that; we want more of these gadgets. But this creativeness is not of satisfaction; it is something totally unknown; it cannot be conceived or speculated upon. It can come into being only when the mind, being fully aware of the total process of the 'me', understands its significance and therefore does not feed it through experience.

Question: Why is it that those who have a secure income and are able to retire from responsible work so often deteriorate and go to pieces psychologically?

KRISHNAMURTI: Is the deterioration merely a matter of secure income? Perhaps the secure income only exaggerates the deterioration which has already taken place. No, sirs, please don't brush it off by laughter. Are we concerned with why the mind deteriorates at a certain stage or with why the mind deteriorates at all? A man who is working, earning money, going regularly to an office is apparently not deteriorating because he is active, but when that activity stops, you perceive the deterioration. The mind that is caught in routine, whether it is the routine of an office, of a ritual, or the routine of a certain dogma, is already deteriorating, is it not? Surely, it is much more worthwhile to find out what are the causes which bring about this deterioration of the mind than to inquire why your neighbor, who has money, goes to pieces when he retires. Please, if we can really understand this one question, perhaps we shall know the eternity of the mind.

Why does the mind deteriorate—not your mind only, but the mind of man? One can see that the deteriorating factor arises when the mind becomes a machine of habit, when its education is merely a matter of memory, and when it is ceaselessly struggling to conform to a pattern, whether imposed or self-created. There is fear, deterioration, a destruction of the mind when it is constantly seeking security or when it is burdened with the desire to fulfill itself. And that is our state, is it not? Either we are caught in habit, in routine—doing the same thing over and over again, practicing virtue, conforming to the pattern of a discipline in order to arrive somewhere, to find psychological or material security—or else we are competing, making tremendous effort in our ambition to achieve worldly success. Surely, that is what each one of us is doing, and therefore we have already set going the mechanism of deterioration. If any of these responses exist in us, at whatever level, we are deteriorating.

Now, can the mind renew itself constantly? Can the mind be creative from moment to moment? I do not mean creativeness in the sense of mere design, expression, capacity, the cultivation of a technique. I am not referring to creativeness in any of those terms. But can the mind experience the unknown? Surely, it is only in the state of unknowableness that there is no deterioration. Any other state is bound to bring old age to the mind. Like any other piece of machinery that is kept running day after day for weeks, months, years, the mind that is always active inevitably deteriorates. As long as you use your mind as a machine to achieve, to produce, to gain, you have the seeds of deterioration, of old age and senility; and whether in a boy of sixteen or in a man of sixty, it is the same process. But of that deteriorating process most of us are not aware. All that we are aware of is that we are caught in the machinery of pleasure and pain, of misery and the struggle to get out of it. So the mind is never still, never unoccupied; it is everlastingly occupied with something: with God, with communism, with capitalism, with growing wealthy, with what one's neighbor thinks, or with the kitchen—oh, innumerable things! Being constantly occupied, it is never free, quiet. It is only the mind that is quiet, not out of dullness, but because it is in that state of silence which is creative—it is only such a mind that ceases to deteriorate. Freedom from deterioration is not possible for the mind that fulfills itself through capacity. As you grow older, capacity becomes dull. You may be an expert player of the piano, but as you grow older, rheumatism sets in, disease comes on, you go blind, or you are destroyed by an accident. The mind which is seeking fulfillment in any direction, at any level, has already within it the seed of destruction. It is the 'me' that is wanting to fulfill itself, to become something; being empty, frustrated, the 'me' seeks fulfillment in my family, my child, my property, my idea, my experience. When one recognizes all this and sees the danger of it, only then is it possible for the mind to be empty from moment to moment, from day to day, uncrippled by the burden of the past or the fear of the future. To live in that moment is not something fantastic, something given only to the few. After all, as I said, each one of us is caught in misery, in strife, in pain, in passing joy, and each one of us must find this unknown; it is not reserved for one and denied to the rest. It is together that we can create a new world, but the new world cannot come into being through revolution on the outside, which is the revolution of decay.

The mind deteriorates as long as it is seeking an end or as long as it is conforming to authority bred of fear. There is a withering away of the mind when there is no self-knowledge, and self-knowledge is not a thing to be learned from a book. It is to be uncovered at every moment of the day, which requires a mind that is extraordinarily alert, and the mind is not alert when it has found an end. So the factor that brings about deterioration lies in our own hands. A mind that is caught in experience, that lives on experience, can never find the unknowable. The unknowable comes into being only when the past is not, and the past is not only when the mind is still.

June 28, 1953

Fifth Talk in The Oak Grove

I think it is particularly important to understand the question of what is knowledge. Most of us seem so eager for knowledge; we are always acquiring, not only property, things, but also ideas. We go from one teacher to another, from one book, from one religion, from one dogma to another. We are always acquiring ideas, and this acquisition we think is important in the understanding of life. So I would like, if I may, to go into the problem and see whether this additive process of the mind does bring about freedom, and whether knowledge can solve any human problem. Knowledge may solve superficial, mechanical problems, but does it free the mind fundamentally so that it is capable of directly perceiving what is true? Surely it is very important to understand this question because in understanding it, perhaps we shall revolt against mere methodology, which is a hindrance except in achieving some mechanical result. I am talking about the psychological process of the mind, and whether it is possible to bring about individual creativeness—which is naturally of the greatest importance, is it not? Does the acquisition of knowledge, as we conceive it, bring about creativeness? Or, to be capable of that state which is creative, must the mind be free from the whole additive process?

Most of us read books or go to talks in order to understand; when we have a problem, we study, or we go to somebody to discuss it, hoping thereby that our problem will be solved or that we will see something new. We are always looking to others or to experience, which is essentially knowledge, in the hope of resolving the many problems that confront us. We turn to the interpreters, those who say they understand a little more—the interpreters, not only of these talks, but also of the various sacred books. We seem to be incapable of tackling the problem directly for ourselves without relying on anyone. And is it not important to find out whether the mind, in its process of accumulation, is ever able to resolve any psychological, spiritual problem? Must not the mind be totally unoccupied if it is to be capable of perceiving the truth of any human conflict?

I hope you will have the patience to go into this problem, not merely as I describe it, but as each one of us is involved in it. After all, why are you here? Obviously, some are merely curious, so we won't concern ourselves with those. But others must be very serious, and if you are serious, what is the intention behind that seriousness? Is it to understand what I am saying—and, not understanding, to turn to another to explain what has been said, thereby bringing about the process of exploitation? Or are you listening to find out if what I say is true in itself, not because I say it or because someone else explains it? Surely, the problems which we discuss here are your problems, and if you can see and understand them directly for yourself, you will resolve them.

We all have many problems, and there must obviously be a change, but is change brought about by the process of the mind? I am talking of fundamental change, not of mere sociological or economic reform. Surely, it is the mind that has created our problems, and can the mind resolve the problems it has created? Does the resolution of these problems lie in acquiring more knowledge, more information, in learning new techniques, new methods, new systems of meditation, in going from one teacher to another? All that is clearly very superficial, and is it not important to find out what makes the mind superficial, what brings about superficiality? With most of us, that is the problem, is it not? We are very superficial; we do not know how to go deeply into our conflicts and difficulties, and the more we turn to books, to methods, to practices, to the acquisition of knowledge, the more superficial we become. That is an obvious fact. One may read innumerable books, attend highly intellectual talks, gather vast stores of information; but if one does not know how to delve within oneself and discover the truth, understand the whole process of the mind, surely all one's efforts will only lead to greater superficiality.

So is it possible for you, while listening, not merely to remain at the superficial, verbal level, but to uncover the process of your own thinking and go beyond the mind? What

I am saying is not very complicated. I am only describing that which is taking place within each one of us, but if you live at the verbal level and are satisfied with the description without directly experiencing, then these talks will be utterly useless. Then you will turn to the interpreters, to those who offer to tell you what I am talking about—which is so utterly silly. It is much better to listen directly to something than to turn to someone else to tell you what it is all about. Cannot one go to the source without interpretation, without being guided to discover what the source is? If one is guided to discover, it is no longer discovery, is it?

Please see this point. To discover what is true, what is real, no guidance is necessary. When you are guided to discover, it is not discovery; you merely see what someone has pointed out to you. But if you discover for yourself, then there is quite a different experience, which is original, unburdened by the past, by time, by memory, utterly free of tradition, dogma, belief. It is that discovery which is creative, totally new, but to come to that discovery, the mind must be capable of penetrating beyond all the layers of superficiality. And can we do it? Because all our problems—political, social, economic, personal—are essentially religious problems; they are reflections of the inward, moral problem, and unless we solve that central problem, all other problems will multiply. That problem cannot be resolved by following anybody, by reading any book, by practicing any technique. In the discovery of reality, methods and systems are utterly valueless because you have to discover for yourself. Discovery implies complete aloneness, and the mind cannot be alone if it is living on explanations, on words, if it is practicing a method or depending on someone else's translation of the problem.

So, realizing that from childhood our education, our religious training, our social environment have all helped to make us utterly superficial, can the mind put aside its superficiality, this constant process of acquisition, negative or positive—can it put all that aside and be not blank but unoccupied, creatively empty, so that it is no longer creating its own problems and seeking the resolution of what it has created? Surely, it is because we are superficial that we do not know how to go very deeply, how to reach great depths within ourselves, and we think we can reach great depths by learning or by listening to talks.

Now, what is it that makes the mind superficial? Please don't merely listen to me but observe, be aware of your own thinking when a question of that kind is put to you. What makes the mind superficial? Why cannot the mind experience something that is true, beyond its own projections? Is it not primarily the gratification which each one of us is seeking that makes the mind superficial? We want at any price to be gratified, to find satisfaction, so we seek methods to achieve that end. And is there such a thing as satisfaction, ever? Though we may be temporarily satisfied and change the object of our satisfaction depending on our age, is there satisfaction at any time? Desire is constantly seeking to fulfill itself, so we go from one satisfaction to another, and getting caught in each new satisfaction with all its complications, we again become dissatisfied and try to disentangle ourselves. We cling to persons, pursue teachers, join groups, read books, take up one philosophy after another, but the central desire is always the same—to be satisfied, to be secure, to become somebody, to achieve a result, to gain an end. Is not that whole process one of the primary causes of the mind's superficiality?

And is not the mind superficial because we think in terms of acquisition? The mind is constantly occupied with acquiring or with putting aside, denuding itself of what it has acquired. There is tension between acquisition and denudation, and we live in that tension, and does not that tension contribute to shallowness of mind?

Another factor which brings about shallowness is the mind's ceaseless occupation with its own troubles, or with some philosophy, or with God, ideas, beliefs, or with what it should do or should not do. As long as the mind is absorbed, concerned, taken up with something, is it not superficial? Surely, only the unoccupied mind, the mind that is totally free, not caught in any problem, that is not concerned with itself, with its achievements, with its pains, with its joys and sorrows, with its own perfection—only such a mind ceases to be shallow. And cannot the mind live from day to day, doing the things it has to do, without this preoccupation?

For most of us, with what is the mind occupied? When you observe your own mind, when you are aware of it, what is it concerned with? With how to make itself more perfect, how to be healthy, how to get a better job, whether it is loved or not loved, whether it is making progress, how to get out of one problem without falling into another—it is concerned with itself, is it not? In different ways it is everlastingly identifying itself with the greatest or with the most humble. And can a mind occupied with itself ever be profound? Is it not one of our difficulties, perhaps the major difficulty, that our minds have become so extraordinarily shallow? If any difficulty arises, we rush to somebody to help us; we have not the capacity to penetrate, to find out; we are not investigators into ourselves. And can the mind investigate, be aware of itself, if it is occupied with any problem? The problems which we create in our superficiality demand not superficial responses but the understanding of what is true, and cannot the mind, being aware of the causes of superficiality in itself, understand them without struggling against them, without trying to put them aside? Because the moment we struggle, that in itself becomes another problem, another occupation which merely increases the superficiality of the mind.

Let me put it this way: If I realize that my mind is superficial, what am I to do? I realize its superficiality through observation. I see how I turn to books, to leaders, to authority in various forms, to Masters, or to some yogi—you know the many different ways in which we seek to be satisfied. I realize all that. Now, is it not possible to put all that aside without effort, without being occupied with it, without saying, "I must put it aside in order to go deeper, be more thoughtful"? This concern to become something more—is it not the constant occupation of the mind and a primary cause of superficiality? That is what we all want—to understand more, to have more property, to have better brains, to play a better game, to look more beautiful, to be more virtuous—always the more, the more, the more. And as long as the mind is occupied with the 'more', can it ever understand *what is?*

Please listen to this. When the mind is pursuing the 'more', the 'better', it is incapable of understanding itself as it is because it is always thinking of acquiring more, of going further, achieving greater results; it cannot understand its actual state. But when the mind perceives what it actually is without comparison or judgment, then there is a possibility of being deep, of going beyond. As long as one is concerned with the 'more' at any level of consciousness, there must be superficiality, and a superficial mind can never find what is real; it can never know truth, God. It can concentrate on the image of God; it can imagine, speculate, and throw up hopes, but that is not reality. So what is needed, surely, is not a new technique, a new social or religious group, but individuals who are capable of going beyond the superficial, and one cannot go beyond the superficial if the mind is occupied with the 'more' or with the 'less'. If the mind is concerned with having more property or less property, if property is its occupation, then obviously it is a very superficial, silly mind; and the mind that is occupied with becoming more virtuous is equally silly because it is concerned with itself and its acquisitions.

So the mind is the result of time, which is the process of the 'more', and cannot the mind be aware of this process and be what it is without trying to change itself? Surely, transformation is not brought about by the mind. Transformation comes into being when the truth is seen, and truth is not the 'more'. Transformation, which is the only real revolution, is in the hands of reality, not within the sphere of the mind.

Is it not important, then, for each one of us not merely to listen to these talks but to be aware of ourselves and remain in that state of awareness without looking to interpreters or leaders, and without desiring something more? In that state of awareness in which there is no choice, no condemnation or judgment, you will see what is taking place, you will know the process of the mind as it actually is, and when the mind is thus aware of itself, it becomes quiet, it is unoccupied, still. It is only in that stillness that there is a possibility of seeing what is true, which brings about a radical transformation.

Question: Why is it that in this country we seem to feel so little respect for anybody?

KRISHNAMURTI: I wonder in what country one feels respect for another? In India they salute most profoundly, they give you garlands, flowers—and ill-treat the neighbors, the servants, the animals. Is that respect? Here, as in Europe, there is respect for the man with an expensive car and a big house; there is respect for those who are considered superior, and contempt for others. But is that the problem? We all want to feel equal to the highest, do we not? We want to be on a par with the famous, the wealthy, the powerful. The more a civilization is industrialized, the more there is the idea that the poor can become the rich, that the man living in a cabin can become the president, so naturally there is no respect for anyone, and I think if we can understand the problem of equality, we may then be able to understand the nature of respect.

Now, is there equality? Though the various governments, whether of the left or of the right, emphasize that we are all equal, are we equal? You have better brains, greater capacity, you are more gifted than I; you can paint, and I cannot; you can invent, and I am only a laborer. Can there ever be equality? There may be equality of opportunity; you and I may both be able to buy a car, but is that equality? Surely, the problem is not how to bring about equality economically but to find out whether the mind can be free from this sense of the superior and the inferior, from the worship of the man who has much, and the contempt for the man who has little. I think that is the problem. We look up to those who can help us, who can give us something, and we look down on those who cannot. We respect the boss, the man who can give us a better position, a political job, or the priest, who is another kind of boss in the so-called spiritual world. So we are always looking up and looking down, and cannot the mind be free from this state of contempt and false respect?

Just watch your own mind, your own words, and you will discover that there is no respect as long as there is this feeling of superiority and inferiority. And do what the government may to equalize us, there can never be equality because we all have different capacities, different aptitudes, but what there can be is quite a different feeling, which is perhaps a feeling of love, in which there is no contempt, no judgment, no sense of the superior and the inferior, the giver and the taker. Please, these are not mere words; I am not describing a state to be desired, and being desired gives rise to the problem, "How am I to get there?"—which again only leads to superficial attitudes. But when once you perceive your own attitude and are aware of the activities of your own mind, then perhaps a different feeling, a sense of affection comes into being, and is it not that which is important?

What matters is not why some people have respect and others do not but to awaken that feeling, that affection, that love, or what name you will, in which this sense of the high and the low will totally cease. And that is not a utopia; it is not a state to be striven after, something to be practiced day after day until you ultimately arrive. I think it is important merely to listen to it, to be aware of it as you would see a beautiful picture, or a lovely tree, or hear the song of a bird; and if one listens truly, the very listening, the very perception does something radical. But the moment the mind interferes, bringing in its innumerable problems, then the conflict arises between 'what should be' and *what is;* then we introduce ideals and the imitation of those ideals, so we never discover for ourselves that state in which there is no desire to be more and therefore no contempt. As long as you and I are seeking fulfillment, there is no respect, there is no love. As long as the mind wants to fulfill itself in something, there is ambition; and it is because most of us are ambitious in different directions, at different levels, that this feeling, not of equality, but of affection, of love, is impossible.

I am not talking of something superhuman, but I think if one can really understand ambition, the desire to become more, to fulfill, to achieve, to shine, if one can live with it, know for oneself all its implications, look at it as one would look at oneself in a mirror, just to see what one is without condemnation—if one can do that, which is the beginning of self-knowledge, of wisdom, then there is a possibility of this affection coming into being.

Question: Is fear a separate, identifiable quality of the mind, or is it the mind itself? Can it be discarded by the mind, or does it come to an end only when the mind ceases altogether? If this question is confusing, can it be asked differently: Is fear always an evil to be overcome, and is it never a necessary blessing in disguise?

KRISHNAMURTI: The question has been asked, and let us try to find out, you and I together, what fear is and whether it is possible to eradicate it. Or, as the questioner suggests, it may be a blessing in disguise. We are going to find out the truth of the matter, but to do that, though I may be talking, you must investigate your own fears and see how fear arises.

We have different kinds of fear, have we not? Fear exists at different levels of our being; there is the fear of the past, fear of the future, and fear of the present, which is the very anxiety of living. Now, what is this fear? Is it not of the mind, of thought? I think of the future, of old age, of poverty, of disease, of death, and of that picture I am afraid. Thought projects a picture which awakens anxiety in the mind, so thought creates its own fear, does it not? I have done something foolish, and I don't want my attention called to it, I want to avoid it, I am afraid of the consequences. This is again a thought process, is it not? I want to recapture the happiness of youth; or perhaps I saw something yesterday in the mountain sunlight which has now escaped me, and I want to experience that beauty again; or I want to be loved, I want to fulfill, I want to achieve, I want to become somebody; so there is anxiety, there is fear. Thought is desire, memory, and its responses to all this bring about fear, do they not? Being afraid of tomorrow, of death, of the unknown, we begin to invent theories that we shall be reborn, that we shall be made perfect through evolution, and in these theories the mind takes shelter. Because we are everlastingly seeking security, we build churches around our hopes, our beliefs and dogmas, for which we are prepared to fight, and all this is still the process of thinking, is it not? And if we cannot resolve our fear, our psychological block, we turn for help to somebody else.

As long as I am thinking in terms of achieving, fulfilling, of not becoming, of dying, I am always caught in fear, am I not? The process of thinking as we know it, with its self-enclosing desire to be successful, not to be lonely, empty—that very process is the seat of fear. And can the mind which is occupied with itself, which is the product of its own fears, ever resolve fear?

Suppose one is afraid, and one knows the various causes that have brought about fear. Can that same mind, which has produced fear, put aside fear by its own effort? As long as the mind is occupied with fear, with how to get rid of it, with what to do and what not to do in order to surmount it, can it ever be free from fear? Surely, the mind can be free from fear only when it is not occupied with fear—which does not mean running away from fear or trying ignore it. First, one must be fully aware that one is afraid. Most of us are not fully aware, we are only vaguely aware of fear, and if we do come face to face with it, we are horrified; we run away from it and throw ourselves into various activities which only lead to further mischief.

Because the mind itself is the product of fear, whatever the mind does to put away fear only increases it further. So can one just be aware of one's fear without being occupied with it, without judging or trying to alter it? To be aware of fear without condemnation does not mean accepting it, taking it to your heart. To be aware of fear without choice is just to look at it, to know there is fear and to see the truth of it; and seeing the truth of fear dissolves fear. The mind cannot dissolve fear by any action of its own; in the face of fear it must be very quiet; it must know and not act. Please listen to this. One must know that one is afraid, be fully conscious of it without any reaction, without any desire to alter it. The alteration, the transformation cannot be brought about by the mind; it comes into being only with the perception of truth, and the mind cannot perceive what is true if it is concerned with fear, if it condemns or desires to be rid of it. Any action of the mind with regard to fear only increases fear or helps the mind to run away from it. There is freedom from fear only when the mind, being fully aware of its own fears, is not active towards them. Then quite a different state comes into being which the mind cannot possibly conceive or invent. That is why it is so important to understand the process of the mind not according to some philosopher, analyst, or religious teacher but as it is actually going on in yourself from moment to moment in all your relationships—when you are quiet, when you are walking, when you are listening to somebody, when you are turning on the radio, reading a book, or talking at table. To be fully aware of oneself without choice is to keep the mind astonishingly alert, and in that awareness there is self-knowledge, the beginning of wisdom. The mind that struggles against fear, that analyzes fear, will never resolve fear, but when there is passive awareness of fear, a different state comes into being in which fear does not exist.

July 4, 1953

Sixth Talk in The Oak Grove

I think that it would be worthwhile and quite important to go into the question of what is true religion; and perhaps, in going into this matter rather deeply, we might be able to discover, directly experience for ourselves, that state which is not of the mind and which must be something unknown, totally new, never experienced before. But to discover and experience that state, it seems to me that we will first have to understand the process of the intellect, the mind. The mind is made up not only of the conscious but also of the many layers of that which we call the unconscious; it is a total process, though for convenience we may divide it as the conscious and the unconscious, with the different gradations of consciousness that lie between the two. To understand the various activities of the mind, surely we must not only inquire at the superficial or verbal level but also go deeply into the process of thought itself.

What I would like to do this morning, if it is possible—and I don't know if it is—is to bring about that state which is not conceivable, which is not imaginable, which cannot be systematized or speculated upon; and surely that requires not a condition of self-hypnosis or mere auto suggestion but rather the gradual unfolding, as I talk, of the process of your own mind. Can we discover together and directly experience that state to which all religions, stripped of their churchianity, their dogmas, their rituals and innumerable stupidities, always refer? I am not going to lead you to discover it because discovery is spontaneous. You must discover it for yourself. What I shall try to do is to describe how that state comes into being, but if you merely follow the verbal description, then you will obviously not comprehend or experience that state which arises only when the mind is no longer projecting or resisting.

As I was saying, we have first to understand the intellect, the process of consciousness, not only the superficial, but also the deeper layers, and to do that we must obviously begin with the verbal reactions and responses. Besides their outward meaning, words like *God, communist, capitalist, greed, progress, death,* have very great significance for most of us, have they not? They have a neurological as well as psychological significance. Words are symbols, and if we do not use words, we have symbols in other forms, like the cross and the religious symbols of India. And is it possible to abstain from reacting, from throwing up barriers in response to symbols? Can the mind, at that superficial level, put aside the imaginative, the speculative, the verbal process, with all its responses? To do so is quite arduous because at present the mind thinks only in terms of words, symbols, images.

And must we not go into the process of desire? Surely, desire is part of the mind, of the intellect, of the intelligence which we use in everyday life. Desire is the very process of the mind, of the mind that accumulates, holds, that has innumerable motives, that pursues sensations, that demands more, that avoids pain and is caught in the urgency of pleasure. The mind is continually seeking a place of safety where it can dwell without disturbance, is it not? It tries to be permanently secure in an idea, in a belief, in an experience, in a relationship. All that is the process of the mind, of what we call the intellect, the individual intelligence; it is all part of consciousness, either open or hidden, and it is all we know.

Now, knowing the total process of itself, can the mind go beyond this process? Can it be quiet so as to discover what is true, what is real, what is God? That is what I would like to go into this morning. Can the mind be aware of its many layers—of the verbal responses, of the purely physical appetites, the biological urges, of the imprint of tradition and environment, of the open and hidden memories—can it be aware of all this without in any way interfering? Thought is always conditioned as long as it is the verbal expression of memory, and until the mind is totally free of this extraordinary accumulation of the past, the unknown is obviously not possible. Until the process of recognition ceases, the new cannot be.

Please, let us talk it over a little more. After all, what we call experience is a process of recognition, is it not? When you see a certain animal, you know it is a dog because you have had previous experience of the species and given it a name. When you meet a friend, you recognize him because you have already experienced the friendship. When there is a psychological experience, that experience has been tasted before, and you have given it a name, and from that there is a further experiencing. The mind can recognize only that which has been experienced; it cannot recognize something new because what is new is not recognizable. So truth, God, or what name you will, must be totally new; it cannot be recognized. If it is recognized, it has already been experienced, and what has been experienced is within the field of time. Please see this clearly and you will understand something. It is not difficult. The words I am using may be difficult, but the feeling, the import of what I am saying is quite simple.

The function of the mind is cognitive, is it not? The mind recognizes, thinks; and its thinking, recognizing, experiencing all come from the background of memory. After all, if I am a Hindu, my conditioning limits my thinking; I think of God, of morality, in terms of tradition, according to what I have read in the various Hindu scriptures. And those who are Christians or Buddhists, or what you will, and who are religiously inclined, are equally conditioned by all that they have been taught.

Now, what we are trying to do—not only now, but always—is to find out if the mind can free itself from its conditioning and thereby experience that which has never been experienced before. Surely, that is reality, that is true religion, is it not? Religion has nothing to do with beliefs, with symbols, with rituals, with the promises, hopes, and fears around which creeds and churches are built. Nor is it a question of morality. The moral person may never know reality—which does not mean that to know reality he must be immoral. Morality which is the result of conscious effort circumscribes the mind. Virtue is necessary only because it gives freedom, but a man who is trying to become virtuous is never free.

So, knowing the whole content of the mind—its denials, its resistances, its disciplinary activities, its various efforts at security, all of which condition and limit its thinking—can the mind, as an integrated process, be totally free to discover that which is eternal? Because without that discovery, without the experiencing of that reality, all our problems with their solutions only lead to further misery and disaster. That is obvious; you can see it in everyday life. Individually, politically, internationally, in every activity we are breeding more and more mischief, which is inevitable as long as we have not experienced that state of religion, that state which is experienceable only when the mind is totally free.

Now, after hearing this, can you, if only for a second, know that freedom? You cannot know it merely because I am suggesting it, for then it would be only an idea, an opinion without any significance. But if you have followed all these talks very seriously, you are beginning to be aware of the process of your own thought, of its direction, its purposes, its motives; and being aware, you are bound to come to a state in which the mind is no longer seeking, choosing, struggling to achieve. Having perceived its own total process, the mind becomes extraordinarily still, without any direction, without any volition, without any action of will. Will is still desire, is it not? The man who is ambitious in the worldly sense has a strong desire to achieve, to be successful, to become famous, and he exercises will for his self-importance. Likewise we exercise will to develop virtue, to achieve a so-called spiritual state. But what I am talking about is totally different; it is devoid entirely of any desire, of any action towards escape, of any compulsion to be this or that.

In examining what I am saying, you are exercising reason, are you not? But reason can lead only so far and no further. We must obviously exercise reason, the capacity to think things out completely and not stop half way. But when reason has reached its limit and can go no further, then the mind is no longer the instrument of reason, of cunning, of calculation, of attack and defense, because the very center from which arise all our thoughts, all our conflicts, has come to an end.

So, now that you have listened to these talks, surely you are beginning to be aware of yourself from moment to moment during the day in your various activities; the mind is coming to know itself with all its deviations, its resistances, its beliefs, its pursuits, its ambitions, its fears, its urge to fulfill. Being aware of all this, is it not possible for the mind, if only for an instant, to be totally still, to know a silence in which there is freedom? And when there is that freedom of silence, then is not the mind itself the eternal?

To experience the unknown, the mind itself must be the unknown. The mind, so far, is the result of the known. What are you but the accumulation of the known, of all your troubles, your vanities, your ambitions, pains, fulfillments, and frustrations? All that is the known, the known in time and space; and as long as the mind is functioning within the field of time, of the known, it can never be the unknown; it can only go on experiencing that which it has known.

Please, this is not something complicated or mysterious. I am describing obvious facts of our daily existence. Burdened with the known, the mind seeks to discover the unknown. How can it? We all talk of God; in every religion, in every church and temple that word is used, but always in the image of the known. It is only the very, very few who leave all the churches, the temples, the books, who go beyond and discover.

At present the mind is the result of time, of the known, and when such a mind sets out to discover, it can discover only what it has already experienced, which is the known. To discover the unknown, the mind has to free itself completely from the known, from the past, not by slow analysis, not by delving step by step into the past, interpreting every dream, every reaction, but by seeing the truth of all this completely, instantaneously, as you are sitting here. As long as the mind is the result of time, of the known, it can never find the unknown, which is God, reality, or what you will. Seeing the truth of that frees the mind from the past. Don't immediately translate freedom from the past as not knowing the way to your home. That is amnesia. Don't reduce it to such infantile thinking. But the mind is freed the moment it sees the truth that it cannot find the real, this extraordinary state of the unknown, when it is burdened with the known. Knowledge, experience, is the 'me', the ego, the self which has accumulated, gathered; therefore, all knowledge must be suspended, all experience must be set aside. And when there is the silence of freedom, then is not the mind itself the eternal? Then it is experiencing something totally new, which is the real, but to experience that, the mind must be that. Please don't say the mind is reality. It is not. The mind can experience reality only when it is totally free from time, and this whole process of discovery is religion. Surely, religion is not what you believe; it has nothing to do with whether you are a Christian or a Buddhist, a Muslim or a Hindu; those things have no significance; they are a hindrance, and the mind that would discover must be totally stripped of them all. To be new, the mind must be alone; for eternal creation to be, the mind itself must be in that state to receive it. But as long as it is full of its own travails and struggles, as long as it is burdened with knowledge and complicated by psychological blockages, the mind can never be free to receive, to understand, to discover.

So, a truly religious person is not one who is encrusted with beliefs, dogmas, rituals. He has no beliefs; he is living from moment to moment, never accumulating any experience, and therefore he is the only revolutionary being. Truth is not a continuity in time; it must be discovered anew at every moment. The mind that gathers, holds, that treasures any experience cannot live from moment to moment discovering the new.

Those who are really serious, who are not dilettantes, not merely playing with all this, have an extraordinary importance in life because it is they who will become a light unto themselves and therefore, perhaps, to others. To talk of God without experiencing, without having a mind that is totally free and thereby open to the unknown, has very little value; it is like grown-up people playing with toys, and when we play with toys, calling it religion, we are creating more confusion, greater misery. It is only when we understand the whole process of thinking, when we are no longer caught in our own thought, that it is possible for the mind to be still, and only then can the eternal come into being.

Question: To help my three children, do I just watch myself? And how am I to instruct them?

KRISHNAMURTI: Is not life, everyday living, a process of educating the children and yourself, too? Please, this question with its answer is not limited to teachers and students; you are all concerned with this because you are parents.

Now, is education merely the imparting of knowledge? Is it a matter of teaching the children how to read, how to add, how to get a job? But that is what we are now chiefly concerned with, is it not? And what is the result? The boy either ends up in the army to be destroyed, or he destroys himself in a job. So what does it mean to educate oneself and the children? Does it mean spending years in learning a technique, and then becoming cannon fodder, or a machine in the social structure? Please just follow this; I am asking you to find out for yourself. Does it mean surrounding oneself with innumerable gadgets, with things or beliefs, in order to safeguard oneself and not to be afraid? Does it mean the superficial covering of the mind with information? But that is what we call education, is it not? We spend enormous sums of money to train a boy, and then he ends up in a war in Korea or in Germany or in Russia. We are everlastingly creating wars, destroying each other, from the most ancient of times until now. So education as we know it has obviously failed; it has no meaning any more. And if education is none of these things for any intelligent man who thinks about it, then what do we mean by education? Does it not mean an integrated view of life which will bring about integrated human beings? And one obviously cannot be an integrated human being if one is an American or a Russian or a Hindu; those are mere labels without much significance. An integrated human being is one who is no longer caught in fear, who is not shaped by society into a particular pattern of thought, either Catholic, communist, or any other. Each sect, each national or religious group wants to educate its children according to a certain formula, and is that education? Will it bring about integrated human beings? To educate the children, must one not begin to free oneself from fear, from all these limitations of thought as the Christian, the communist, or the idealist?

Surely, to educate oneself and others, one must become aware of oneself, of one's thoughts, of one's motives, of one's contempt, and fears; one must become aware of the words one uses, and of the psychological response of the mind to words like *American, Russian, German.* To educate others, one must begin to educate oneself, and is that not the right process of education? True education exists when the educator is being educated as well as the children, and that implies freedom for the child as well as for yourself. Freedom is not at the end of a long course of discipline, coercion. There is no freedom at the end of compulsion; the outcome of compulsion is still compulsion. If you dominate the child, compel him to fit into a pattern, however idealistic, will he be free at the end of it? If we want to bring about a true revolution in education, there must obviously be freedom at the very beginning, which means that both the parent and the teacher must be concerned with freedom, and not with how to help the child to become this or that.

The right kind of education also implies freedom from competition, does it not? We give marks, compare children and encourage competition because when there is the competitive spirit it is much easier to discipline the child, and through fear he is forced to conform, to study more. But if we want to create the right kind of education, we will be concerned with freeing the mind so that it is able to look at life with an integrated outlook and meet all its complications as they arise from moment to moment. Surely, that is far more important than the mere drudgery of learning. Book knowledge may or may not come in, but what we are concerned with is to bring about a new human being who is no longer coerced, no longer competitive, no longer seeking success, but who understands *what is* and is therefore freeing himself from *what is.* But that requires an extraordinary patience, an integrated understanding which comes only through self-knowledge, and that is why it is so important that both the educator and the educated, the teacher and the taught, should be fully aware of the process of the mind, of their own being.

I believe it used to cost twenty-five cents to kill a Roman soldier or for the Roman soldier to kill some other soldier, and now to kill a soldier, it costs something like a hundred thousand dollars. We go on developing mere technique, the ways of memory, of the cunning intellect, and there is no revolt against all this. And when we do revolt, we become pacifists, idealists, or adopt some other label. There can be fundamental revolution only when there is an integrated outlook on life, when each individual is a total being; and that totality, that integration of the individual cannot exist as long as there is fear, competition, ambition, this constant urge to fulfill oneself in some activity, all of which implies 'me' against the whole. The world is ours, the riches of the earth are yours and mine. No one can be prosperous while others are starving, but to see this requires an integrated outlook, and we cannot have that integrated view of life as long as you remain an American and I a Hindu. We are human beings, but we cannot partake of this earth if you are competing with me and I with you. As long as you and I are ambitious to fulfill, to become, we must be in constant conflict with each other. If you see all this not merely verbally but inwardly, deeply, I assure you, you will be in revolt and then, perhaps, we shall be able to produce a new culture, a new world.

Question: The basic struggle throughout history, as in the modern world, seems to be the clash between the forces of tradition and conservatism on the one hand, and the progressive forces on the other. To which side should one give one's support in this great battle to advance human welfare?

KRISHNAMURTI: Cannot we look at this problem without taking sides? Because the moment you take sides, you have not an integrated outlook, you are not free. If you are a progressive and I am a conservative, we clash, we are against each other. Instead of looking at the problem from your point of view or from my point of view, can we not find out what it is that makes the mind conservative or progressive? Do you understand the problem? If I am conservative and you are progressive, we must inevitably be in conflict. I want to conserve, to retain, to keep things very much as they are, and you want to bring reform, you want to produce revolution. We are in constant battle with each other, and so we never solve the problem. But if you and I are intent on solving the human problem, then we will be neither progressive nor conservative; we will be concerned with the problem itself, not with how you look at it or how I look at it. I hope the question is now clear, but the question will never be clear if we have already taken sides. So let us inquire into the conservative and the progressive mind.

Both the conservative and the progressive desire change. That is obvious. It is only the most stupid, the totally blind who want no change at all. Those who have all the things of this world, a large bank account, comfort, luxury, who are satisfied and want everything guarded—such people do not want change. But those who observe, who are aware of the world problem, not just the American or Indian problem, who see this whole human struggle—they all want change. There is starvation in Asia of which you know nothing. Millions and millions have only half a meal a day, and not even that. There is famine, disease, superstition, the degradation of poverty, the multiplication of children, ever-increasing populations, poor soil. Naturally they are clamoring for change. And there must obviously be a change from war. Something must be done to stop all wars so that man can be free to educate himself, to live peacefully, harmoniously, creatively. So, if we are at all thoughtful, we all want change, the conservative as well as the progressive.

The problem, then, is not whether to support the conservative or the progressive but how to bring about change. Isn't it? Please, one can answer superficially, but I want to tackle this problem fundamentally, deeply. What brings about change? Do revolutions bring about change? There have been revolutions in the past, the French and the more recent ones, and have they brought about change? They may have brought about superficial political changes, but not a basic change of mind and heart, not a fundamental, integrated change in which the individual is no longer nationalistic, no longer French, Russian, German, Hindu, but a human being. So, when we are inquiring into change, revolution, must we not ask if the mind, regardless of whether it is conservative or progressive, can ever bring it about? Does change, revolution, come into being through a process of the mind, or does it come about entirely differently? Have you ever observed how you change as an individual human being? When do you change? Surely, not when you are trying to change through the exercise of thought. You change in spite of yourself, when the mind is no longer planning to change.

It is very, very important to understand this, so please have the patience to inquire into it. If I am greedy, envious, how am I to change? Can I change by volition? When I try to get rid of greed, is not that very effort the result of greed in another form? When I say, "I must not be greedy," why do I say it? Because it no longer pays me to be greedy; it causes me pain, so now I have a different motive, a different urge; there is a new sensation which I am after; therefore, in discarding greed, I am still greedy. As long as change is the result of thought, it is not change, regardless of whether that thought is conservative or progressive. Change, revolution can come into being only when calculated thought has come to an end. Please think it over, see the truth of what I am saying. The change that is brought about by thought, by calculation, is a modified continuity. All political revolutions are merely a modified continuity, a reaction to the past, and therefore not a change at all.

So, if they are concerned with change, both the progressive and the conservative must inquire whether thought can ever bring it about. Change comes into being when there is the perception of what is true, and the perception of what is true is not of the mind. The mind may translate history according to its prejudices, according to its bourgeois or proletarian instincts, but the revolt of those who have nothing, like the conservatism of those who have everything, is always a reaction, and reaction is not change. Change comes about when the mind sees what is true, and it cannot see what is true as long as it is thinking in terms of the progressive or the conservative. You and I must be concerned directly with the problem of change. Change cannot be brought about by any act of will, by any application of knowledge; it comes into being only when reality is seen by you and me. And reality can be seen only when the mind is no longer caught in reaction, when it is neither dreaming of utopia nor wanting to conserve everything as it is. There is transformation when you and I are truly religious, and that is the only revolution, the only permanent change.

July 5, 1953

Seventh Talk in The Oak Grove

It seems to me that it is one of the most difficult things to live simply, and perhaps this evening we can go into it not just at the superficial level but deeply, and try to find out what, in essence, it means to live simply. If one is at all alive, life has innumerable problems. Every problem seems to breed several more. There is apparently no end to problems, not only at the conscious level, but also at the deeper levels of consciousness. We never seem to escape or solve any problem without introducing other problems. But if we could understand what it is to live simply or to think simply, then perhaps we might be able to produce in ourselves a state of being in which we would not bring about problem after problem.

Why is it that the mind accumulates? Why do we store up knowledge? Why is it that experience conditions us? If we can inquire into this accumulative process of the mind, it may help us to understand what it is to think directly, simply; and in perceiving why the mind gathers, holds, accumulates, perhaps we shall be able to dissolve our many difficulties as they arise.

We think that by gathering knowledge, by having experience, we shall be able to understand life with all its complex struggles. But what happens when we accumulate knowledge, experience? We are always translating any incident, any crisis, any reaction, in terms of our past experience, which is memory. With this burden of the past, we are incapable of looking at things directly—and perhaps there lies the crux of our difficulty. We never meet anything anew, but always in terms of the old, of what we have known. It is because we never meet each problem directly and understand it for ourselves that we go on introducing other problems, creating further struggles.

Now, our conception of a simple life is to possess only a few things or to have no possessions at all, but surely, that is not a simple life. We look up to those who lead a simple life in the physical sense, who have few clothes and no property, as though that were something marvelous. Why? Because we in ourselves are attached to things, to property. But is living a simple life merely a matter of denudation, the putting aside of physical things? Or is it much deeper? Though we may have but few things, inwardly we are always gathering, accumulating; we are bound to beliefs, to dogmas, to every form of experience and memory, and there is in us a ceaseless conflict between various wants, longings, hopes, desires. All this indicates not a simple life but a very complex inward life. So I think it is important to find out why the mind accumulates, consciously as well as unconsciously, why it cannot meet every incident, every reaction as though it were something new, fresh. Why must it translate each experience in terms of the old, in terms of what it has known? The mind is always accumulating experiences, reactions, storing them away as memory in order to use them for its own security. And is understanding, is intelligence the result of innumerable experiences? Or is it the capacity to look at things anew, to face life from moment to moment without the darkening effect of experience, of the past?

As I said the other day, please do not listen to all this in order to understand what I am talking about but rather to find out how you are thinking. You are not here merely to follow my description of a certain state of mind but to discover how your own mind operates when any new experience arises.

Take, for example, the problem of fear. Can you and I understand fear and dissolve it without bringing in the accumulation of the past? Most of us are afraid of various things: of tomorrow, of what the neighbors say, of being poor, of not fulfilling, of death. Now, what is this fear? Can we not go into it, understand it very simply, and thereby be free from fear—not everlastingly, but as it arises from moment to moment, from day to day—so that the mind is not burdened with the anxiety of tomorrow? Fear, after all, is a reaction, is it not? I have done something of which I am ashamed, I have made a mistake which I do not want somebody to discover, and of that I am afraid. So fear is a reaction, and it is no good fighting fear, trying to overcome it, to analyze or avoid it. Fear is the shadow of the thing I have done, so the problem is not fear, but my approach to what I have done. Now, can I look anew at what I have done? That is, can I, knowing the cause of fear, look at it very simply without accumulating, without making the understanding of the cause a technique of how to meet fear? Do you follow? When, knowing the cause of fear, the mind tries to understand that cause in order to protect itself against further fears, the fears of tomorrow, it introduces the complex process of self-protection, and therefore it is never able to meet each experience clearly, simply, directly.

Now, cannot the mind observe the cause, the incident which has produced fear, without interpretation, without judgment? Can it not merely look at the cause of fear, listen to it, let it tell its whole story without interpreting, accepting or denying it, without trying to hide it, without taking refuge or running away from it? I think it is this that brings about the simplicity which is so essential in understanding. If we are capable of looking at the cause of the problem very simply, without translating or condemning it, then I think it is possible to be free moment by moment not only from fear but from envy, jealousy, the desire to be successful, and all the other human problems that inevitably arise. Problems will always arise; there are bound to be reactions as long as we live, so is it not necessary to have the capacity to meet them as they arise from day to day without accumulating experience, which limits our thinking and prevents our understanding of the problem?

Simplicity of thought, of mind, is essential, but there cannot be simplicity as long as the accumulative process of self-protection is going on, and this self-protective process of thought exists not only at the conscious level but also at the various unconscious levels of our being. It is because we want to protect ourselves that knowledge, experience, becomes so vastly important to us. When we are confronted with a problem, we are never completely denuded of the past. And is it possible for you and me to empty the mind of the past, of the accumulated knowledge of yesterday?

Please, I think it is rather important to go into this and understand it. Burdened with the past, the mind creates its own problems, does it not? And can the mind begin to meet every problem anew, observe it as it arises without bringing in all the shadows of past experience? Surely, that is our problem—to look at every incident, every reaction without prejudice, without bias, without interpreting it according to the things we have learned, which is the desire to protect ourselves. Can the mind be free from all that and look directly at each problem as it arises? If it can, then there is no death, then every human problem can be resolved—but not to its satisfaction, not to its gratification. The moment we introduce the desire to be satisfied, we are accumulating, which brings about fear. But cannot we look at the problem, whatever it is, without judgment, without evaluation? To evaluate a problem implies memory, judgment, weighing, calculating, all of which indicates that the mind is constantly protecting itself. The desire to protect, to safeguard oneself, is conscious as well as unconscious, and knowing this whole process, can the mind at the same time put it all aside and look at the problem directly? It can do that only when you and I understand the necessity of freeing oneself from fear.

Fear corrupts, it shadows all our actions; where there is fear, there is no love. We know that theoretically; we have read about it, but, being aware that one is afraid of innumerable things, cannot one go into it completely? Cannot one find out the cause of fear and really understand it without fighting, without translating, judging, or interpreting *what is?* And when the mind is aware of *what is,* not only at the conscious level, but as the total process of one's whole being, is there not a release, a freedom from the cause which has produced fear? But there is no release if there is not the intention to understand *what is,* to look at it, to be familiar with it, to listen to its whole content, to see its flow, its movement.

So, simplicity of thinking does not come about through the accumulation of knowledge. On the contrary, the more you know, the less simple the mind is, and the mind must be extraordinarily simple to understand *what is. What is* is never the same, it varies from moment to moment, and its movement cannot be understood by a mind that is burdened with condemnation, with judgment, with self-protectiveness, and fear of the future.

Please, I think it is very important to find out if one can really observe *what is* without resentment, without recoil. After all, what are we? We are the result of many reactions, responses, conditioning influences, desires, fears, and in this turmoil the mind is caught; it is always in battle, in conflict. And to put an end to this ceaseless struggle, to this misery and pain, must we not understand simply, from moment to moment, the movement of *what is?* If I am greedy or angry or envious, surely I must understand that as it is and not try to resolve it, overcome it, because the very overcoming is a struggle, a new conflict, and hence there is no release from *what is.* But if I am aware not only of my envy but also of the deeper cause to which it is a response, and of the desire to be free from envy—if I am aware of that total process without judgment, choicelessly, then I think such awareness does bring about the clarification and the resolution of that cause. This requires not practice or discipline but watchfulness, alertness of mind, and the mind cannot be alert if it is constantly choosing, condemning, judging, escaping, or trying to alter *what is.*

Simplicity is the understanding of *what is,* and the understanding of *what is* comes into being only when the mind is no longer fighting, struggling with *what is,* no longer trying to mold it according to its fancies, desires, hopes, and fears. In understanding *what is,* the movements of the self, the 'me', the ego, are revealed, and that, surely, is the beginning of self-knowledge—self-knowledge not only at the conscious level but at those levels where the self is so deeply hidden and from which it comes out occasionally, spontaneously, when you are off guard.

When we are aware of ourselves, is not the whole movement of living a way of uncovering the 'me', the ego, the self? The self is a very complex process which can be uncovered only in relationship, in our daily activities, in the way we talk, the way we judge, calculate, the way we condemn others and ourselves. All that reveals the conditioned state of our own thinking, and is it not important to be aware of this whole process? It is only through awareness of what is true from moment to moment that there is discovery of the timeless, the eternal. Without self-knowledge, the eternal cannot be. When we do not know ourselves, the eternal becomes a mere word, a symbol, a speculation, a dogma, a belief, an illusion to which the mind can escape. But if one begins to understand the 'me' in all its various activities from day to day, then in that very understanding, without any effort, the nameless, the timeless comes into being. But the timeless is not a reward for self-knowledge. That which is eternal cannot be sought after; the mind cannot acquire it. It comes into being when the mind is quiet, and the mind can be quiet only when it is simple, when it is no longer storing up, condemning, judging, weighing. It is only the simple mind that can understand the real, not the mind that is full of words, knowledge, information. The mind that analyzes, calculates, is not a simple mind.

To be creative, the mind must be denuded of all its accumulations, and without that creativeness, our life is very empty; though it may be full of activity, of resolutions and determinations, they have very little significance. But the mind that sees this whole process of accumulation as a means of self-protection, that is aware of its implications without trying to alter it or put it aside—such a mind, being simple, quiet, understands *what is,* and in that there is an astonishing release, a freedom in which there is reality.

Question: You say that only a still mind can solve the problem of fear, but how can the mind be still when it is afraid?

KRISHNAMURTI: There are several problems involved in this question. First, how to make the mind still in order to resolve fear?

And can the mind which is afraid ever be still? And does stillness of mind come about through any technique? After all, that is what disturbs many people—the "how", the method, the technique of arriving at peace. The "how" implies habit, maintaining a certain attitude day after day, repeating a certain action, conforming to an established plan, disciplining the mind to be still. And is quietness, stillness of mind, the result of a habit? Is it the outcome of constant practice? Or does stillness of the mind come about only when there is freedom, when there is the understanding of *what is?*

Surely, if I want peace of mind, I can never have it. It is because I want a still mind that I go through various practices which I hope will bring it about, but such a mind is dead. A dead mind is very still, but it is not a mind in which creativeness can come into being. So there is no "how." All that the mind can do is to be aware that it is seeking a method because it wants something. If you want to be rich, you accumulate money, you choose your friends, you move among people who can help you get what you want. Similarly, if you want peace of mind, if you feel the urgency of it, you try to find out how you can arrive at that; you listen to various teachers, you practice disciplines, you read certain books—always with the intention of having a quiet mind—but your mind merely becomes dull. Whereas, if you are aware of this whole process of your thinking, of the unconscious as well as the conscious, if you see all your thoughts from moment to moment without condemnation or judgment, just watching each thought as it arises without rejecting or laying by, then you will find there is a freedom in which stillness comes into being without your volition, without any action of your will.

The problem, then, is not how to free the mind from fear, or how to have a quiet mind in order to dissolve fear, but whether fear can be understood. Though I may be afraid of many things—of my boss, of my wife or husband, of death, of losing my bank account, of what my neighbors say, of not fulfilling, of losing my self-importance—fear itself is the result of a total process, is it not? That is, the 'me', the self, the ego, in its activity, projects fear. The substance is the thought of the 'me', and its shadow is fear, and it is obviously no good battling the shadow, the reaction. The 'me' is protecting itself, longing, hoping, desiring, struggling, constantly comparing, weighing, judging; it wants power, position, prestige; it wants to be looked up to, and can that 'me', which is the source of fear, cease to be, not everlastingly, but from moment to moment? When that feeling arises, can the mind be aware of it, examine it without condemnation, judgment, choice? Because, the moment you begin to judge, to evaluate, it is part of the 'me' that is directing and so conditioning your thinking, is it not?

So, can I be aware of my greed, of my envy, from moment to moment? These feelings are expressions of the 'me', of the self, are they not? The self is still the self at any level you may place it; whether it is the higher self or the lower self, it is still within the field of thought. And can I be aware of these things as they arise from moment to moment? Can I discover for myself the activities of my ego when I am eating, talking at table, when I am playing, when I am listening, when I am with a group of people? Can I be aware of the accumulated resentments, of the desire to impress, to be somebody? Can I discover that I am greedy and be aware of my condemnation of greed? The very word *greed* is a condemnation, is it not? To be aware of greed is also to be aware of the desire to be free from it and to see why one wants to be free from it—the whole process. This is not a very complicated procedure; one can immediately grasp the whole significance of it. So one begins to understand from moment to moment this constant growth of the 'me', with its self-importance, its self-projected activities—which is basically, fundamentally, the cause of fear. But you cannot take action to get rid of the cause; all you can do is to be aware of it. The moment you want to be free from the ego, that very desire is also part of the ego, so you have a constant battle in the ego over two desirable things, between the part that wants and the part that does not.

As one becomes aware at the conscious level, one also begins to discover the envy, the struggles, the desires, the motives, the anxieties that lie at the deeper levels of consciousness. When the mind is intent on discovering the whole process of itself, then every incident, every reaction becomes a means of discovery, of knowing oneself. That requires patient watchfulness—which is not the watchfulness of a mind that is constantly struggling, that is learning how to be watchful. Then you will see that the sleeping hours are as important as the waking hours because life then is a total process. As long as you do not know yourself, fear will continue and all the illusions that the self creates will flourish.

Self-knowledge, then, is not a process to be read about or speculated upon; it must be discovered by each one from moment to moment so that the mind becomes extraordinarily alert. In that alertness there is a certain quiescence, a passive awareness in which there is no desire to be or not to be, and in which there is an astonishing sense of freedom. It may be only for a minute, for a second—that is enough. That freedom is not of memory; it is a living thing, but the mind, having tasted it, reduces it to a memory and then wants more of it. To be aware of this total process is possible only through self-knowledge, and self-knowledge comes into being from moment to moment as we watch our speech, our gestures, the way we talk, and the hidden motives that are suddenly revealed. Then only is it possible to be free from fear. As long as there is fear, there is no love. Fear darkens our being, and that fear cannot be washed away by any prayer, by any ideal or activity. The cause of fear is the 'me', the 'me' which is so complex in its desires, wants, pursuits. The mind has to understand that whole process, and the understanding of it comes only when there is watchfulness without choice.

July 11, 1953

Eighth Talk in The Oak Grove

I would like to talk over this morning a problem which I think is sufficiently important—that of the constant urge in each one of us to seek a permanent state which nothing will disturb. It is really quite a complex problem, and may I suggest that you listen to it passively, without acceptance or rejection, as one would listen to the song of a bird. Surely, if one would try to understand a very complex problem, there must be a certain alertness in which the mind is passive but not hypnotized by words. This does not in any way imply that you must accept what I am saying. On the contrary, mere acceptance, or conformity to what you consider to be the truth, has no significance at all. What has significance is to discover for yourself what is true, and you cannot discover what is true if your mind is constantly agitated by comparison, or by remembering what somebody else has said, or what you have read in various books. All that must intelligently be put aside so that one can listen with a passive awareness in which there is no self-projection, no defensive or antagonistic spirit. One cannot find out what is true if one is overanxious or in any way distracted. To see the truth of anything requires a peculiar attention, does it not? It is an attention which is effortless, as when you are listening to something which you really love.

Are not most of us seeking permanency at different levels of our consciousness? If we are merely worldly, we want permanency in name, in form, permanency in our good looks, in furniture, in property. That is, desire is seeking a permanent state in which there will be no disturbance of any kind, and if we are very superficial, we look for that permanency in the social order, either of the left or of the right. If we are not caught up in that kind of worldliness, then we seek permanency in what we call love, in our relationship with certain people, and if we go beyond that, we seek permanency in belief, in ideas, in knowledge, dogma, tradition. And there is also the desire to find a permanency in which there is no action from oneself. The mind says, "I surrender my will to God; He knows best; therefore, let Him function." One immolates oneself to what one considers to be God or to the idea of the group, of the nation. Whether our activities are imposed by external circumstances or are self-imposed through fear, through hope, through various forms of utopian illusion, the fundamental desire is to find a permanency in which the mind can take shelter and feel safe.

So desire is constantly seeking a state of permanency, a state in which there will be complete self-fulfillment through property, through persons, or through ideas, and in which the mind can never be disturbed. Is that not what most of us are after, consciously or unconsciously? We want to fulfill, to find permanent security, and this very urge gives rise to anxiety, to fear, and to various forms of destructive activity which we then try to reform, control, discipline.

Now, is it possible for the mind not to seek permanency, not to pursue a state which it has conceived to be happiness, reality? Can the mind be free from the experience of yesterday so that it does not permanently condition the present? And is there an action, a state of being, which is not the outcome of desire, which is beyond time, which has no continuity? To find out if there is such a state, surely the mind must inquire into and understand the process of its own desire. As long as one is seeking any kind of permanence, any kind of security, every experience becomes a hindrance to further understanding, all knowledge a block to further discovery. Surely, then, if you and I would discover whether there is or is not the timeless, we must first understand how the mind is seeking, through property, relationship, or belief, a condition in which it can dwell securely day after day. In whatever guise, that is, in essence, what we are after, is it not? Our life is very complex, fluctuating, changing; there is uncertainty, pain, sorrow. Realizing all that, consciously or unconsciously we want the opposite, something quite different from *what is;* and that is why we build churches, pursue utopias, cling to dogmas, beliefs. We may see the fallacy of all that and consciously reject it, we may reason out that there is nothing permanent—and there is nothing permanent—but unconsciously, deep down, the human urge, the individual urge, is to find something which is beyond the conflict of desire.

Now, is there such a thing as security? Is there a permanency which continues everlastingly in spite of calamities, in spite of death? Is there something which the mind can cling to? If through education, culture, tradition, through the conditioning of certain beliefs, one asserts that there is or is not, surely that response has no validity. A man who would really inquire into this question must obviously free himself from his conditioning, and that is one of our greatest difficulties, is it not?

The mind, which is thought, is constantly seeking in many subtle ways to have a permanent, unvarying state in which it can continue day after day. Though we don't say so, that is what we consciously or unconsciously demand, and thought finds the means to produce that permanency. Thought creates the thinker, and then the thinker becomes the permanent entity who guides and controls thought. But the thinker is the thought; there is no thinker apart from thought.

Thought is seeking security at various levels, and when it seeks outward security, it is inviting insecurity. When you build up armaments in the hope of creating security for yourselves in this world, your security is destroyed by war. The mind that has found some measure of security becomes conservative; it wants to hold, to build, to continue as it is without being disturbed; it changes only under compulsion, when the pressure of the inevitable forces it to do so. But there is no such thing as security, permanency, that is, a state of complete conservation.

Inwardly, psychologically, the whole process of memory, which is the accumulation of experience, of knowledge, is a means through which the 'me', the ego, can find security and perpetuate itself. Deep down there is the unconscious desire to fulfill, so we try various forms of fulfillment, various activities, jobs, functions. And is there fulfillment for the 'me'? Can I ever fulfill myself? Surely, the 'me' is only an idea; it has no reality. The 'me' that is seeking prosperity, wealth, position, pleasure, the 'me' that is avoiding pain, that is constantly endeavoring to increase, to become, to grow—that entity is merely an idea; it is a desire which has identified itself with a particular form of thought. So, is there ever fulfillment for you and me? And as long as each one of us is trying to fulfill, we are antagonistic, in competition with each other. You want to fulfill yourself through beauty, through harmony, and I want to fulfill myself through violence, through irresponsibility, through so-called freedom. Are we not antagonistic to each other? You are seeking peace, and I am ambitious. Can the man who is pursuing peace and the man of ambition live together in the same social order? Obviously not. To seek fulfillment in peace, or in anything else, is not to be peaceful, and as long as each one of us is seeking fulfillment, there must be conflict. And yet, for most of us, the desire for fulfillment is an intense urge which must at all costs be satisfied. At all the different levels of our being, waking or sleeping, we are constantly seeking a state which nothing can disturb, a continuity of thought as the 'me'—the 'me' with experiences, the 'me' that has suffered, the 'me' that has gathered so much information, knowledge. Not having found outward security, the 'me' proceeds to find that state at other levels beyond the superficial. So we meditate in order to achieve peace, to have a quiet mind. We think that a still mind will give us the state of permanency which we have not found in any other direction, and then the question arises, "How am I to be still?" So a whole new problem begins, and in that we get caught.

Surely, the thought that wants to be still can never free itself from conflict because it is the very center of the 'me'. It is thought as the 'me' which identifies itself with the group, with the nation. You forget the 'me' by throwing yourself into this or that activity. The 'me' is forgotten, but the activity remains. Being an escape from the 'me', your activity must be protected, and so there is antagonism, there are battles between various activities, between various national groups. And if you do not indulge in some activity or in nationalism, you become a religious entity, identifying yourself with a particular belief which then becomes immensely important because you are part of it.

Now, without going into too many details, all this is a true statement of an obvious fact, and if you really see the truth of what I am saying, surely your mind is no longer consciously or deeply seeking any state; it is beginning to be aware of everything as it arises and is trying to understand it without storing up that understanding for use on future occasions. So there is a certain sense of freedom, and when you come to that point, you will find that there is an action taking place which is not the outcome of desire. Ordinarily we know only the activity of desire, which is the activity of the mind identified as the 'me'. That 'me' is very petty, very small, narrow, shallow; though it may extend widely through identification, it is still very shallow, and therefore it can never find that which is real. A petty mind seeking God will find a god which is also petty. A superficial mind, however much it may discipline itself and assert that it must love, be compassionate, kind, gentle, will still be superficial.

Now, if the mind can see the truth of all this, then perhaps it will discover quite a different state—a state of silence which is not self-projected, which is not the outcome of any desire, compulsion, or fear. In that silence there is no activity of the mind, and therefore there is no continuity. That which is continuous is the result of time; it is a process of time. Time is the mind, the mind that desires a continuity. Desiring continuity in experience, the mind is made continuous through memory, and such a mind can never find anything new; it can never meet reality, the unknowable.

So the mind is the result of time; it is the outcome of memory, of knowledge, of experience; and can such a mind, being aware of its own total process, cease to project and remain silent? In that silence, surely, great depths are known which the conscious mind can never experience and retain because the moment the conscious mind interferes and takes pleasure in that experience, there is born the experiencer apart from the experienced, and so the division begins. There is then the conflict of the experiencer who is always pursuing that which is beyond himself. That is why it is very important, it seems to me, to understand this whole process of desire—the desire that is always creating the duality of the 'me' who is the experiencer apart from the experienced, the thinker who is always dominating, controlling, shaping thought, pursuing the more pleasurable experience.

Seeing all this, can thought, which is a very complex process, come to an end so that there is stillness of mind? In that stillness there are depths which the mind cannot possibly conceive, but a still mind knows those things. When the mind can experience without retaining, without storing up the experience as memory, only then is it capable of receiving that which is timeless, eternal; and without a glimpse of that, life is a series of empty struggles, an everlasting process of conflict and misery. Understanding does not come through escape but through constant watchfulness in which there is no condemnation or comparison. Condemnation and comparison are of desire. When it is free of desire, watchfulness becomes clear, simple; there is immediate perception without analysis or judgment. Being choicelessly aware, the mind comes unknowingly to that state where there is stillness, and then it is possible for reality to be.

Question: What significance has physical death in the life of the individual? Is it not the great liberator from all our miseries?

KRISHNAMURTI: Does death solve all our problems? And why is it that so many of us are afraid of death? The older we grow, the more anxious we become. Why? And does death, the coming to an end of the physical state, resolve our complex thoughts? Has not thought continuity? It may not continue in me, but thought is continuous, and thought which is continuous can never find release from its misery. So, being afraid of death, we have theories, hopes of a continuity; we say there must be reincarnation, that I must be born next life for a greater opportunity. I am not finished, and what is the value of all my accumulations, of the knowledge and experiences I have gathered unless I can fulfill myself in the next life, or be resurrected in the future, or find a place in heaven? We are always afraid of the unknown, of the tomorrow, and so we set about finding ways and means of avoiding that finality. Or we reason logically, saying that everything comes to an end and is reborn; I die, I dissolve physically so that I can be born again in another form or nourish another entity. Reasonably, logically, we pierce through the fear of death and are satisfied. Or we are satisfied through belief in a future life, in something after death to which the mind can cling. So the mind is everlastingly seeking its own continuity, but that which is continuous is the known, and the known can never find the unknowable. That is our problem, is it not? In the midst of living, we are dying because we are the result of the known. We never for a moment put aside all the things that we know and become completely denuded of the past; we never allow the mind to be totally empty, consciously and unconsciously naked, inwardly stripped of all its experiences, of all its beliefs, of all its learning, so that the unknown can be.

After all, what is it that we know? Actually, what do you know? You know the way to your house; you have certain information, certain political or economic data; you know how to run a job. You know your name, your insurance, the make of your car; and you are a little bit aware of your own desires and appetites, of the experiences and reactions which are the outcome of your conditioning. Beyond that, what else do you know? You know the everlasting struggle to be something; if you are conceited, proud, you try to be humble, and so on. That is all we know. We move within the field of the known, the known of pleasure and pain, and with that mind we try to convince ourselves that there is no death by inventing theories—the belief in reincarnation, in resurrection—all the innumerable illusions that the mind creates in order to escape from its own knowing quality. So while we are living, we are dying in the field of the known.

Surely, if you would find out what is immortal, what is beyond the mind, then the mind, which is the known, must come to an end; it must die to itself. You have read of all these things, or you have listened to me quite often, and yet the mind is continually seeking an answer, asking what lies beyond death. All the stupid societies thrive on your appetite to know what lies beyond, and when they tell you, you are satisfied, at least temporarily. But the real problem, which is fear of the unknown, is still there like a canker.

So, realizing that the mind can function only within the field of the known, cannot one remain completely and passively aware of the known without making a positive movement into the unknown? Which means, really, being open to death, to the unknown, the real. One carries on with the known as best one can and knows its limitations completely, and knowing its limitations, there is no projection into the future, into the tomorrow. Then there is no fear of the unknown; then death is not something to be afraid of—which does not mean you have a new theory, a new explanation, that you must form new groups to discuss what lies beyond, which is infantile. But when you see the limitations of the mind, of the known, when you see that you are limited and are totally aware of it, consciously as well as in the deeper layers of your consciousness, there is a complete cessation of the activity of the mind; the mind as thought, as "I know," ceases. Then there is a possibility of the unknown coming into being. But you cannot invite the unknown; you cannot invite God, truth, or what name you will. When you do, it is already the known. What is known is purgatory, hell; the unknown is heaven. But the unknowable has no relation with the known; it comes into being only when the mind is completely still. Mind as thought must come to an end, must die, and only then is it possible for that which is eternal to be.

July 12, 1953

Questions

Ojai, 1952

Rajghat, 1952

Poona, 1952

Bombay, 1953

London, 1953

Ojai, 1953

Index

CPSIA information can be obtained
at www.ICGtesting.com
Printed in the USA
JSHW021125220222
23102JS00001B/8

9 781934 989401